FEMINIST
THOUGHT

FIFTH EDITION

FEMINIST THOUGHT

A MORE COMPREHENSIVE INTRODUCTION

Rosemarie Tong
University of North Carolina, Charlotte

and

Tina Fernandes Botts
California State University, Fresno

WESTVIEW
PRESS

Westview Press
Hachette Book Group
1290 Avenue of the Americas
New York, NY 10104
www.westviewpress.com

Fifth Edition: July 2017
Published by Westview Press, an imprint of Perseus Books, LLC, a subsidiary of Hachette Book Group, Inc.

The Hachette Speakers Bureau provides a wide range of authors for speaking events. To find out more, go to www.hachettespeakersbureau.com or call (866) 376-6591.

The publisher is not responsible for websites (or their content) that are not owned by the publisher.

Print book interior design by Trish Wilkinson

Library of Congress Cataloging-in-Publication Data

Names: Tong, Rosemarie, author. | Botts, Tina Fernandes, author.
Title: Feminist thought : a more comprehensive introduction / Rosemarie Tong,
    University of North Carolina, Charlotte, and Tina Fernandes Botts,
    California State University, Fresno.
Description: Fifth edition. | Boulder, CO : Westview Press, [2017] | Includes
    bibliographical references.
Identifiers: LCCN 2016058505| ISBN 9780813349954 (pbk.) | ISBN 9780813350707
    (ebook)
Subjects: LCSH: Feminist theory.
Classification: LCC HQ1206 .T65 2017 | DDC 305.4201—dc23
LC record available at https://lccn.loc.gov/2016058505

ISBNs: 978-0-8133-4995-4 (paperback), 978-0-8133-5070-7 (ebook)

Contents

Conclusion   277

Preface

The two of us have enjoyed working together on the fifth edition of *Feminist Thought*—even though one of us was in Charlotte, North Carolina, retired as an emeritus professor of philosophy, and the other was an assistant professor of philosophy at California State University, Fresno. Committed to making the fifth edition of the book the best yet, we expanded it from seven to ten chapters. Although Chapter 1 on liberal feminism, Chapter 3 on Marxist and socialist feminisms, Chapter 8 on ecofeminism, and Chapter 9 on existentialist, poststructural, and postmodern feminisms remain somewhat the same, we added better critiques and more recent data. We have recast Chapter 2 on radical feminism to better accommodate some of our most recent ideas about sexuality and particularly reproduction. In addition, we now have two chapters on women-of-color feminism. One focuses on women of color in the United States and the other on women of color worldwide (global, postcolonial, and transnational). We have also split Chapter 6 on psychoanalytic and care-focused feminism into two chapters: Chapter 6 on psychoanalytic feminism and Chapter 7 on care-focused feminism. Finally, we have added Chapter 10 on third-wave feminism and feminist queer theory and significantly updated and reconfigured our bibliography.

This fifth edition of *Feminist Thought* contains several substantial changes in addition to many cosmetic ones. We believe that nothing currently on the market is more inclusive of the rich diversity and intersectionality of feminist thought.

Acknowledgments

As usual we have relied on the help of many people to bring this book to market. First, we wish to acknowledge each other as responsive, responsible, and self-critical coauthors. Second, we want to thank everyone at Westview Press who cheerfully and skillfully aided us. In particular, we want to thank our editors, Elizabeth Hansen and Nikki Ioakimedes; our publisher, Cathleen Esposito; and our editorial director, Grace Fujimoto. In addition, we give special thanks to our project editor, Michael Clark, for shepherding our project through the production process, and our copyeditor, Jennifer Kelland, for polishing our manuscript. Their help unified and improved our two distinct styles. Finally, we wish to thank our patient and conscientious typist, Pamela Eudy, who kept track of our many draftings and redraftings. We cannot overemphasize her dedication to the fifth edition.

Introduction

The Diversity of Feminist Thinking

While working on the fifth edition of *Feminist Thought*, we have become increasingly convinced that feminist thought resists categorization into tidy schools. "Interdisciplinary," "intersectional," and "interlocking" are the kinds of adjectives that best describe feminist thinking. There is an exhilaration in the way we feminists move from one idea to the next, revising our thoughts in midstream. Yet, despite the very real challenges that accompany trying to categorize the thought of an incredibly diverse and large array of feminist thinkers, feminist thought is old enough to have a history complete with a set of labels: liberal, radical, Marxist/socialist, women-of-color, global, postcolonial, transnational, psychoanalytic, care-focused, ecofeminist, existentialist, poststructural, postmodern, third-wave, and queer. To be sure, this list of labels is incomplete and contestable. It probably does not capture the full range of feminism's intellectual and political commitments to women and society in general. Yet feminist thought's traditional labels remain serviceable. They signal to the public that feminism is not a monolithic ideology and that all feminists do not think alike. The labels also help mark the number of different approaches, perspectives, frameworks, and standpoints that a variety of feminists have used to shape both their explanations for women's oppression and their proposed solutions for its elimination.

Because so much of mainstream feminist theory reacts against traditional liberal feminism, liberalism is as good a place as any to begin a survey of feminist thought. This perspective received its classic formulation in Mary

1

Wollstonecraft's *A Vindication of the Rights of Woman*,[1] John Stuart Mill's "The Subjection of Women,"[2] and the nineteenth-century women's suffrage movement. Its main thrust, an emphasis still felt in such groups as the National Organization for Women (NOW), is that female subordination is rooted in a set of customary and legal constraints that block women's entrance to and success in the public sphere. To the extent that society holds the false belief that women are, by nature, less intellectually and physically capable than men, it tends to discriminate against women in the academy, the forum, and the marketplace. As liberal feminists see it, this discrimination against women is unfair. Women should have as much chance to succeed in the public realm as men do. Gender justice, insist liberal feminists, requires us, first, to make the rules of the game fair and, second, to ensure that none of the runners in the race for society's goods and services are systematically disadvantaged.

But is the liberal feminist program robust enough to undo women's oppression? Radical feminists think not. They claim that power, dominance, hierarchy, and competition characterize the patriarchal system. It cannot be reformed but only ripped out, root and branch. Radical feminists insist that it is not enough for us to overturn patriarchy's legal and political structures on the way to women's liberation; we must also thoroughly transform its social and cultural institutions (especially the family and organized religion).

As in the past, we remain impressed by the diverse modalities of thinking that count as radical feminist thought. Although all radical feminists focus on sex, gender, and reproduction as the loci for the development of feminist thought,[3] some stress the pleasures of sex (be it heterosexual, lesbian, or autoerotic) and view as unalloyed blessings for women not only the old reproduction-controlling technologies but also the new reproduction-assisting technologies. In contrast, other radical feminists emphasize the dangers of sex, especially heterosexual sex, and regard as harmful to women the new reproduction-assisting technologies and, in a different way, the old reproduction-controlling technologies. As in the previous edition of *Feminist Thought*, we sort this varied array of radical feminist thinkers into two groups: radical-libertarian and radical-cultural feminists.[4]

With respect to issues related to sexuality, radical-libertarian feminists argue that no specific kind of sexual experience should be prescribed as the best.[5] Every woman should be encouraged to experiment sexually with herself, with other women, and with men. Although heterosexuality can be dangerous for women within a patriarchal society, women must nonetheless feel free to follow their own desires, even if that means embracing men.

Radical-cultural feminists disagree. They stress that through pornography, prostitution, sexual harassment, rape, and woman battering,[6] through foot binding, suttee, purdah, clitoridectomy, witch burning, and gynecology,[7] men have controlled women's sexuality for male pleasure. Thus, to become liberated, women must escape the confines of heterosexuality and create a distinct female sexuality through celibacy, autoeroticism, or lesbianism.[8] Only alone, or with other women, can women discover the true pleasure of sex.

Radical feminist thought is as diverse on issues related to reproduction as it is on matters related to sexuality. Radical-libertarian feminists claim biological motherhood drains women physically and psychologically.[9] Women should be free, they say, to use the old reproduction-controlling technologies and the new reproduction-assisting technologies on their own terms—to prevent or terminate unwanted pregnancies or, alternatively, to have children when they want them (pre- or postmenopausally), how they want them (from their own womb or that of another woman), and with whom they want them (a man, a woman, or alone). Some radical-libertarian feminists go further than this, however. They look forward to the day when ectogenesis (extracorporeal gestation in an artificial uterus) entirely replaces the natural process of pregnancy.

In contrast to radical-libertarian feminists, radical-cultural feminists claim biological motherhood is the ultimate source of women's power.[10] Women, in their view, determine whether the human species continues—whether there is life or no life. Women must guard and celebrate this life-giving power, for in its absence, men will have even less respect and use for women than they do now.[11]

Unconvinced by the liberal and radical feminist agendas for women's liberation, Marxist and socialist feminists claim it is impossible for anyone, especially women, to achieve true freedom in a class-based society, where the wealth produced by the powerless many ends up in the hands of the powerful few. With Friedrich Engels,[12] Marxist and socialist feminists insist that women's oppression originated with the introduction of private property, an institution that obliterated whatever equality of community humans had previously enjoyed. Private ownership of the means of production by relatively few persons, originally all male, inaugurated a class system whose contemporary manifestations are corporate capitalism and imperialism. Reflection on this state of affairs suggests that capitalism itself, not just the larger social rules that privilege men over women, is the cause of women's oppression. If all women—rather than just the exceptional ones—are ever to be liberated, a socialist system in which the means of production belong to everyone must replace the capitalist system. No longer economically dependent on men, women will be just as free as men are.

Socialist feminists agree with Marxist feminists that capitalism is the source of women's oppression and with radical feminists that patriarchy is the origin. Therefore, the way to end women's oppression, in socialist feminists' estimation, is to kill the two-headed beast of capitalist patriarchy or patriarchal capitalism (take your pick). Motivated by this goal, socialist feminists seek to develop theories that explain the relationship between capitalism and patriarchy.

During the first stage of theory development, socialist feminists offered several so-called two-system explanations of women's oppression. These two-system theories included those forwarded by Juliet Mitchell and Alison Jaggar. In *Woman's Estate*, Mitchell claimed that women's condition is determined not only by the structures of production (as Marxist feminists think) but also by the structures of reproduction and sexuality (as radical feminists believe) and the socialization of children (as liberal feminists argue).[13] She stressed that women's status and function in all these structures must change if women are to achieve full liberation. Still, Mitchell ultimately gave the edge to capitalism over patriarchy as women's worst enemy.

Like Mitchell, Alison Jaggar attempted to achieve a synthesis between Marxist and radical feminist thought. Acknowledging that all feminist perspectives recognize the conflicting demands made on women as wives, mothers, daughters, lovers, and workers,[14] Jaggar insisted that socialist feminism is unique because of its concerted effort to interrelate the myriad forms of women's oppression. She used the unifying concept of alienation to explain how, under capitalism, everything (work, sex, play) and everyone (fellow workers, family members, and friends) that could engender women's integration as persons becomes instead a cause of their disintegration. Together with Mitchell, Jaggar insisted there are only complex explanations for women's subordination. Yet, in contrast to Mitchell, she named patriarchy rather than capitalism as the worst evil visited on women.

After Mitchell and Jaggar, another group of socialist feminists aimed to develop new explanations of women's oppression that pinpointed neither capitalism nor patriarchy alone as the primary source of women's limited well-being and freedom. Iris Marion Young[15] and Heidi Hartmann[16] constructed explanations for women's oppression that viewed capitalism and patriarchy as interacting to the point of full symbiosis. To a greater or lesser extent, these thinkers addressed the question of whether capitalism could survive the death of patriarchy, or vice versa. Although the nuances of their theories were difficult to grasp, Young and Hartmann—like their predecessors Mitchell and Jaggar—pushed feminists to address issues related to women's unpaid, underpaid, or disvalued work.

We need to point out that for all their insights into women's condition(s), pre-1980s feminists, especially in the Anglo-American world, were almost entirely white, bourgeois, heterosexual, and oriented toward events in the Western, now so-called Northern, world. In this fifth edition of *Feminist Thought*, we try to devote adequate attention to the ways in which women of color, working-class women, lesbian women, and, most recently, transwomen in the United States and elsewhere have shaped a variety of feminisms that have helped women everywhere become freer and more equal to men in their rights and responsibilities. Owing to the addition of Tina Fernandes Botts (a woman-of-color feminist) as an author of this text, we believe that we have better articulated some of the concerns, issues, and ideas of women of color in this edition.

Specifically, in this edition, we have enhanced Chapters 4 and 5 to reflect the contemporary centrality of women-of-color feminisms in feminist thought and to highlight the concept of intersectionality. In Chapter 4, we focus on women of color in the United States, specifically Black/African American, Latin American/Latina/Chicana, Asian American, and Indigenous women. Although there certainly exist many more varieties of women of color in the United States, we use our representative units of analysis to provide a sampling of the unique experiences of oppression of each of these groups of women and to highlight their distinct vantage points. At the same time, we understand that these different groups of women share the common experience of having been racialized (assigned a nonwhite race) inside the history and ongoing presence of racial hierarchy in the culture of the United States. At least in this sense, the experiences of oppression and patriarchy of women of color in the United States differ importantly from those of nonracialized (white) women, and we think it is important to continue to interrogate this state of affairs for as long as it continues.

Moving from the United States to the world stage, in Chapter 5 we discuss global, postcolonial, and transnational feminism, all of which we understand as related but distinct approaches to worldwide feminist concerns. As we observe a continuum beginning with global feminism and moving into postcolonial and then transnational feminism, the ideological vantage point shifts from emphasis on such notions as universal human rights and women's rights (global feminism), to the situated needs of different groups of women of color in developing countries (postcolonial feminism), to full-blown critiques of the possibility of women from different countries coalescing to address problems of mutual concern (transnational feminism).[17]

To the degree that most of the feminists considered up to this point focus on the macrocosm (patriarchy, capitalism, nationalism) in their respective explanations of women's oppression, psychoanalytic and care-focused feminists analyze the microcosm of the individual. They claim the roots of women's oppression are embedded deeply in the female psyche. Initially, psychoanalytic feminists focused on Sigmund Freud's work, looking within it for a better understanding of sexuality's role in the oppression of women. According to Freud, in the so-called pre-Oedipal stage, all infants are symbiotically attached to their mothers, whom they perceive as omnipotent. The mother-infant relationship is an ambivalent one, however: sometimes mothers give too much (their presence is overwhelming), whereas other times they give too little (their absence disappoints).[18]

The pre-Oedipal stage ends with resolution of the so-called Oedipus complex, the process by which the boy gives up his first love object, the mother, to escape (symbolic) castration at the hands of the father. According to some psychoanalytic feminists, the Oedipus complex is the root of male rule, or patriarchy, and nothing more than the product of men's imagination—a psychic trap that everyone, especially women, should try to escape. Other psychoanalytic feminists object that unless we are prepared for reentry into a chaotic state of nature, we must accept some version of the Oedipus complex as the experience that integrates the individual into society. In accepting some version of the Oedipus complex, Sherry Ortner noted, we need not accept the Freudian version, which labels the qualities of authority, autonomy, and universalism as male and those of love, dependence, and particularism as female.[19] These labels, meant to privilege the male over the female, are not essential to the Oedipus complex. Rather, they are simply the consequences of a child's actual experience with men and women. As Ortner saw it, dual parenting (as recommended also by Dorothy Dinnerstein and Nancy Chodorow) and dual participation in the workforce would change the gender valences of the Oedipus complex.[20] Authority, autonomy, and universalism would no longer be the exclusive property of men; love, dependence, and particularism would no longer be the exclusive property of women, an insight shared by even Lacanian-rooted[21] psychoanalytic feminists Julia Kristeva[22] and Luce Irigaray.[23]

The fourth edition of *Feminist Thought* discussed such thinkers as Carol Gilligan[24] and Nel Noddings[25] in the chapter on psychoanalytic feminism. We have now decided it is more appropriate to devote a separate chapter to care-focused feminism. Unlike psychoanalytic feminists, care-focused feminists do not emphasize boys' and girls' psychosexual development. Instead, they stress boys' and girls' psychomoral development. And also unlike psychoanalytic feminists, care-focused feminists are not necessarily burdened by some of the more sexist features of (traditional) psychoanalytic theory.

Also distinguishing care-focused feminists from psychoanalytic feminists is (obviously) their focus on the nature and practice of care. More than any other group of feminist thinkers, care-focused feminists investigate why, to a greater or lesser degree, women are usually associated with emotions and the body and men with reason and the mind. On a related note, care-focused feminists seek to understand why women as a group are usually linked with interdependence, community, and connection, whereas men as a group are usually linked with independence, selfhood, and autonomy. These thinkers offer a variety of explanations for why societies divide realities into things feminine and things masculine. But whatever their explanation for men's and women's differing gender identities and behaviors, care-focused feminists regard women's hypothetically greater capacities for care as a human strength, so much so that they privilege an ethics of care over the reigning ethics of justice in the Western world. In addition, care-focused feminists provide insightful explanations for why women as a group disproportionately shoulder the burden of care in virtually all societies and why men as a group do not routinely engage in caring practices. Finally, care-focused feminists provide plans and policies for reducing women's burden of care so that they have as much time and energy as men to develop themselves as full persons.[26]

Related to care-focused feminism, ecofeminism offers a particularly demanding conception of the self's relationship to the other. According to ecofeminism, we human beings are connected not only to one another but also to the nonhuman world: animal and even vegetative. Thus, ecofeminism entails the view that we do not sufficiently acknowledge our responsibilities to the nonhuman, albeit living, world. As a result, we do things like deplete the world's natural resources, pollute the environment, and stockpile arms centers with tools of mass destruction. In so doing, we delude ourselves that we are controlling nature and enhancing ourselves, when, as ecofeminist Ynestra King observed, nature is already rebelling.[27] Ecofeminists insist that the only way not to destroy ourselves is to strengthen our relationships with the nonhuman world.[28]

In this fifth edition of *Feminist Thought*, we continue to treat existentialist feminism together with poststructural and postmodern feminism. Looking into women's psyches more deeply even than psychoanalytic and care-focused feminists, Simone de Beauvoir provided an ontological-existential explanation for women's oppression. In *The Second Sex*, a key theoretical text of twentieth-century feminism,[29] she argued that women are oppressed by virtue of their otherness from men. Woman is the other because she is not-man. While man is the free, self-determining being who defines the meaning of his existence, woman is the other, the object whose meaning is determined for her. To become a self, a subject, woman must, like man, transcend the definitions, labels, and essences limiting her existence. She must make herself be whomever she wants to be.

Poststructural and postmodern feminists turn de Beauvoir's understanding of otherness on its head. Woman is still the other; however, rather than interpreting this condition as something to reject, poststructural and postmodern feminists embrace it. They claim woman's otherness enables individual women to stand back and criticize the norms, values, and practices that the dominant male culture (patriarchy) seeks to impose on everyone, particularly those who live on its periphery. Thus, otherness, for all its associations with being excluded, shunned, unwanted, abandoned, and marginalized, has its advantages. It is a way of existing that allows for change and difference. Women are not unitary selves, essences to be defined and then ossified. On the contrary, women are free spirits, capable of "performing" their own way of being gendered, as Judith Butler, among others, has said.[30]

In Chapter 10 we discuss third-wave and queer feminisms. Third-wave feminists understand themselves as responding to the concerns of as many different kinds of women as possible. In other words, they strive to include the plurality of available feminist vantage points. They desire to shape a new kind of feminism that is not so much interested in getting women to want what they *should* want as in responding to what women of all varieties say they *do* want. Third-wave feminists describe the context in which they practice feminism as one of "lived messiness." Rebecca Walker speculates, for example, that third-wave feminists are not as judgmental as their second-wave feminist predecessors. She stresses that because "the lines between Us and Them are often blurred," third-wave feminists seek to create identities that "accommodate ambiguity" and "multiple positionalities."[31]

Queer feminism offers a rich and dynamic way of questioning gender and sexuality. Queer feminists put particular pressure on how our society tries to fit everyone into a male/female binary and also on the ways people self-identify as men, women, both, or neither. The future of queer feminism promises to raise new aspects of the already contested concept of woman. According to queer feminism, for example, transmen and transwomen help everyone better appreciate how gender appears in increasingly diverse societies.

Although reconciling the pressures for diversity and difference with those for integration and commonality poses a major challenge, contemporary feminists seem up to the task. Each year, we better understand the reasons why women worldwide continue to be the "second sex" and how to change this state of affairs. In this fifth edition of *Feminist Thought*, we have tried to discuss the strengths and weaknesses of each of the feminist perspectives presented here. In so doing, we have aimed to respect what each feminist perspective has contributed to the shaping of feminist thought. At the end of this book, readers looking for one winning view will be disappointed. Although all feminist perspectives cannot be equally correct, there is no need here for a definitive final say. Instead there is always room for growth, improvement, reconsideration, and expansion for true feminist thinkers. This breathing space helps keep us from falling into the authoritarian trap of having to know it all.

1

Liberal Feminism

Liberal feminism originated during the "first wave" of feminist activity, roughly from the mid-nineteenth century through the 1950s; came into full flower in the so-called "second wave" of feminist activity, roughly from the 1960s through the 1980s; and began to transform and restructure itself at the start of the so-called "third wave" of feminist activity, approximately from the 1990s to the present. The first wave of liberal feminism centered on women's suffrage; the second wave concentrated on gender equity and equal opportunity for women; and the third wave shifted focus to egalitarian concerns, equality of outcome, and intersectionality theory.

Conceptual Roots

In *Feminist Politics and Human Nature*,[1] Alison Jaggar observed that liberal political thought generally locates our uniqueness as human beings in our capacity for rationality. The belief that reason distinguishes us from other animals is, however, relatively uninformative, so liberals have attempted to define the concept in various ways, stressing either its moral or its prudential aspects. A definition of reason as the ability to comprehend the rational principles of morality stresses the value of individual autonomy. In contrast, defining reason as the ability to determine the best means to achieve some desired end emphasizes the value of self-fulfillment.[2]

Whether liberals define reason largely in moral or prudential terms, they nevertheless concur that a just society allows individuals to exercise their autonomy and to pursue their conceptions of the good life. Liberals justify the Western system of individual rights as constituting a framework within

11

which each person can choose a particular set of goods, provided one does not deprive others of theirs. Such a priority defends religious freedom, for example, not on the grounds that it will increase the general welfare or that a godly life is inherently worthier than a godless one but simply on the assumption that people have a right to practice or not practice their own brand of spirituality. The same holds for all rights liberals generally identify as fundamental.

The idea that the right takes priority over the good complicates the construction of a just society. For if it is true, as most liberals claim, that resources are limited and each individual, even when restrained by altruism, has an interest in securing as many available resources as possible, then creating political, economic, and social institutions that maximize the individual's freedom without jeopardizing the community's welfare poses a challenge.

When it comes to state interventions in the private sphere (family or home), most liberals agree that the less the state intrudes into our bedrooms, bathrooms, kitchens, recreation rooms, and nurseries, the better.[3] The thinking is that all people need a place where, among family and friends, they can shed their public personae and be themselves. When it comes to state intervention in the public sphere (civil or political society),[4] however, a difference of opinion emerges between classical liberals on the one hand and egalitarian liberals on the other.[5]

Classical liberals think the state should limit its intrusions or interventions to protecting civil liberties or fundamental rights (e.g., property and voting rights; freedom of speech, religion, and association). They also think that the state should let individuals earn as much as they want within the free market. Classical liberals believe we achieve the ideal of equality through equality of opportunity. In contrast, egalitarian liberals believe the state should focus on minimizing economic disparities as well as protecting civil liberties. As they see it, differences based on initial advantage, talent, and sheer luck influence individual participation in the market. At times, these differences are so great as to constitute liabilities, and in the absence of offsetting adjustments, some individuals cannot earn their fair share of what the market has to offer. On this view, egalitarian liberals call for state intervention in the economy, for instance, by providing legal services, school loans, food stamps, low-cost housing, Medicaid, Medicare, Social Security, and Temporary Assistance for Needy Families (TANF). The idea is to prevent the market from inhibiting access to basic social goods for those at a disadvantage through no fault of their own. For egalitarian liberals, therefore, we achieve the ideal of equality through equality of outcome.

Most contemporary liberal feminists favor egalitarian over classical liberalism. In fact, when feminist Susan Wendell described contemporary liberal feminist thought, she stressed its "commit[ment] to major economic reorganization and considerable redistribution of wealth."[6] Very few, if any, contemporary liberal feminists favor the elimination of state-funded safety nets for society's most vulnerable members, for example.

Because it would be impossible to discuss all liberal feminist movements and organizations in a single book, we focus here on a representative set of classical and egalitarian liberal feminists. More specifically, we present Mary Wollstonecraft, John Stuart Mill, Harriet Taylor, the women's suffragists in the United States, Betty Friedan, and the members of the National Organization for Women (NOW) as examples of classical liberal feminists. In contrast, we present Martha Nussbaum and Elizabeth Anderson as egalitarian liberal feminists. We aim to accurately characterize the overall goal of liberal feminism, which, like Nussbaum, we view as the creation of "a just and compassionate society."[7]

Before the "First Wave": Equal Education

Mary Wollstonecraft

Mary Wollstonecraft (1759–1799) wrote at a time when the economic and social position of bourgeois (upper- and middle-class) European women was in decline. Up until the eighteenth century, women as well as men had done productive work (work that generated income to support a family). But then the forces of industrial capitalism began to draw labor out of the private home and into the public workplace. This industrialization moved slowly and unevenly, having the greatest impact on working-class white women who needed to work outside the home to survive. In contrast, bourgeois white women had little incentive to work outside the home or, if they had servants, even inside it. They relied on their well-to-do husbands or fathers to support them. African American women were generally already in the workforce, laboring as slaves.[8]

In *A Vindication of the Rights of Woman*,[9] Mary Wollstonecraft compared women of privilege to members of "the feathered race," birds confined to cages with nothing to do but preen and "stalk with mock majesty from perch to perch."[10] Bourgeois white ladies were, in Wollstonecraft's estimation, kept women who sacrificed health, liberty, and virtue for whatever prestige, pleasure, and power their husbands (or fathers or other male relations) could provide. As she saw it, these women, not allowed to exercise outdoors lest their skin tan, lacked healthy bodies. Not permitted to make their own decisions, they lacked liberty. Discouraged from developing their powers of reason, they lacked virtue.

Although Wollstonecraft did not talk about socially constructed gender roles per se, she denied that women are, by nature, more pleasure seeking and pleasure giving than men. She reasoned that if confined to the same cages as women, men would develop the same kind of "female" characteristics.[11] Denied the chance to develop their rational powers, to become moral persons with concerns, causes, and commitments beyond personal pleasure, men would, like women, become overly "emotional," a term Wollstonecraft associated with hypersensitivity, extreme narcissism, and excessive self-indulgence.

Accordingly, Wollstonecraft abhorred philosopher Jean-Jacques Rousseau's *Emile*.[12] In this classic of educational philosophy targeting the literate bourgeoisie, Rousseau portrayed the development of rationality as the most important educational goal for boys but not for girls. He was committed to sexual dimorphism, the view that rational man is the perfect complement for emotional woman, and vice versa.[13] As he saw it, men should be educated in such virtues as courage, temperance, justice, and fortitude, whereas women should be educated in patience, docility, good humor, and flexibility. Thus, Rousseau's ideal male student, Emile, studies the humanities and the social and natural sciences, whereas Rousseau's ideal female student, Sophie, dabbles in music, art, fiction, and poetry while refining her homemaking skills. Rousseau hoped sharpening Emile's mental capacities and limiting Sophie's would make of Emile a self-governing citizen and a dutiful head of family and of Sophie an understanding, responsive wife and a caring, loving mother.

Wollstonecraft agreed with Rousseau's projections for Emile but not with those for Sophie. Drawing on her familiarity with bourgeois white women, she predicted that, fed a steady diet of "novels, music, poetry, and gallantry," Sophie would become a detriment rather than a complement to her husband, a creature of poor sensibility rather than good sense.[14] Her hormones surging, her passions erupting, her emotions churning, Sophie would show no practical sense in performing her wifely and, especially, her motherly duties.

Wollstonecraft's cure for Sophie was to provide her, like Emile, with the kind of education that permits people to develop their rational and moral capacities, their full human potential. At times, Wollstonecraft constructed her argument in favor of educational parity in utilitarian terms. She claimed that unlike emotional and dependent women, who routinely shirked their domestic duties and indulged their carnal desires, rational and independent women tended to be "observant daughters," "affectionate sisters," "faithful wives," and "reasonable mothers."[15] The truly educated woman would be a major contributor to society's welfare. Wollstonecraft's line of reasoning in *A Vindication of the Rights of Woman* is remarkably similar to that of eighteenth-century philosopher Immanuel Kant in *Groundwork of the Metaphysics of Morals*—namely, that unless people act autonomously, they act as less than fully human persons.[16] Wollstonecraft insisted that women as well as men deserve an equal chance to develop into autonomous agents.

Repeatedly, and somewhat problematically, Wollstonecraft celebrated reason, usually at the expense of emotion. As Jane Roland Martin said, "In making her case for the rights of women . . . [Wollstonecraft] presents us with an ideal of female education that gives pride of place to traits traditionally associated with males at the expense of others traditionally associated with females."[17] Wollstonecraft never questioned the value of traditional male traits. On the contrary, she simply assumed that they were good and traditional female traits were rationally and morally deficient.

Throughout the pages of *A Vindication of the Rights of Woman*, Wollstonecraft urged women to become autonomous decision makers. But beyond insisting that the path to autonomy passes through the academy, she provided women with little concrete guidance.[18] Although Wollstonecraft toyed with the idea that women's autonomy might depend on their economic and political independence from men, in the end she decided well-educated women did not need to be economically self-sufficient or politically active to be autonomous. In fact, she dismissed the women's suffrage movement as a waste of time because she saw the whole system of legal representation as merely a "convenient handle for despotism."[19]

Despite the limitations of her analysis, Wollstonecraft presented a vision of a woman strong in mind and body, a person who is not a slave to her passions, her husband, or her children. For Wollstonecraft, the ideal woman is less interested in self-indulgence than in exercising self-control.[20] To liberate herself from the oppressive roles of emotional cripple, petty shrew, and narcissistic sex object, a woman must obey the commands of reason and discharge her wifely and motherly duties faithfully.

Wollstonecraft most wanted personhood for women. She claimed that a woman should not be reduced to the "toy of man, his rattle," which "must jingle in his ears whenever, dismissing reason, he chooses to be amused."[21] In other words, a woman is not a mere instrument of a man's pleasure or happiness. Rather, she is, as Kant would say, an end in herself, a rational agent whose dignity consists in having the capacity for self-determination.[22]

"First Wave" Liberal Feminism: Equal Liberty and the Suffrage

Harriet Taylor and John Stuart Mill

Writing approximately one hundred years later, Harriet Taylor and John Stuart Mill joined Wollstonecraft in celebrating rationality. But they conceived of it not only morally, as autonomous decision making, but also prudentially, as calculative reason, or the use of the mind to achieve goals. Unlike Wollstonecraft, Taylor and Mill claimed that permitting individuals to pursue their own preferences maximized liberty, provided the individuals did not hinder, obstruct, or harm others in the process. Taylor and Mill also departed from Wollstonecraft in insisting that to achieve equality between the sexes, society must provide women with the same political rights and economic opportunities (as well as the same education) enjoyed by men.

Taylor and Mill authored, either separately or together, several essays on equality between women and men. Scholars generally agree that the two co-authored "Early Essays on Marriage and Divorce" (1832), that Taylor wrote "Enfranchisement of Women" (1851), and that Mill wrote "The Subjection of Women" (1869). The question of these works' authorship is significant because Taylor's and Mill's views sometimes diverged.[23] For example, Harriet Taylor accepted the traditional view that maternal ties were stronger than paternal ones. She also assumed that in the event of divorce, mothers would bear the responsibility of rearing any children to adulthood—and thus cautioned women to have few. In contrast, Mill urged couples to marry late, have children late, and live in extended families or commune-like situations so as to minimize divorce's disrupting effects on children's lives.[24]

Although Taylor, unlike Mill, did not contest traditional assumptions about male and female child-rearing roles, she did challenge those about women's supposed preference for marriage and motherhood over a career or occupation. Mill contended that even after being fully educated and enfranchised, most women would choose to remain in the private realm, where they would serve primarily to "adorn and beautify" rather than to "support" life.[25] In contrast, in "Enfranchisement of Women," Taylor argued that women needed to do more than read books and cast ballots; they also needed to partner with men "in the labors and gains, risks and remunerations of productive industry."[26] Thus, Taylor predicted that if society gave women a bona fide choice between either devoting their lives "to one animal function and its consequence"[27] (childbearing and child rearing) or writing great books, discovering new worlds, and building mighty empires, many women would happily leave domestic life behind.

Whereas the foregoing passages from "Enfranchisement" suggest Taylor thought a woman had to choose between housewifery and mothering on the one hand and working outside the home on the other, other passages indicate she believed a woman had a third option: namely, adding a career or occupation to her domestic and maternal roles and responsibilities. In fact, Taylor claimed a married woman could not be her husband's true equal unless she had the confidence and sense of entitlement that come from contributing "materially to the support of the family."[28] Decidedly unimpressed by Mill's 1832 argument that women's economic equality would depress the economy and subsequently lower wages, Taylor wrote, "Even if every woman, as matters now stand, had a claim on some man for support, how infinitely preferable is it that part of the income should be of the woman's earning, even if the aggregate sum were but little increased by it, rather than that she should be compelled to stand aside in order that men may be the sole earners, and the sole dispensers of what is earned."[29] In short, Taylor seems to have thought that to be their husband's partners rather than their servants, wives must earn an income outside the home.

In further explaining her view that married as well as single women should work outside the home, Taylor admitted that married women, especially those with children, would need domestic help. Realizing that women could not work full-time both outside and inside the home without exhausting themselves, Taylor conceded that working women with children would need several domestic helpers to ease their burdens.[30] In critic Zillah Eisenstein's estimation, Taylor's words reveal her privileged status. Circa 1850, only bourgeois white women could afford to hire household staff.[31] Thus, Taylor's solution offered relatively rich women of European descent a way to "have it all" but did not account for the needs of poor women and women of color. Never did she wonder who would care for the families of low-paid female servants in bourgeois homes. Would these working-class domestics manage to find women poorer than themselves to look after their children? Or would their children simply have to fend for themselves? And what of slave women who had no choice about performing domestic service, especially nannying for their owners?

So, like Wollstonecraft, Taylor wrote not to all women so much as to a certain privileged class of married women of European descent. Nonetheless, it seems fair to say that Taylor's writings helped smooth the entrance of bourgeois white women into the working world, as did Mill's. He argued in "The Subjection of Women" that by recognizing women's rational powers as equal to men's, society would reap significant benefits: public-spirited citizens for society itself, intellectually stimulating spouses for husbands, a doubling of the "mass of mental faculties available for the higher service of humanity," and a multitude of very happy women.[32] Although Mill's case for the liberation of women did not rest on his proving that *all* women could do anything men could do, it did depend on his demonstrating that some "exceptional" women could.[33]

Unlike Wollstonecraft, who put no "great stress on the example of a few women who, from having received a masculine education, have acquired courage and resolution,"[34] Mill used the life stories of exceptional women to strengthen his claim that male-female distinctions were not absolute but instead differences of average. The average woman's inability to do something the average man could do, said Mill, did not justify a law or taboo barring all women from attempting that thing.[35]

Moreover, for Mill even if all women were worse than all men at something, this still did not justify forbidding them from trying to do that thing, for "what women by nature cannot do, it is quite superfluous to forbid them from doing. What they can do, but not so well as the men who are their competitors, competition suffices to exclude them from."[36] Although Mill believed women would fare quite well in any competitions with men, he conceded that occasionally a biological sex difference might tip the scales in favor of men. Like Wollstonecraft, however, he denied the existence of general intellectual or moral differences between women and men: "I do not know a more signal instance of the blindness with which the world, including the herd of studious men, ignore and pass over all the influences of social circumstances, than their silly depreciation of the intellectual, and silly panegyrics on the moral, nature of women."[37]

Overall, Mill went further than Wollstonecraft in challenging men's alleged intellectual superiority. Stressing the sameness of men's and women's mental abilities, Wollstonecraft nonetheless entertained the thought that women might not be able to attain the same degree of knowledge as men.[38] Mill expressed no such reservation. He insisted intellectual achievement gaps between women and men simply resulted from men's more thorough education and privileged position. In fact, Mill was so eager to establish that men were not intellectually superior to women that he tended to err in the opposite direction, valorizing women's attention to detail, use of concrete examples, and intuitiveness as superior cognitive skills not often found in men.[39]

Unlike Taylor, and despite his high regard for women's intellectual abilities, Mill assumed most women would continue to choose family over career even under ideal circumstances—with marriage a free contract between real equals, legal separation and divorce easily available to wives, and jobs open to unwed women. He also assumed that women's choice of family over career was entirely voluntary and involved their consent to temporarily give their other interests in life lower priority: "Like a man when he chooses a profession, so, when a woman marries, it may in general be understood that she makes choice of the management of a household, and the bringing up of a family, as the first call upon her exertions, during as many years of her life as may be required for the purpose; and that she renounces not all other objects and occupations, but all which are not consistent with the requirements of this."[40] Mill's words attest to his apparent belief that most women would choose family life over career or professional pursuits.

As noted, Taylor disagreed with Mill that truly liberated women would want to stay home to rear children. Yet, like Mill, Taylor was fundamentally a reformer, not a revolutionary. To be sure, by inviting married women with children as well as single women to work outside the home, Taylor did challenge the traditional division of labor where men earned the money and women managed its use. But she did not ask husbands to do their fair share of housework. Thus was born the "double day" for women: eight hours of work outside the home and then eight hours of work inside the home.

Suffrage and the Abolitionist Movement: Elizabeth Stone, Lucretia Mott, Elizabeth Cady Stanton, and Sojourner Truth

During the first wave of the women's rights movement, women's suffrage was often tied to the abolitionist movement, though not always in ways that successfully addressed race, either as a stand-alone concern or in terms of how gender and other axes of oppression might intersect.[41]

When people began to work in earnest for the abolition of slavery, a reluctance on the part of many white male abolitionists to link the rights of enslaved persons of African descent to white women's rights became evident. Rejecting a view of white women as oppressed in the same way as slaves, many white male abolitionists persuaded white female abolitionists to disassociate white women's liberty struggles from the liberty struggles of enslaved men of African descent. In fact, most white male abolitionists deemed the voting rights of men of African descent more important than those of white women, to say nothing of the voting rights of women of African descent.[42]

Assuming their male counterparts would reward them for being team players, the American women who attended the 1840 World Anti-Slavery Convention in London thought they would play a major role at the meeting. They could not have been more wrong. Not even Lucretia Mott and Elizabeth Cady Stanton, two of the most prominent leaders of the US women's rights movement, spoke at the meeting. Although several male delegates of African descent participated at the convention, the British organizing committee rejected the credentials of all female delegates (of whatever racioethnic background) and permitted no woman to share actively in the proceedings.[43] Angered by this silencing of women, Mott and Stanton vowed to hold a women's rights convention on their return to the United States. Eight years later, in 1848, three hundred women and men met in Seneca Falls, New York, and produced a Declaration of Sentiments and twelve resolutions.

Modeled on the Declaration of Independence, the Declaration of Sentiments stressed the issues Mill and Taylor had wanted to emphasize in England, particularly the need for reforms in marriage, divorce, property, and child-custody laws. The twelve resolutions emphasized women's rights to express themselves in public—to speak out on the burning issues of the day, especially "in regard to the great subjects of morals and religion,"[44] which women were supposedly more qualified to address than men. The Seneca Falls Convention failed to endorse only one of the twelve resolutions unanimously: the ninth, Susan B. Anthony's Women's Suffrage Resolution, which read, "Resolved, that it is the duty of the women of this country to secure to themselves their sacred right to the franchise."[45] Many convention delegates hesitated to press such an "extreme" demand for fear that all of their demands would be rejected. Still, with the help of African American male abolitionist Frederick Douglass, Resolution Nine did manage to pass.

Assessing the Seneca Falls Convention, recent critics have observed that, with the exception of Lucretia Mott's hastily added resolution to secure for women "an equal participation with men in the various trades, professions, and commerce,"[46] the nineteenth-century meeting failed to address class concerns, such as those that troubled underpaid white female mill and factory workers. Moreover, the convention did not address the specific concerns of women of African descent or of any racioethnic background other than white European. In the same way that the abolitionist movement had focused on the rights of men of African descent to the exclusion of their female counterparts, the nineteenth-century women's rights movement focused too much on the rights of privileged white women, again neglecting the concerns of women from other racioethnic and economic backgrounds. Yet, despite this lack of consideration on the part of first-wave feminists, many women of color made significant contributions to the nineteenth-century women's rights and suffrage movements. For example, African American abolitionist Sojourner Truth, discussed in greater depth in Chapter 4, delivered her famous speech on behalf of women at an 1851 women's rights convention in Akron, Ohio. Responding to male hecklers who taunted that it was ludicrous for women to desire the vote when they could not even step over a puddle or get into a horse carriage without male assistance, Truth exclaimed that no man had ever extended such help to her. Neither her "womanhood" nor her "female nature," said Truth, had ever prevented her from working, acting, or functioning as well as a man.[47]

The Civil War began just as the women's rights movement was gaining momentum. Seeing in this tragic war their best opportunity to free the slaves, male abolitionists again asked female abolitionists to put women's causes on the back burner, which they reluctantly did. But the end of the Civil War did not bring women's liberation, and women of all racioethnic backgrounds increasingly found themselves at odds with recently emancipated men of African descent. Concerned that the struggle to secure the rights of men of

African descent would again eclipse that for women's rights, the male as well as female delegates to an 1866 national women's rights convention decided to establish an Equal Rights Association. Cochaired by Frederick Douglass and Elizabeth Cady Stanton, the association had as its announced purpose the unification of the suffrage struggles of predominately white women and of men of African descent. Considerable evidence, however, indicates that Stanton and some of her coworkers actually "viewed the organization as a means to ensure that [African American] men would not receive the franchise unless and until [white] women were also its recipients."[48]

Unmoved by Douglass's observation that because of their extreme vulnerability, men of African descent needed the vote even more than white women, Anthony and Stanton, among others, successfully argued for the dissolution of the Equal Rights Association for fear that it might endorse passage of the Fifteenth Amendment, which would enfranchise men of African descent but not white women. Elizabeth Cady Stanton reportedly said, "I will cut off this right arm of mine before I will ever work for or demand the ballot for the Negro and not the [white] woman."[49]

Upon the dissolution of the Equal Rights Association, Anthony and Stanton established the National Woman Suffrage Association. At approximately the same time, Lucy Stone, who had serious philosophical disagreements with Stanton and especially Anthony about the role of organized religion in women's oppression, founded the American Woman Suffrage Association. Henceforward, the US women's rights movement would be split in two.

In the main, the National Woman Suffrage Association forwarded a revolutionary feminist agenda for women, whereas the American Woman Suffrage Association pushed a reformist feminist agenda. Most American women gravitated toward the more moderate American Woman Suffrage Association. By the time these two associations merged in 1890 to form the National American Woman Suffrage Association, the wide-ranging, vociferous women's rights movement of the early nineteenth century had transformed into a single-issue, relatively tame women's suffrage movement. From 1890 until passage of the Nineteenth Amendment in 1920, the National American Woman Suffrage Association confined almost all of its activities to gaining the vote for women. Victorious after fifty-two years of concerted struggle, many of the exhausted suffragists chose to believe that simply by gaining the vote, women had become men's equals.[50]

"Second Wave" Liberal Feminism: Equal Rights

For nearly forty years after passage of the Nineteenth Amendment, feminists went about their work relatively quietly in the United States. Then, around

1960, a rebellious generation of feminists loudly proclaimed as fact what suffragists Stanton and Anthony had always believed: to be fully liberated, women needed economic opportunities and sexual freedoms as well as civil liberties. Like their grandmothers, some of these young women pushed a reformist, liberal agenda, whereas others forwarded a more revolutionary, radical program of action.

By the mid-1960s the second wave of US feminism was well underway. Most liberal feminists had joined one of the emerging women's rights groups, such as the National Organization for Women, the National Women's Political Caucus, and the Women's Equity Action League. These groups generally worked to improve women's status "by applying legal, social, and other pressures upon institutions ranging from the Bell Telephone Company to television networks to the major political parties."[51] In contrast, most radical feminists had banded together in one or another women's liberation groups. Much smaller and more personally focused than the liberal women's rights groups, these radical women's liberation groups aimed to increase women's consciousness about women's oppression. The groups embraced the spirit of the revolutionary New Left, striving not to reform what they regarded as an elitist, capitalistic, competitive, individualistic system but to replace it with an egalitarian, socialistic, cooperative, communitarian, sisterhood-is-powerful system. Among the largest of these radical women's liberation groups were the Women's International Terrorist Conspiracy from Hell, the Redstockings, the Feminists, and the New York Radical Feminists. Although Maren Lockwood Carden correctly noted in her 1974 book, *The New Feminist Movement*, that the ideological contrasts between the women's rights and women's liberation groups of the 1960s had blurred by the mid-1970s,[52] women's rights groups remained less revolutionary than women's liberation groups.

Because this chapter focuses on liberal feminists, we reserve discussion of radical feminist "women's lib" for Chapter 2. Here we concentrate on the history of twentieth-century liberal women's rights groups and their mostly legislative activities. Between the passage of the Nineteenth Amendment and the advent of the second wave of US feminism during the 1960s, only two official feminist groups—the National Woman's Party and the National Federation of Business and Professional Women's Clubs—promulgated women's rights. Despite their efforts, however, discrimination against women did not end, largely because the importance of women's rights had not yet been impressed on the consciousness (and conscience) of the bulk of the US population. This changed with the eruption of the civil rights movement. Sensitized to the myriad ways in which US systems, structures, and laws oppressed people of color, many of those active in or at least sympathetic to the civil rights movement recognized similarities in discrimination against persons of African descent and against women, resulting in increased sympathy for all women's liberation.

In 1961, President John F. Kennedy established the Commission on the Status of Women, which produced much new data about women and resulted in the formation of the Citizens' Advisory Council, various state commissions on the status of women, and the passage of the Equal Pay Act. When Congress passed the 1964 Civil Rights Act—amended with the Title VII provision to prohibit discrimination based on sex, as well as race, color, religion, or national origin, by private employers, employment agencies, and unions—a woman shouted from the congressional gallery, "We made it! God bless America!"[53] Unfortunately, the jubilation of women in general was short-lived; the courts were reluctant to enforce Title VII's "sex amendment." Women felt betrayed by the system, and their joy morphed into an anger that feminist activists used to mobilize women to fight for their civil rights with new vigor.

Among these feminist activists was Betty Friedan (1921–2006), who reflected on how she and some of her associates reacted to the courts' refusal to take Title VII's "sex amendment" seriously: "The absolute necessity for a civil rights movement for women had reached such a point of subterranean explosive urgency by 1966, that it only took a few of us to get together to ignite the spark—and it spread like a nuclear chain reaction."[54] That spark was the formation of the National Organization for Women by Friedan, Anna Pauline (Pauli) Murray, the first female Episcopal priest of African descent, and Shirley Chisholm, the first major-party person of African descent to run for president of the United States of America.[55] Murray's *States' Laws on Race and Color, and Appendices* was deemed required reading for civil rights lawyers of the time;[56] and Chisholm used her position in the US Senate to lobby for women's and minorities' rights.[57]

Considered the first explicitly feminist group in the United States to challenge sex discrimination, NOW saw women's inequality in all spheres of life: social, political, economic, and personal. After considerable behind-the-scenes maneuvering, NOW's three hundred charter members, male and female, elected Friedan—viewed as a home-breaker because of her then controversial book *The Feminine Mystique* (see below)—as the organization's first president in 1966.

Although NOW's first members included radical and conservative feminists as well as liberal feminists, it quickly became clear that the organization's essential identity and agenda were fundamentally liberal; that is, NOW simply aimed to make women the equals of men. Its 1967 Bill of Rights demanded the following rights and opportunities for women:

I. That the U.S. Congress immediately pass the Equal Rights Amendment to the Constitution to provide that "Equality of rights under the law shall not be denied or abridged by the United States or by any State on account of sex," and that such then be immediately ratified by the several States.

II. That equal employment opportunity be guaranteed to all women, as well as men, by insisting that the Equal Employment Opportunity Commission enforces the prohibitions against racial discrimination.

III. That women be protected by law to ensure their rights to return to their jobs within a reasonable time after childbirth without the loss of seniority or other accrued benefits, and be paid maternity leave as a form of social security and/or employee benefit.

IV. Immediate revision of tax laws to permit the deduction of home and child-care expenses for working parents.

V. That child-care facilities be established by law on the same basis as parks, libraries, and public schools, adequate to the needs of children from the pre-school years through adolescence, as a community resource to be used by all citizens from all income levels.

VI. That the right of women to be educated to their full potential equally with men be secured by Federal and State legislation, eliminating all discrimination and segregation by sex, written and unwritten, at all levels of education, including colleges, graduate and professional schools, loans and fellowships, and Federal and State training programs such as the Job Corps.

VII. The right of women in poverty to secure job training, housing, and family allowances on equal terms with men, but without prejudice to a parent's right to remain at home to care for his or her children; revision of welfare legislation and poverty programs which deny women dignity, privacy, and self-respect.

VIII. The right of women to control their own reproductive lives by removing from the penal code laws limiting access to contraceptive information and devices, and by repealing penal laws governing abortion.[58]

NOW's list of demands pleased the organization's liberal members but angered both its conservative and its radical members, albeit for different reasons. Whereas conservative members objected to the push for permissive contraception and abortion laws, NOW's failure to support women's sexual rights, particularly the right to choose between heterosexual, bisexual, and lesbian lifestyles, alienated radical members. Moreover, NOW's 1967 Bill of Rights lacked any mention of important women's issues such as domestic violence, rape, and sexual harassment.[59]

Although Friedan acknowledged that "the sex-role debate . . . cannot be avoided if equal opportunity in employment, education and civil rights are ever to mean more than paper rights,"[60] she still insisted "that the gut issues of this revolution involve employment and education and new social institutions and not sexual fantasy."[61] Worried that NOW would radicalize its traditional liberal focus, Friedan, among other feminist activists, strongly opposed the organization's public support of lesbianism, going so far as to term lesbians a "lavender menace"[62] because, as she saw it, they alienated mainstream society from feminists in general.

Friedan's concerns about the lavender menace notwithstanding, NOW eventually endorsed four resolutions favorable to lesbian women. Presented at NOW's 1970 Congress to Unite Women, they read as follows:

1. Women's Liberation is not a lesbian plot.
2. Whenever the label lesbian is used against the movement collectively or against women individually, it is to be affirmed, not denied.
3. In all discussions of birth control, homosexuality must be included as a legitimate method of contraception.
4. All sex education curricula must include lesbianism as a valid, legitimate form of sexual expression and love.[63]

As we will see in Chapter 2, lesbian women's role in the feminist movement remained strong. Moreover, NOW began to stress its aim to serve not only the women most likely to survive and thrive in a traditionally male system but any woman who believed women's rights should equal men's. Thus, NOW increasingly focused its energies on what many feminists term the "sameness-difference debate": Is gender equality best achieved by stressing women's oneness as a gender or their diversity as individuals; similarly, is it best achieved by emphasizing the similarities or the differences between women and men? The varied answers to these basic questions continue to shape and reshape NOW's political agenda.

Toward "Third-Wave" Liberal Feminism: Sameness Versus Difference and Egalitarianism

Sameness Versus Difference

Betty Friedan

It is instructive to reflect further on Betty Friedan's career as a writer not only because of her identification with NOW but also because of her own evolution as a thinker. Friedan initially took for granted that all women are the same as men, but later she concluded quite differently. Like most twentieth-century liberal feminists, Friedan gradually accepted both the radical feminist critique that liberal feminists are prone to co-optation by the "male establishment" and the conservative feminist critique that liberal feminists are out of touch with the bulk of US women who hold the institutions of marriage, motherhood, and the family in high regard.[64] When she wrote her 1963 classic, *The Feminine Mystique*,[65] Friedan seemed oblivious to any other perspective than that of bourgeois, heterosexual, literate white women who found the traditional roles of wife and mother unsatisfying. She wrote that in lieu of more meaningful goals, these women spent too much time cleaning their already tidy homes, improving their already attractive appearances, and indulging their already spoiled children.[66] Focusing on this unappealing picture of family life in affluent US suburbs, Friedan concluded that contemporary housewives needed to find meaningful work in the full-time, public workforce. Wives' and mothers' partial absence from home would enable husbands and children to become more self-sufficient, capable of cooking their own meals and doing their own laundry.[67]

Although Friedan may have explained why marriage and motherhood were not enough for bored, stay-at-home wives and mothers, critics thought *The Feminine Mystique* failed to address a host of issues deeper than "the problem that has no name"—Friedan's tag for the dissatisfaction supposedly felt by privileged housewives in the United States. Like Taylor and Mill before her, Friedan sent bourgeois white women out into the workplace without summoning men of any class or racioethnicity to share in domestic duties and without addressing the situation of white working-class women and women of color who were already toiling in the public realm.

By the time she wrote *The Second Stage*,[68] about twenty years after *The Feminine Mystique*, Friedan had come to believe that these critics were right. Often it is very difficult for women, even bourgeois white women, to combine marriage, motherhood, and full-time work outside the home. Observing the ways in which some members of her daughter's generation ran themselves ragged in the name of feminism—trying to be full-time career women as well as full-time housewives and mothers—Friedan concluded that the "superwomen" of the 1980s were no less oppressed (albeit for different reasons) than the stay-at-home mothers of the 1960s had been. Increasingly, Friedan urged feminists to ask themselves whether women either can or should try to meet not simply one but two standards of perfection: that set in the workplace by traditional men, who had wives to take care of all their nonworkplace needs, and that set in the home by traditional women, whose whole sense of worth, power, and mastery came from being ideal housewives and mothers.[69]

Rather than despairing over these and other women's choices, however, Friedan used them as talking points to convince feminists of the 1980s to move from what she termed first-stage feminism to second-stage feminism. She noted that this latter form of feminism would require women to work with men to escape the excesses of the new feminist mystique, "which denied the core of women's personhood that is fulfilled through love, nurture, [and] home," as well as those of the feminine mystique, "which defined women solely in terms of their relation to men as wives, mothers and homemakers."[70] Together, women and men might develop the kind of social values, leadership styles, and institutional structures needed to permit both sexes to achieve fulfillment in both the public and the private worlds.

In some ways, the difference between the Friedan of *The Feminine Mystique* and the Friedan of *The Second Stage* mirrors the difference between a feminist who believes women need to be the same as men to be equal to them and one who believes women, though different from men, can still be men's equals, provided society values things "feminine" as much as things "masculine." *The Feminine Mystique* sent the overall message that women's liberation hinged on women's becoming like men. For this reason, Friedan peppered its pages with such comments as "If an able American woman does not use her human energy and ability in some meaningful pursuit (which necessarily means competition, for there is competition in every serious pursuit of our society), she will fritter away her energy in neurotic symptoms, or unproductive exercise, or destructive 'love.'"[71]

Eighteen years after the publication of *The Feminine Mystique*, however, Friedan's message to women had substantially changed. In *The Second Stage*, she described as culturally feminine so-called Beta styles of thinking and acting, which emphasize "fluidity, flexibility and interpersonal sensitivity," and as culturally masculine so-called Alpha styles of thinking and acting, which stress "hierarchical, authoritarian, strictly task-oriented leadership based on instrumental, technological rationality."[72] Rather than offering women of the 1980s the same advice she had offered 1960s women—namely, minimize your feminine Beta tendencies and maximize your masculine Alpha tendencies—Friedan counseled just the opposite: embrace your womanhood. She said that women did not need to deny their differences from men to achieve equality with them. Thus, Friedan urged women of the 1980s to stop "aping the accepted dominant Alpha mode of established movements and organizations" and start using their "Beta intuitions" to solve the social, political, and economic problems of the day.[73]

To the degree that *The Feminine Mystique* advised women to overcome their femininity, *The Second Stage* urged them to embrace their womanhood. But *The Second Stage* did more than this. It also encouraged women and men alike to work toward an androgynous future in which all human beings manifest both traditionally masculine and traditionally feminine traits. Once she decided that androgyny was in all human beings' best interest, Friedan stayed committed to her vision. Indeed, she devoted many pages of her third major book, *The Fountain of Age*,[74] to singing androgyny's praises. Specifically, she urged aging (Alpha) men to develop their passive, nurturing, or contemplative feminine qualities and aging (Beta) women to develop their bold, assertive, commanding, or adventurous masculine qualities. Insisting that people over fifty should explore their "other side"—whether masculine or feminine—Friedan noted that women over fifty who went back to school or work or actively engaged in the public world reported this time as the best of their lives. Men over fifty who started to focus on the quality of their personal relationships and interior lives reported a similar satisfaction in older age.

The more she emphasized the concept of androgyny, however, the more Friedan seemed to move toward humanism and away from feminism. Increasingly, she described feminist "sexual politics" as the "no-win battle of women as a whole sex, oppressed victims, against men as a whole sex, the oppressors."[75] In addition, she urged women to join with men to create a "new [human] politics that must emerge beyond reaction."[76] Eventually, Friedan claimed that because "human wholeness" is the true "promise of feminism," feminists should move beyond a focus on women's issues (issues related mostly to women's reproductive and sexual roles, rights, and responsibilities) to work with men on "the concrete, practical, everyday problems of living, working and loving as equal persons."[77] In a shift that appears to be more than mere coincidence, NOW's focus also moved in the humanist direction suggested by Friedan.

Catharine MacKinnon

The sameness-versus-difference debate did not end with Friedan, however. On the contrary, lawyer Catharine MacKinnon gave it especially strong treatment in the latter part of the twentieth century. MacKinnon argued that neither the "sameness" nor the "difference" approach to sex equality works to support women's equality. The sameness approach does not work because it measures women against a male ideal. In *Toward a Feminist Theory of the State*, MacKinnon argued that laws designed to effectuate sex equality are insufficient. Under the guise of neutrality, they operate on the assumption that maleness and masculinity are the standard toward which all women should strive.[78] The difference approach does not work much better, however: it reinforces stereotypes about what women are, how they are, and how they behave. Rather than supporting women's equality, according to MacKinnon, the difference approach reinforces what political theorist Iris Marion Young has called the "five faces of oppression": "Exploitation (essentially, having one's surplus labor extracted by another), marginalization (being expelled from useful participation in social life, including productive work), powerlessness (lack of autonomy and respectability), cultural imperialism (being subjected to universalized dominant group norms), and violence (existing in a social context that makes violence against one's group allowable or acceptable)."[79] In short, the difference approach to women's equality does not work, in MacKinnon's view, because Western society equates difference with being undeserving of respect and consideration from the privileged group from which one differs.

Egalitarianism

One way to better understand the difference between classical liberal feminists and contemporary egalitarian liberal feminists is to focus on a concrete issue, such as affirmative action policy. Classical liberal feminists believe that after discriminatory laws and policies have been removed from the books, thereby formally enabling women to compete equally with men, not much else can or should be done about "birds of a feather flocking together"— about male senior professors, for example, favoring a male candidate for a faculty promotion over an equally qualified female candidate. In contrast, egalitarian liberal feminists urge society to break up that "old flock (gang) of mine," especially when failure to make feathers fly results in significant gender asymmetries with respect to the rank of full professor, for example. One typical 2000s study found that "only one in eight women has attained full rank compared to nearly nine out of ten men."[80] The same study found that in engineering, nearly three in five men had become full professors as compared to only one in five women. In view of such statistics, egalitarian feminists advocate for selecting female school and job applicants over equally qualified male applicants (so-called affirmative action).[81] Egalitarian liberal feminists insist that to the degree such policies are viewed as temporary (that is, curative), they are not problematic. As soon as women and men have equal social status and economic clout, affirmative action policies will be unnecessary. Indeed, egalitarian feminists stress, when women achieve de facto as well as de jure equality with men, policies advantaging women over men will be unfair.

Elizabeth Anderson

Elizabeth Anderson is a contemporary egalitarian feminist who favors what she terms "democratic equality" over "luck" egalitarianism.[82] Whereas the luck egalitarian thinks the fundamental injustice in need of correction is the "natural inequality of the distribution of luck"[83] among individuals, the democratic equality egalitarian thinks that eliminating bad luck is only the first move in the game. To construct a just society, people must, in Anderson's view, aim to establish a community of equals, which integrates principles of distribution with "the expressive demands of equal respect."[84] For Anderson, democratic equality depends on deprivileging bourgeois, heterosexual white men.

Martha Nussbaum

Martha Nussbaum, another contemporary egalitarian feminist, insists that to be equal men and women must have the same resources and opportunities in life. In her view all people need ten "central human functional capabilities" to live a flourishing life:[85] the ability to live to the end of a human life, to have good health, to move freely, to use their senses, to have emotional attachments to others, to plan their own lives, to have a social basis for self-respect, to laugh and enjoy life, to live in harmony with nature, and to exhibit political autonomy. The central idea of Nussbaum's "capabilities approach" to human flourishing is that morality and equality demand that the state provide everyone with access to these capabilities.

"Third-Wave" Liberal Feminism: Intersectionality

Importantly, in recent years liberal feminism has taken a turn toward intersectionality (see Chapter 4), which holds that to properly treat the oppression of women, we must understand it as situated within a grander matrix of interlocking and overlapping oppressions. A nonexhaustive list of the various forms of oppression encompassed by intersectionality includes those based on gender, sex, sexuality, race, ethnicity, disability status, and socioeconomic status. As part of its self-restructuring, liberal feminism currently grapples with its historical racioethnic and socioeconomic exclusivity and actively attempts to include the experiences and perspectives of women historically marginalized from its ranks. Consider, for example, NOW. The organization's points of focus started to evolve rapidly throughout the 1980s, 1990s, and 2000s. NOW held its first Lesbian Rights Conference in 1984, its first Global Feminist Conference in 1992, its first Women of Color and Allies

Summit in 1998, and its first Women with Disabilities and Allies Summit in 2003.[86] During this same period, NOW's leadership also began to change. More women of color, lesbians, and bisexual, transsexual, and transgender women joined the organization and contributed to its direction.

Critiques of Liberal Feminism

Critique One: Reason, Freedom, and Autonomy Are Not as Good as They Sound

Among other feminist philosophers, Alison Jaggar formulated a powerful critique of both classical and egalitarian liberal feminism. She argued that the rational, free, and autonomous self favored by liberals is not neutral between the sexes but is, on the contrary, a male self. Jaggar claimed that because liberals, including liberal feminists, locate human beings' specialness in rationality and autonomy, they are normative dualists—thinkers committed to the view that the functions and activities of the mind are somehow better than those of the body.[87] Eating, drinking, excreting, sleeping, and reproducing are not, in this view, quintessential human activities because most other animal species also engage in them. Instead, the capacity to think, reason, calculate, deliberate, and comprehend sets human beings apart from the rest of animal creation.

Jaggar then posited that because of the original sexual division of labor, liberal thought increasingly emphasized mental over bodily activities and functions. Given their undemanding reproductive and domestic roles, men had plenty of free time to cultivate the life of the mind; for them the body is that which interferes with thinking. In contrast, because of their heavy reproductive and domestic roles, women had little time for themselves. Their days and nights were spent caring for other people, especially infants, the aged, and the infirm. Thus, women focused on their own and others' bodies, viewing thinking as a luxury they could not afford. Not surprisingly, men took over the field of philosophy, said Jaggar. Their way of seeing themselves as "minds" came to dominate Western culture's collective pool of ideas about human nature. As a result all liberals, male or female, nonfeminist or feminist, tend to accept as truth the priority of the mental over the bodily, even when their own daily experiences contradict this belief.

(Classical) liberal feminists' adherence to some version of normative dualism is problematic for feminism, according to Jaggar, not only because normative dualism leads to a devaluation of bodily activities and functions but also because it usually leads to both political solipsism and political skepticism. (Political solipsism sees rational, autonomous person as essentially isolated, with needs and interests separate from, and even in opposition to, those of every other individual. Political skepticism holds that the fundamental questions of political philosophy—what constitutes human well-being and fulfillment, and what are the means to attain it?—have no shared answer.) Thus, valuing the mind over the body and stressing the independence of the self from others creates a politics that puts an extraordinary premium on liberty—on the rational, autonomous, independent, self-determining, isolated, and separated person's ability to think, do, and be whatever he or she deems worthy.[88]

Jaggar criticized the political solipsism that results from liberalism on empirical grounds, noting it makes little sense to think of people as individuals existing prior to the formation of community through some sort of contract. She observed, for example, that any pregnant woman knows a child is related to others (at least to her) even before it is born. The baby does not—indeed could not—exist as a lone atom prior to subsequent entrance into the human community. Human infants are born helpless and require great care for many years. Jaggar explained that because a single adult cannot adequately provide this care, humans live in social groups that cooperatively bring offspring to maturity. She said, "Human interdependence is . . . necessitated by human biology, and the assumption of individual self-sufficiency is plausible only if one ignores human biology."[89] Thus, Jaggar insisted, liberal political theorists need to explain not how and why isolated individuals come together but how and why communities dissolve. Competition, not cooperation, is the anomaly.

To add force to her empirical argument, Jaggar observed that political solipsism makes no sense conceptually. Here she invoked Naomi Scheman's point that political solipsism requires belief in abstract individualism.[90] The abstract individual's emotions, beliefs, abilities, and interests can supposedly be articulated and understood without any reference whatsoever to social context. Kant's person is this type of abstract individual—a pure reason unaffected by either the empirical-psychological ego or the empirical-biological body. However, Kant's philosophy notwithstanding, said Scheman, we are not abstract individuals but flesh-and-blood people "embedded in a social web of interpretation that serves to give meaning"[91] to our twitches and twinges, our moans and groans, our squeals and screams. Apart from this interpretative grid, we are literally self-less—that is, socially constituted wants and desires determine our very identities. We are, fundamentally, the selves our communities create, an observation that challenges the classical liberal myth of the self-sufficient individual.

Political skepticism collapses together with political solipsism, according to Jaggar, because the former also depends on an overly abstract and individualistic conception of the self. In contrast to those liberals or liberal feminists who insist the state should refrain from privileging any one conception of human well-being over another, Jaggar argued that the state should serve as more than a traffic cop who, without commenting on drivers' stated destinations, merely makes sure their cars do not collide. Whether we like it or not, she said, human biology and psychology dictate a set of basic human needs, and societies that treat these basic needs as optional cannot expect to survive, let alone to thrive. Thus, said Jaggar, the state must do more than keep traffic moving; it must also block off certain roads even if some individuals want to travel down them.

Critique Two: Women Should Not Try to be Like Men

Jean Bethke Elshtain, a communitarian political theorist, developed an even stronger critique of liberal feminism. Like Jaggar, Elshtain claimed liberal feminists are wrong to emphasize individual interests, rights, and personal freedom over the common good, obligations, and social commitment because "there is no way to create real communities out of an aggregate of 'freely' choosing adults."[92] In addition, more so than Jaggar, Elshtain criticized liberal feminists for putting an apparently high premium on so-called male values. She accused the Friedan of the 1960s of equating male being with human being, manly virtue with human virtue. Specifically, she identified what she considered liberal feminism's three major flaws: (1) claiming women can become like men if they set their minds to it, (2) claiming most women want to become like men, and (3) claiming all women should want to become like men, to aspire to "masculine" values.

With respect to the claim that women can become like men, Elshtain pointed to the general liberal feminist belief that male-female differences are the products of culture rather than biology, of nurture rather than nature. She claimed liberal feminists refuse to entertain the possibility that some sex differences are biologically determined, for fear that affirmative answers could be used to justify the repression, suppression, and oppression of women. For this reason, many liberal feminists have, in Elshtain's estimation, become "excessive environmentalists"—that is, people who believe that gender identities are the exclusive product of socialization, easily changeable at society's will.[93]

Liberal feminism also has a tendency, continued Elshtain, to overestimate the number of women who want to be like men. She denied the view that any woman who wants to be only a wife and mother is a benighted and befuddled victim of patriarchal "false consciousness." Patriarchy, in Elshtain's estimation, is simply not powerful enough to make mush out of millions of women's minds. If it were, feminists could not have provided a cogent explanation for the emergence of feminist "true consciousness" out of pervasive patriarchal socialization. Elshtain observed that liberal feminists' attempt to reduce wifing and mothering to mere roles is misguided. If, after investing years of physical and emotional energy into being a wife and mother, a woman hears she made the wrong choice, that she could have done something significant with her life instead, she is not likely to have a positive reaction. It is one thing to suggest that a person try a new hairstyle; it is quite another to advise a person to pursue a more purposeful destiny.

Finally, as Elshtain saw it, liberal feminists are wrong to sing "a paean of praise to what Americans themselves call the 'rat race,'"[94] to tell women they should absorb traditional masculine values. Articles written for women about dressing for success, making it in a man's world, not crying in public, avoiding intimate friendships, being assertive, and playing hardball serve only to erode what may, according to Elshtain, ultimately be women's best feature—namely, their learned ability to create and sustain community through involvement with friends and family. Women ought to resist membership in the "rat race" culture, said Elshtain. Rather than encouraging one another to mimic the traditional behavior of so-called successful men, who spend a minimum of time at home and a maximum of time at the office, women ought to work toward the kind of society in which men as well as women have as much time for friends and family as for business associates and professional colleagues.

Although she came close here to forwarding the problematic thesis that every wife and mother is necessarily a good woman, Elshtain insisted maternal thinking "need not and must not descend into the sentimentalization that vitiated much Suffragist discourse."[95] Fearing that full participation in the public sphere would threaten female virtue, the suffragists reasoned "the vote" was a way for women to reform the evil, deceitful, and ugly public realm without ever having to leave the supposed goodness, truth, and beauty of the private realm. As Elshtain saw it, had the suffragists not constructed a false polarity between male vice and female virtue, they might have secured women's right to vote in the only world available to them: a flawed world in need of women's best qualities.[96]

In assessing Elshtain's critique of liberal feminism, late-twentieth-century liberal feminists found several reasons to fault her communitarian line of thought. In particular, they saw her as adopting an "overly romanticized view of a traditional community, where the status quo is not only given but often embraced,"[97] and where, therefore, women's traditional roles remain largely unchanged even if supposedly more valued by society as a whole. They also saw her as accepting the values of a community without critically examining its exclusionary potentialities or asking what kind of communities constitute an environment in which women can thrive.

Critique Three: Liberal Feminism Inadequately Addresses Issues of Race, Class, and Sexual Orientation

Feminist critics of liberal feminism (particularly classical liberal feminism) fault it not only for valorizing a male (e.g., rational, autonomous, isolated) ontology of self and an individualist politics (e.g., an emphasis on the rights of individuals instead of groups) but also for focusing only, or mainly, on the interests of upper- and middle-class, heterosexual, white women.

For example, African American political theorist and activist Angela Davis commented that a significant number of women of African descent experience the housewife role as liberating rather than oppressive.[98] Indeed, stressed Davis, many women of African descent, particularly poor ones, would happily trade their travails for the "problem that has no name" (that is, the privileged [white] woman's dissatisfaction with her traditional housewife role). In response to this inherent lack of diversity, many second-wave women-of-color feminists formed their own groups, including the Comisión Femenil Mexicana Nacional, the North American Indian Women's Association, and the Combahee River Collective (discussed in greater depth in Chapter 4), which sought to grapple with oppression in multiple spheres, including both gender and race.

Moreover, classism has historically permeated liberal feminism. As mentioned above, seemingly oblivious to the privileged status of the women she addressed in *The Feminine Mystique*, Friedan simply assumed all or most women were supported by men and therefore wished to work for other than financial reasons. Later, when she came into increased contact with single mothers trying to support their families on meager wages or paltry social benefits, Friedan realized just how hard life can be for a poor woman working in a factory as opposed to a wealthy woman driving to a PTA meeting. Even in *The Second Stage*, although Friedan tried to address some of the economic concerns of women who had to work, her primary audience remained well-educated, financially comfortable white women whom she wished to rescue from the hardships of the so-called double day.

Similarly, in *The Fountain of Age* (1993) Freidan more directly targeted relatively well-to-do and healthy, as opposed to relatively poor and frail, older people. Although inspiring, her anecdotes about people remaking their lives after the age of fifty are, as one commentator noted, mostly tales about "life-long achievers with uncommon financial resources."[99] This group's experience contrasts with that of US citizens whose work years have worn them out physically and psychologically and who find it extremely difficult to survive, let alone thrive, on a small, fixed income. As such people age, especially if they are infirm, their main enemy is not self-image. On the contrary, it is "unsafe neighborhoods, unmanageable stairs, tight budgets and isolation."[100]

Finally, in addition to coming under attack for not addressing racism and classism adequately, liberal feminism has earned repeated accusations of heterosexism. As noted above, when lesbians working within the women's rights movement in the late 1960s decided publicly to avow their sexual identity, Betty Friedan and other key leaders of NOW feared that a vocal and visible lesbian constituency might further alienate the public from "women's rights" causes. Therefore, they remained relatively silent about homophobia in society at large for far too many years.

Conclusion

One response to the perceived limitations of liberal feminism would be to dismiss it as a movement of the past, too focused on the needs of bourgeois white women to the exclusion of other women, especially women of color. In essence, Ellen Willis did precisely this in her 1975 article "The Conservatism of *Ms.*,"[101] which faulted the magazine, then the most widely recognized liberal feminist publication, for imposing a pseudofeminist "party line." After describing this line at length, Willis noted its overall message denied women's pressing need to overthrow patriarchy and capitalism and affirmed women's supposed ability to make it in the "system." Whatever *Ms.* offered women, insisted Willis, it was not feminism.

In response to this sort of criticism, *Ms.*, like NOW, has attempted to evolve since the mid-1970s. Its editors have featured articles on the intersectional nature of the oppression of women. Specifically, it has reported on such topics as overseas sweatshops, sex trafficking, and global human rights, thereby grappling with concerns beyond those of privileged white women.[102]

According to Anne Phillips, Martha Nussbaum forcefully defended liberalism (and by implication liberal feminism) from three main complaints: (1) it is too "individualistic," (2) its conception of equality is too "abstract and formal," and (3) it overemphasizes the role of reason in human life to the neglect of emotion.[103] Nussbaum argued that, in fact, liberalism was correct in just the right sort of way. It regards the individual as the basic unit for the construction of society, a notion that serves to protect the interests and rights of women and other oppressed people. The collective—be it the state or the family—should not subsume the individual to its ends, purposes, or goals. Rather, people should be recognized as separate selves who are "hungry and joyful and loving and needy *one by one*, however closely [they] may embrace one another."[104]

Questions for Discussion

1. Does liberal feminism survive the concerns of its critics? If so, in what way is this the case? If not, how might liberal feminism better address these concerns?
2. What are some practical ways in which women may achieve a balance of public and private pursuits? Consider various groups of women (e.g., single mothers, racial minorities, married women, lesbians, economically disadvantaged women).
3. Is there value in attaining legal equality (e.g., the right to vote) when social equality (e.g., the right to food) is still lagging?
4. Why do liberal feminists, most of whom are white, have so much trouble overcoming their Eurocentric biases?
5. What are the main differences between first- and second-wave liberal feminism and between second- and third-wave liberal feminism?

2

Radical Feminism

Radical feminists believe that true gender or sex equality is impossible within a patriarchal system. For these feminists, since the system is teeming with oppressive patriarchal norms, assumptions, and institutions, truly emancipatory reform is only possible through a radical reordering of society that eliminates male supremacy. Indeed, second-wave radical feminists who formed groups such as the Redstockings, the Feminists, New York Radical Women (NYRW), and New York Feminists perceived themselves as revolutionaries rather than reformers. They proclaimed, "The personal is political," offering stories from their own lives to illustrate the kinds of challenges faced by women in a society rife with patriarchy.[1]

For example, NYRW refused to join the 1968 Jeannette Rankin Brigade peace march in Washington, DC, a large gathering of women's groups united to oppose the Vietnam War, because its members saw the march as only a reaction to those who governed patriarchal America. NYRW felt that by appealing to Congress, the brigade was keeping its "traditional passive role of reacting to men instead of gaining real political power."[2] This same group of feminists also protested the 1968 Miss America Pageant, calling it a "cattle auction" and tossing bras, girdles, *Playboy* magazines, mops, and other items that represented women's oppression into a trash can.[3] Similarly, the Redstockings (a neologism combining "bluestocking," a negative term for brainy women, with "red," for its close linkage to the revolutionary Left) engaged in proactive activism. The group was famous for its speakouts and street theater dramatizations on the issue of abortion rights.[4]

Radical feminists introduced to women at large the practice of consciousness-raising. Women came together in small groups and shared with each other their personal experiences as women. In these groups, throughout the 1960s and 1970s, many women discovered that their supposedly individual experiences were not unique but widely shared by women of various backgrounds. According to philosopher Valerie Bryson, consciousness-raising revealed the linkages between the trauma of a woman who had been raped or forced to resort to an illegal abortion and the experiences of the wife whose husband refused to do his share of housework, the secretary whose boss expected her to flatter important male clients, and the female student whose professor promised her good grades if she had sex with him.[5]

Key to radical feminism was the insistence that men's control of women's sexual and reproductive lives and their self-identity, self-respect, and self-esteem constituted the most fundamental of all the oppressions. These feminists split themselves into two general camps, sometimes called radical-libertarian feminists and radical-cultural feminists.

Radical-Libertarian Feminism in General

Radical-libertarian feminists claimed that an exclusively feminine gender identity is likely to limit women's development as full human persons. Thus, they encouraged women to become androgynous—that is, to embody both (good) masculine and (good) feminine characteristics or, more controversially, any potpourri of masculine and feminine characteristics, good or bad, that struck their fancy.

Joreen Freeman

Among the first radical-libertarian feminists to celebrate the androgynous woman was Joreen Freeman. She wrote, "What is disturbing about a bitch is that she is androgynous. She incorporates within herself qualities defined as 'masculine' as well as 'feminine.' A Bitch is blatant, direct, arrogant, at times egoistic. She has no liking for the indirect, subtle, mysterious ways of the 'eternal feminine.' She disdains the vicarious life deemed natural to women because she wants to live a life of her own."[6] In other words, the androgynous woman does not limit herself to being a sweet girl with little in the way of power. Instead, she embraces as part of her gender identity whatever characteristics permit her to lead life on her own terms.

Freeman's views did not go unchallenged, however. Among others, Alice Echols rejected as wrongheaded Freeman's celebration of androgyny. She said that Freeman's androgynous woman was far too masculine to constitute a good role model for women. Still, Echols credited Freeman for expressing

radical-libertarian feminists' desire to free women from the apparent or perceived constraints of female biology.[7]

Gayle Rubin

Gayle Rubin, another radical-libertarian feminist, saw the sex/gender system
as a "set of arrangements by which a society transforms biological sexuality
into products of human activity."[8] So, for example, patriarchal society uses
certain facts about male and female biology (chromosomes, anatomy, hormones) as the basis for constructing a set of masculine and feminine gender
identities and behaviors that serve to empower men and disempower women.
According to Rubin, in the process of accomplishing this task, patriarchal society convinced itself that its cultural constructions are somehow natural and
therefore that people's normality depends on their ability to display whatever
gender identities and behaviors are culturally linked with their biological sex.
The task for feminists is therefore to contest the normativity of "naturalness"
and to proclaim the fluidity of all categories of gender.

Kate Millett

Kate Millett, yet another prominent radical-libertarian feminist, agreed with
Rubin that the roots of women's oppression are buried deep in patriarchy's
sex/gender system. In *Sexual Politics* (1970), Millett claimed the male-female
sex relationship is the paradigm for all power relationships: "Social caste su-
persedes all other forms of inegalitarianism: racial, political, or economic,
and unless the clinging to male supremacy as a birthright is finally forgone,
all systems of oppression will continue to function simply by virtue of their
logical and emotional mandate in the primary human situation."[9] Because
male control of the public and private worlds maintains patriarchy, male
control must be eliminated if women are to be liberated. But this is no easy
task. To eliminate male control, men and women must eliminate gender—
specifically, sexual status, role, and temperament—as it has been constructed
under patriarchy.

Patriarchal ideology exaggerates biological differences between men
and women, making certain that men always have the dominant, or masculine, roles and women always have the subordinate, or feminine, ones.
This ideology is so powerful, said Millett, that men usually secure the apparent consent of the very women they oppress. They do this through institutions, such as the academy, the church, and the family, each of which
justifies and reinforces women's subordination to men, resulting in many

women's internalization of a sense of inferiority to men. Should a woman refuse to accept patriarchal ideology by casting off her "femininity"—that is, her submissiveness/subordination—men will use coercion to accomplish what conditioning has failed to achieve. Intimidation is everywhere in patriarchy, according to Millett. The streetwise woman realizes that if she wants to survive in patriarchy, she had better act feminine, or else she may be subjected to "a variety of cruelties and barbarities."[10]

Millett singled out authors D. H. Lawrence, Henry Miller, and Norman Mailer as some of the most articulate leaders of patriarchy's 1930s–1960s assault on women. She claimed that readers typically took these writers' descriptions of relationships, in which men sexually humiliate and abuse women, as prescriptions for ideal sexual conduct. Millett considered this view of heterosexual relationships to be pornographic, arguing that pornography often functions in much the same way as advertising does. The perfectly slim bodies of the models who grace the covers of the fashion magazine *Vogue* become standards for average women. Nobody has to articulate an explicit law: "Thou shalt mold thine lumpen body in the image of one of America's top models." Women simply know what is expected of them, what it means to be beautiful. In the same way, women exposed to pornographic authors simply know what is expected of them, what it means to be sexually exciting as opposed to sexually uptight.

In addition to these literary pornographers, Millett identified two other patriarchal groups—neo-Freudian psychologists and Parsonian sociologists—as leading the assault on feminists. Although Sigmund Freud's openness about sexuality, his willingness to talk about what people do or do not do in the bedroom, initially appeared as a progressive step toward better, more various, and more liberating sexual relations, Millett claimed Freud's disciples used his writings to "rationalize the invidious relationship between the sexes, to ratify traditional roles, and to validate temperamental differences."[11] In a similar vein, the followers of Talcott Parsons, a well-known sociologist, used his writings to argue that distinctions between masculine and feminine traits are biological/natural rather than social/cultural and that without rigid gender dimorphism, society could not function as well as it does now. Convinced that gender identities and behaviors are not "an arbitrary imposition on an infinitely plastic biological base" but rather "an adjustment to the real biological differences between the sexes,"[12] Parsons's disciples confidently asserted that women's subordination to men is natural.

Millett ended her discussion of prominent sexists on an optimistic note. In the 1970s, women were, she believed, regrouping their forces. Twentieth-century feminists were determined not to repeat their nineteenth-century predecessors' mistakes. Millett observed in contemporary feminism a determined effort to destroy the so-called sex/gender system—the basic source of women's oppression—and to create a new androgynous society in which men and women are equals at every level of existence. Interestingly and importantly, she noted that creating this ideal society would require women to temporarily separate from men so that both men and women could better appreciate the value of women. A truly androgynous society is one in which both sexes value female worth as highly as male worth, said Millett.[13]

Shulamith Firestone

Like Millett, radical-libertarian feminist Shulamith Firestone claimed the material basis for the sexual/political ideology of female submission and male domination was rooted in the reproductive roles of men and women. However, Firestone believed Millett's solution to this problem—elimination of the sexual double standard that permits men but not women to experiment with sex and inauguration of a dual-parenting system that gives fathers and mothers equal child-rearing responsibilities—was inadequate. It would, in her estimation, take far more than such modest reforms in the sex/gender system to free women's (and men's) sexuality from the biological imperatives of procreation and to liberate women's (and men's) personalities from the socially constructed and rigid constraints of femininity and masculinity. In fact, said Firestone, it would take a major biological and social revolution to effect this kind of human liberation: artificial (ex utero) reproduction would need to replace natural (in utero) reproduction, and so-called intentional families, whose members chose each other for reasons of friendship or even simple convenience, would need to replace the traditional biological family constituted in and through its members' genetic connections to one another.

Firestone maintained that with the end of the biological family would come the breakup of the Oedipal family situation, which prohibits, among other things, parent-child incest. No longer would there be concerns about so-called inbreeding as people reverted to their natural "polymorphous perversity"[14] and again delighted in all types of sexual behavior. Genital sex, so important for the purposes of biological sex, would become just one kind of sexual experience—and a relatively unimportant one—as people rediscovered the erotic pleasures of their oral and anal cavities and engaged in sexual relations with members of the same as well as the opposite sex.

Firestone believed that people associate science and technology with men and the humanities and the arts with women. Thus, for her the "masculine response" to reality is the "technological response": "objective, logical, extroverted, realistic, concerned with the conscious mind (the ego), rational, mechanical, pragmatic and down-to-earth, stable."[15] In contrast, the "feminine response" to reality is the "aesthetic response": "subjective, intuitive, introverted, wishful, dreamy or fantastic, concerned with the subconscious (the id), emotional, even temperamental (hysterical)."[16] Firestone claimed that only when the aforementioned biological revolution eliminates the need to maintain rigid lines between male and female, masculine and feminine, will people be able to bridge the gap between the sciences and the arts. People will find themselves living in an androgynous society in which the categories of the technological and the aesthetic, together with the categories of the masculine and the feminine, have disappeared through what Firestone termed "a mutual cancellation—a matter-antimatter explosion, ending with a poof!"[17] At last, claimed Firestone, the male technological mode would be able to "produce in actuality what the female aesthetic mode had envisioned"[18]—namely, a world in which we use our knowledge to create not hell but heaven on earth; in which men no longer have to toil by the sweat of their brow to survive and in which women no longer have to bear children in pain and travail.

Radical-Cultural Feminism in General

Radical-cultural feminists, in contrast to radical-libertarian feminists, did not support androgyny as a feminist ideal. As they saw it, the androgynous woman was not a full human person but only a woman who had embraced some of the worst features of masculinity. According to Echols, radical-cultural feminists replaced the goal of androgyny with a summons to affirm women's "femaleness."[19] Far from believing, as radical-libertarian feminists did, that women should exhibit both masculine and feminine traits and behaviors, radical-cultural feminists deemed it better for women to be strictly female. Women, they said, should not try to be like men. On the contrary, they should try to be more like women, emphasizing the values and virtues culturally associated with women ("interdependence, community, connection, sharing, emotion, body, trust, absence of hierarchy, nature, immanence, process, joy, peace and life") and deemphasizing the values and virtues culturally associated with men ("independence, autonomy, intellect, will, wariness, hierarchy, domination, culture, transcendence, product, asceticism, war and death").[20] Moreover, and in the ideal, women should appreciate that, despite cultural variations among them, they all share one and the same female nature, and the less influence men have on it, the better.[21] Indeed, some radical-cultural feminists thought women's essential nature better than men's and that women ought to govern men, a stance that pitted them against liberal feminists, who advocated sexual equality.

Mary Daly

Radical-cultural feminist Mary Daly offered a different message than Firestone in her first major book, *Beyond God the Father: Toward a Philosophy of Women's Liberation.*[22] She focused on God as the paradigm for all patriarchs, arguing that unless both women and men dislodge God from their consciousness, women will never be empowered as full persons. She repeatedly claimed that if anyone ever had a power-over-others complex, it is the transcendent God who appears in Judaism, Islam, and especially Christianity. This God is so remote and aloof that he dwells in a place beyond earth, suggesting that power over others inevitably leads to separation from others. Curiously, most alien to this transcendent God, this total being, is the natural world he called into existence out of total nothingness. Thus, women, associated with nature on account of their reproductive powers, play the role of object/other/it against both God's and men's role of subject/self/I.[23]

Importantly, in *Beyond God the Father*, Daly observed what she described as the Unholy Trinity of Rape, Genocide, and War combining in their one patriarchal person the legions of sexism, racism, and classism. In her second major book, *Gyn/Ecology: The Metaethics of Radical Feminism* (1978),[24] she articulated this claim more fully, arguing that this Unholy Trinity, this single patriarchal person, has but one essential message: necrophilia, defined as "obsession with an usually erotic attraction toward and stimulation by corpses, typically evidenced by overt acts (as copulation with a corpse)."[25] Whereas Daly emphasized in *Beyond God the Father* that women cannot thrive as long as they subscribe to the morality of victimization, she stressed in *Gyn/Ecology* that women cannot even survive as long as they remain in patriarchy. Men not only twist women's minds but also try to destroy their bodies through such practices as "Hindu suttee, Chinese foot-binding, African female circumcision [*sic*], European witch burning, and Western gynecology."[26]

In *Gyn/Ecology*, Daly decided to reject several concepts she had used in *Beyond God the Father*, including that of androgyny, which she came to view as twisted, as idealizing someone like "John Travolta and Farrah Fawcett-Majors Scotch-taped together."[27] The more Daly reflected on the traditional understanding of femininity, the more convinced she became that women should not strive to be feminine. Instead she claimed that because patriarchy had constructed the positive feminine qualities of nurturance, compassion, and gentleness as well as the negative feminine qualities of pettiness, jealousy, and vanity, women should reject the supposedly good aspects of femininity as well as the obviously bad ones. All feminine characteristics are "man-made constructs" shaped for the purposes of trapping women deep in the prison of patriarchy, said Daly.[28]

According to critic Ann-Janine Morey-Gaines, Daly used Jerzy Kosinski's image of a "painted bird" to articulate in detail the differences between "femininity" and "femaleness." Kosinski described a keeper who imprisons a nondescript bird simply by painting its feathers a glittering color. Eventually, the bird's ordinary and natural-looking counterparts destroy her out of jealousy. Reversing Kosinski's image, Daly claimed that when it comes to women, it is not the artificial, painted birds (whom Daly looked upon as tamed, domesticated, feminized females) but the natural, plain-looking birds (whom Daly called "wild females") who are in trouble. For Daly, painted birds are the women who permit "Daddy" to deck them out in splendor, to cosmetize and perfume them, to girdle and corset them. They are the women whom "Daddy" dispatches to destroy real, natural women—that is, the women who refuse to be what the patriarchs want them to be, who insist on being themselves no matter what, and who peel patriarchal paint off their minds and bodies.[29]

By the time she wrote the last page of *Gyn/Ecology*, Daly had completely replaced the ideal of the androgynous person with the ideal of the wild female who dwells beyond masculinity and femininity. To become whole, a woman needs to strip away the false identity—femininity—patriarchy has constructed for her. Then and only then, said Daly, will she experience herself as the self she would have been had she lived her life in a matriarchy rather than a patriarchy from the very beginning.

In another major book, *Pure Lust: Elemental Feminist Philosophy*,[30] Daly continued her transvaluation of values. In this book Daly said that men have "fed on" women, making them weak, frail, even anorexic. To grow strong, women must resist the trap of androgyny. Utterly dependent on their God-given helpmates, patriarchs offer women androgyny in a last-ditch effort to keep them by their side: "Come, join forces with us. Masculinity and femininity together!" Women should not, said Daly, be deceived by such inviting words, which are simply a ploy on the part of men to appropriate for themselves that which is best about women.

In *Pure Lust*, Daly provided women with new meanings for some of the old terms that had thwarted women's liberation. The word "lust" is a case in point. Daly wrote, "The usual meaning of *lust* within the lecherous state of patriarchy is well known. It means 'sexual desire, especially of a violent self-indulgent character: lechery, lasciviousness.'"[31] Lust, then, is evil, said Daly, but only because we live in a society with a slavish morality that resents women. If we lived instead in a nonpatriarchal society, continued Daly, lust would have good meanings, such as "vigor," "fertility," "craving," "eagerness," and "enthusiasm."[32] Thus, said Daly, the lusty women of *Pure Lust* are the wild females of *Gyn/Ecology*, the undomesticated women who refuse to be governed by the rules of men's "sadosociety," which is "formed/framed by statues of studs, degrees of drones, canons of cocks, fixations of fixers, precepts of prickers, regulations of rakes and rippers . . . boreocracy."[33]

Controversies Between Radical-Libertarian and Radical-Cultural Feminists

Sexuality

On the topic of sex per se (as opposed to the sex/gender system), Ann Ferguson wrote insightfully on the topic of types of radical feminists. To avoid an unnecessarily confusing discussion of Ferguson's work, we substitute "radical libertarian" and "radical cultural" for the terms she uses. According to Ferguson, radical-libertarian feminists view sexuality as follows:

> 1. Heterosexual as well as other sexual practices are characterized by repression. The norms of patriarchal bourgeois sexuality repress the sexual desires and pleasures of everyone by stigmatizing sexual minorities, thereby keeping the majority "pure" and under control.
> 2. Feminists should repudiate any theoretical analyses, legal restrictions, or moral judgements that stigmatize sexual minorities and thus restrict the freedom of all.
> 3. As feminists we should reclaim control over female sexuality by demanding the right to practice whatever gives us pleasure and satisfaction.
> 4. The ideal sexual relationship is between fully consenting, equal partners who negotiate to maximize one another's sexual pleasure and satisfaction by any means they choose.[34]

In contrast, again according to Ferguson, radical-cultural feminists view sexuality as follows:

> 1. Heterosexual sexual relations generally are characterized by an ideology of sexual objectification (men as subjects/masters; women as objects/slaves) that supports male sexual violence against women.
> 2. Feminists should repudiate any sexual practice that supports or normalizes male sexual violence.
> 3. As feminists we should reclaim control over female sexuality by developing a concern with our own sexual priorities, which differ from men's—that is, more concern with intimacy and less with performance.
> 4. The ideal sexual relationship is between fully consenting, equal partners who are emotionally involved and do not participate in polarized roles.[35]

As we shall see, these two contrasting views on sexuality led to many lively debates between radical-libertarian and radical-cultural feminists.

Pornography and Prostitution

Pornography

The use, abuse, and misuse of pornography is one sexual issue that continues to divide radical-libertarian and radical-cultural feminists. In the past, as today, radical-libertarian feminists urged women to use pornography to overcome their fears about sex, to arouse sexual desires, and to generate sexual fantasies. They claimed that women should feel free to view and enjoy all sorts of pornography, including violent pornography. Some radical-libertarian feminists even invited women to engage in rape fantasies in which men "had their way" with women in bed. An actual rape differs from a rape fantasy, they said. The same woman who derives sexual pleasure from playing Scarlett O'Hara–Rhett Butler sex games with her boyfriend would protest loudly were he actually to attempt to rape her. Just because a woman wants to explore whether power games are part of what makes sex "sexy" for her does not mean that she wants to serve as an object of male violence in real life.[36] Rather than condemning pornography, said radical-libertarian feminists, feminists should engage in an entirely open-minded and nondefensive examination of it, saving their rage for rapists.

Ironically, radical-libertarian feminists' defense of pornography only served to increase radical-cultural feminists' opposition to it. Radical-cultural feminists stressed that sexuality and gender are the products of the same oppressive social forces. There is no difference between gender discrimination against women in the boardroom and the sexual objectification of women in the bedroom. In both instances, the harm done to women is about men's power over them. Pornography is nothing more than patriarchal propaganda about woman's supposedly proper role as man's servant, helpmate, caretaker, and plaything, according to radical-cultural feminists. Whereas men exist for themselves, women exist for men. Men are subjects; women are objects.

Wanting to prove that exposure to pornographic representations directly causes men either to harm women's persons or to defame their characters, radical-cultural feminists sought protection for women in antidiscrimination laws. They followed the lead of feminist thinkers like Andrea Dworkin and Catharine MacKinnon, who defined pornography as "the graphic sexually explicit subordination of women through pictures or words that also includes women dehumanized as sexual objects, things, or commodities; enjoying pain or humiliation or rape; being tied up, cut up, mutilated, bruised, or physically hurt; in postures of sexual submission or servility or display; reduced to body parts, penetrated by objects or animals, or presented in scenarios of degradation, injury, torture; shown as filthy or inferior; bleeding, bruised, or hurt in a context that makes these conditions sexual."[37]

Radical-cultural feminists claimed that because pornographers systematically depict women as less fully human and, therefore, less deserving of respect and good treatment than men, they should be viewed as agents of sexual discrimination, guilty of violating women's civil rights.[38] For this reason, any woman (or man, child, or transsexual) should be granted a legal cause of action against a particular pornographer or pornographic business if she is coerced into a pornographic performance, has pornography forced on her, or is assaulted or attacked because of a particular piece of pornography. Further, any woman should be able to bring civil suit against traffickers in pornography on behalf of all women.[39] According to many radical-cultural feminists, emptying the pockets of pornographers is the best way for feminists to fight the misogynistic ideology pornographers willingly spread.

Although some radical-cultural feminists, most especially MacKinnon and Dworkin, initially succeeded in having antipornography ordinances passed in such cities as Minneapolis and Indianapolis, a coalition of radical-libertarian and liberal feminists, called the Feminist Anti-censorship Taskforce (FACT), joined nonfeminist free speech advocates to work against them. Largely because of FACT's efforts, the US Supreme Court eventually declared the Minneapolis and Indianapolis antipornography ordinances unconstitutional.[40] During the period that FACT worked to defeat the legislation, its membership insisted that phrases such as "explicit subordination of women" have no context-free, fixed meaning.[41]

Shocked by radical-libertarian feminists' seeming acceptance of pornography, including violent pornography, radical-cultural feminists then accused radical-libertarian feminists of false consciousness, of buying the bill of goods men are eager to sell women. Soon bitter debates about sexuality broke out between radical-libertarian and radical-cultural feminists, reaching fever pitch at the 1982 Barnard College Conference on Sexuality. A coalition of radical-libertarian feminists, including lesbian practitioners of sadomasochism and butch-femme relationships, bisexuals, workers in the sex industry (prostitutes, porn models, exotic dancers), and heterosexual women eager to defend the pleasures of sex between consenting men and women, accused radical-cultural feminists of prudery. To this charge, radical-cultural feminists responded that, on the contrary, they were thoughtful women who could tell the difference between "erotica," a term denoting sexually explicit depictions and descriptions of women being integrated, constituted, or focused during loving or at least life-affirming sexual encounters, and "thanatica," which refers to sexually explicit depictions and descriptions of women being disintegrated, dismembered, or disoriented during hate-filled or even death-driven sexual encounters.

Radical-libertarian feminists faulted radical-cultural feminists for presenting vanilla sex—gentle, touchy-feely, side-by-side (no one on top or bottom) sex—as the only kind of sex that is good for women. Why, asked radical-libertarian feminists, should women be limited to a particular flavor of sex? Given free rein, some women may choose vanilla sex, but others may prefer rocky-road sex—encounters where pain punctuates pleasure, for example. No woman should be told that if she wants to be a true feminist, she must limit herself to only certain sorts of sexual encounters.[42] To this line of reasoning, radical-cultural feminists again replied that radical-libertarian feminists were not true feminists but deluded pawns of patriarchy who had willfully closed their ears to pornography's women-hating message. Before too long, the Barnard conference collapsed, as the gulf between radical-libertarian and radical-cultural feminists widened.

Over thirty years have passed since the 1982 Barnard College Conference on Sexuality unraveled. However, the debate about what counts as "feminist sex" continues, with what seems like a radical-libertarian view predominating. Consider a blog post by KaeLyn titled "Feminist Porn: Sex, Consent, and Getting Off." KaeLyn stated, "I have talked to many feminist women who struggle to balance what really happens behind closed doors and what they feel the bedroom politics of a 'good feminist' should be. Enjoying BDSM, strap-on sex and sex toys, genderplay, rape and incest taboo, mainstream pornography, and other deviant sexual taboos with a consensual partner does not make a bad feminist or a hypocrite. To the contrary, feminism is what gave me permission to love sex, with myself and with others, to embrace my sexual orientations, and find out what turns me on. . . . How is that not feminist?"[43]

Of the ninety-eight people who commented on the post, most agreed to a greater or lesser extent with KaeLyn. For example, commenter Ashley said that radical-cultural feminists can be "judgmental," offering a "negative take on bdsm and kink."[44] Clearly not agreeing with radical-cultural feminists' position on sexual relations, Ashley concluded her comment with the following statement: "Sometimes recognizing power dynamics and playing with them/challenging them is a lot more radical than pretending that sex is (or should be) all Enya, clouds and puppy dog tails."[45] Despite a few heated exchanges, the overall tenor of the comments on the post was civil, respectful, and thoughtful rather than argumentative or hostile.

Prostitution

Another sexual issue that continues to divide radical-libertarian and radical-cultural feminists is whether prostitution is a profession, and an acceptable one at that, or simply an example of women's general sexual oppression. As noted above, Dworkin and MacKinnon condemned pornography as a powerful source of women's oppression. In doing so, they presented prostitution as a live enactment of pornography. Most radical-cultural feminists concurred with this view, but radical-libertarian feminists rejected it. They said that prostitution is simply sex work, a kind of liberating labor that undermines those traditional patriarchal moral values that prevent women from expressing their sexuality freely. One organization espousing this view called itself COYOTE (for "Call Off Your Old Tired Ethics") and had quite a following in the late 1970s and early 1980s.[46]

Later in the 1990s and 2000s, radical-cultural feminists, among others, once again presented prostitution as bad for women, emphasizing the evils of global sex trafficking. Allying with faith-based groups like the International Justice Mission, these contemporary radical-cultural feminists sought to rescue girls and women from sexual slavery. Unfortunately, some of the tactics they used backfired, in many radical-libertarian feminists' estimation. In a 2016 *New York Times Magazine* article, Emily Bazelon reported that in India and Indonesia a crackdown on prostitution resulted in girls and women being "deported, detained in abusive institutions and coerced into sex with the police."[47] In addition, it resulted in the weakening of efforts to stop the spread of HIV/AIDS. When US President George W. Bush earmarked $15 billion for the prevention and treatment of HIV/AIDS in developing countries, many pro-women activists refused the funds because of the strings attached, said Bazelon. Fund recipients had to sign an "antiprostitution pledge" that prohibited them from distributing free condoms to prostitutes.[48] Pro-women activists protested to the Bush administration that it is better to protect a woman from HIV/AIDS than to prevent her from selling her sexual services.

Currently, the debate over prostitution/sex work in the United States is generally presented as "a choice between international legal systems," said Bazelon.[49] One approach to prostitution/sex work—called the "Nordic model" because it originated in Sweden and was then adopted in Norway and Iceland (before spreading to Canada and Northern Ireland)—emphasized punishing the men who bought sex as opposed to the girls and women who sold it.[50] But women pro-women activists in Amnesty International claimed that this seemingly women-friendly policy did not work. Coming down hard on the johns had the effect of driving prostitution underground, where protections for prostitutes against rapists and sex abusers are virtually nonexistent.

In contrast to the Nordic model, the model adopted in 1999 by Australia and in 2003 by New Zealand repealed the countries' respective criminal laws against prostitution, "freeing consenting adults to buy and sell sex and allowing brothels to operate much like other businesses."[51] Subsequent to the repeal of these laws, "the rate of sex work 'stayed flat,' condom use among prostitutes rose above 99 percent, and depression and stress among sex workers decreased," said Bazelon.[52] According to Amnesty International, Australia and New Zealand gave prostitutes more power "to operate independently, self-organize in informal cooperatives and control their own working environments."[53]

Although the traditional radical-cultural feminist argument that "legalizing prostitution will harm women by leading to more sexual inequality"[54] still has force, it seems to be losing ground to the radical-libertarian feminist position that legalizing prostitution in a truly women-friendly way will safeguard the well-being of people who sell and buy sex. Commented Bazelon, "In this fight over whose voices to listen to, who speaks for whom and when to use the power of the criminal law, the sex-workers' rights movement is a rebellion against punishment and shame. It demands respect for a group that has rarely received it, insisting that you can only really help people if you respect them."[55]

Artificial Reproduction Versus Natural Reproduction

Radical-libertarian and radical-cultural feminists have different views not only about sexual identity and behavior, with rare exception (see Marge Piercy below), but also about reproduction. Radical-libertarian feminists believe women should substitute artificial for natural modes of reproduction whenever feasible. They are convinced that the less women are physically involved in reproduction, the more time and energy they will have to engage in society's productive processes. Baby making is definitely not in the best interests of women who want successful careers, in radical-libertarian feminists' estimation.

Shulamith Firestone

In *The Dialectic of Sex*, radical-libertarian feminist Shulamith Firestone claimed that patriarchy, defined as the systematic subordination of women, is rooted in the biological inequality of the sexes. Her reflections on women's reproductive role led her to a feminist revision of the materialist theory of history offered by Karl Marx and Friedrich Engels. So focused were Marx and Engels on economic class struggle as the driving force of history that they paid scant attention to what Firestone termed "sex class." She proposed to make up for this oversight by developing a feminist version of historical materialism centered on sex class rather than economic class.

To appreciate Firestone's co-optation of Marxist method, we have only to contrast her definition of historical materialism with Engels's. Engels defined historical materialism as "that view of the course of history which seeks the ultimate cause and great moving power of all historical events in the economic development of society, in the changes of the modes of production and exchange, in the consequent division of society into distinct classes, and in the struggles of these classes against one another."[56] Firestone reformulated Engels's definition as follows: "Historical materialism is that view of the course of history which seeks the ultimate cause and the great moving power of all historical events in the dialectic of sex: the division of society into two distinct biological classes for procreative reproduction, and the struggles of these classes with one another; in the changes in the modes of marriage, reproduction and child care created by these struggles; in the connected development of other physically-differentiated classes (castes); and in the first division of labor based on sex which developed into the (economic-cultural) class system."[57] In other words, for Firestone, relations of reproduction, rather than production, are the driving forces in history. The original class distinction is rooted in men's and women's differing reproductive roles; economic and racial class differences derive from sex class differences.

In much the same way that Marx concluded workers' liberation requires an economic revolution, Firestone concluded women's liberation requires a biological revolution.[58] Like the proletariat who must seize the means of production to eliminate the economic class system, women must seize control of the means of reproduction to eliminate the sexual class system. Just as the ultimate goal of the communist revolution is, in a classless society, to obliterate class distinctions, the ultimate goal of the feminist revolution is, in an androgynous society, to obliterate sexual distinctions. As soon as technology overcomes the biological limits of natural reproduction, said Firestone, the biological fact that some persons have wombs and others have penises will "no longer matter culturally."[59] Sexual intercourse will no longer be necessary for human reproduction. Eggs and sperm will be combined in vitro, and embryos will be gestated outside of women's bodies.

No matter how much educational, legal, and political equality women achieve and no matter how many women enter public industry, Firestone insisted, nothing fundamental will change for women as long as natural reproduction remains the rule and artificial or assisted reproduction the exception. Natural reproduction is in the best interests of neither women nor the children so created, argued Firestone. The joy of giving birth—invoked so frequently in this society—is a patriarchal myth. In fact, pregnancy is "barbaric," and natural childbirth is "at best necessary and tolerable" and at worst "like shitting a pumpkin."[60] Moreover, said Firestone, natural reproduction is the root of further evils, especially the vice of possessiveness that generates feelings of hostility and jealousy among human beings. Engels's *Origin of the Family, Private Property, and the State* was incomplete not so much because he failed adequately to explain why men became the producers of surplus value, said Firestone, but because he failed adequately to explain why men wish so intensely to pass their property on to their biological children. If humans are to put an end to divisive hierarchies, reasoned Firestone, they must overcome precisely this vice of possessiveness—the favoring of one child over another on account of his or her being the product of one's own ovum or sperm.

Marge Piercy

Marge Piercy developed Firestone's last point in her science fiction novel *Woman on the Edge of Time*.[61] Although a radical-cultural feminist, Piercy argued that, done in a women-controlled way, artificial reproduction can serve women and society well. Piercy tells the story of her feminist utopia from the perspective of Connie Ramos, a late-twentieth-century, middle-aged, working-class Chicana with a history of what society regards as "mental illness" and "violent behavior." She has been trying desperately to support herself and her daughter, Angelina, on a pittance. One day, near the point of exhaustion, Connie loses her temper and hits Angelina. As a result of this one outburst, a criminal court finds her an unfit mother and takes her beloved daughter away. Depressed and despondent, angry and agitated, Connie is committed by her family to a mental hospital, where she is selected as a human research subject for brain-control experiments. Just when things can get no worse, a person named Luciente psychically transports Connie to a future world called Mattapoisett—a world that does not define women in terms of reproductive functions and in which both men and women delight in rearing children. In Mattapoisett, there are neither men nor women; rather, everyone is a "per" (short for "person").

Artificial reproduction makes Piercy's futuristic world imaginable. In Mattapoisett, babies are birthed by the "brooder." Female ova, fertilized in vitro with male sperm selected for a full range of racial, ethnic, and personality traits, are gestated in an artificial placenta. Unable to comprehend why Mattapoisett women rejected the experience that meant the most to her—physically gestating, birthing, and nursing an offspring—Connie is initially repelled by the brooder. She sees the embryos "all in a sluggish row . . . like fish in the aquarium."[62] She not only regards them as less than human but pities them because no woman loves them enough to carry them in her own womb and, bleeding and sweating, bring them into the world.

Yet Connie eventually becomes a supporter of artificial reproduction. She learns from Luciente that the women of Mattapoisett reluctantly gave up natural reproduction only when they realized it was the ultimate cause of all isms, including sexism: "It was part of women's long revolution. When we were breaking all the old hierarchies. Finally there was the one thing we had to give up too, the only power we ever had, in return for no power for anyone. The original production: the power to give birth. Cause as long as we were biologically enchained, we'd never be equal. And males never would be humanized to be loving and tender. So we all became mothers. Every child has three. To break the nuclear bonding."[63] Women's relinquishing their monopoly on the power to give birth destroyed the original paradigm for power relations, and all residents of Mattapoisett found themselves in a position to reconstitute human relationships in ways that defied the hierarchical ideas of better-worse, higher-lower, stronger-weaker, and especially dominant-submissive.

Piercy's utopia is more radical than a Marxist one because she eliminates the family as a biological as well as an economic unit. Individuals possess neither private property nor their own biological children. Indeed, children are not viewed as belonging to their biological mothers and fathers, to be brought into the world in their parents' likeness and reared according to their idiosyncratic values. The people of Mattapoisett view children as precious human resources for the entire community, to be treasured on account of their uniqueness. Each child is reared by three co-mothers (one man and two women or two men and one woman), assisted by "kidbinders," a group of individuals who excel at mothering. Child rearing is a communal effort, with each child having access to large-group experiences at child-care centers and small-group experiences in the separate dwellings of each of their co-mothers.[64]

As nicely as Piercy reformulated some of Firestone's more controversial ideas, radical-cultural feminists nonetheless challenged her views as well as Firestone's. They claimed that Mattapoisett is an undesirable social ideal for today's women because women's oppression is not likely to end if women give up the only source of men's dependence on them. "Technological reproduction," said Azizah al-Hibri, "does not equalize the natural reproductive power structure—it *inverts* it. It appropriates the reproductive power from women and places it in the hands of men who now control both the sperm and the reproductive technology that could make it indispensable. . . . It 'liberates' them from their 'humiliating dependency' on women in order to propagate."[65] That is, far from liberating women, reproductive technology further consolidates men's power over women; it gives them the ability to have children without women's participation. Even though some women use other women's eggs and wombs to procreate and some women adopt other women's children, society continues to define a mother as someone who is genetically, gestationally, and socially related to the children she rears with or without a spouse or partner. Indeed, most women who go to infertility clinics do so because they want Connie's experience of carrying a fetus for nine months "heavy under their hearts," bearing a baby "in blood," and nursing a child.[66]

Mary O'Brien

Viewing natural reproduction through the lens of male alienation from the gestational process and female immersion in it, another radical-cultural feminist, Mary O'Brien, noted that until the advent of artificial reproduction, the "reproductive consciousness" of a man differed from that of a woman in at least three ways. First, the woman experienced the process of procreation as one continuous movement taking place within her body, whereas the man experienced this same process as a discontinuous movement taking place outside his body. After the act of sexual intercourse, through which he impregnated the woman, the man had no other procreative function. Second, the woman, not the man, necessarily performed the fundamental labor of reproduction—pregnancy and birthing. At most, the man could attend childbirth classes with the woman and try to imagine the feeling of being pregnant and giving birth. Third, the woman's connection to her child was certain—she knew, at the moment of birth, the child was flesh of her flesh. In contrast, the man's connection to the child was uncertain; he could never be absolutely sure, even at the moment of birth, whether the child was in fact genetically related to him. For all he knew, the child was the genetic progeny of some other man. Therefore, observed O'Brien, birthing naturally gives women a reproductive edge over men and an intensely intimate relationship to their children, which makes women, not men, the true authorities about how children should be reared.[67]

Adrienne Rich

In *Of Woman Born*,[68] yet another radical-cultural feminist, Adrienne Rich, noted that men realize patriarchy cannot survive unless they can control women's power to bring or not bring life into the world. Rich described how men tried to take the birthing process into their own hands. Male obstetricians replaced female midwives, substituting their "hands of iron" (obstetrical forceps) for midwives' hands of flesh (female hands sensitive to the female anatomy), she said.[69]

In addition, Rich cataloged the ways in which male physicians tried to write the rules not only for giving birth but also for being pregnant. Male experts (think here of Dr. Spock) told women how to act during pregnancy—when to eat, sleep, exercise, have sex, and the like. In some instances, males even dictated to women how to feel during childbirth. The overall effect of men's intrusion into the birthing process was to confuse women, because men's rules for women's pregnancies often clashed with women's intuitions about what was best for their bodies, psyches, and babies.

To the degree men deprived women of control over their own pregnancies, said Rich, women experienced pregnancy as a mere event, as something that simply happened to them. Indeed, confessed Rich, she herself felt out of control and alienated during her pregnancy.[70] She concluded that if women reclaimed their pregnancies from male authorities, they would no longer have to sit passively, waiting for their physicians to deliver their babies to them. Instead, women would actually direct the childbirth process, experiencing its pleasures as well as its pains. In Rich's estimation, childbirth does not have to feel like "shitting a pumpkin."[71] On the contrary, it can feel a great deal more exhilarating and certainly far less dehumanizing than this.

Margaret Atwood

Rich's concerns about the ways in which male authorities have used medical science to control women's reproductive powers reached new heights in radical-cultural feminist Margaret Atwood's *The Handmaid's Tale.*[72] In the Republic of Gilead, Atwood's dystopia, women are reduced to one of four functions. There are the Marthas, or domestics; the Wives, or social secretaries and functionaries; the Jezebels, or sex prostitutes; and the Handmaids, or reproductive prostitutes. One of the most degrading Gileadean practices, from a woman's perspective, is a ritualistic form of sexual intercourse in which the so-called Commander pretends to have sex with his Wife. The Wife, who is infertile, lies down on a bed with her legs spread open. The Wife's Handmaid, one of the few fertile women in Gilead, puts her head between the spread legs of the Wife. Then the Commander engages in sexual intercourse with the Handmaid. If the Handmaid gets pregnant, the Commander and his Wife lay claim to the child she is gestating. Adding to the oddity of this arrangement is the fact that on the day the Handmaid gives birth to the child, the Wife simulates labor pains, as other Wives and Hand-maids in Gilead gather round the Wife and her Handmaid in a rare moment of female bonding.

After one such birthday, the central character, Offred—whose name literally means "to be of Fred"—recalls better times and speaks in her mind to her mother, who had been a feminist leader: "Can you hear me? You wanted a woman's culture. Well, now there is one. It isn't what you meant, but it exists. Be thankful for small mercies."[73] Of course, they are *very* small mercies, for with the exception of birthdays—those rare occasions when a Handmaid manages to produce a child—women have little contact with one another. The Marthas, Wives, Jezebels, and Handmaids are segregated from one another, and the contact women do have—even within an assigned class—is largely silent, for women are permitted to speak to one another only when absolutely necessary.

Gena Corea

Like Atwood, radical-cultural feminist Gena Corea was suspicious of what the new reproductive technologies and their concomitant social arrangements promise women. Corea claimed that if men control the new reproductive technologies, they will use them not to empower women but to further empower themselves. To reinforce her point, she drew provocative analogies between Count Dracula and physician Robert Edwards, a codeveloper of in vitro fertilization (IVF). Corea suggested that just as Dracula never had enough blood to drink, Edwards never had enough eggs to use in experiments. Indeed, Edwards routinely attended the hysterectomies his colleagues performed, for the sole purpose of collecting the eggs they discarded after the surgeries. Fearing that male infertility experts such as Edwards do not have women's best interests at heart, Corea ended her essay "Egg Snatchers" with a question: "Why are [men] splitting the functions of motherhood into smaller parts? Does that reduce the power of the mother and her claim to the child? ('I only gave the egg. I am not the real mother.' 'I only loaned my uterus. I am not the real mother.' 'I only raised the child. I am not the real mother.')"[74]

Interestingly, the debate on the best kind of human reproduction continues. On the positive side, many radical-libertarian feminists argue that reproductive technology gives women a chance to cooperate with each other to produce a child that would not otherwise exist.[75] Pro-assisted reproduction champions point, for example, to lesbian couples who use in vitro fertilization so that donor sperm can fertilize the egg of one member of the lesbian couple, and the other member can gestate the resulting embryo. Due to this technological process, both members of the lesbian couple can claim a biological connection to their child.[76]

In response to contemporary radical-libertarian feminists, contemporary radical-cultural feminists point out that many women feel compelled to use IVF, for example, so that they can have a baby no matter the risk to their health.[77] They also observe that while in their twenties some young women are coaxed into freezing their eggs so that they can get pregnant in their early forties.[78] As egg freezing and postmenopausal pregnancy get normalized, say these radical-cultural feminists, women's bodies will increasingly have to do technology's bidding.

Biological Motherhood: Negative Versus Positive Assessments

Although commentators do not always distinguish between biological and social motherhood, the difference between these two dimensions of mothering is important. If we accept philosopher Alison Jaggar's extension of the term "mothering" to "any relationship in which one individual nurtures and cares for another,"[79] then a person need not be a biological mother to be a social mother. Nevertheless, patriarchal society simply assumes that the woman who bears a child is best suited to rear it. Viewing this tenet as often placing unreasonable demands on women's bodies and energies, most radical-libertarian feminists argued against glorifying motherhood.

Ann Oakley: A Case Against Biological Motherhood

The radical-libertarian feminist case against biological motherhood has at least two versions: a weaker, more general one offered by Ann Oakley and a stronger, more specific one offered by Shulamith Firestone. As Oakley saw it, biological motherhood is a myth based on the threefold belief that "all women need to be mothers, all mothers need their children, all children need their mothers."[80]

The first assertion, that all women need to be mothers, gains its credibility, according to Oakley, from the socialization of girls and from popular psychoanalytic theory that provides "pseudoscientific backing" for that process. If parents did not give their daughters dolls, if the schools, the churches, and the media did not stress the wonders of biological motherhood, if psychiatrists, psychologists, and physicians did not do everything in their power to transform abnormal girls (i.e., "masculine" girls who do not want to be mothers) into normal girls (i.e., "feminine" girls who do want to be mothers), then girls would not grow into women whose sense of self-worth depends on having a biological child. For Oakley, women's supposed need to mother "owes nothing" to women's "possession of ovaries and wombs" and everything to their social and cultural conditioning.[81]

The second assertion, that mothers need their children, rests on the belief that unless a woman's maternal instinct is satisfied, she will become increasingly frustrated. In Oakley's view, there is no such thing as a maternal instinct. Women do not naturally experience a desire to have a biological child, and no hormonally based drives "irresistibly draw the mother to her child in the tropistic fashion of the moth drawn to the flame"[82] during and after pregnancy. To support her contention that the supposed instinct for mothering is learned, Oakley pointed to a study that observed 150 first-time mothers. Few knew how to breast-feed, and those who did had seen either their own mother or another woman nurse a baby. Additionally, Oakley noted that most women who abuse or neglect their offspring were themselves abused or neglected as children. Never having seen another woman mother properly, these women never learned the behavior repertoire society associates with adequate mothering. Mothers, in short, are not born; they are made.

The third assertion, that children need their biological mothers, is, according to Oakley, the most oppressive feature of the myth of biological motherhood. Children do not require rearing by the women who bear them; instead, they should be reared by those adults who have their best interests at heart and the wherewithal to pursue them.[83] In an ideal world, adults would have to be licensed to secure the privilege of rearing one or more children. Biological connections alone would not authorize parenthood.

In Oakley's estimation, biological motherhood is not a natural female need, any more than being reared by their biological mother is a natural need of children. Therefore, she concluded, biological motherhood is a social construct, a myth with an oppressive purpose. To avoid accusations of selfishness and even abnormality, women who would be happier not having children at all become mothers reluctantly, and women who might be better off sharing their child-rearing responsibilities make of mothering an all-consuming, individualistic task. No wonder, said Oakley, so many mothers are unhappy—a burden made all the heavier because society looks with disfavor on any woman who expresses dissatisfaction with her maternal role.

Shulamith Firestone: Another Case Against Biological Motherhood

Although Shulamith Firestone's negative assessment of biological motherhood did not substantively differ from Oakley's, it was harsher in tone. In *The Dialectic of Sex*, Firestone suggested that the desire to bear and rear children is less the result of an "authentic liking" for children and more a "displacement" of ego-extension needs. For a man, a child is a way to immortalize his name, property, class, and ethnic identification; for a woman, a child is a way to justify her homebound existence as absolutely meaningful. At times, a father's need for immortality or a mother's need for meaning becomes pathological. When this happens, said Firestone, the less-than-perfect child inevitably suffers.[84]

Firestone believed that if adults, especially women, did not feel a duty to reproduce, they might discover in themselves an authentic desire to live in close association with children. People do not need to be biological parents to lead child-centered lives, said Firestone. Ten or more adults could agree, for example, to live with three or four children for as long as the children needed a stable family structure. Firestone did not think adults have a natural desire to be any closer to children than this kind of household arrangement permits. Instead, she believed adults have been socialized to view biological reproduction as life's raison d'être because without this grandiose sense of mission and destiny, the pains of childbearing and the burdens of child rearing would prove overwhelming. Now that technology promises to liberate the human species from the burdens of reproductive responsibility, adults should decide how much time and energy they want to spend with and on children.[85]

Adrienne Rich: The Case for Biological Motherhood

Although radical-cultural feminist Adrienne Rich agreed with some of Firestone's analysis, she criticized Firestone for condemning biological motherhood "without taking full account of what the experience of biological pregnancy and birth might be in a wholly different political and emotional context."[86] Rich sharply distinguished between biological motherhood understood as "the *potential relationship* of any woman to her powers of reproduction and to children" and biological motherhood understood as "the *institution*, which aims at ensuring that that potential—and all women—shall remain under male control."[87] As Rich saw it, there is a world of difference between women's deciding who, how, when, and where to mother and men's making these decisions for them.

Rich agreed with Firestone that women should be liberated from biological motherhood as institutionalized under patriarchy. If success is measured in terms of patriarchy's ability to determine not only women's gender behavior but also their gender identity through "force, direct pressure . . . ritual, tradition, law and language, customs, etiquette, education, and the division of labor," then institutionalized biological motherhood is one of patriarchy's overwhelming achievements, reasoned Rich.[88]

Within patriarchy, women learn that mothering is their exclusive job. This view of women's role blocks their access to the public realm of culture. It also fails to acknowledge their right to have and fulfill their own wants and needs. Good mothers should have no personal friends or plans unrelated to their families. They should be on the job twenty-four hours a day and love every minute of it. Ironically, observed Rich, this very expectation causes some women to act in anything but motherly ways. The constant needs of a child can tax a mother's patience and, with no relief from the father or any other adult, make her feel angry, frustrated, and bitter: "I remember being uprooted from already meager sleep to answer a childish nightmare, pull up a blanket, warm a consoling bottle, lead a half-asleep child to the toilet. I remember going back to bed starkly awake, brittle with anger, knowing that my broken sleep would make the next day hell, that there would be more nightmares; more need for consolation, because out of my weariness I would rage at those children for no reason."[89] Rich's point was not that mothers do not love their children but that, like children, mothers have their own physical and psychological needs.

Rich also argued that the institution of biological motherhood prevents women from rearing their children as women think they should be reared. She recounted squabbles with her own husband about the best way to raise their two sons. Under patriarchy, she wrote, most men demanded sons for the wrong reasons: "as heirs, field-hands, cannon-fodder, feeders of machinery, images and extensions of themselves, their immortality."[90] What is worse, most husbands have demanded that their wives help them raise their sons to be "real men"—that is, aggressive and competitive. Rich recalled a seashore vacation she spent with her two boys but without her husband. She and her sons lived spontaneously for several weeks, ignoring most of the established rules of patriarchy. They ate the wrong food. They stayed up past bedtime. They wore wrinkled clothes. They giggled at silly jokes. And they were enormously happy.

Genetic, Gestational, and Rearing Connections to Children

The attention of radical-cultural and radical-libertarian feminists has recently centered on surrogate, or gestational, motherhood—a contractual arrangement in which a third party is hired and usually paid to bear a child whom the contracting couple will rear.[91] The birth mother (the woman whose gestational services have been contracted) is either the full biological mother of the child (both the genetic and the gestational mother) or, more often, the gestational but not the genetic mother of the child.

In general, radical-cultural feminists opposed contracted motherhood on the grounds that it creates destructive divisions among women—for instance, between economically privileged and disadvantaged women. Advantaged women can hire disadvantaged women to meet their reproductive needs, adding gestational services to the child-rearing services poor women traditionally have provided to rich women (think here of wet-nursing). Another potential division exists among child begetters, child bearers, and child rearers. According to Gena Corea, for example, reproduction is currently being segmented and specialized as if it were simply a mode of production. As she envisions it, in the future, no one woman will beget, bear, and rear a child. Rather, genetically superior women will beget embryos in vitro, strong-bodied women will bear these test-tube babies to term, and sweet-tempered women will rear these newborns from infancy to adulthood.[92] This division of labor could actually give rise to a dystopia similar to the one Atwood described in *The Handmaid's Tale*.

In addition to lamenting how contracted motherhood might harm women's relationships to each other and to their children, radical-cultural feminists bemoaned its rooting of parental rights either in persons' genetic contribution to the procreative process or in their professed intention to rear children. Basing parental rights exclusively on genetic contribution means that a surrogate mother genetically unrelated to the child in her womb has no parental rights to it after it is born. Only if she is the genetic as well as the gestational mother does she have grounds for claiming parental rights to the child—rights that must be balanced against those of the child's genetic father. Similarly, basing parental rights exclusively on a persons' professed intention to rear a child implies that because the surrogate mother has expressed no such intentions contractually, she has no grounds for claiming parental rights, even if she is genetically related to the child.

According to radical-cultural feminists, men have reason to base all parental rights on either genes or intentions. After all, until a man takes an active part in the rearing of his child, he can only have a genetic or an intentional relationship with his offspring. Unlike his wife or other female partner, he cannot experience the kind of relationship a pregnant woman can with her child. For this reason, said radical-cultural feminists, patriarchal society unfairly dismisses the gestational relationship as unimportant, as a mere biological event with no special parental meaning. But in truth, they continued, the gestational connection is of extraordinary importance. The child's gestator proves through her concrete actions, some of which may cause her inconvenience and even pain, her commitment to the child's well-being. When parental claims are in question, said radical-cultural feminists, the kind of lived commitment a gestational parent has made to a child should count at least as much as the contemplated commitment of a genetic or intentional parent.

Radical-libertarian feminists disagreed with radical-cultural feminists' assessment of contracted motherhood, arguing that such arrangements, if handled properly, can bring women closer together. They observed that some contracting mothers and couples live near each other, so they can all share in the rearing of the child they have collaboratively produced.[93] Thus, we need not view contracted motherhood as a male-directed and -manipulated specialization and segmentation of the female reproductive process; we can see it as women getting together (as in the case of mothers carrying their daughters' fetuses to term) to achieve, in unison, something they could not accomplish without each other's help. As long as women control collaborative-reproduction arrangements, contracted motherhood increases rather than decreases women's reproductive freedom, in radical-libertarian feminists' estimation.

Believing it does women a disservice to overstate the importance of the gestational connection, radical-libertarian feminists objected to the radical-cultural feminist position on contracted motherhood for two reasons. First, if women want men to spend as much time caring for children as women now do, then they should not repeatedly remind men of women's special connection to infants. Doing so implies that they are more suited to parenting tasks than men. Second, if women want to protect their bodily integrity from the forces of state coercion, then they should not stress the symbiotic nature of the maternal-fetal connection lest the state try to control their pregnancies. If a pregnant woman can be said to harm her fetus by drinking large quantities of alcohol or using illicit drugs, society may urge that she be treated, voluntarily or involuntarily, for her addictions. Should treatment fail, society may even recommend that a pregnant woman be punished for negligently, recklessly, or intentionally engaging in lifestyle behavior resulting in serious, largely irreparable damage to her unborn child. For this reason, if no other, radical-libertarian feminists believe that less emphasis on the specialness of the mother-fetus relationship will better serve women's interests.[94]

Lesbian Separatist Feminism

Another topic that divided radical-libertarian feminists from radical-cultural feminists was lesbianism, particularly separatist lesbianism, which maintained that women should have as few dealings with men as possible. As noted in Chapter 1's discussion of the National Organization for Women, lesbianism first surfaced as an issue within the women's movement during the 1970s. Ironically, at the Second Congress to Unite Women, a group of lesbian women wearing T-shirts emblazoned with Betty Friedan's words "lavender menace" staged a protest. This controversial act did not surprise conference organizers and attendees, however. They had anticipated trouble following publication of Anne Koedt's provocative "The Myth of the Vaginal Orgasm."[95] In this essay, Koedt claimed that many women believe their orgasms during heterosexual intercourse are vaginal when in fact they are clitoral. Koedt also noted that many men fear "becom[ing] sexually expendable if the clitoris is substituted for the vagina as the center of pleasure for women."[96] Viewing men's fear of sexual expendability as alarmist, Koedt said that even if all women recognized that they did not need men as sexual partners for physiological reasons, some women would still want men as sexual partners for psychological reasons.

Viewing Koedt as wrong to suggest that some (perhaps many) sexually liberated women might prefer vaginal to clitoral sex, radical-cultural feminists argued that a truly sexually liberated woman would not want to have sex with men[97] and that all genuine feminists would instead profess lesbianism as their sexual practice. Women should free themselves from the false idea that a woman is deviant, abnormal, sick, crazy, or bad because she wants sex with women instead of men.

For a time, radical-cultural feminists' reaction to Koedt's essay predominated in feminist circles, so much so that many heterosexual feminists felt like traitors if they wanted to have sex with men. Deirdre English, a radical-libertarian feminist of this period, reported finding it "fascinating and almost funny"[98] that so many heterosexual feminists she knew "seemed to accept the idea that heterosexuality meant cooperating in their own oppression and that there was something wrong with being sexually turned on to men. How many times have I heard this? 'Well, unfortunately, I'm not a lesbian but I wish I was, maybe I will be.'"[99] The so-called political lesbian was born: a woman who does not find herself erotically attracted to women but who tries as hard as possible to want sex from them. Among other radical cultural feminists, Charlotte Bunch urged all women to become political lesbians. She said that as long as heterosesexual women regard lesbianism as merely a private choice, "as a bedroom issue, they hold back the development of politics and strategies that would put an end to male supremacy and they give men an excuse for not dealing with their sexism. . . . Lesbianism is the key to liberation and only women who cut their ties to male privilege can be trusted to remain serious in the struggle against male dominance. Those who remain tied to men, individually or in political theory, cannot always put women first."[100] Affirming this position, feminist philosopher Bat-Ami Bar On said that Bunch presented lesbianism, first and foremost, as a political stance and only secondarily as a private "bedroom" choice.[101]

Like radical-cultural feminists, radical-libertarian feminists saw heterosexuality as a flawed institution that has harmed many women. Still, they insisted it would be just as wrong for radical-cultural feminists to impose lesbianism on women as it had been for patriarchy to impose heterosexuality on them.[102] Men's having sex with women was not, in and of itself, bad for women, in radical-libertarian feminists' estimation. Rather, the harm stemmed from men's having sex with women in a particular way: "fucking for a minute and a half and pulling out."[103] Many women found pleasure in sex with men when men made women's sexual satisfaction just as important as their own, said radical-libertarian feminists.

Radical-libertarian feminists also stressed that individual men were not women's primary oppressors. On the contrary, women's main enemy was the patriarchal system, the product of centuries of male privilege, priority, and prerogative. Thus, unlike those radical-cultural feminists who urged women to stop relating to men on all levels beginning with the sexual, radical-libertarian feminists rejected a separatist agenda. Instead they exhorted women to confront individual men about their male chauvinism to get them to renounce the unfair privileges patriarchy had bestowed upon them.[104] These feminists recalled that even the Women's International Terrorist Conspiracy from Hell (WITCH), one of the most radical feminist groups of the 1960s, had urged women not to renounce men or heterosexuality entirely but to relate to men only on gynocentric terms: "You are pledged to free our brothers from oppression and stereotyped sexual roles (whether they like it or not) as well as ourselves. You are a Witch by saying aloud, 'I am a Witch' three times, and *thinking about that.* You are a Witch by being female, untamed, angry, joyous, and immortal."[105]

According to most contemporary radical feminists (cultural as well as libertarian), women in the 2000s need not live together on the fringes of society or have sex only with one another to be liberated. Freedom comes to women as the result of women's giving one another the power of self-definition and the energy to rebel continually against any individual man, group of men, or patriarchal institution seeking to disempower or otherwise weaken women. This is a long task, however. Most contemporary radical feminists admit that Adrienne Rich's 1980s article "Compulsory Heterosexuality and Lesbian Existence" still holds sway. In this article, Rich argued that male power has suppressed female sexuality in eight ways: (1) by denying women their own sexuality, (2) by forcing male sexuality upon women, (3) by controlling women's reproductive capacities, (4) by controlling the manner in which women rear their children, (5) by confining women physically and/or limiting their movement, (6) by using women as virtual commodities in certain "male transactions," (7) by "cramp[ing] [women's] creativeness," and by (8) limiting or withholding women's access to large areas of social knowledge and culture.[106] Although this eightfold (male) oppression of women is much weakened today, vestiges of it remain, in contemporary radical-cultural feminists' estimation.

Critiques of Radical Feminism

Critique One: Woman's Nature Is Not Necessarily the Root of Her "Goodness"

Jean Bethke Elshtain claimed that radical-cultural feminists wrongly suggested that males and females are, on either the biological or the ontological level, two kinds of creatures: the men corrupt and the women innocent. Such a biology or ontology denies the individuality and history of actual men and women. It implies that some sort of a priori essence makes human beings important and real.

Elshtain deemed essentialism—the conviction that men are men and women are women, both with immutable natures—an analytic dead end and a political hazard. As she saw it, in essentialist arguments oppressors have historically told the oppressed to accept their lot in life because "that's just the way it is." Essentialist arguments served to justify slavery, to resist the Nineteenth Amendment (which gave women the vote), and to sustain colonialism by arguing in a supposedly "altruistic" manner that "the natives are unable to run their own governments."[107]

Also at issue in Elshtain's critique is the radical-cultural feminist understanding of patriarchy. Elshtain faulted Mary Daly for implying that no matter when and where it appears, patriarchy, be it in the form of Hindu suttee, Chinese foot binding, African female circumcision, or Western gynecology, is about men's hating women. Claiming that all these various practices boiled down to the same thing, said Elshtain, showed little or no awareness of the rich diversity of different societies.[108] As a Western feminist searching for signs of patriarchy in Asia and Africa, Daly sometimes failed to recognize her own cultural baggage, said Elshtain. As an outsider, she was not always privy to the contextual meaning of certain rituals and customs for their female participants. Female circumcision, also known as genital mutilation, is a case in point. For Daly, this practice reflects women's deprivation by patriarchal forces of a wide range of sexual experiences; for the women circumcised/mutilated, it may represent something else: a passage into womanhood or a means of rebelling against supposedly civilized, Christian, colonial powers. To Daly's objection (and ours) that these women are not ready, willing, or able to see the harm being done to them, Elshtain responded that perhaps Daly's vision, rather than these women's, was clouded.[109]

Admitting that Daly and other radical-cultural feminists usually wrote about patriarchy metaphorically rather than historically, Elshtain conceded that, as a metaphorical term, "patriarchy" is a useful analytical tool for women who are just beginning to rethink their political and personal experiences of oppression. But beyond this, it becomes a blunt instrument. If chanted incessantly, the formula "men over women; women for men" becomes monotonous and even meaningless. In Elshtain's estimation, the tendency of radical-cultural feminists to view all patriarchies as equally evil (misogynistic) contributes to the "broken record effect" characterizing some feminist texts.[110]

Elshtain speculated that the absolute condemnation of patriarchy by radical-cultural feminists might stem from their fear that women may have certain things—even ugly things—in common with men. Unable to accept their own masculine qualities, radical-cultural feminists projected these rejected qualities onto men to shield themselves from the more awful parts of their own personalities. This defensiveness, said Elshtain, led radical-cultural feminists toward a utopian vision of an all-women community. Man encompasses evil; woman encompasses good. Because the essence of womanhood is supposedly about the positive force of power-to rather than the negative force of power-over, a world of women would supposedly be warm, supportive, nurturing, and creative.

Elshtain believed that if her controversial critique was on target, radical-cultural feminists were in for a disappointment. Given that women, like men, are human beings, vice as well as virtue would inevitably appear in an all-women community. Elshtain asked radical-cultural feminists to reconsider the concept of "pure voice," the idea that the victim, in her status as victim, speaks in a pure voice: "I suffer, therefore I have moral purity."[111] Victorian men used exactly this belief about women's moral purity to keep them on high pedestals, away from the world of politics and economics, observed Elshtain.

Critique Two: Radical Feminists Focus on Reproductive Technologies Mainly Available to White, Middle- and Upper-Class, Heterosexual Women

Many critics of radical feminism in both its libertarian and cultural forms also faulted it for focusing too much on issues such as egg donation, surrogacy, and other expensive, hard-to-access artificial (assisted) modes of procreation. They urged radical feminists to focus instead on the kinds of reproductive issues that concern most women—contraception and sterilization, for example.

By the mid-1970s, most US women realized that oral contraceptives posed risks as well as benefits[112] and that estrogen and progesterone were not necessarily women's best friends. Some women, worried about the so-called Pill's side effects, turned to the intrauterine device (IUD), which, as they saw it, had the benefit of being nonhormonal as well as forgettable once inserted.

In the United States, women's romance with IUDs ended, however, when a heated controversy broke out about one type, the Dalkon Shield. Shaped like a crab, with little spines and a multifilament tail-spring to maximize opportunity for monitoring its position in the uterus, the Dalkon Shield was initially hailed as a new, improved IUD. Unfortunately, its crab-like qualities also made it difficult and painful to insert, wear, and remove, and its filamentous string facilitated the passage of infectious bacteria into the uterus. Indeed, studies showed that Dalkon Shield users were at much higher risk for pelvic inflammatory disease (PID) and septic abortions than were women who wore other IUDs.[113] Over the years, Dalkon Shield victims or their survivors reported fourteen deaths, 223 septic abortions, and thousands of PID cases, many of them resulting in infertility, to the Food and Drug Administration. Eventually, more than 300,000 claims were filed in a class-action suit against the A. H. Robins Company, manufacturer of the Dalkon Shield, alleging that the company had continued marketing the device after becoming aware of its dangers. After paying out $378.3 million in 9,230 lawsuits, A. H. Robins filed for bankruptcy in 1985.[114]

Put on alert by this event, the National Women's Health Network (NWHN) became very vigilant as other pharmaceutical companies brought new contraceptives to the US market. It insisted that all be subject to rigorous clinical testing before being sold and that US researchers avoid the use of women in developing countries, where research practices are relatively unregulated, as "guinea pigs."[115]

As concerned as the NWHN was about the safety of contraceptives, however, it worried even more about women's lack of control over their use.[116] For example, unlike many older means of birth control (condoms, spermicides, and the rhythm method), newer methods are not strictly in women's hands. Physicians or other health-care practitioners have the power and presumably the skills to prescribe oral contraceptives, insert IUDs, inject Depo-Provera, or implant Norplant in women's bodies. Women must go to them for help.

That women must rely on physicians or other health-care practitioners for access to a full range of contraceptives renders them dependent on the medical establishment for full exercise of their reproductive freedom. Further, the effectiveness of long-lasting contraceptives and sterilization has prompted legislators as well as health-care practitioners to force them on certain women (usually poor women and women of color). Indeed, most contemporary US feminists, of whatever school of thought, have serious reservations about sterilization procedures in particular. They point to their long history of abuse in the United States, beginning in the late nineteenth century and officially ending as late as the 1960s, with the repeal of most state eugenics laws as unconstitutional. These laws generally targeted developmentally disabled individuals and worked in tandem with sterilization programs focused on indigent and African American women in particular. In poorer states, sterilizations were so common that they were called "Mississippi appendectomies." Many poor women and/or women of color did not understand that once their "appendix" was removed, they could no longer bear children.[117]

Critique Three: Radical Feminists Often Dichotomize in Ways That Are Unhelpful to the Overall Feminist Agenda

According to Marxist-socialist feminist Ann Ferguson, both the radical-libertarian and the radical-cultural feminist perspectives on sexuality fail on account of their ahistoricity.[118] Radical-cultural feminists wrongly claim that sexuality, whether conceived as emotional intimacy or physical pleasure,[119] is the same for all women. Rather, "sexuality is a bodily energy whose objects, meaning and social values are historically constructed."[120] Ferguson used her own lesbian sexuality as a case study in the historical construction of human sexuality in general. She said her current (and therefore, by implication, changeable) way of loving resulted from two factors: "first, the historical and social contexts in my teenage years which allowed me to develop a first physical love relationship with a woman, and, second, the existence of a strong self-identified lesbian-feminist oppositional culture [today] which allowed me to turn toward women again from an adult life hitherto exclusively heterosexual."[121] Ferguson speculated that had she grown up in a more restrictive sexual environment or in a less feminist era, she probably would not have wished for lesbian lovers. After all, she said, "one's sexual objects are defined by the social contexts in which one's *on-going* gender identity is constructed in relation to one's peers."[122]

Like radical-cultural feminists, radical-libertarian feminists are guilty of ahistoricism, in Ferguson's estimation, but in a different way. Seeming to think that women can always give free or true consent, they make no distinction between real and apparent consent. But, Ferguson said, depending on a woman's "social context," she may in fact be a "victim of false consciousness." Thus we must challenge the supposed freedom of an economically dependent housewife to consent to sadomasochistic (S-M) sex with her husband or of a high-school student to have sex with her teacher.[123]

Conclusion

Assuming that women's sexual and reproductive desires, needs, behaviors, and identities are largely the product of their time and place in history, we can claim that (1) neither heterosexuality nor lesbianism is either inherently pleasurable or inherently dangerous for women, and (2) neither natural reproduction nor artificial reproduction is either inherently empowering or inherently disempowering for them. Contemporary radical feminists, whether libertarian or cultural, wonder what kind of sexual and reproductive practices people would adopt in a society that structured all economic, political, and kinship systems to create equality between men and women and, as far as possible, between adults and children. In such an egalitarian world, would men and women engage in "male breadwinner/ female housewife sex prostitution," or would they instead develop forms of egalitarian heterosexuality seldom imagined, let alone practiced, in our very unequal, patriarchal world? Would some lesbians continue to engage in S-M and butch-femme relationships, or would all lesbians find themselves turned off by such practices? Would women use more or less in the way of contraceptives? Would couples contract for gestational mothers' services or instead prefer to adopt? Would there be more or fewer children? Would most people choose to reproduce "artificially" or the old-fashioned, natural way?

The answers to the kinds of questions just posed will be found in a future world that radical feminists imagine and not, for the most part, in the present world radical feminists experience. For now, radical feminists continue to take the lead in developing approaches to sexuality and reproduction that permit women to understand both the pleasures and the dangers of sex and both the liberating and enslaving aspects of reproduction and mothering. The one-sided approaches of the past seem to constitute part of the problem of human oppression rather than a remedy for it. The sooner that either/or approaches to sexuality and reproduction give way to both/ and approaches, the sooner men and women will stop playing the destructive game of male domination and female subordination.[124]

Questions for Discussion

1. Discuss the helpfulness of understanding the totality of human oppression without first considering the specific case of women's oppression.
2. In your estimation, are there still sexist writers and filmmakers? If so, who are they, and what, if anything, should be done about them?
3. Imagine a world in which technology has erased biological differences. Would this technologically advanced society necessarily embrace gender equality?
4. Compare and contrast the benefits and drawbacks of both traditional one-on-one child rearing and the "kid-minding" Marge Piercy proposed. Is bloodline ever morally relevant when considering maternal and/or paternal responsibilities?
5. What kind of social and political policies regarding mothering and reproduction would you recommend adopting in a society where all economic, political, and kinship systems were egalitarian?

3

Marxist and Socialist Feminisms

Although possible, distinguishing between Marxist and socialist feminist thinking is quite difficult. The differences between these two schools of thought seem more a matter of emphasis than of substance. Classical Marxist feminists work within the conceptual terrain laid out by Karl Marx, Friedrich Engels, Vladimir Lenin, and other nineteenth-century thinkers. They regard classism rather than sexism as the fundamental cause of women's oppression. In contrast, socialist feminists are not certain that classism is women's worst or only enemy. They write in view of the Soviet Union's twentieth-century failure to achieve socialism's ultimate goal—namely, the replacement of class oppression and antagonism with "an association, in which the free development of each is the condition for the free development of all."[1] Post-1917 communism in the Soviet Union and later in the Eastern Bloc was not true socialism but simply a new form of human oppression. Women's entry into the productive workplace did not make them men's equals either there or at home. For these and related reasons, socialist feminists moved beyond relying on class as the sole category for understanding women's subordination to men. Increasingly, they have tried "to understand women's subordination in a coherent and systematic way that integrates class and sex, as well as other aspects of identity such as race/ethnicity or sexual orientation."[2]

Some Traditional Marxist Concepts and Theories

To appreciate the differences between classical Marxist and contemporary socialist feminism, we need to understand the Marxist concept of human nature. As noted in Chapter 1, liberals believe that several characteristics distinguish human beings from other animals: a set of abilities, such as the capacity for rationality and the use of language; a set of practices, such as religion, art, and science; and a set of attitude and behavior patterns, such as competitiveness and the tendency to put oneself over others. Marxists reject the liberal conception of human nature, claiming instead that our ability to produce our means of subsistence makes us different from other animals. We are what we are because of what we do—specifically, what we do to meet our basic needs through productive activities such as fishing, farming, and building. Unlike bees, beavers, and ants, whose activities are governed by instinct and which cannot willfully change themselves, we create ourselves in the process of intentionally transforming and manipulating nature.[3]

For the liberal, the ideas, thoughts, and values of individuals account for change over time. For the Marxist, material forces—the production and re-production of social life—are the prime movers in history. In laying out a full explanation of how change takes place over time, an explanation usually termed "historical materialism," Marx stated, "The mode of production of material life conditions the general process of social, political, and intellectual life. It is not the consciousness of men that determines their existence, but their social existence that determines their consciousness."[4] In other words, Marx believed a society's total mode of production—that is, its forces of production (the raw materials, tools, and workers that actually produce goods) plus its relations of production (the ways in which production is organized)—generates a superstructure (a layer of legal, political, and social ideas) that in turn reinforces the mode of production. Adding to Marx's point, Richard Schmitt later emphasized that we should read the statement "human beings create themselves" not as "men and women, as *individuals*, make themselves what they are" but instead as "men and women, through production *collectively*, create a society that, in turn, shapes them."[5] So, for example, people in the United States think in certain ways about liberty, equality, and freedom because their mode of production is capitalist.

Like Marxists in general, Marxist and socialist feminists claim that social existence determines consciousness. For them, the observation that "women's work is never done" is more than an aphorism; it is a description of the nature of woman's work. Always on call, women form a conception of themselves they would not have if their roles in the family and the workplace did not keep them socially and economically subordinate to men. Thus, Marxist and socialist feminists believe we need to analyze the links between women's work status and women's self-image to understand the unique character of women's oppression.[6]

The Marxist Theory of Economics

To the degree Marxist and socialist feminists believe women's work shapes their thoughts and thus "female nature," these thinkers also believe capitalism is a system of power as well as exchange relations. When viewed as a system of exchange relations, capitalism is described as a commodity or market society in which everything, including one's own labor power, has a price, and all transactions are fundamentally exchange transactions. But when viewed instead as a system of power relations, capitalism is described as a society in which every kind of transactional relation is fundamentally exploitative. Thus, depending on one's emphasis, the worker-employer relationship is either an exchange relationship in which items of equivalent value are freely traded—labor for wages—or as a workplace struggle in which the employer, who has superior power, takes advantage of workers in any number of ways.

Whereas liberals view capitalism as a system of voluntary exchange relations, Marxists and socialists view it as a system of exploitative power relations. According to Marx, we determine the value of any commodity based on the amount of labor, or actual expenditure of human energy and intelligence, necessary to produce it.[7] To be more precise, the value of any commodity equals the direct labor incorporated into the commodity by workers, plus the indirect labor stored in workers' artificial appendages—the tools and machines made by the direct labor of their predecessors.[8] Because all commodities are worth exactly the labor necessary to produce them, and because workers' labor power (capacity for work) is a commodity that can be bought and sold, the value of workers' labor power is exactly the cost of whatever it takes (food, clothing, shelter) to maintain them throughout the workday. But there is a difference between what employers pay workers for their mere capacity to work (labor power) and the value that workers actually create when they put their work capacity to use in producing commodities.[9] Marx termed this difference "surplus value," and from it employers derive their profits. Thus, capitalism is an exploitative system because employers pay workers only for their labor power and not for the human energy they expend and the intelligence they transfer into the commodities they produce.[10]

At this point in an analysis of Marxist economic thought, it seems reasonable to ask how employers get workers to labor for more hours than are necessary to produce the value of their subsistence, especially when workers received no compensation for this extra work. As Marx explained in *Capital*, the answer is simple: employers have a monopoly on the means of production, including factories, tools, land, and modes of transportation and communication. Workers must choose between being exploited and having no work at all. It is a liberal fiction that workers freely sign mutually beneficial contractual agreements with their employers. Capitalism is just as much a system of power relations as it is one of exchange relations. Workers are free to contract with employers only in the sense that employers do not hold a gun to their heads when they sign on the dotted line.

Interestingly, employers can exploit workers under capitalism for another, less discussed reason. According to Marx, capitalist ideologies lead workers and employers to focus on capitalism's surface structure of exchange relations.[11] By means of this ideological ploy, which Marx called the "fetishism of commodities," workers gradually convince themselves that even though their money is very hard earned, there is nothing inherently wrong with the specific exchange relationships into which they have entered, because life, in all its dimensions, is simply one colossal system of exchange relations.

That liberal ideologies, typically spawned in capitalist economies, present practices such as prostitution and surrogate motherhood as contractual exercises of free choice is thus no accident, according to Marxist and socialist feminists. The liberal ideologies claim that women become prostitutes and surrogate mothers because they prefer this work over other available jobs. But, as Marxist and socialist feminists see it, when a woman, especially if she is poor, illiterate, and unskilled, chooses to sell her sexual or reproductive capacities, chances are her choice is more coerced than free. After all, if one has little else of value to sell besides one's body, one's leverage in the marketplace is quite limited.

The Marxist Theory of Society

Like the Marxist analysis of power, the Marxist analysis of class has provided both Marxist and socialist feminists with some of the conceptual tools necessary to understand women's oppression. Marx observed that every political economy—the primitive communal state, the slave era epoch, the precapitalist society, and the bourgeois society—contains the seeds of its own destruction. Thus, according to Marx, there are within capitalism enough internal contradictions to generate a class division dramatic enough to overwhelm the very system that produced it. Specifically, there exist many poor and propertyless workers who live very modestly, receiving subsistence wages for their exhausting labor, while their employers live in luxury. When both these groups of people, the haves and the have-nots, become conscious of themselves *as* classes, said Marx, class struggle ensues and ultimately topples the system that produced these classes.[12] It is important to emphasize the dynamic nature of class. Classes do not simply appear. They are slowly and painstakingly formed by similarly situated people who share the same wants and needs. According to Marx, people who belong to any class initially have no more unity than do "potatoes in a sack of potatoes."[13] But through a long and complex process of struggling together about issues of local and later national interest to them, a group of individuals gradually becomes a unity, a true class. Because class unity is difficult to achieve, its importance cannot be overstated, said Marx. As soon as a group is fully conscious of itself as a class, it has a better chance of achieving its fundamental goals. There is power in group awareness.

Class consciousness is, in the Marxist framework, the opposite of false consciousness, a state of mind that impedes the creation and maintenance of true class unity. False consciousness causes exploited people to believe they are as free to act and speak as their exploiters. The bourgeoisie is especially adept at fooling the proletariat. For this reason, Marxists discredit egalitarian, or welfare, liberalism, for example, as a ruling-class ideology that tricks workers into believing their employers actually care about them. As Marxists see it, fringe benefits such as generous health-care plans and paid maternity leave are not gifts employers generously bestow on workers but rather a means to pull the wool over their eyes. Grateful for the benefits their employers give them, workers minimize their own hardships and suffering. Like the ruling class, they begin to perceive the status quo as the best possible world for workers and employers alike. The more benefits employers give them, the less likely workers will be to form a class capable of recognizing their true needs as human beings.

Because Marxist and socialist feminists wish to view women as a collectivity, Marxist teachings on class and class consciousness play a large role in Marxist and socialist feminist thought. Much debate within the Marxist and socialist feminist community has centered on the following question: Do women, per se, constitute a class? Given that some women are wives, daughters, friends, and lovers of bourgeois men, whereas other women bear these relationships to proletarian men, women do not constitute a single class in the strict Marxist sense. Yet bourgeois and proletarian women's domestic experiences, for example, may bear enough similarities to motivate unifying struggles such as the 1970s wages-for-housework campaign, which we will discuss later. Thus, many Marxist and socialist feminists believe women can gain a consciousness of themselves as a class of workers by insisting, for example, that domestic work be recognized as real—that is, productive—work. The observation that wives and mothers usually love the people for whom they work does not mean that cooking, cleaning, and child care are not productive work. At most it means that wives' and mothers' working conditions are better than those of people who work for employers they dislike.[14]

By keeping the Marxist conceptions of class and class consciousness in mind, we can understand another concept that often plays a role in Marxist and socialist feminist thought: alienation. Like many Marxist terms, "alienation" is difficult to define simply. In *Karl Marx,* Allen Wood suggested we are alienated "if we either experience our lives as meaningless or ourselves as worthless, or else are capable of sustaining a sense of meaning and self-worth only with the help of illusions about ourselves or our condition."[15] Robert Heilbroner added that alienation is a profoundly fragmenting experience. Things or persons that are or should be connected in some significant way are instead viewed as separate. As Heilbroner saw it, this sense of fragmentation and meaninglessness is particularly strong under capitalism.

As a result of invidious class distinctions, as well as the highly specialized and highly segmented nature of the work process, human existence loses its unity and wholeness in four basic ways, according to Heilbroner. First, workers are alienated from the product of their labor. Not only do they have no say in what commodities they will or will not produce, but the fruits of their labor are snatched from them. Therefore, the satisfaction of determining when, where, how, and to whom to sell these commodities is denied the workers. What should partially express and constitute their being-as-workers confronts them as a thing apart, a thing alien.[16]

Second, workers are alienated from themselves because when experienced as something unpleasant, to be gotten through as quickly as possible, work is deadening. When the potential source of workers' humanization becomes the actual source of their dehumanization, workers may undergo a major psychological crisis. They may start feeling like hamsters on a hamster wheel, going nowhere.[17]

Third, workers are alienated from other human beings because the structure of the capitalist economy encourages and even forces workers to see one another as competitors for jobs and promotions. When the source of workers' solidarity (the experience of other workers as cooperators, friends, people to be with) becomes instead the source of their isolation (the experience of other workers as competitors, enemies, people to avoid), workers become disidentified with one another, losing an opportunity to add joy and meaning to their lives.[18]

Fourth, workers are alienated from nature because the kind of work they do and the conditions under which they do it make them see nature as an obstacle to their survival. This negative perception of nature sets up an opposition where, in fact, a connectedness should exist—the connectedness among all elements in nature. The elimination of this type of alienation, entailing a return to a humane kind of work environment, is yet another important justification for the overthrow of capitalism.[19]

Building on the idea that in a capitalist society human relations take on an alienated nature in which "the individual only feels himself or herself when detached from others,"[20] socialist feminist Ann Foreman claimed that this state of affairs is worse for women than for men:

> The man exists in the social world of business and industry as well as in the family and therefore is able to express himself in these different spheres. For the woman, however, her place is within the home. Men's objectification within industry, through the expropriation of the product of their labour, takes the form of alienation. But the effect of alienation on the lives and consciousness of women takes an even more oppressive form. Men seek relief from their alienation through their relations with women; for women there is no relief. For these intimate relations are the very ones that are essential structures of [their] oppression.[21]

As Foreman saw it, women's alienation is profoundly disturbing because women experience themselves not as selves but as others. All too often, said Foreman, a woman's sense of self depends entirely on her family and friends' appreciation of her. If they express loving feelings toward her, she will be happy, but if they fail to give her even a thank-you, she will be sad. Thus, Marxist and socialist feminists aim to create a world in which women can experience themselves as whole persons, as integrated rather than fragmented beings, as people who can be happy even when unable to make their families and friends happy.

The Marxist Theory of Politics

Like the Marxist theories of economics and society, the Marxist theory of politics offers Marxist and socialist feminists insights to help liberate women from the forces that oppress them. As noted previously, class struggle takes a certain form within the workplace because the interests of the employers are not those of the workers. Whereas it is in the employers' interests to use any tactics necessary (harassment, firing, violence) to get workers to labor ever more effectively and efficiently for fewer wages than their work is worth, it is in the workers' interests to use any countertactics necessary (sick time, coffee breaks, strikes) to limit the extent to which employers use their labor power to produce sheer profit for themselves.

The relatively small, everyday class conflicts occurring within the capitalist workplace serve as preliminaries to the full-fledged, large-scale class struggles that Marx envisioned. As noted earlier, Marx predicted that as workers became increasingly aware of their common exploitation and alienation, they would achieve class consciousness. United, they could to fight their employers for control over the means of production (e.g., the nation's factories). If they managed to win this fight, Marx claimed that a highly committed, politically savvy, well-trained group of revolutionaries would subsequently emerge from the workers' ranks. Marx termed this special group of workers the "vanguard" of the full-scale revolution for which he hoped. More than anything else, Marx desired to replace capitalism with socialism, a nonexploitative, nonalienating political economy through which communism, "the complete and conscious return of man himself as a social, that is, human being,"[22] could come into existence.

Under capitalism, Marx suggested, people are largely free to do what they want within the confines of the system, but they have little say in determining the confines themselves. "Personality," said Marx, "is conditioned and determined by quite definite class relationships."[23] Decades later, Richard Schmitt elaborated on Marx's powerful statement:

> In as much as persons do certain jobs in society, they tend to acquire certain character traits, interests, habits, and so on. Without such adaptations to the demands of their particular occupations, they would not be able to do a great job. A capitalist who cannot bear to win in competition, or to outsmart someone, will not be a capitalist for long. A worker who is unwilling to take orders will not work very often. In this way we are shaped by the work environment, and this fact limits personal freedom for it limits what we can choose to be.[24]

In contrast, in Marxists' view, to people living under capitalism, those living under communism are free not only to do, but also to be, what they want, because they have the power to see clearly and change the system that shapes them.

If we read between these lines, we can appreciate another of Marxism's major appeals to Marxist and socialist feminists. It promises to reconstitute human nature in ways that preclude all the pernicious dichotomies that have made slaves of some and masters of others. Marxism also promises to make people free, a promise women would like to see kept. There is, after all, something very liberating about the idea of women and men constructing together the social structures and social roles that will permit both genders to realize their full human potential.

The Marxist Theory of Family Relations

Although the fathers of Marxism did not take women's oppression as women nearly as seriously as they did women's (and certainly men's) oppression as workers, some of them did offer explanations for why women are oppressed qua women. With the apparent blessing of Marx, Engels wrote *The Origin of the Family, Private Property, and the State* (1845), in which he showed how changes in the material conditions of people affect the organization of their family relations. He argued that before the family, or structured conjugal relations, there existed a primitive state of "promiscuous intercourse."[25] In this early state, every woman was fair game for every man. All were essentially married to all. In the process of natural selection, suggested Engels, various kinds of blood relatives were gradually excluded from consideration as eligible marriage partners.[26] As fewer and fewer women in the tribal group became available to any given man, individual men began to put forcible claims on individual women as their possessions. As a result, the pairing family, in which one man marries one woman, came into existence.

Noting that when a man took a woman, he came to live in her household, Engels interpreted this state of affairs as a sign of women's economic power. Because women's work was vital for the tribe's survival and because women produced most of the material goods (e.g., bedding, clothing, cookware, tools) that could be passed on to future generations, Engels concluded that early pairing societies were probably matrilineal, with inheritance and lines of descent traced through the mother.[27] Later, Engels speculated that pairing societies may have been not merely matrilineal but also matriarchal, with women ruling at the political, social, and economic levels.[28] But his main and less debatable point remained that any power women held in past times was rooted in their position in the household, at that time the center of production.[29] Only if the site of production changed would women lose their advantaged position.[30] As it turned out, said Engels, a site change did occur. The "domestication of animals and the breeding of herds" outside the household led to an entirely new source of wealth for the human community.[31] Men gained control of the tribe's animals (Engels did not tell us why or how),[32] and the male-female power balance shifted in favor of men, as men learned to produce more than enough animals to meet the tribe's needs for milk and meat.

Surplus animals constituted an accumulation of wealth that men used as a means of exchange between tribes. Possessing more than enough of a valuable socioeconomic good, men found themselves increasingly preoccupied with the issue of property inheritance. Directed through the mother's line, property inheritance was originally a minor matter of the bequest of a "house, clothing, crude ornaments and the tools for obtaining and preparing food—boats, weapons and domestic utensils of the simplest kinds."[33] As production outside the household began to outstrip production within it, the traditional sexual division of labor between men and women, which had supposedly arisen out of the physiological differences between the sexes—specifically, the sex act[34]—took on new social meanings. As men's work and production grew in importance, not only did the value of women's work and production decrease, but so did the status of women within society. Because men now possessed things more valuable than the things women possessed, and because men, for some unexplained reason, suddenly wanted their own biological children to get their possessions, men exerted enormous pressure to convert society from matrilineal to patrilineal. As Engels phrased it, mother right had "to be overthrown, and overthrown it was."[35]

Engels presented the "overthrow of mother right" as "the world-historic defeat of the female sex."[36] Having produced and staked a claim to wealth, men took control of the household, reducing women to the "slaves" of men's carnal desire and "mere instrument[s] for the production of [men's] children."[37] In this new familial order, said Engels, the husband ruled by virtue of his economic power: "He is the bourgeoisie and the wife represents the proletariat."[38] Engels believed men's power over women stemmed from the fact that men, not women, controlled private property. The oppression of women would cease only with the dissolution of the institution of private property.

The emergence of private property and the shift to patrilineage also explained, for Engels, the transition to the monogamous family. Before the advent of technologies such as in vitro fertilization, it was always possible to identify the biological mother of a child. If the child came out of a woman's body, the child was the biological product of her egg and some man's sperm. In contrast, before the development of DNA testing, the identity of a biological father was uncertain because a man other than her husband could have impregnated the mother. Thus, to secure their wives' marital fidelity, men imposed the institution of heterosexual monogamy on women, the purpose of which was, according to Engels, to provide a vehicle for the guaranteed transfer of a father's private property to his biological children. Male dominance, in the forms of patrilineage and patriarchy, is simply the result of the class division between the propertied man and the propertyless woman. Engels commented that monogamy was "the first form of the family to be based not on natural but on economic conditions."[39] In his estimation, the monogamous family is the product not of love and commitment but of power plays and economic exigencies.

Because Engels viewed monogamous marriage under capitalism as an economic institution that has nothing to do with love and everything to do with the transfer of private property, he insisted that emancipation of wives from their husbands would require first that women become economically independent of men. He stressed that the first presupposition for the emancipation of women is "the reintroduction of the entire female sex into public industry," and the second is the socialization of housework and child rearing.[40] Remarkably, Engels believed that proletarian women experience less oppression than do bourgeois women. As he saw it, the bourgeois family consists of a relationship between a husband and a wife in which the husband agrees to support his wife, provided she promises to remain sexually faithful to him and to produce only his legitimate heirs. "This marriage of convenience," observed Engels, "often enough turns into the crassest prostitution—sometimes on both sides, but much more generally on the part of the wife, who differs from the ordinary courtesan only in that she does not hire out her body, like a wageworker, on piecework, but sells it into slavery once and for all."[41]

In contrast to the bourgeois marriage, the proletarian marriage is not, in Engels's estimation, a mode of prostitution, because the material conditions of the proletarian family differ substantially from those of the bourgeois family. Not only is the proletariat's lack of private property significant in removing the primary male incentive for monogamy—namely, the reproduction of legitimate heirs for one's property—but the general employment of proletarian women as workers outside the home also leads to a measure of equality between husband and wife. This equality, according to Engels, provides the foundation of true "sex-love." In addition to these differences, the household authority of the proletarian husband, unlike that of the bourgeois husband, is not likely to receive the full support of the legal establishment. For all these reasons, Engels concluded that with the exception of "residual brutality" (spouse abuse), all "the material foundations of male dominance had ceased to exist" in the proletarian home.[42]

Classical Marxist Feminism: General Reflections

Evelyn Reed

Affirming the ideas of Marx and Engels, classical Marxist feminists tried to use a class rather than a gender analysis to explain women's oppression. A good example of classical Marxist feminism appeared in Evelyn Reed's "Women: Caste, Class, or Oppressed Sex?"[43] Stressing that the same capitalist economic forces and social relations that "brought about the oppression of one class by another, one race by another, and one nation by another"[44] also brought about the oppression of one sex by another, Reed resisted the view that women's oppression as women is the worst kind of oppression for all women. Although she agreed that relative to men, women occupy a subordinate position in a patriarchal or male-dominated society, she did not think that all women were equally oppressed by men or that no women were guilty of oppressing men or other women. On the contrary, she thought bourgeois women capable of oppressing both proletarian men and women. In a capitalist system, money is most often power.

Not found in Reed is any manifesto urging all women to band together to wage a "caste war" against all men.[45] Rather, she encouraged oppressed women to join oppressed men in a "class war" against their common capitalist oppressors, female as well as male.[46] Reed deemed misguided the insistence that all women, simply by virtue of possessing two X chromosomes, belong to the same class. On the contrary, she maintained that "women, like men are a multiclass sex."[47] Specifically, proletarian women have little in common with bourgeois women, who are the economic, social, and political, as well as sexual, partners of the bourgeois men to whom they are linked. Bourgeois women are united not with proletarian women but with bourgeois men "in defense of private property, profiteering, militarism, racism—and the exploitation of other women."[48]

Clearly Reed believed that the primary enemy of at least proletarian women is not patriarchy but, first and foremost, capitalism. Optimistic about male-female relations in a postcapitalist society, Reed maintained that "far from being eternal, woman's subjection and the bitter hostility between the sexes are no more than a few thousand years old. They were produced by the drastic social changes which brought the family, private property, and the state into existence."[49] With the end of capitalist male-female relationships, both sexes would thrive in a communist society that enabled all its members to cooperate with one another in communities of care.[50]

Margaret Benston

Unable to find in Reed's theory a satisfying explanation for why, on average, women were not faring as well as men in the productive workforce, some Marxist feminists turned their attention to the work women did in the domestic realm—work that men typically did not do. Trying to explain why women were saddled with their families' domestic work, whether or not they participated in the productive workforce, Margaret Benston defined women as that class of people "responsible for the production of simple use-values in those activities associated with the house and family."[51] As she saw it, women must break out of this class to be liberated but could not do so unless their domestic labor was socialized: "Women, particularly married women with children, who work outside the home simply do two jobs; their participation in the labor force is only allowed if they continue to fulfill their first responsibility in the home. . . . Equal access to jobs outside the home, while one of the preconditions for women's liberation, will not in itself be sufficient to give equality for women; as long as work in the home remains a matter of private production and is the responsibility of women, they will simply carry a double work-load."[52]

To bring women into the productive workforce without simultaneously socializing the jobs of cooking, cleaning, and child care would exacerbate women's oppressed condition, claimed Benston. To be sure, she conceded, the socialization of domestic work might lead to women doing the same sorts of "female" work both inside and outside the home. But the simple fact that women would be doing this "female" work outside their own homes for wages over which they had control would constitute an advancement for women, insisted Benston.

Wages for Housework

Mariarosa Costa and Selma James

Agreeing with Benston that the socialization of domestic work would be necessary to achieve full liberation for women in a socialist society, Mariarosa Dalla Costa and Selma James nonetheless argued that in a capitalist society, the best (or at least the most efficient) way for women to achieve economic parity with men might not be for women to enter the productive workforce and for domestic labor to be socialized, but instead for women to stay at home and demand wages for the "real"—that is, productive—work they did there. Unlike most classical Marxist feminist thinkers, Dalla Costa and James claimed that women's work inside the home does generate surplus value.[53] They reasoned that women's domestic work is the necessary condition for all other labor, from which, in turn, surplus value is extracted. By providing not only food and clothes but also emotional comfort to current (and future) workers, women keep the cogs of the capitalist machine running. Therefore, argued Dalla Costa and James, men's employers should pay women wages for the housework they do.[54] Let housewives get the cash that would otherwise fatten employers' wallets.[55]

Acknowledging that domestic labor could be viewed as productive work, most Marxist feminists nonetheless concluded that, for a number of reasons, paying women wages for housework was neither as feasible nor as desirable as Dalla Costa and James seemed to think. First, if required to pay housewives wages for housework, employers would probably pay lower wages in general. Under such circumstances, the total capitalist profit margin would remain high, and the material conditions of workers would not improve. Second, not all or even most women in advanced capitalist economies are stay-at-home domestic workers. Many married women and men work outside the home, as do many single men and women. Would employers be required to compensate all workers for their at-home domestic work? If so, would employers have any way to monitor the quantity and quality of this domestic labor? Third, if required to pay all their workers for domestic work, most small companies would probably go out of business. Back in 1972, the height of the wages-for-housework campaign, the Chase Manhattan Bank estimated that "for her average 100-hour workweek, the housewife should be paid $257.53."[56] In that same year, noted Ann Crittenden Scott, "white males had average incomes of $172 a week; white females had average incomes of $108 a week."[57] By 2015, over forty years later, annual median earnings per week in the United States were $726 for women and $895 for men.[58] Add to these median wages new wages for domestic labor done by employees in their own homes, and there is little question that most small or even large companies could not sustain such a hit.[59]

On balance, it does not seem feasible to pay anyone, including wives, girlfriends, mothers, and daughters, wages for housework. But even if doing so were feasible, would it be desirable? Many Marxist and other feminists in the 1970s were not confident that wages for housework would liberate women. Carol Lopate, among others, argued that paying women for housework would have the net effect of keeping them isolated in their own homes with few opportunities to do anything other than routinized and repetitive work:

> The decrease in house size and the mechanization of housework have meant that the housewife is potentially left with much greater leisure time; however, she is often kept busy buying, using, and repairing devices which are theoretically geared toward saving her time. Moreover, the trivial, manufactured tasks which many of these technological aids perform are hardly a source of satisfaction for housewives. Max-Pacs may give "perfect coffee every time," but even a compliment about her coffee can offer little more than fleeting satisfaction to the housewife. Finally, schools, nurseries, day care, and television have taken from mothers much of their responsibility for the socialization of their children.[60]

Additionally, paying women wages for domestic work would give women little impetus to work outside the household. As a result, the traditional sexual division of labor would be strengthened. Women outside the home would have little incentive to do "men's work."[61] One thinks here of the stereotypical stay-at-home supermom who is at the beck and call of her children to shuttle them to and from multiple sports events, club meetings, parties, mall visits, and the like.

Contemporary Socialist Feminism: General Reflections

The more Marxist feminists realized that, like everyone else, they had unreflectively assumed domestic work to be women's work, the more concerned they became that the advent of communist/socialist societies had not resulted in the socialization of this labor. Rather than an approximately equal number of men and women doing domestic work for wages, it was business as usual. That is, women continued to do domestic work "for free," whether or not they had a paid job outside the home. Unable to explain in exclusively economic terms why domestic work is viewed as women's work in socialist as well as capitalist societies, many Marxist feminists concluded that domestic work is assigned to women in all societies simply because all women belong to the same sex class—namely, the second (female) sex, which is thought to exist to serve the first (male) sex.

The Marxist feminists who decided that, in addition to economic class, women's sex class plays a role in women's oppression began to refer to themselves as socialist feminists or materialist feminists. This evolving group of feminist thinkers initially aimed to develop one theory powerful enough to explain the complex ways in which capitalism and patriarchy allied to oppress women. This effort gave rise, as might be predicted, not to a unitary theory but to a variety of theories that sorted themselves into two types: (1) two-system explanations of women's oppression, and (2) interactive-system explanations of women's oppression.

Contemporary Two-System Explanations of Women's Oppression

Two-system explanations of women's oppression typically combine a Marxist feminist account of class power with a radical feminist account of sex status.[62] According to Chris Beasly, some two-system explanations adhere to the Marxist base-superstructure model that views economics as "the fundamental motor of social relations,"[63] shaping the form of society, including its ideologies and psychologies. These explanations claim that, at root, women have more to fear from capitalist forces than from patriarchal forces. In contrast, other two-system explanations that are less committed to the Marxist base-superstructure model imply that patriarchy, not capitalism, may be women's ultimate worst enemy.

Juliet Mitchell

In the early 1970s, Juliet Mitchell sketched a plausible two-system explanation of women's oppression. In *Woman's Estate*,[64] she abandoned the classical Marxist feminist position that a woman's condition is simply a function of her relation to capital, of whether she is part of the productive workforce. In place of this monocausal explanation, Mitchell suggested that women's status and function are multiply determined by their role in not only production but also reproduction, the socialization of children, and sexuality: "The error of the old Marxist way was to see the other three elements as reducible to the economic; hence the call for the entry into production was accompanied by the purely abstract slogan of the abolition of the family. Economic demands are still *primary*, but must be accompanied by coherent policies for the other three elements (reproduction, sexuality and socialization), policies which at particular junctures may take over the primary role in immediate action."[65]

In attempting to determine which of these elements most oppressed 1970s US women, Mitchell concluded that they had not made enough progress in the areas of production, reproduction, and the socialization of children. She noted that even though women were just as physically and psychologically qualified as men for high-paying, prestigious jobs, employers continued to confine women to low-paying, low-status work.[66] Moreover, said Mitchell, despite the widespread availability of safe, effective, and inexpensive reproduction-controlling technologies, women often failed or refused to use them. As a result, the causal chain of "maternity—family—absence from production and public life—sexual inequality" continued to bind women to their subordinate status. Furthermore, although 1970s US women had far fewer children than US women did at the turn of the century, the modern women spent no less time socializing them.[67] In fact, the pressures to be a perfect mother, always attentive to her child's every physical and psychological need, seemed to be increasing.

Interestingly, like radical-libertarian feminists, Mitchell thought 1970s US women had made major progress in the area of sexuality. She claimed that unlike previous generations, 1970s US women felt freer to express and act upon their sexual desires publicly. Still, Mitchell acknowledged that, pushed to its extreme, women's newly won sexual liberation could mutate into a form of sexual oppression. Whereas turn-of-the-century US society may have condemned sexually active women as "wanton whores," 1970s US society tended to celebrate them as "sex experimenters" or healthy role models for sexually repressed women to emulate. Commenting on this state of affairs, Mitchell observed that too much sex, like too little, can be oppressive.[68] Women can be made to feel that something is wrong with them if they are not sexually active or sexually preoccupied.

Mitchell speculated that patriarchal ideology, which views women as lovers, wives, and mothers rather than as workers, is almost as responsible as capitalist economics for women's position in society. She claimed that even if a Marxist revolution destroyed the family as an economic unit, women would not automatically become men's equals. Because of how patriarchal ideology has constructed men's and women's psyches, women would probably continue to remain subordinate to men until their and men's minds had been liberated from the idea that women are somehow less valuable than men.

Alison Jaggar

Like Mitchell, Alison Jaggar provided a two-system explanation of women's oppression. But in the final analysis, instead of identifying capitalism as the primary cause of women's low status, she reserved this honor for patriarchy. Capitalism oppresses women as workers, but patriarchy oppresses them as women, an oppression that affects women's identity as well as their activity. A woman is always a woman, even when she is not working. Rejecting the classical Marxist doctrine that a person must participate directly in the capitalist relations of production to be considered truly alienated, Jaggar claimed, as did Foreman, that all women, no matter their work role, are alienated in ways that men are not.[69]

Jaggar organized her discussion of women's alienation under the headings of sexuality, motherhood, and intellectuality. In the same way that wage workers may be alienated from the product(s) on which they work, women, viewed simply as women, may be alienated from the "product(s)" on which they typically work: their bodies. Women may insist that they diet, exercise, and dress only to please themselves, but in reality they most likely shape and adorn their flesh primarily for the pleasure of men. Moreover, women do not have final or total say about when, where, how, or by whom their bodies will be used, because their bodies can be suddenly appropriated through acts ranging from the male gaze to sexual harassment to rape. Likewise, to the same degree that wage workers can be gradually alienated from themselves— their bodies beginning to feel like things, mere machines from which labor power is extracted—women can be gradually alienated from themselves. To the degree that women work on their bodies—shaving their underarms, slimming their thighs, augmenting their breasts, painting their nails, and coloring their hair—they may start to experience their bodies as objects or commodities. Finally, just as many wage workers compete with one another for their employers' approbation and rewards, many women compete with one another for men's power and wealth.[70]

In the same vein as Adrienne Rich (see Chapter 2), Jaggar continued that motherhood may also be an alienating experience for women, especially when mostly or exclusively men decide the policies and laws that regulate women's reproductive choices. For example, societies that heavily use children's labor power may pressure women to bear as many offspring as physically possible. In contrast, societies that view children as an economic burden for parents to support may discourage women from having large families. Indeed, women may be pressured or even forced to use contraception, undergo sterilization, or have an abortion.[71]

Furthering her analysis, Jaggar said women may be alienated from the product as well as the process of their reproductive labor. Raising the same type of concerns that some radical-cultural feminists raised about gestational surrogacy, Jaggar claimed that such arrangements do not do full justice to the gestational mother, whose reproductive work shapes the embryo into a viable human infant to which she may become emotionally as well as physically bonded. Should not this circumstance give her some parental claim to the child, even though she did not provide the "raw material," the egg? asked Jaggar.[72]

Child rearing, like childbearing, may also be an alienating experience for women when scientific experts (most of whom are men) take charge of it, stressed Jaggar.[73] She saw the pressures on mothers as enormous because, with virtually no assistance, they are supposed to execute every edict issued by child-rearing authorities, some of whom have never experienced the daily demands of child rearing. Echoing the thoughts of Rich in *Of Woman Born*, Jaggar explained how contemporary child-rearing practices may ultimately alienate or estrange mothers from their children. The extreme mutual dependence of mother and child encourages the mother to define the child primarily with reference to her own needs for meaning, love, and social recognition. She sees the child as her product, as something that should improve her life and often instead stands against her, as something of supreme value, whose life is viewed as more important than hers, for example, by antiabortionists. The social relations of contemporary motherhood often make it impossible for a woman to see her child as part of a larger community to which both the child and she belong.[74]

Finally, women may be alienated from their own intellectual capacities, according to Jaggar. Many women feel so unsure of themselves that they hesitate to express their ideas in public for fear that their thoughts do no merit articulation; they remain silent when they should loudly voice their opinions. Worse, when women do express themselves forcefully and with passion, their ideas are often rejected as irrational or the product of mere emotion. To the extent that men set the terms of thought and discourse, suggested Jaggar, women cannot be at ease in the world of theory.[75]

Jaggar concluded that although the overthrow of capitalism might end women's as well as men's exploitation in the productive workforce, it would not necessarily end women's alienation from everything and everyone, especially themselves.[76] Only the overthrow of patriarchy would enable women to become full persons.

Contemporary Interactive-System Explanations of Women's Oppression

In contrast to two-system explanations, which, as just noted, tended to identify either class or sex as the primary source of women's oppression, interactive-system explanations strove to present capitalism and patriarchy as coequal partners colluding in a variety of ways to oppress women. Interactive-system thinkers included Iris Marion Young and Heidi Hartmann, both of whom used such terms as "capitalist patriarchy" or "patriarchal capitalism" in their work. Aiming not to view one system as more fundamental than the other, Young and Hartmann wrote about how capitalism and patriarchy work together to cause and then maintain women's oppression.

Iris Marion Young

According to Iris Marion Young, as long as classical Marxist feminists try to use class as their central category of analysis, they will fail to explain why women in socialist countries are often just as oppressed as women in capitalist countries. Precisely because class is a gender-blind category, said Young, it cannot provide an adequate explanation for women's specific oppression. Only a gender-sighted category such as the "sexual division of labor" has the conceptual power to do this.

Young reasoned that whereas class analysis looks at the system of production as a whole, focusing on the means and relations of production in the most general terms possible, a sexual division-of-labor analysis pays attention to the characteristics of the individuals who do the producing in society. In other words, a class analysis calls only for a general discussion of the respective roles of the bourgeoisie and the proletariat, whereas a sexual division-of-labor analysis requires a detailed discussion of who gives and who takes the orders, who does the stimulating work and who counts the beans, who works more or fewer hours, and who gets paid relatively high or relatively low wages. Therefore, as compared with a class analysis, a sexual division-of-labor analysis can better explain why women usually take the orders, count the beans, work part-time, and get paid relatively low wages, whereas men usually give the orders, do the stimulating jobs, work full-time, and get paid relatively high wages.

Because she believed capitalism and patriarchy are necessarily linked, Young insisted that a sexual division-of-labor analysis is a total substitute for, not a mere supplement to, class analysis. We do not need one theory (Marxism) to explain gender-neutral capitalism and another theory (feminism) to explain gender-biased patriarchy, said Young. Rather, we need a single theory—a socialist feminist theory—to explain gender-biased (i.e., patriarchal) capitalism. "*My thesis,*" wrote Young, "*is that marginalization of women and thereby our functioning as a secondary labor force is an essential and fundamental characteristic of capitalism.*"[77]

Young's controversial thesis marked a major departure from the more traditional Marxist view that workers, be they male or female, are interchangeable. She argued that capitalism is very much aware of its workers' gender and, we may add, race and ethnicity. Because a large reserve of unemployed workers is necessary to keep wages low and to meet unanticipated demand for goods and services, capitalism has both implicit and explicit criteria for determining who will constitute its primary, employed and secondary, unemployed workforces. For a variety of reasons, not the least being a well-entrenched gender division of labor, capitalism's criteria identify men as "primary" workforce material and women as "secondary." Because women are needed at home in a way men are not—or so patriarchy believes—men are freer to work outside the home than women are.

Under capitalism as it exists today, women experience patriarchy as unequal wages for equal work, sexual harassment on the job, uncompensated domestic labor, and the pernicious public-private split. Earlier generations of women also experienced patriarchy, but they lived it differently, depending on the dynamics of the reigning economic system. As with class society, reasoned Young, patriarchy should not be considered a system separate from capitalism just because it existed first. In fact, class and gender structures are so intertwined that neither actually precedes the other. A feudal system of gender relations accompanied a feudal system of class arrangements, and the social relations of class and gender grew up together and evolved over time into the forms we now know (e.g., the capitalist nuclear family). To say gender relations are independent of class relations is to ignore how history works.

Heidi Hartmann

Reinforcing Young's analysis, Heidi Hartmann noted that a strict class analysis leaves largely unexplained why women rather than men play the subordinate and submissive roles in both the workplace and the home. Understanding not only workers' relation to capital but also women's relation to men, said Hartmann, required integrating a feminist analysis of patriarchy with a Marxist analysis of capitalism. In her estimation, the partnership between patriarchy and capitalism is complex because their interests in women are not always the same. In the nineteenth century, for example, proletarian men wanted proletarian women to stay at home, where women could "personally service" men.[78] In contrast, bourgeois men wanted proletarian women to work for next to nothing in the productive workforce, grateful for the opportunity to earn "pin money" to supplement their partners' puny take-home pay. Only if all men—be they proletarian or bourgeois—could find some mutually agreeable way to handle this particular "woman question" could the interests of patriarchy and capitalism be harmonized.

To some degree the tension between bourgeois and proletarian men's best interests was ameliorated when bourgeois men (e.g., factory owners) offered to pay proletarian men (e.g., factory workers) a (family) wage large enough to enable proletarian wives and mothers to stay at home, said Hartmann. Bourgeois men struck this bargain with proletarian men for two reasons: (1) stay-at-home housewives would produce and maintain healthier, happier, and therefore more productive male workers than working wives would, and (2) women and children could always be persuaded at a later date to enter the workforce for low wages should male workers demand high wages. For a time, this arrangement worked well enough, but over time, the size of the family wage shrank, and many proletarian men could no longer pay all their families' bills. Consequently, many proletarian women decided to enter the workforce to earn not "pin money" but enough income to help their male partners defray the family's actual living costs.[79] Regrettably, these women typically came home to male partners who had little or no interest in helping with domestic work. Hartmann concluded that women were in a no-win situation when it came to work-related issues. Everywhere women turned, the sexual division of labor disadvantaged them. The only hope for women was to break the symbiotic relationship between capitalism and patriarchy. Thus, Hartmann claimed, women's real enemy was the unitary system of capitalist patriarchy/patriarchal capitalism.

Contemporary Women's Labor Issues

The preceding discussion suggests that the distinctions some socialist feminists make between two-system and interactive-system explanations for women's oppression are somewhat forced and probably of more theoretical than practical interest to the average woman. Yet we cannot overstate the relevance of contemporary socialist feminism's overall message for women. Worldwide, women's oppression correlates strongly to the fact that women's work, be it in- or outside the home, is still unpaid, underpaid, or disvalued, a state of affairs that largely explains women's lower status and power nearly everywhere.

Although we could elaborate much more about women's domestic work, suffice it to say that according to a 2010 United Nations Development Programme report, "The omission of unpaid care work from national accounts leads to sizeable undercounts in all countries. By applying the wage rate of a general household worker to the number of hours that people spend on housework, the United Nations Research Institute for Social Development estimates that the omissions equal 10 to 39 percent of GDP. Incorporating unpaid work in national accounts would better reflect the realities of time use, especially for women."[80] Whether they live in developing or developed, socialist or capitalist countries, women still do the majority of unpaid work in the home, even when they also do full- or part-time paid work outside the home. As of 2009, US women did 25.9 hours to US men's 16.8 hours of domestic work a week. Moreover, US women did 3.9 hours of child care a day, compared to US men's 1.8 hours. When these hours are added to US working women's forty-hour-a-week shift, it seems clear that women are indeed working nearly a double day.[81] Add to this workload the amount of hours some women spend caring for relatives, typically 21.9 hours a week, and one begins to wonder how long women can maintain this kind of pace.[82]

The amount of housework women do is a global as well as local phenomenon. In 2014, said the World Bank Group, "by virtually every global measure, women [were] more economically excluded, dropping from 75 to 55 percent of the global workforce."[83] One of the main reasons given for women exiting the workforce was their increased caregiving responsibilities in the home. Worldwide, women spend at least twice as much time on unpaid domestic work such as child care and housekeeping than they spend on paid work in the factory or office, for example.[84] It does not help the situation that, globally, "one in three girls in developing countries is married before reaching her eighteenth birthday."[85] Girls that marry early are less likely to work outside the home than women who complete a higher education degree, which at least qualifies them to work outside the home.[86]

Gender Pay Gap

Most, though not all, countries have a gender pay gap, in the estimation of Shawn Meghan Burn. Japan's is particularly egregious. In 2011, Japanese women between the ages of thirty and thirty-four earned only 69 percent of Japanese men's wages.[87] Interestingly, the situation was dramatically different in Sweden, where women earned approximately 83 percent of men's wages.[88] In the United States in 2015, women earned 91 percent as much as men in Washington, DC, and only 66 percent of what men earned in Louisiana.[89] What is more, evidence indicates that the wage gap is widening between US men and women.[90] Christina Huffington pointed out that, on average, US women receive seventy-seven cents for every dollar paid to men—the gap is even worse for African American and Latin American/Latina/Chicana women.[91] Indeed, Hispanic women showed the largest pay gap, earning only 54 percent of white men's earnings.[92]

Some of the most frequently cited reasons for the gender pay gap are (1) the concentration of women in low-paying, female-dominated jobs, (2) the high percentage of women who work part-time rather than full-time, and (3) outright wage discrimination against women. Worldwide, women tend to engage in service work (teaching, nursing, child care, elder care), clerical work, agricultural work (picking fruit), and light industrial work (producing clothes, shoes, toys, and electronic devices), while men tend to engage in heavy industrial, transportation, management, administration, and policy work.

Although US women have gained some access to high-paying, male-dominated jobs like law and medicine, their numbers in these professions remain under 50 percent. A variety of reports done between 2012 and 2015 show that only one-third of lawyers and physicians in the United States are women.[93] Also worrisome is the fact that women in the workforce continue to hit the so-called glass ceiling—that is, "the invisible but effective barrier which prevents women from moving beyond a certain point on the promotion ladder."[94] For example, in the United States, women chief executive officers, especially in Fortune 500 companies, are still in the minority. As of January 25, 2015, there were only twenty-five female Fortune 500 CEOs, with Mary Barra, the head of General Motors, ranked seventh on the list.[95] In contrast, the numbers of women in less lucrative and prestigious jobs, such as human resources and accounting, are legion.[96] Similarly, it is no accident that just 33.8 percent of physicians and surgeons are female[97] or that female registered nurses comprise 91.1 percent of the total number of nurses in the United States.[98] Another notable statistic, once again related to the area of legal services, reveals that US women are more likely than US men to work as relatively low-paid paralegals. Indeed, in the United States, women make up 84.3 percent of all paralegals and legal assistants.[99] Add to all these statistics the fact that men make up 75 percent of those in high-paid computer and mathematical occupations and over 94 percent of all high-paid mechanical engineers.[100] Experts on women's work equity underscore the importance of the statistics just enumerated. Unless their presence in high-paying, high-status occupations and professions in the United States rises to the 50 percent mark, women are unlikely to be treated as well as men in these fields.

Beyond US women's relative absence in certain high-paying jobs, another explanation for the gender pay gap is women's tendency to limit the time they devote to work in the productive workforce. Far more women than men work part-time,[101] and far more women than men leave the productive workforce for months or even years to tend to family matters.[102] Thus, over time, women earn less than men simply because they work fewer hours and years than men typically do. For example, it is estimated that female physicians lose an average of $350,000 over a lifetime of work because of their spending less time in the workforce as compared to their male counterparts.[103]

Although it is tempting to attribute the current gender pay gap to women's decision to work fewer hours or years in the paid workforce, this explanation does not address the question contemporary socialist feminists have since forcefully asked: Why do women limit their paid work outside the home in ways that men do not? Do women not want to work long hours outside the home? Do they view the money they earn as luxury money they can forsake? Or do they think it is their responsibility rather than men's to take time off work to rear their children properly or to care for sick relatives and aging parents, or both?

In addition to not answering why women, rather than men, limit their time in the workforce, the human-capital approach does not explain why many employers prefer to hire women as part-timers. Are female part-time workers—who, by the way, are usually not entitled to employer-paid benefit packages—easily motivated to work longer hours than they should? Acculturated to help out in a pinch, women who work part-time may work longer and harder than their contracts specify simply because they do not want to let other people down.

Feminist solutions to the gender pay gap vary, depending on which aspects get put under the microscope or require the most attention. Liberal feminists prefer the remedy of equal pay for equal work. They invoke legislation such as the US Equal Pay Act of 1963, which mandates that women's pay should equal men's when their positions are equal.[104] Although the Equal Pay Act sounds like an ideal tool for US women, it may not be. Equal

Pay Act civil suits put the burden of proof on plaintiff, who must prove that her work position is the same as that of a comparable male employee. Such proof might be relatively easy to secure in some lines of work, such as mail carrier or flight attendant, but it is far harder to secure in a profession such as law or medicine, where different labels such as "associate," "assistant," and "partner" can serve to make two virtually identical positions sound quite different.[105] Moreover, the usefulness of the Equal Pay Act as a reference point for gender-based civil suits seems predicated on women's gaining access to slots in male-dominated jobs or professions. The act does little, if anything, to question the sexual division of labor per se—that is, to question why the kinds of work men typically do tend to be valued more than the kinds of work women typically do.

Viewing liberal feminists' preference for an equal-pay-for-equal-work remedy for the gender pay gap as a capitulation to the view that women must be like men (in this instance, must work like men) to be valued like men, many contemporary socialist feminists have joined with many radical-cultural feminists to endorse a comparable-worth remedy for the gender pay gap, which they see as an opportunity not only to secure better wages for women but also to force society to reconsider why it pays some people so much and others so little.[106]

Many social scientists are convinced that as long as women remain in traditionally female-dominated jobs and, more significantly, as long as society continues to assign less value to these jobs than to male-dominated jobs, the gender pay gap will persist. We need to ask ourselves why, in 2014, women in western Australia had to work ninety-eight extra days a year to make the same pay as men for the same work[107] and, on the average, sixty-four extra days to achieve pay equity with men for comparable work.[108] Do such pay differentials exist because supervising construction workers (a "male" job) is so much more physically, psychologically, and intellectually demanding than is counseling troubled people (a "female" job)? Or do they exist simply because most construction managers are men and most social workers are women?

Convinced that gender considerations factor into how much or how little workers are paid, comparable-worth advocates demand that employers evaluate their employees objectively by assigning so-called worth points to the four components found in most jobs: (1) "knowledge and skills," or the total amount of information or dexterity needed to perform the job; (2) "mental demands," or the extent to which the job requires decision making; (3) "accountability," or the amount of supervision the job entails; and (4) "working conditions," such as how physically safe the job is.[109] When Norman D. Willis and Associates used this index to establish the worth points for various jobs performed in the state of Washington in the 1980s, the company found the following disparities: "A Food Service I, at 93 points, earned an average salary of $472 per month, while a Delivery Truck Driver I, at 94 points, earned $792. A Nurse Practitioner II, at 385 points, had average earnings of $832, the same as those of a Boiler Operator, with only 144 points. A Homemaker I, with 198 points and an average salary of $462, had the lowest earnings of all evaluated jobs."[110] After reflecting on the Willis and Associates study, a federal court judge in Tacoma ruled that the state was in violation of Title VII of the 1964 Civil Rights Act prohibiting discrimination by type of employment and level of compensation and should eliminate pay gaps within its systems.[111]

On the average, contemporary socialist feminists support a comparable-worth approach to further reducing the gender pay gap for two reasons—one addressing the feminization of poverty and the other the low value put on the kinds of work women traditionally do. According to Teresa Amott and Julie Matthaei, for example, we need to ask ourselves questions such as the following: "Why should those whose jobs give them the most opportunity to develop and use their abilities also be paid the most? The traditional argument—that higher pay must be offered as an incentive for workers to gain skills and training—is contradicted by the fact that our highly paid jobs attract many more workers than employers demand. And given unequal access to education and training, a hierarchical pay scheme becomes a mechanism for the intergenerational transmission of wealth privilege, with its historically-linked racism, sexism, and classism."[112]

Seemingly, the comparable-worth remedy for the gender pay gap has more potential to destabilize capitalist forces than does the equal-pay-for-equal-work remedy. The question is whether consumerism writ large has made it all too difficult for a sufficient number of people to challenge the status quo.

Women's Work in the Global Market

In recent years, contemporary socialist feminists have moved beyond analyzing the gender pay gap in developed countries to discussing women's working conditions in these regions. The forces of so-called globalization—described by the World Bank as the "growing integration of economies and societies around the world"[113]—have created very large, profit-driven multinational corporations, most with their point of origin in one or more developed countries and their point of destination in one or more developing countries. Interestingly, multinationals in developing countries prefer to hire women not only because so many women need work but also because their manual dexterity and cultural docility make them ideal sweatshop workers.

To better understand how much profit, say, a US multinational can make by moving its plants to a developing country, we need read only some late-1990s statistics compiled by Shawn Meghan Burn:

> The *maquiladoras* of Mexico's border towns are but one example of women in the global factory. There, over 2,000 multinational corporations have drawn over a half million workers, two-thirds of them women, who get paid between $3.75 and $4.50 a day. In El Salvador, women employees of the Taiwanese *maquilador* Mandarin are forced to work shifts of 12 to 21 hours during which they are seldom allowed bathroom breaks; they are paid about 18 cents per shirt, which is later sold for $20 each. Mandarin makes clothes for the Gap, J. Crew, and Eddie Bauer.
>
> In Haiti, women sewing clothing at Disney's contract plants are paid 6 cents for every $19.99 *101 Dalmatians* outfit they sew; they make 33 cents an hour. Meanwhile, Disney makes record profits and could easily pay workers a living wage for less than one half of 1 percent of the sales price of one outfit. In Vietnam, 90 percent of Nike's workers are females between the ages of 15 and 28. Nike's labor for a pair of basketball shoes (which retail for $149.50) costs Nike $1.50, 1 percent of the retail price.[114]

The executives of US multinationals defend such low wages as higher than those the workers would otherwise receive. Another argument is that the wages the multinationals pay are, at least, a living wage—that is, a wage sufficient to meet the subsistence needs of a family. But such claims, particularly the second one, are not always true. Other statistics compiled by Burn revealed, for example, that in the 1990s Nicaraguan sweatshop workers earned in the range of $55 to $75 a month—less than half of the $165 a month their families needed to meet their most basic needs.[115] To be sure, some multinationals do pay their workers—female and male—living wages, but they seem to be more the exception than the rule, according to Burn.

Disturbed by the situation just described, contemporary socialist feminists have recently taken a lead in trying to improve not only pay but working conditions in sweatshops. Some of the strategies they have used involve the unionization of workers (even more difficult to achieve in today's developing nations than it was in the early days of union organizing in the United States) and consumer boycotts of sweatshop imports.[116]

Another phenomenon that concerns not only contemporary socialist feminists but also other types of feminists is the number of women who migrate from poor countries to do care work in rich countries. For example, in the United States, most elder-care workers who do home-based care are either native-born women of color or female migrant workers. Ron Hoppe, a founder of WorldWide HealthStaff Associates, pointed out that mainstream Americans, especially men, are not much interested in working for his company, which cannot pay its employees any more than fast-food businesses do. Most of the people willing to work for him are migrants, many of them from "caring" cultures and all of them accustomed to working long hours for less money than Americans expect.[117]

Relying on migrant women to do low-paid care work seems to be the order of the day. No matter how poor a country is, if there is a country poorer, then that country may be a source of female caregivers willing to work for very low wages. Countries high up on the economic ladder see little or no reason not to rely on poor countries to supply them with care workers. For example, in the United Kingdom, 35 percent of the nurses who work in the elder-care environment are migrants, and most of them work for low wages. In London, more than 60 percent of the people who do elder-care work are migrants.[118] These workers, nearly exclusively women, come from Zimbabwe, Poland, Nigeria, the Philippines, and India. Their employers like their "work ethic" and their "warmth, respect, empathy, trust, and patience in the care relationship."[119] They also like the fact that these people are willing to work for wages that native-born elder-care workers would find outrageously low.

Like the United Kingdom, Taiwan has an exceptionally high demand for migrant care workers. Since the early 1980s, significant numbers of undocumented migrant women have worked in Taiwanese households,[120] thereby enabling Taiwanese women in the paid workforce to keep their jobs. Comments Pei-Chia Lan, "The filial duty of serving aging parents is transferred first from the son to the daughter-in-law (a gender transfer); later, it is outsourced to migrant care workers (a market transfer)."[121] Due to citizen pressure, the Taiwanese government decided to document large numbers of migrant care workers. Specifically, in 1992, Taiwan started to grant work permits to "domestic caretakers" who agreed to care for severely ill or disabled people, children under the age of twelve, or elders over the age of seventy.[122] Moreover, it began to describe the importation of care workers from the Philippines and Indonesia in particular "as a solution to the growing demand for paid care work among both nuclear households and the aging population."[123]

In addition to taking advantage of female migrant care workers' willingness to work for low wages, rich countries often fail to acknowledge the deficits of care they create in poor countries. Families of female migrant care workers suffer a loss of care from their own mothers, daughters, and sisters. Women leave their children and/or their elderly parents behind, to be cared for in makeshift ways, and doctors and nurses from developing countries leave their posts for high-paying jobs in developed countries, thereby weakening the already fragile health-care system of their respective native lands.[124]

Critiques of Marxist and Socialist Feminisms

Critique One: Marxist Feminism Provides an Unsatisfying Analysis of Women's Oppression

Arguably, classical or strict Marxist feminists believe that the overthrow of capitalism will bring equality between men and women. This belief, held by Evelyn Reed, was discredited by many Russian feminists after the Communist Russian Revolution of 1917. Feminist critics were quick to point out that the entrance of women into the productive workforce brought them neither economic independence nor a view of themselves as self-confident, purposeful agents. Rather than meaningful, high-wage employment, most Russian women found in the workplace dronelike, exhausting work that was typically less valued than men's work. Not wanting to jeopardize Communist plans to totally destroy capitalism, most Marxist feminists kept quiet publicly about their employment situation. However, in private they complained about such workplace disadvantages as (1) the relegation of most women to low-status "women's work" (i.e., secretarial work, rote factory work, and service work, including jobs related to cooking, cleaning, and attending to the basic needs of the young, the old, and the infirm), (2) the creation of "female professions" and "male professions," (3) the payment of lower wages to women than to men, and (4) the treatment of women as a "colossal reserve of labor forces" to use or not use, depending on the state's need for workers.[125]

Critique Two: Socialist Feminism Needs to Be More "Materialistic"

Concerned by Juliet Mitchell's turn to the theories of psychoanalysis for a better explanation of women's oppression than standard socialism can provide, some socialist feminists insisted on the need to return to more traditional Marxist concerns.[126] A socialism that fails to look at the concrete and specific material ways in which women are oppressed does not motivate people outside the intellectual bastions of the academy to demand equality with men as their right, they said. Indeed, Stevi Jackson recently wrote that only a return to materialism can save socialist feminism from undeserved neglect:

> A materialist analysis is as relevant now as it ever was. While accepting that traditional Marxists had little to say about gender divisions,

that one theory cannot explain the whole of human life, the method of analysis Marx left us remains useful. There are good reasons why materialist perspectives remain necessary to grapple with the complexities of a postcolonial world, with the intersections of gender, ethnicity, and nationality. It seems evident that the material foundations and consequences of institutionalized racism, the heritage of centuries of slavery, colonialism and imperialism and the continued international division of labour are at least as important as culturally constituted difference. We live our lives now within a global system characterized by extremely stark material inequalities. The continued vitality of approaches which deal with such inequalities is crucial for feminist politics and theory.[127]

Jackson's point is compelling not only for socialist feminists but for all feminists—indeed, all human beings.

Conclusion

Although Marxist and socialist feminisms are not as popular today as in their 1970s heyday, they continue to provide insight into women's condition. In other words, the failure of communism and dismantling of the former Soviet Union does not render all types of Marxist and socialist feminism irrelevant. On the contrary, said Nancy Holmstrom,

the socialist feminist project is more pressing than ever. . . . The brutal economic realities of globalization impact everyone across the globe—but women are affected disproportionately. Displaced by economic changes, women bear a greater burden of labor throughout the world as social services have been cut, whether in response to structural adjustment plans in the third world or to so-called welfare reform in the United States. Women have been forced to migrate, are subject to trafficking, and are the proletarians of the newly industrializing countries. On top of all this they continue to be subject to sexual violence and in much of the world are not allowed to control their own processes of reproduction. How should we understand these phenomena and, more importantly, how do we go about changing them? *Feminist theory that is lost in theoretical abstractions or that depreciates economic realities will be useless for this purpose.* Feminism that speaks of women's oppression and its injustice but fails to address capitalism will be of little help in ending women's oppression. . . . Socialist feminism is the approach with the greatest capacity to illuminate the exploitation and oppression of most of the women of the world.[128]

Only when women earn as much as men for the same job, have equal status in the workplace, and do no more than their fair share of domestic work will Marxist and socialist feminist take a rest. This day is not likely to come soon, however, if we look at women's condition worldwide. Poverty remains a major issue for millions of women globally, and it will take enormous social, political, and cultural changes to alter the status quo. Importantly, more and more contemporary Marxist and socialist feminists are engaging in intersectional thinking. For example, Barbara Ehrenreich, a socioeconomically advantaged, well-educated, white woman, adopted the "material life conditions of a poor woman."[129] In *Nickeled and Dimed: On (Not) Getting By in America*, Ehrenreich revealed the issues that preoccupy women who work for minimum wages to be quite different from those that bother well-heeled women.[130] Viewing women differentially according to their class helps Marxist and socialist feminists clarify the different ways in which rich and poor women are oppressed in capitalist countries.

Questions for Discussion

1. Discuss some tangible examples of how human beings "create themselves" through collective production. How does the capitalist mode of production impact women's historical and modern experiences?
2. Do you believe women constitute a class in the Marxist sense? Weigh the similarities and differences between bourgeois and proletarian women. Consider the benefits and drawbacks of viewing all women as belonging to a single class.
3. Explain the four Marxist forms of alienation. Are women more or less alienated than men? Examine forms of alienation involving women's self-concepts, relationships, careers, and political representation.
4. What concerns did women laborers raise after the Russian Revolution? What were the concerns of those women involved with the wages-for-housework campaign? How were the difficulties in implementing material solutions to their issues complementary?
5. Speculate about the sexual division of labor. Why do you think male-dominated careers tend to be valued more (monetarily and, arguably, socially) than female-dominated careers? Could the "worth point" system resolve such disparities, or is such a system still subjective? In what other ways might we mediate arbitrary valuation of work?

4

Women-of-Color Feminism(s)
in the United States

The term "of color" is ambiguous. For some, it simply means "nonwhite."[1] For others, it has important sociological, historical, and political implications. For this second group, the term stresses the common experience of groups of persons (across a variety of cultural and ethnic backgrounds) who have been racialized (that is, assigned a nonwhite race) inside white cultural hegemony. The experience of being racialized includes, among other things, (1) having one's non-Western culture devalued, (2) having what W. E. B. DuBois called "double consciousness,"[2] (3) being pressured to assimilate to the dominant (white) culture, (4) being denied access to "white privilege,"[3] and (5) being expected to be more competent than nonracialized persons. Being a person of color, in other words, entails living in a constant state of vigilance regarding when and where the fact of one's having been racialized as nonwhite might pop up and operate as a barrier to the liberal ideal of the autonomous self. It also entails, however, claiming one's unique cultural heritage and opposing white cultural hegemony when it presents itself as operating in opposition to that cultural heritage, or to one's autonomy.

Women of color are persons who have had the female experience within this group of persons, an experience understood as consisting of oppression both as a woman and as a person of color. For many women of color, mainstream feminism (in all its forms, but particularly first- and second-wave feminism) fails to take the experiences of women of color seriously. Operating as if every woman's experience mirrors that of women who have benefited from birth from white privilege, mainstream feminism fails to adequately acknowledge and address the concerns of women of color.

For women of color, the female experience is constituted by encounters not only with patriarchy but also with racial oppression. In the lived experience of women of color, on this view, the point at which patriarchy ends and racial oppression begins is altogether unclear. Instead, each woman of color is a site of multiple forms of oppression that operate upon her simultaneously, creating a new form of oppression such that the whole experience is an entirely different animal than the sum of its parts. The idea that women of color are living sites of multiple forms of oppression (i.e., at a minimum, discrimination on the bases of race and gender) is a key theme in women-of-color feminisms.

Feminism has only just recently reappropriated the term "women of color" to capture the similarity of experience attendant to being racialized within Eurocentric cultural imperialism (no matter what the nonwhite race ascribed). Of course, it would be nearly impossible to create an exhaustive list of these individual group experiences, particularly because many women of color belong to not one but multiple historically oppressed subgroups. Still, we can discuss some of the main groups of women-of-color feminisms, as well as some of the major works of prominent women-of-color feminists.

Women-of-Color Feminism(s) and the "First Wave"

In the same way that the abolitionist movement focused on the rights of African American[4] men to the exclusion of the rights of African American women, first-wave feminism focused on the rights of white women to the exclusion of the concerns of women from other racioethnic backgrounds. Nonetheless, many women of color made significant contributions to the nineteenth-century women's rights and suffrage movements. These included Sojourner Truth (briefly mentioned in Chapter 1), Anna Julia Cooper, Mary Church Terrell, Amy Jacques Garvey, Harriet Ann Jacobs, Zora Neale Hurston, Harriet Tubman, Maria W. Stewart, Jarena Lee, and Mary Ellen Pleasant. Importantly, these women-of-color feminists were "first wave" in the sense of the era in which they worked: they were primarily concerned with women's suffrage. But they were also nonliberal in that they did not share with first-wave liberal feminists the idea that women could be understood as a demographic monolith; instead, they concerned themselves primarily with suffrage for women of color and understood that the problems faced by women of color differed from those faced by their white sisters.

Women-of-Color Feminism(s) and the "Second Wave"

Most feminist consciousness-raising groups of the second wave were sorely lacking in raciocultural diversity, most often being compromised almost entirely of white women. In response to this, many second-wave women-of-color feminists formed their own groups. These included the Combahee River Collective (CRC), the Comisión Femenil Mexicana Nacional (CFMN), and the North American Indian Women's Association. Founded by Black feminist lesbians in Boston, Massachusetts, in 1974, the Combahee River Collective, whose name refers to an act of resistance by Harriet Tubman in South Carolina in 1863, originally met less formally at the 1973 regional conference of the National Black Feminist Organization (NBFO), from which they split a year later.[5] These feminists experienced much disillusionment with second-wave liberal feminism and also had concerns about the civil rights for minorities, Black nationalism, and the Black Panther movements.[6] The CRC created a platform that took issue with various forms of oppression, including racial, sexual, heterosexual, and class oppression.[7] Similarly, the Comisión Femenil Mexicana Nacional, a group of Chicana feminists, was instrumental in building bilingual schools for children and obtaining a ban on the compulsory sterilization of Hispanic women.[8] Yet another women-of-color group, the North American Indian Women's Association, the first national Native American women's group, was founded in 1970 and shared many of the same concerns as the CRC and CFMN.[9]

In contrast to many white feminists, most second-wave feminists of color denied that the most fundamental oppression is that based on gender. They leaned more toward the view that multiple and interlocking systems of oppression (including racism, homophobia, and class oppression) impact women's lives negatively and significantly. In fact, many women-of-color feminists (who have more to worry about than men's "sexism" per se) understand the distinction made in Chapter 2 between radical-libertarian and radical-cultural feminism as hair-splitting. For example, the CRC indicated that its members' collective task as Black feminists was to develop an "integrated analysis and practice" of grappling with oppression based on "the fact that the major systems of oppression are interlocking."[10] For these Black feminists, then, sexism was neither the prototypical nor the most problematic form of oppression. Instead, all forms of oppression were co-constitutive, such that the proper concern of Black feminism was to untangle and dismantle oppression itself, not just the oppression of women qua women.[11] Moreover, for these feminists, racism in the white feminist movement was a matter of concern and deep hurt.[12]

During the six years of its existence (1974–1980), the CRC expressed the thought that US African American women had more in common with "Third World" people and the US white working-class (male as well as female) than with privileged, "First World" US white feminists. Among the issues that concerned the CRC most were not only women's reproductive rights[13] but also general social matters like universal health care, school de-segregation, police brutality against African American men in particular, and construction jobs for African American people.[14]

Women-of-Color Feminism(s) and the "Third Wave"

The heyday of multiculturalism in the United States occurred between the early 1970s and the late 1990s. During this period, multiculturalism was understood, generally, as a political and intellectual movement that called for public institutions to better recognize the unique collective social identities of certain historically oppressed groups in the United States. Depending on how the term "multiculturalism" was used, the term "women of color" fell in and out of favor with feminists. Originally, the term had a unifying effect, but later it took on negative connotations. It began to represent an attempt on the part of white feminists to lump all nonwhite women together, as if the differences between various groups of nonwhite women and their respective experiences of oppression and patriarchy were inconsequential. Importantly, the term has come back into favor as an acknowledgment that the experiences of racialized women as nonwhite differ from those of non-racialized (white) women in the United States.

As the third wave of feminism progressed, the conviction that women-of-color feminism(s) were essential to feminist theorizing grew in popularity. Gradually, the idea that forms, modes, or axes of oppression (such as race, gender, class, sexuality, and ability status) overlap and fuse in the lives of oppressed people came to the fore. In many ways, this insight was a phenomenon looking for a name. Then, in 1989, Kimberlé Crenshaw coined the term "intersectionality" to highlight the ways in which existing institutional structures fail to address the unique needs of women of color.[15] Her point was that these institutions acknowledge gender discrimination against white women but not the unique kind of discrimination experienced by women of color as a consequence of how racial and gender discrimination intersect in their lived experience.

Crenshaw noted that "women of color are situated within at least two subordinated groups that frequently pursue conflicting political agendas."[16] Specifically, antiracist discourse has failed to address the intersections of race and gender discrimination, resulting in the reinforcement of the subordination of women of color. In addition, mainstream feminist discourse has failed women of color because its resistance strategies often replicate and reinforce (or, at a minimum, simply neglect) the subordination of people of color. For example, while mainstream feminism gives a great deal of attention to the general problem of sexual harassment in the workplace, it usually overlooks the particular problem of the racialized sexual harassment experienced by women of color in the workplace. When a white male boss sexually harasses an African American, female worker, his action evokes memories of the slave period in US history, when white masters, if they had the desire, raped their African American, female slaves. Through the concept of intersectionality, then, women-of-color feminisms highlight that oppression is sociohistorically situated and multidimensional. To be effective, the solutions to the problems taken up by feminism must resist simplistic analysis and instead reflect the complexity of the historicity of the women who experience them.

Distinct Women-of-Color Feminism(s)

As already stressed, mainstream feminist thought tends to lump the thinking of all women of color together, as if feminist thought can be divided between white (official, central, universal) feminism and all other (outlaw, peripheral, particular) feminisms. In the process, it tends to gloss over the unique experiences and viewpoints of different groups of feminists of color, such as Black feminists, Latin American/Latina/Chicana feminists, Asian American feminists, and Indigenous feminists, thereby weakening the power and message of each group. In what follows, we attempt to address this problem by treating each unique area of women-of-color feminism individually and on its own terms.

Black Feminism

As a distinct feminist presence, Black feminism goes as far back as first-wave feminism. Women like Sojourner Truth were at the center of the demand for female equality in America from the start. Truth articulated the key idea in Black feminism that the experiences of African American women are both the same as and different from those of white American women. Later, in her 1892 book, *A Voice from the South: By a Woman from the South*, Anna Julia Cooper voiced the related view that African American women should be self-determining and act as moral leaders for the purpose of uplifting the African American community.[17] Similarly, Ida Wells-Barnett, a newspaper editor who published several writings of her own, was a member with W. E. B. DuBois of the Niagara Movement (an African American civil rights organization founded in 1905). She also was a founding member of the National Association for the Advancement of Colored People and a lifelong activist in the antilynching crusade.[18] Each of these women (and countless others) articulated and exemplified the distinctively Black feminist mind-set that being a woman and being powerless are not necessarily coextensive. Through the way they lived their lives, these women problematized the idea of what it meant to be a woman (white, powerless, frail, irrational, ineffectual). In other words, Black feminism has from the beginning sought to accomplish one of mainstream (white) feminism's ostensible goals—namely, the deconstruction of stereotypical notions of womanhood.

Sojourner Truth

Importantly, we can understand Black feminism to begin with Sojourner Truth (née Isabella Baumfree). Born into slavery in approximately 1797, Truth planted the seeds of distinctively Black feminist thought when she famously asked during the height of first-wave feminism, "Ain't I a woman?"[19] Truth escaped from slavery in 1826 and ultimately became a noted abolitionist and women's rights activist. Taking the stage to speak at the Women's Convention in Akron, Ohio, in 1851, just three years after the Women's Rights Convention in Seneca Falls, New York, Truth articulated the complex nature of what it meant to be a nineteenth-century African American woman. She highlighted two cornerstones of Black feminism of the era: (1) lest anyone forget, African American women are women, and (2) the experiences of African American female slaves differ from those of free and well-treated, bourgeois white women.[20] Forcefully, Truth called attention to the unique womanhood of African American women.[21] Her enigmatic words "Ain't I a woman?" engaged what became a core issue in late-twentieth and early-twenty-first-century feminism—namely, how to understand the female experience and feminism in such a way as to generate solidarity (universality of vision) and therefore power, while accommodating the wide variety of experiences of women of different racial and ethnic backgrounds, socioeconomic levels, sexualities, and histories of oppression.

Key to Truth's distinctively Black feminism was her experience of herself as powerful, not powerless. Women should seize their rights, emphasized Truth, not beg for them. Action was the path to women's liberation, not talk. Articulating a similar sentiment at a convention in 1878, Truth stated, "If women would live as they ought to, they would get their rights as they went along."[22]

Truth's statements emphasized again and again her view that white women's barriers to true power and equality lay not outside but inside themselves. To her, white women seemed to think that to become powerful, they needed the acquiescence of white men. But from Truth's perspective, if you want power, you take it. You don't ask permission.[23]

The willingness of Sojourner Truth to alienate the affections of those in power (white men) in pursuit of equality, as compared to the seeming unwillingness of white women to do so, arguably gets to the heart of the difference between the African American and white female experiences even in contemporary times. From the perspective of many Black feminists, white women access power in large part through their association with white men. If white women alienate white men, they lose the "white privilege" they enjoy as a consequence of marrying or working with white men.[24] This reality creates a political barrier between Black feminists and white women in two ways. First, many Black feminists perceive white women as less committed to true equality, causing the former to break off from mainstream (white) feminism to create their own movement(s).[25] Second, many Black feminists perceive white women as untrustworthy, due to their seeming indifference to women of color's particular concerns. Indeed, many commentators root the divide between white feminists and feminists of color in how white women's silence on issues unique to women of color increases the power of white men.[26]

Truth also articulated early on another theme in Black feminism, one that Crenshaw later called "intersectionality," or the view that oppression operates simultaneously along a variety of avenues with the result that the oppression associated with being female is inseparable, at least for women of color, from that associated with being ascribed a socially inferior race.[27] Truth's work as both an abolitionist and a women's rights activist often gave her opportunities to express versions of this view. Just after the Civil War, for example, it appeared that African American men would get the vote but women would not. Interestingly, African American supporters of women's rights predominately deemed it more important for African American men, rather than women of any skin color, to get the vote. Truth choose not to take sides, claiming that all African American people, male or female, deserved the vote.

Audre Lorde

Building on Truth, twentieth-century feminist Audre Lorde introduced other lines of thought crucial to understanding the viewpoint of Black feminists in the United States. She stressed that African American women should regard their otherness from white women as a strength not a weakness. Alluding to the days of slavery, Lorde said, "Those of us who stand outside the circle of this society's definition of acceptable women; those of us who have been forged in the crucibles of difference . . . know that survival is not an academic skill. It is learning how to stand alone, unpopular and sometime reviled. It is learning how to take our differences and make them strengths. For the master's tools will never dismantle the master's house."[28]

Lorde's point was that mere tolerance of the differences in experience that African American women bring to the table of feminism is insufficient to overcome the oppression that they face. Rather, for real change to occur, difference must be respected, affirmatively valued, and "seen as a fund of necessary polarities between which our creativity can spark like a dialectic."[29] Indeed, for Lorde, "difference is that raw and powerful connection from which our personal power is forged."[30] Weary of explaining her African American woman's experience to white audiences, Lorde urged other African American women to stop doing so as well and to start asking white women to explain their differences from women of color. Difference, after all, is necessarily judged from a particular vantage point.

Clearly Lorde was used to the role of outsider. She experienced racism, heterosexism, poverty/classism, ageism, and ableism and expressed her sufferings and pains in and through her writings, especially her poetry. As many of Lorde's reviewers have said, "Anyone who has ever been in love can respond to the straightforward passion and pain, sometimes one and the same in Lorde's poems,"[31] which she began writing when only in high school. Among Lorde's best-known poetry books is *Coal.*[32] Insisting on communicating her authentic self to others, she often used the metaphor of coal to articulate her blackness and to explain how extreme pressure (i.e., experiences of adversity) can transform coal into diamonds. She further elaborated on her African American identity in "Poetry Is Not a Luxury," where Lorde claimed that her power—which is also women's power—is "neither white nor surface" but instead "dark . . . ancient . . . and deep."[33] She also insisted in this same work that poetry is "a bridge across our fears of what has never been before."[34]

For Lorde, black is literally beautiful. She embraced the blackness of her West Indian heritage as well as of her skin. Refusing to buy into white society's white/black binary, according to which everything that is good is white and everything that is bad is black, Lorde insisted instead that the patriarchal world, which resists warrior women, has gotten it wrong. It is very good to be African American and not so good to be white, especially if one suffers from the disease of the oppressor, racism. Throughout Lorde's work one feels her anger toward racists and racism. Indeed, feeling is vital to Lorde and should be celebrated as welcome relief from the kind of abstract reason that seems to rule white society. Commented Lorde, "When we view living, in the European mode, only as a problem to be solved, we then rely solely upon our ideas to make us free, for these were what the white fathers told us were precious. But as we become more in touch with our own ancient, [African], non-European view of living as a situation to be experienced and interacted with, we learn more and more to cherish our feelings, and to respect those hidden sources of our power from where true knowledge and therefore lasting action comes."[35]

In one of her most moving works, *The Cancer Journals*, Lorde recorded her battle with breast cancer. When she expressed disinterest in being fitted for a prosthesis, a nurse commented to Lorde that her appearance would damage the morale of the other postmastectomy women in the doctor's office. Lorde wrote that she "couldn't believe her ears."

> Here we were, in the offices of one of the top breast cancer surgeons in New York City. Every woman there either had a breast removed, might have to have a breast removed, or was afraid of having to have a breast removed. And every woman there could have used a reminder that having one breast did not mean her life was over, nor that she was less a woman, nor that she was condemned to the use of a placebo in order to feel good about herself and the way she looked. . . . Yet a woman who has one breast and refuses to hide that fact behind a pathetic puff of lambs wool which has no relationship nor likeness to her own breasts, a woman who is attempting to come to terms with her own changed landscape and changed timetable of life and with her own body and pain and beauty and strength, that woman is seen as a threat to the "morale" of a breast surgeon's office.[36]

Authenticity was all important to Lorde, who spoke cogently, creatively, and confidently about her black American lesbian sexuality as one of the main sources of her power. Just because she no longer had her right breast, she said, did not mean she was no longer beautiful or incapable of fighting racism everywhere, including in white feminist circles.

Perhaps the most distinguishing feature of Lorde's work was her insistence that people learn to accept the role of contradiction in their lives. In an interview with Carla M. Hammond, Lorde said,

> There's always someone asking you to underline one piece of yourself— whether it's *Black, woman, mother, dyke, teacher,* etc.—because that's the piece that they need to key into. They want to dismiss everything else. But once you do that, then you've lost because then you become acquired or bought by that particular essence of yourself, and you've denied yourself all of the energy that it takes to keep all those others in jail. Only by learning to live in harmony with your contradictions can you keep it all afloat. You know how fighting fish do it? They blow bubbles and in each one of those bubbles is an egg and they float the egg up to the surface. They keep this whole heavy nest of eggs floating, and they're consistently

repairing it. It's as if they live in both elements. That's something that we have to do, too, in our own lives—keep it all afloat.[37]

bell hooks

Underlining Lorde's point that sexism, racism, and classism feed on each other, bell hooks provided a definition of feminism that is profound in its simplicity. She stated, "Feminism is a movement to end sexism, sexual exploitation and oppression."[38] hooks preferred this definition of feminism to others as it makes clear that feminism is not about being antimale. Rather it is about both men and women getting rid of the sexist thinking they have been steeped in since they were little children. According to hooks, men can be feminists so long as they are fighting together with women, black as well as white, against capitalist patriarchy. She declared that "to ensure the continued relevance of feminist movement in our lives, visionary feminist theory must be constantly made and re-made so that it addresses us where we live, in our present. Women and men have made great strides in the direction of gender equality. And those strides toward freedom must give us the strength to go further. . . . Feminism is for everybody."[39]

hooks took a complex position on lesbians. She distinguished between "women-identified" and "male-identified" women. Of these two types of women, male-identified women were more likely to fall into the trap of desiring the high status and wealth of successful white men. Even though hooks criticized those lesbians who mimicked bad heterosexual relations of domination and subordination, she firmly believed that "feminism is the theory, lesbianism is the practice."[40] For hooks, lesbian women must be at the center and not the periphery of the feminist movement.

hooks started writing her first book, *Ain't I a Woman: Black Women and Feminism*, when she was only nineteen years old, but it took her a total of six years to finalize and two more years to get published.[41] Her refusal to use footnotes led some critics to dismiss her work as not worth reading. Fortunately, other critics found her books both refreshing and groundbreaking. Indeed, in 1992 *Publishers Weekly* proclaimed *Ain't I a Woman* "one of the twenty most influential women's books in the last 20 years."

Important in hooks's work is her frequently articulated distinction between faux (fake) and real feminism. She was especially exercised by successful businessperson Sheryl Sandberg's 2013 book *Lean In: Women, Work, and the Will to Lead*.[42] Sandberg claimed that merely by strength of will and staying power, any US woman so inclined can climb the corporate ladder to its ozone regions. Sandberg failed to realize that although it may be relatively easy for an extremely wealthy, happily married, white woman to become a

Fortune 500 CEO, a poor woman of color in a bad relationship and with only a high school education would almost never be able to equal that accomplishment. Moreover, said hooks, it is one matter to become equal to a privileged white man and quite another to become equal to a disadvantaged African American man. For hooks, as long as classism and racism exist, sexism will thrive.

Kimberlé Crenshaw

Although Lorde, hooks, and many other feminists addressed the reality of intersectionality, Kimberlé Crenshaw highlighted its importance in a particularly forceful way. A lawyer by trade, Crenshaw focused on how antidiscrimination laws look at issues of gender and race separately. Oftentimes she brought up the case of *DeGraffenreid v. General Motors*, in which African American women protested that they were the victims of "compound discrimination" because only white women, white men, and African American men were hired and retained for desirable jobs. This objection notwithstanding, the Supreme Court ruled that (1) because it hired African American men, General Motors' hiring policies were not racist, and (2) because it hired white women, its policies were not sexist. In other words, because the court treated matters of race and gender separately rather than together (intersectionally), African American women lost their case.

Crenshaw also described other ways the law fails women, so much so that African American women turn on each other. She cited the Anita Hill/ Clarence Thomas case as an example. Lawyer Anita Hill alleged that African American judge Clarence Thomas, then a candidate for the Supreme Court, had sexually harassed her. Not wanting to deny Thomas a seat on the Supreme Court (usually entirely white), many African American women protested on his behalf. In doing so, they robbed Anita Hill of her voice. Had the Senate Judiciary Committee viewed the case intersectionally, Hill would probably have won the day. As it turned out, she did not get to talk much about the way African American women experience sexual harassment from African American as well as white men.

In an interview with Bim Adewunmi, Crenshaw emphatically stated, "In every generation and in every intellectual sphere and in every political movement, there have been African American women who have articulated the need to think and talk about race through a lens that looks at gender, or think and talk about feminism through a lens that looks at race."[43] Crenshaw thought that at this stage of the struggle for equality, African American women should take the lead, even if doing so required them to explain and/ or justify themselves to African American men as well as white men and women. She said, "It's up to us [African American women]. Granted, the space has to be open and there has to be a sense of receptivity among the sisterhood, but I really don't want other women to feel that it's their responsibility to theorize what's happening to us. It's up to us to consistently tell those stories, articulate what difference the difference makes, so it's incorporated within feminism and within anti-racism. I think it's important that we do that apart because we don't want to be susceptible to the idea that this is just about the politics of recognition."[44]

Later Crenshaw expressed reservations about US President Barack Obama's five-year, $200 million program aimed at giving African American boys and young men of color summer jobs, mentorships, and some other benefits. Although government support for African American girls and women of color was also made available, the level was small compared to Obama's 2014 "My Brother's Keeper" program, said Crenshaw.[45] To be sure, African American boys and young men of color are noticeably poorer and unhealthier than a preponderance of white women and white men. Yet they are well-off compared to African American women. Therefore, in Crenshaw's estimation, President Obama should have developed something like a "My Sister's Keeper" program in conjunction with his program for boys.[46]

Patricia Hill Collins

Furthering the thoughts of Lorde, hooks, and Crenshaw, philosopher Patricia Hill Collins wrote that in the United States, African American women's oppression is systematized and structured along three interdependent dimensions. First, the economic dimension of [African American] women's oppression relegates them to "ghettoization in service occupations."[47] Second, the political dimension denies them the rights and privileges routinely extended to all white men and many white women, including the very important right to an equal education. Third, the ideological dimension imposes a freedom-restricting set of "controlling images" on African American women, serving to justify as well as explain whites' treatment of them.[48]

Reiterating some of hooks's observations, Collins said, "From the mammies, Jezebels, and breeder women of slavery to the smiling Aunt Jemimas on pancake mix boxes, and the ubiquitous [African American] prostitutes, and ever-present welfare mothers of contemporary popular culture, the nexus of negative stereotypical images applied to African-American women has been fundamental to Black women's oppression."[49] Collins theorized that the ideological dimension was more powerful in maintaining African American women's oppression than either the economic or political dimensions. She emphasized that "race, class, and gender oppression could not continue without powerful ideological justification for their existence."[50] For this very reason, Collins urged Black feminists to release themselves from demeaning and degrading stereotypes imposed on them by whites.

Perhaps Collins is best known for her feminist epistemology. According to Eve Browning Cole, Collins's theory of knowledge has four components. First, "it adheres to concrete experience as a criterion of meaning, making knowledge and subjective wisdom the arbiters of epistemic significance."[51] With respect to situated knowledge, subjugated knowledge, and partial perspectives, Collins claimed that Lorraine Hansberry was on the right track when she wrote, "I believe that one of the most sound ideas in dramatic writing is that in order to create the universal, you must pay very close attention to the specific. Universality, I think, emerges from the truthful identity of what is."[52] Rather than abstract, objective, and impartial, knowledge should be concrete, subjective, and partial. Any knowledge we have is the product of our personal experiences filtered through the lens of our society, in Collins's estimation.

The second component of knowledge for Collins, said Cole, is dialogue as "a method of validating knowledge claims."[53] Eschewing both the "ostensibly objective norms of science" and "relativism's claims that groups with competing knowledge claims are equal," Collins applauded Elsa Barkley Brown for saying that "all people can learn to center in another experience, validate it, and judge it by its own standards without need of comparison or need to adopt that framework as their own."[54] Collins hearkened back to the "Afrocentric call-and-response tradition whereby power dynamics are fluid, everyone has a voice, but everyone must listen and respond in order to be allowed to remain in the community."[55] One can have one's own position without viewing it as the absolute norm for everybody.

Collins made a third point about Black feminist epistemology, said Cole, that it goes hand in hand with an ethic of caring that cherishes each person's contribution to the community.[56] The word "cherish" is important here because it conveys an affectionate affirmation of the so-called other. Relationships, particularly the mother-daughter relationship, are pivotal in Black feminist thought, as any reading of Alice Walker's *In Search of Our Mothers' Gardens: Womanist Prose* shows.

According to Cole, the final feature of Collins's Black feminist epistemology is an ethic of personal accountability that holds one responsible for one's knowledge claims. Repeatedly, Collins theorized that "African-Americans [should] reject the Eurocentric, masculinist belief that probing into an individual's personal viewpoint is outside the boundaries of discussion."[57] A person is literally as good as his or her word, provided that it expresses his or her authentic self. Accountable people actually do what they say they will do. Thus, political activism flows from one's knowledge claims, argued Collins.

In short, words really count for Collins. She explained that the arcane style of writing used by some contemporary feminists freezes out women (and men) who lack the education privileged people have. Even though she risked not being taken seriously by the mostly white and male guardians of the so-called canon of knowledge, Collins wrote in a personal way and from her heart. She deliberately chose the language of ordinary people to express her ideas. Unlike those who have traditionally filled the "core curriculum" with the works of so-called dead white men, Collins used personal anecdotes, hip-hop music, and folklore to serve the best interests of her readers, particularly those marginalized by mainstream society.

Latin American/Latina/Chicana Feminism

Overlapping to a considerable degree with Black feminism, Latin American/Latina/Chicana feminism nevertheless has distinct themes and insights. Like Black feminism, it calls for recognition of the alterity (otherness) and uniqueness of the experiences of women of color, particularly as distinct from the experiences of mainstream (white, Western, Eurocentric) feminists. On its own terms, Latin American/Latina/Chicana feminism is primarily concerned with cross-cultural dialogue and the extent to which it is limited by differing levels of power among the parties to the conversation.

The term "Chicano" began as a slur against Mexican immigrants but evolved into a symbol of self-determination and ethnic pride for Mexican Americans. Built upon the Mexican American civil rights movement of the 1940s, the 1960s Chicano movement demanded equal civil rights for people classified as "Hispanic." Chicana feminism began as a critique of the gender inequalities many Chicana feminists saw within the Chicano movement, dominated as it was by Chicano men. Over time, it developed a piercing critique of the traditional submissive role of Mexican American women in Chicano culture.[58] Established in 1973, the Comisión Femenil Mexicana Nacional was one of the first Chicana feminist organizations to press for Chicana women's rights.

Gloria Anzaldúa and Cherríe Moraga

Chicana feminists Gloria Anzaldúa and Cherríe Moraga challenged the racism of second-wave feminists of European descent in *This Bridge Called My Back: Writings by Radical Women of Color*, a collection of essays and poems focused on, as they put it, "a positive affirmation of the commitment of women of color to [their] *own* feminism."[59] Described at the time of its publication as having the "profoundest implications for radical theory and practice,"[60] *This Bridge Called My Back* is currently understood as a classic in early intersectionality theory, highlighting the intimate links between sexism and the wide array of other forms of oppression, especially racism and homophobia.

In *Borderlands/La Frontera: The New Mestiza*, Anzaldúa presented herself as a mestiza, or a woman of mixed Spanish and Indigenous background, living between two cultures, Anglo and Mexican. She used both prose and poetry to convey a central theme—namely that the Western belief "in objectivity with its habit of separating the self from others in order to make objects of them is the root of all violence."[61] Latin American women in Latin American culture, Latina/Chicana women in white American culture, and lesbians in heterosexual culture all experience themselves as "the other" in their respective mainstream (male, white, and/or heterosexual) societies, said Anzaldúa. Describing these women as living a life of alienation or isolation, Anzaldúa portrayed them as prisoners inside cultural narratives not of their own making. To highlight the sense of disconnection and internal conflict experienced by such women, she wrote in many different forms of the Spanish and English languages, creating a sense in the reader of the kind of disjunction and disharmony that, for her, characterizes the Latin American/Latina/Chicana feminist experience.[62]

Although both Anzaldúa and Moraga frequently expressed anger about how whites treat Latin American/Latina/Chicana women, their overall message was inclusive of all people, including white, bourgeois, heterosexual women. It became almost mandatory for traditional white feminists to use their work in their own course syllabi and writings. Arguably, Latin American/Latina/Chicana feminism will become even more central to feminist discourse in the United States as the Hispanic population continues to grow at fast rates.[63]

Cristina Herrera

Following Anzaldúa and Moraga's lead, Latin American/Latina/Chicana feminist Cristina Herrera wrote about what she saw as the central task of contemporary Chicana feminism—namely, the rewriting of female and maternal archetypes that hold Chicanas back from gender equality. These archetypes include La Virgen de Guadalupe (the Catholic Blessed Virgin Mary), La Llorona (the Weeping Woman), and La Malinche (Doña Marina).[64] For Herrera, the dominant, patriarchal Chicano culture has traditionally portrayed the mother-daughter relationship negatively. The bond between these "three mothers" and Chicana women, for Herrera, should be reclaimed and reinterpreted so as to heal the mother-daughter bond and facilitate Chicana empowerment.[65] Mothers should protect their daughters from abusive men who would quash their spirit.

Ofelia Schutte

Adding to Herrera's work, Ofelia Schutte elaborated on the concept of otherness that all women of color experience in the United States. For Schutte, the confrontation with alterity that occurs in cross-cultural exchanges involves a decentering of the self that "allows us to reach new ethical, aesthetic, and political ground."[66] But when differentials of power mark these supposed dialogues (as in attempts at dialogue between dominant and subaltern cultures), the result can be "cross-cultural incommensurability."[67] Listeners and speakers simply cannot understand each other's perspectives.

Chela Sandoval

Chela Sandoval, yet another Latin American/Latina/Chicana feminist, made several unique points. Inspired by Donna Haraway's "cyborg feminism," she rejected binary thinking in favor of an "ideology-praxis"[68] rooted in the experience of women of color. According to Sandoval, oppositional consciousness poses five challenges to the dominant order of power: "equal rights," "revolutionary," "supremacist," "separatist," and "differential."[69] Of these, the fifth, "differential," is the most important. Gaining a so-called oppositional consciousness that separates different groups of women from each other requires alienation, perseverance, and reformation on the part of both feminist theorists and feminist activists. As Sandoval saw it, disadvantaged US and "Third World" feminists are particularly good at challenging white, bourgeois, heterosexual thinking, thereby freeing themselves from the clutches of old colonialist thinkers.

Maria Lugones

Furthering the thinking other Latin American/Latina/Chicana feminists, Maria Lugones also captured how it feels to be a woman of color in the United States. In a dialogue with white feminist Elizabeth Spelman, Lugones, who immigrated to the United States from Argentina, pointed out that although Latin American women in the United States must participate in the Anglo world, Anglo US women do not have to participate in the Latin American world. An Anglo woman can go to a Latin American neighborhood for a church festival, for example, and if she finds the rituals and music overwhelming, she can simply get into her car, drive home, and forget the evening. A Latin American woman cannot escape the dominant Anglo culture so easily, however, for it sets the basic parameters of her survival as a member of one of its minority groups. Still, Lugones's work highlights the agency of Latin American women, pointing out that although Western society views the Latin American woman as a woman of color, in her own home, among her family and friends, she perceives herself as herself instead of an-*other*.[70]

Asian American Feminism

Asian American feminism shares with other women-of-color feminisms a sense of the experience of having been racialized as nonwhite within the broader culture of the United States. However, it has distinct features. Specifically, Asian American feminism often condemns both white and women-of-color feminisms for ignoring the experiences of Asian women. According to one Asian American feminist, Chen Chao-ju, "Asian American feminists condemn mainstream feminist scholarship, as well as feminist discourses on women of color, for marginalizing and for ignoring Asian American women's experiences and call for attention to the difference that Asian American women's difference makes."[71] In addition, Asian American feminism often allies itself with postcolonialist critiques of Western imperialism.[72] Arguing that white feminist discourse grants visibility to Asian women only by labeling them as different and categorizing them according to a series of cultural stereotypes such as submissive, timid, unenlightened, exotic, seductive, available, and bound in ahistorical Asian traditions, Chen stresses that mainstream (white) feminists stigmatize Asian women's experiences, which in turn fosters unequal relationships of power between and among women. On this view, within mainstream white feminism, Asian women exist as the perennial other.

Grace Lee Boggs

Asian American feminists have a long history in the United States. Born to Chinese immigrants in 1915, Grace Lee (later Grace Lee Boggs) won a regent's scholarship to Barnard College and earned a PhD in philosophy from Bryn Mawr. She founded many community organizations and political movements and spent her life fighting against racism and for human rights.[73] Boggs translated works by Karl Marx and collaborated with revolutionaries C. L. R. James, Raya Dunayevskaya, and others in critiques of the Soviet Union.[74] Upon her marriage to James Boggs, an African American autoworker, writer, and radical activist, she began an effort to combat racism and effect social change that lasted for the rest of her life. "What we tried to do is explain that rebellion is righteous, because it's the protest of a people against injustice," Boggs told Bill Moyers during a PBS interview in 2007.[75] According to Moyers, Boggs dedicated her life to trying to "make America work for everyone," stating often, "If we stick to [the] categories of race, class, and gender, we're stuck," meaning that solutions to the problem of oppression were beyond such categorization.

Yuri Kochiyama

Born Mary Yuriko Nakahara, Yuri Kochiyama was another lifelong champion of civil rights causes in the African American, Latino, Indigenous, and Asian American communities.[76] After the Japanese attack on Pearl Harbor, her family was moved to a California internment camp set up to isolate Japanese Americans from the rest of the US population. After World War II Kochiyama moved to New York City, where she became involved in the civil rights movement. A friend of Malcom X, Kochiyama became a Black nationalist, worked to end the war in Vietnam, and in the 1980s pushed for a formal government apology and reparations for Japanese American internees.[77] Kochiyama was present when a group of Puerto Rican *independentistas* seized the Statue of Liberty in 1977, and she played a key role in black radical activism in New York during the same period.[78] Her dedication to social causes continued throughout her lifetime, inspiring many generations of activists, especially within the Asian American community.[79]

Leslie Bow

Following in Kochiyama's footsteps, Leslie Bow wrote of the Asian American experience in the segregated South and of how the legal segregation of African Americans framed the Asian experience of oppression during the Jim Crow era.[80] The legacy of segregation (of African Americans), wrote Bow, to this day frames race relations in the United States, both as a matter of differential access to rights and as a struggle between black and white. Since Asian Americans, during the Jim Crow era, were construed as a "third race" inside America's black/white binary, they were neither white nor nonwhite but "situated in between" US racial categories, a kind of other's other, "partly colored," very much like Indigenous Americans and mestizas.

Bow identified Asian Americans (as well as Indigenous Americans and mestizas) as "interstitial populations," or populations between the primary racial categories understood to exist in the United States (black and white).

According to Bow, the legacy of the segregated South and the "racial anomalies" it produced within its entrenched black/white binary is a "productive site for understanding the investments that underlie a given system of relations; what is unaccommodated becomes a site of contested interpretation."[81] In this way, the Asian American experience can be understood as a force for the destruction of hierarchy. Said Bow, "The interstices between black and white forces established perspectives and definitions into disorientation. The racially interstitial can represent the physical manifestation of the law's instability, its epistemological limit, the point of interpellation's excess."[82]

According to Bow, the Asian American immigration experience often serves as a way to reproduce a dominant narrative of post–civil rights movements and racial representations—a "progressive chronology of racial uplift that buttresses a liberal vision of ethnic incorporation"—rather than as a way to destroy oppressive hierarchies.[83] Examining the question of whether the interstitial racial status of Asian Americans was sustained within the binary caste system containing only "Negroes" and "whites" in the segregated South, Bow noted that it did not withstand the test of time. Instead, Asian Americans underwent a "shift in status from colored to white, in the course of one generation."[84]

Citing an influential study conducted on Chinese people in Mississippi in the mid-twentieth century, Bow pointed out that in *Glum v. Rice*, a 1927 case, the US Supreme Court ruled that the Chinese people were colored. By 1967, however, the Chinese had become "card-carrying white people."[85] Among other proof, there was the "W" on their driver's licenses. So, in response to the black/white binary of the segregated South, rather than its destroying racial hierarchy, the racial status of Asian Americans can be understood to have become productive of that hierarchy, in Bow's estimation. Asian Americans became a part of what has been called the "colonial sandwich": Europeans at the top, Asians in the middle, and Africans at the bottom.[86] The lessons for feminism are clear, said Bow: "The space between the social enactment of identity and its idealization reveals the structures that consolidate social power in its multiple manifestations."[87] Although racial interstitiality can theoretically operate in the service of dismantling hierarchy, in practice it often does not, the Asian American experience being a case in point.

Mitsuye Yamada

Mitsuye Yamada made a similar point about the gap between theory and practice, this time as regards the feminist ideal and its reality. While noting that Asian American women need white feminist leaders ("the women who coordinate programs, direct women's buildings, and edit women's publications throughout the country")[88] to accomplish political objectives that are important to them, she was dismayed to find her white feminist audiences often responding to her as though they had "never known an Asian Pacific woman who [was] other than the passive, sweet, etc., stereotype of the Oriental 'woman.'"[89] White feminists want to believe that all women—white or nonwhite—are equal to white men. In reality historical and psychological forces have made it easier for white women to achieve equality with white men than for women of color to accomplish the same feat. White women enjoy perks not available to women of color. The browner a woman's skin color, the less likely she will achieve parity with white men.

This is a problem for feminism, according to Yamada, because "a movement that fights sexism in the social structure must deal with racism."[90] In response, many Asian Pacific women involved in radical politics have moved not into the upper echelons of women's organizations but into groups active in promoting ethnic identity. These women can be found in ethnic studies programs in universities, ethnic theater groups, or ethnic community agencies. However, "this doesn't mean," stressed Yamada, that "[Asian Pacific women] have placed [their] loyalties on the side of ethnicity over womanhood."[91] She continued, "The two are not at war with one another; we shouldn't have to sign a 'loyalty oath' favoring one over the other."[92] Invoking a central problem of women-of-color feminisms (that women of color are intersectional sites of multiple forms of oppression), Yamada noted, "women of color are often made to feel that we must make a choice between [loyalty to race/ethnicity and loyalty to womanhood]."[93] Pointedly, Yamada explained, "As a woman of color in a white society and as a woman in a patriarchal society, what is personal to me is political."[94] Furthermore, Yamada expressed the frustration experienced by many women-of-color feminists when she stated, "These [connections between different forms of oppression] are connections we expected our white sisters to see. . . . They should be able to see that political views held by women of color are often misconstrued as being personal rather than ideological. Views critical of the system held by an 'out group' are often seen as expressions of personal angers against the dominant society. (If they hate it so much here, why don't they go back?)"[95]

Indigenous Feminism

Reasoning like many of their African American, Latin American/Latina/Chicana, and Asian American sisters, many Indigenous or Native women

distance themselves from the label "feminist" for the reason that, within Indigenous communities and academic circles, feminism carries a stigma because of its association with whiteness.[96] According to Indigenous feminists,
the concerns of other women of color, as well as those of white women,
often differ and conflict.[97] Moreover, for these women, Indigenous feminism
rests on the idea that the United States is a settler colonial nation-state and
that settler colonialism is a gendered process.[98] Maile Arvin, Even Tuck, and
Angie Morrill, three Indigenous, women-identified scholars, have expanded
on these ideas and laid out five challenges that Indigenous feminisms offer to
mainstream feminist discourse: (1) a problematization of settler colonialism
and its intersections, (2) a refusal to be erased and wanting more than to
be (merely) included, (3) an active seeking of alliances that directly address
differences, (4) a recognition of Indigenous ways of knowing, and (5) a stress
on sovereignty.[99]

Paula Gunn Allen

Addressing all five of the challenges listed above, the Women of All Red
Nations (WARN) formed in the mid-1970s as a spin-off of the American Indian Movement (AIM).[100] Unhappy with the mostly supporting roles offered
to women in AIM, Indigenous women formed WARN to address issues facing them, such as reproductive rights, land treaties, and the Native American
Rights Fund.[101] Thinkers such as Paula Gunn Allen concretized WARN's
philosophy. In "Kochinnenako in Academe: Three Approaches to Interpreting a Keres Indian Tale," Allen analyzed the female-centered Yellow Woman
("Kochinnenako") stories of the Keres of the Laguna and Acoma Pueblos in
New Mexico. The women paint their faces yellow—the color of women and
of corn—on certain ceremonial occasions.[102] Allen compared three different
interpretations of the Kochinnenako story "Sha-ah-cock and Miochin or the
Battle of the Seasons": (1) a traditional Keres interpretation, (2) a "modern
feminist"/mainstream/Eurocentric interpretation with a "radical feminist"
variant, and (3) a "feminist-tribal" interpretation. In the process, Allen highlighted some key components of the theoretical divide between mainstream
(white) and Indigenous feminists.

One key component is the different assumptions about what it means to
be a woman. In the traditional Keres interpretation, the power of the female
is central to the story. In the "modern feminist"/mainstream/Eurocentric
interpretation (which entails "the Western romantic view of the Indian, and
the usual antipatriarchal bias that characterizes the feminist analysis"), the
woman has low status in the culture, is unhappy in her marriage, and thinks

her husband is "cold and disagreeable, and she cannot love him."[103] Tacked on to the "modern feminist" ("liberal feminist") account of the story, said Allen, is a "radical feminist" one, which reads the story as one of women's resistance to racism and oppression. Allen summarized the "modern feminist," "radical feminist" interpretations as containing two claims: that women are essentially powerless and that conflict is basic to human existence. But Keres thought contains neither of these assumptions, said Allen. Whereas "modern feminism" sees marriage in the story as an institution developed to establish and maintain male supremacy, from the Keres perspective, Yellow Woman's agency is central both to her marriage and to the story. Allen wrote, "The contexts of Anglo-European and Keres Indian life differ so greatly in virtually every assumption about the nature of reality, society, ethics, female roles, and the sacred importance of seasonal change that simply telling a Keres tale within an Anglo-European narrative context creates a dizzying series of false impressions and unanswerable (perhaps even unposable) questions."[104] Western (technological, industrialized) minds cannot adequately interpret tribal materials, said Allen, because they "see the world in ways that are alien to tribal understandings."[105] Whereas tribal peoples see their world in a "unified-field fashion" and write their literature in an "accretive and fluid" style, mainstream (white) perception and literature are masculinist, "single-focused," linear, and fixed. Most importantly, whereas from a mainstream perspective (whether "modern" or "radical") woman is a victim, from a tribal perspective she is both an agent and an empowerer of change. Allen argued, then, that Indigenous feminism exists outside the continuum (in Eurocentric feminism) between the "modern" and "radical forms," offering instead a third alternative that dramatically challenges the very concept of what it means to be a woman.

In the traditional Indigenous culture undiluted by Western influences, woman is not powerless but powerful, according to Allen. "Agency is Kochinnenako's ritual role [in the story]; it is through her ritual agency that the orderly, harmonious transfer of primacy between Summer and Winter people is accomplished."[106] Also, because the "modern feminist" version of the story reads the Yellow Woman in a Eurocentric light (as a powerless victim), the very act of interpreting Yellow Women stories through Eurocentric eyes "will provide a tribally conscious feminist with an interesting example of how colonization works, however consciously or unconsciously, to misinform both the colonized and the colonizer" in ways that negatively alter the self-perception of the Indigenous woman."[107] Allen hinted that the relationships between Indigenous men and women became "severely disordered" as a result, leading to "frightening" levels of wife abuse, rape, and battery of women in recent years.[108]

Luana Ross

Although the relationship between feminism and Indigenous women has been historically rocky, recent years have produced a flurry of feminist scholarship on the topic of Indigenous feminism. All recent works emphasize the necessity of recognizing the feminism of Indigenous women as unique and as a phenomenon entirely separate from mainstream, Eurocentric feminism. A representative piece is "From the 'F' Word to Indigenous/Feminisms" by Luana Ross, which opens as follows (quoting Kate Shanley): "Just as sovereignty cannot be granted but must be recognized as an inherent right to self-determination, so Indian feminism must also be recognized as powerful in its own terms, in its own right."[109]

Ross's piece provides a succinct account of recent thinking in Indigenous feminism, highlighting the work of key thinkers such as anthropologist Beatrice Medicine, who was a charter member of the American Indian Women's Service League in Seattle in 1954, and Kate Shanley. Although Medicine did not specifically define her work as feminist, it nonetheless provided some of the earliest studies of Indigenous women seen through the eyes of an Indigenous woman and presented a new image of Indigenous women as strong and capable.[110] In contrast to Medicine, Shanley was one of the first Indigenous women to identify herself publicly as "feminist," according to Ross. Shanley worked on issues that all women face, such as equal pay, children's health and welfare, reproductive rights, and domestic violence. But, argued Ross, her promotion of the cause of tribal sovereignty made her work uniquely Indigenous.[111] In an interesting twist on the presumed relationship between white and Indigenous women (one of oppressor and oppressed), Paula Gunn Allen noted in "Who Is Your Mother? Red Roots of White Feminism" that, according to Ross, all Indigenous peoples are traditionally feminist. If feminists were to acknowledge this fact, said Allen, they could make great strides toward the desirable goal of giving equal civil rights and respect to Indigenous people.[112]

Critiques of Women-of-Color Feminism(s) in the United States

Critique One: "Of Color" Is an Objectifying Label

For some US feminists, the idea of a feminism designed especially for a group of persons called "women of color"—let alone multiple feminisms designed especially for different subsets of women of color—is problematic. Many argue, for example, that to identify a group of persons set apart from others on the basis of color or race reifies the concept of biological race and thereby undermines the third-wave project of moving past restrictive, limiting categories regarding race or gender. But we can also view the appropriation of the term "of color" as a mechanism to identify those who have been on the receiving end of racially motivated oppression. Additionally, it can reveal a commonality among a multiplicity of women, on the basis of which they might collectively generate political power. In recent years, these two positions have reached a compromise, so that a feminist identifying herself as "of color" can be understood not as reifying the concept of biological race but as acknowledging that one of the axes of oppression she faces is racialized oppression.

Critique Two: "Of Color" Increases Feminists' Difficulty in Banding Together to Achieve Economic, Social, and Political Goals

Many white feminists find it hard to understand why women of color don't just join with them to fight sexism. In particular, many white feminists fault those feminists who prefer to call themselves womanist. According to noted novelist Alice Walker, however, African American women and other women of color experience a different and more intense form of oppression than white women do.[113] Among other things, she said a womanist is

> a woman who loves other women, sexually and/or nonsexually. Appreciates and prefers women's culture, women's emotional flexibility (values tears as natural counterbalance of laughter), and women's strength. Sometimes loves individual men, sexually and/or nonsexually. Committed to survival and wholeness of entire people, male and female. Not a separatist, except periodically, for health. Traditionally a universalist, as in: "Mama, why are we brown, pink, and yellow, and our cousins are white, beige and black?" Ans. "Well, you know the colored race is just like a flower garden, with every color flower represented." Traditionally capable, as in: "Mama, I'm walking to Canada and I'm taking you and a bunch of other slaves with me." Reply: "It wouldn't be the first time."[114]

Arguably, a womanist is the best type of feminist a woman can be because her view of life and love transcends all divisive categories.

Critique Three: Intersectionality Is a Limited Concept

Since intersectionality came into being roughly in the early 1990s, the axes of oppression identified at that time have multiplied. Whereas race, gender, class, and sexuality were the primary axes of oppression initially understood to intersect and shape particular women's experiences, recently such factors as religion, nationality, and citizenship status have joined the list. Some levy the critique that the concept of intersectionality itself pertains to a bygone era. The implication is that the categories of race, gender, class, sexuality, and even religion or nationality are problematically based in second-wave notions about clearly defined races, genders, and so on. Race and gender cannot "intersect," on this view, unless the theoretical (and actual) boundaries between different races and genders are fairly clearly defined in the first place.

As noted above, interstitiality has recently been offered in place of intersectionality as an organizing concept to explain the complex web of sociohistorical and sociolegal forces at work in the creation of identity, particularly as it is shaped by oppression. Interstitiality means different things for different feminists. For some, the concept invokes the ill-defined but nevertheless existent space between the existing identity categories of race, gender, and so on. For others, it highlights the unlimited number of identity categories that can overlap and interact in the formation of identity. Perhaps, however, intersectionality and interstitiality are not incompatible concepts and can be understood as different names for the same phenomenon. Interstitiality seems to add to intersectionality, however, an emphasis on the nonessential nature of any singular group identity marker.

Conclusion

We can understand women-of-color feminisms as a way of conceptualizing feminist work outside the white mainstream. Women of color and their work have been present in each wave of feminist theorizing in the United States. In the first wave, their work focused primarily on suffrage for women of color, understood as a different project with a different set of concerns than the problem of suffrage for white women. In the second wave, their work offered a form of radical feminism, focusing on a desire to change the system itself in a way that unpacked and addressed the problem of racism and how that problem affected women. In the third wave, the work of women of color is central to the feminist project, encompassing, as it always has, the idea (sometimes known as intersectionality) that the oppression of women does not occur in a vacuum. Women come in a variety of colors and from a variety of sociocultural backgrounds; women's oppression is not monolithic, and white women's experiences are no more important than those of women of color in understanding the problems women face as a group. Of particular concern in the third wave is treating each kind of women-of-color feminism on its own, with an explicit acknowledgment of its own terms, thereby valuing the importance of difference in the greater feminist project of addressing the needs of all women.

Most forms of mainstream (white) feminism attempt to extrapolate historically Western feminist concerns onto women color, motivated by the universalist belief that the concerns of US bourgeois, white women mirror those of all other women. But there may be an insurmountable barrier between feminist experience and the problem of racial oppression. So, while the feminist of color can fairly concede that there is some overlap among the concerns of women worldwide (e.g., general concerns about safety or reproductive issues), as the section on Indigenous feminism highlights, membership in the one or more specific racial or ethnic groups of which each woman is a part may significantly affect each embodied experience of patriarchy. This "particularity" may exist especially where the racial or ethnic group in question has a specific history of having been oppressed. And how can this not be the case? To the extent that a woman has been racialized, she has been oppressed in a way that is both unique to the particular racial classification(s) assigned to her and common to the experience of being female. In other words, patriarchal oppression as experienced by each group of women of color in the United States has its own features and challenges.

Although part of the point of writing a separate chapter on women-of-color feminisms in the United States was simply to highlight the unique experiences of oppression and patriarchy of various groups of women of color, another was to express an increasingly felt need to let women of color speak for themselves, to identify their agency as well as their right to define their own concerns and to work among themselves to find feasible solutions to them. The contemporary feminist project is no longer respectably conceivable from the standpoint of the Anglo-European feminists who styled themselves as solely responsible for the first and second waves of feminism. Although the efforts, challenges, and theoretical schemas of these brave and trailblazing women certainly played a key role in conceptualizing the feminist project, the new project—the project for the future—includes all women in all their varied and beautiful and powerful forms. It must necessarily be conceived from and examined from a vantage that opens panoramically onto the situated and distinct perspectives of women of all colors—that is, onto women-of-color feminisms in all their situated complexities.

Questions for Discussion

1. Explain why the idea that women of color should participate in the mainstream world necesarily infringes upon their interests and rights.

2. Explain the notion that some women are more equal than others. Is it possible for some women to remain affluent and privileged— at the expense of other, marginalized women (or men, for that matter)—and still consider themselves true feminists? Why or why not?

3. What importance, if any, do you see in identifying multiple forms of women-of-color feminism?

4. Why is the rejection, inherent in women-of-color feminisms, of a universal female identity significant?

5

Women-of-Color Feminism(s) on the World Stage: Global, Postcolonial, and Transnational Feminisms

In Latin American and Southeast Asia, as well as Europe and North America, an increasing number of women say they prefer active engagement in the paid workforce to bearing and rearing children.[1] What is more, opting not to reproduce is a growing trend, particularly in some European countries, where studies indicate that from 12 to 16 percent of young women plan to remain childless.[2] Contemporary feminism functions in this changing world. Purely Eurocentric, bourgeois, heterosexual feminism seems archaic, a matter for historians to discuss and for women and other marginalized segments of the world population to move beyond. Fortunately, global, postcolonial, and transnational feminisms are doing just this. Because of their similar nomenclatures, these three feminisms might seem to boil down to the same thing, but they don't quite. Indeed, for all their commonalities, they have some important differences.

Global Feminism in General

Serena Parekh and Shelley Wilcox provide one of the most succinct definitions of globalization: "In its broadest sense, globalization refers to the economic, social, cultural, and political processes of integration that result from the expansion of transnational economic production, migration, communications, and technology."[3] Global feminists make it their business to explain and address the challenges and choices globalization presents for women in

133

particular. For the most part, they largely concern themselves with issues of women's health, education, and welfare, putting great emphasis on human and women's rights. In addition, and for the most part, global feminists have staunch faith in the possibility of finding definitive solutions to universal feminist concerns.

Seeking Common Ground

Global feminism stresses the links between the various kinds of oppression women experience throughout the world. Charlotte Bunch expresses well the vantage point of many global feminists:

> To make global feminist consciousness a powerful force in the world demands that we make the local, global and the global, local. Such a movement . . . must be centered on a sense of connectedness among women active at the grass roots in various regions. For women in industrialized countries, this connectedness must be based in the authenticity of our struggles at home, in our need to learn from others, and in our efforts to understand the global implications of our actions, not in liberal guilt, condescending charity, or the false imposition of our models on others. Thus, for example, when we fight to have a birth control device banned in the United States because it is unsafe, we must simultaneously demand that it be destroyed rather than dumped on women in the Third World.[4]

Global feminists believe that "the oppression of women in one part of the world is often affected by what happens in another, and . . . no woman is free until the conditions of oppression of women are eliminated everywhere."[5] They view feminism as the process through which women can discuss their commonalities and differences as honestly as possible in an effort to secure the following two long-term goals, in Bunch's opinion:

1. The right of women to freedom of choice, and the power to control our own lives within and outside of the home. Having control over our lives and our bodies is essential to ensure a sense of dignity and autonomy for every woman.

2. The removal of all forms of inequity and oppression through the creation of a more just social and economic order, nationally and internationally. This means the involvement of women in national liberation struggles, in plans for national development, and in local and global struggles for change.[6]

Reproductive-controlling technologies (e.g., contraception, sterilization, and abortion) and reproduction-aiding technologies (e.g., intrauterine donor insemination and in vitro fertilization) are of particular concern to global feminists. Reflecting on the myriad ways in which government authorities seek to manipulate and control women's reproductive powers worldwide, global feminists note that although many women in developing countries want access to safe and effective contraceptives and abortions so that they can control the size of their families, this preference does not necessarily apply to all women in developing countries. In the first place a sizeable number of women want large families, even though responsibility for the care of many children may preclude or limit their participation in the paid workforce.

In the second place, it is not always in women's best interests to use reproductive-controlling technologies—for example, when contraceptives are unsafe. It is one thing for women to use potentially harmful contraceptives in the United States, where follow-up medical care is generally available. But it is quite another for women to have access to such contraceptives in cultural settings with no provisions for follow-up care. Specifically, Shawn Meghan Burn compared the distribution of some hormonal contraceptives in different countries: "In most Western countries, the Pill is prescribed by a physician, and a woman must have a Pap smear once a year to get her prescription renewed. This permits screening for . . . side effects . . . and for screening out those women for whom the Pill is contraindicated. . . . However, in some countries (including Brazil, Mexico, and Bangladesh), the Pill is sold without a prescription in pharmacies and stores. Depo-Provera is sold over the counter in Nigeria and even along the roadside. Long distances to health-care facilities often preclude the monitoring that increases the safety and effectiveness of contraceptive methods."[7]

Despite the correctness of Burn's observations, guaranteed safety is not always a paramount consideration when a woman doesn't want a child at a certain time in her life.[8] Indeed, she may want a contraceptive that she knows is somewhat risky, provided she can secure it conveniently, privately, and at low cost.[9] Not every woman wants her spouse, partner, or parent(s) to know she is using artificial means of birth control.

In the third place, in the same way that access to contraceptives is not always an unalloyed blessing for women, easy access to sterilization may not always be in women's best interests either. Worldwide, sterilizations are often less than fully voluntary. For example, during Indira Gandhi's years as prime minister of India, the country set the world record for vasectomies at 10 million in 1974, largely as a result of government policies that gave material goods to poor, illiterate men in exchange for their agreement to be sterilized. Indian government authorities not only failed to secure anything approximating genuine informed consent from most of these men prior to the procedure but also often neglected to give them the promised materials goods afterward. When these facts became known, the public lost confidence in Gandhi's government. Indian citizens protested that poor people should not be seduced with prizes, such as money, food, clothes, and radios, into giving up their reproductive rights.[10] Interestingly, the sterilization scandal played a key role in Gandhi's overthrow as prime minister; however, it did not dissuade government authorities in other developing countries from offering their people similarly enticing sterilization policies. For example, over twenty years later, Bangladesh's sterilization incentive program gave people not only several weeks' wages but also *saris* for women and *lungis* (pants) for men.[11]

In the fourth place, as with contraception and sterilization, access to affordable and safe abortion services is very important for women. Even in countries where contraceptives are available and affordable, women (and men) do not always elect to use them, for any number of reasons, including religious teachings that contraception is wrong. Although relatively few countries completely outlaw abortion, twenty-six out of a sample of seventy-two developing countries prohibit the procedure except to save the mother's life.[12] As a result, many women undergo illegal, sometimes fatal abortions. Worldwide, about 68,000 women a year die after subjecting themselves to unsafe procedures.[13] The situation for women is particularly perilous in sub-Saharan Africa, Central Asia, Southeast Asia, and Latin America, according to Burn.[14]

Still, access to abortion is not in and of itself always in women's overall best interests. According to global feminists, women in the former Soviet Union, for example, had an average of twelve to fourteen abortions over their lifetimes because contraceptives, although legal, were extremely difficult to obtain. Apparently, cost-benefit studies concluded it was less expensive for the government to provide multiple abortions to women rather than safe, effective, and monitored contraceptives. Governing bodies simply ignored the toll that multiple abortions took on women's bodies and psyches. Even today health-care practitioners in the former Soviet Union reportedly often treat abortion seekers judgmentally and disrespectfully.[15]

Abortion is readily available in countries that want to control the size of their populations. But abortion-friendly policies such as the now eroded one-child policy in China have resulted in women's having multiple abortions to make sure their one child is a boy. In China, most people still prefer boys to girls. In the past, Chinese women got pregnant as many times as necessary to produce at least one male child. If women produced too many daughters on the way to delivering a son, the families sometimes resorted to infanticide or child abandonment. Nowadays, due to the advent of technologies such as ultrasound and amniocentesis, many Chinese people elect to abort female fetuses rather than to kill or abandon a female baby. Indeed, the increased use of highly effective sex-selection techniques in China has engendered an enormous sex-ratio imbalance there: in 2012 it was 1.06 males for every 1 female.[16] Although a low supply of females might be expected to increase women's status, instead it seems to increase their vulnerability. In the rural sections of China, for example, men allegedly kidnap women and force them into marriage. Even worse, some poor families have resorted to selling their prepubescent daughters to men in search of a bride.[17] Realizing they have a serious "bachelor" problem on their hands, Chinese government officials have recently relaxed the one-child policy and inaugurated a girls-are-as-good-as-boys campaign. They have also outlawed prenatal tests for purposes of sex selection, though illegal tests are still available and affordable.[18]

As in China, in India parents' preference for a male child has resulted in a sex-ratio imbalance (1.12 males born for every 1 female).[19] As a result, authorities in that country have also decided to ban the use of prenatal tests for sex-selection purposes. The ban, however, has not been uniformly enforced. In addition, many women, particularly in rural regions, continue to engage in female infanticide because daughters are costly in India.[20] Parents must provide wedding dowries for their daughters. These are no trivial matter. On the contrary, they can be so large as to threaten the livelihood of the girls' parents. Moreover, mothers-in-law and other family members may reportedly mistreat and even physically beat and burn young brides whose parents fail to pay the negotiated dowry.

Complicating the situation in India is the fact that when it banned ultrasound and amniocentesis for sex-selection purposes, the government did not ban all sex-selection techniques. Because of a lacuna in the law, Gametrics, a US company with clinics in many developing countries, started to market heavily a preconception sex-selection technology that separates Y from X chromosomes. Women who want a baby boy and can afford the technology are inseminated with androsperm only. Reflecting on this costly technology, Maria Mies commented, "This example shows clearly that the sexist and racist ideology is closely interwoven with capitalist profit motives, that the logic of selection and elimination has a definite economic base. Patriarchy and racism are not only ethically rejectable ideologies, they mean *business* indeed."[21]

Women's Rights as Human Rights

Susan Moller Okin

According to Nancy Holmstrom, global feminists want to develop a "feminist" humanism that combines "the respect for differences characteristic of progressive movements since the 1960s with the universalistic aspirations of earlier liberatory traditions."[22] For example, feminist political theorist Susan Moller Okin claimed that feminists must talk about women's needs generically as well as specifically.[23] Conceding that as a group, women do not experience gender inequality to the same extent and degree, Okin nonetheless insisted that all women do experience it in some way or another, for the same reasons and with the same consequences. Because virtually all societies regard women as the "second sex"—as existing to some degree for men's sexual pleasure, reproductive use, and domestic service and for all of society's care—women throughout the world tend to have not only less sexual freedom and reproductive choice than men but also worse socioeconomic and health status.

Okin's and similar views were voiced beginning in the 1970s at international women's conferences in Mexico City (1975), Copenhagen (1980), Nairobi (1985), and Beijing (1995). At these conferences, women from both developed and developing countries revealed that their quality of life was diminished simply by virtue of their female sex. They discussed how their respective countries' sex, reproduction, marriage, divorce, child-custody, family-life, and work laws worsened their situations and how women and girls, far more than men and boys, were sexually vulnerable, unhealthy, uneducated, and poor.[24]

Martha Nussbaum

As noted above, global feminists are very concerned with women's rights and welfare on the world stage. In this connection, liberal feminist Martha Nussbaum claimed that individuals may demand as a matter of "right" from the state those arrangements, goods, and services that will enable them to develop two sets of functional human capabilities: (1) those that, if left undeveloped, render a life not human at all, and (2) those that, if left undeveloped, render a human life less than a good life.[25]

As we saw in Chapter 1, Nussbaum's list of functional human capabilities included noncontroversial ones, such as life, bodily health, and bodily integrity. But her list also included more controversial functional human capacities, such as the ability to play and to relate to nonhuman animals. Thus, some global feminists viewed Nussbaum's list as reflecting the needs of only "highly educated, artistically inclined, self-consciously and voluntarily Western women."[26] To this criticism, Nussbaum responded that she did not wish to impose her "good life" on any woman; she just wanted other women to have the means they need to choose their own version of the good life.

Many global feminists remained skeptical of Nussbaum's response, however. To justify their stance, they pointed to passages from Nussbaum's writings, such as the following:

> The capabilities approach insists that a woman's affiliation with a certain group or culture should not be taken as normative for her unless, on due consideration, with all the capabilities at her disposal, she makes that norm her own. We should take care to extend to each individual full capabilities to pursue the items on the list and then see whether they want to avail themselves of these opportunities. Usually they do, even when tradition says they should not. Martha Chen's work with [Indian] widows . . . reveals that they are already deeply critical of the cultural norms that determine their life quality. One week at a widows' conference in Bangalore was sufficient to cause these formerly secluded widows to put on forbidden colors and to apply for loans; one elderly woman, "widowed" at the age of seven, danced for the first time in her life, whirling wildly in the center of the floor. . . . Why should women cling to a tradition, indeed, when it is usually not their voice that speaks or their interests that are served?[27]

Nussbaum's suggestion that one week at a conference might undo years of enculturation struck some global feminist critics as wishful thinking. Commented Vivienne Jabri of King's College Centre for International Relations, Department of War Studies,

> The practical implication of Nussbaum's approach . . . is the production of subjects whose emancipation is defined in terms of their full participation in the global liberal order. Apart from the banality of the certainties expressed, there is here a form of "epistemic violence" that astounds. In representing her discourse as a baseline for an international feminism, Nussbaum reiterates a late-modern form of colonial mentality that leaves the subject of its discourse shorn of history and complexity. This subject is hence denied a presence. This form of international feminism is ultimately a form of disciplining biopolitics, where the distribution of female bodies is ultimately what can constitute their freedom as consumers within the global marketplace, where, to use [Gayatri Chakravorty] Spivak, "to be" is to be gainfully employed.[28]

Postcolonial Feminism in General

Closely related to global feminism, postcolonial feminism harkens back to the era when developed countries sought to colonize developing countries for their own purposes, such as extracting nonrenewable resources like oil for their own use. Actively engaged in directly combating the ongoing and deleterious effects of colonialism, postcolonial feminists concern themselves primarily with cautioning formerly colonized peoples against allowing their former colonizers to define, control, regulate, marginalize, stigmatize, belittle, or in any other way devalue them and their culture.[29] Postcolonial feminists, in other words, refuse to let Eurocentric standards define or assess either themselves or their problems. They take issue with the West's division of countries into "First World" (i.e., heavily industrialized and market-based countries located primarily in the Northern Hemisphere) and "Third World" (i.e., economically struggling countries located primarily in the Southern Hemisphere). In particular, they examine how this division operates to disempower, delegitimize, and disadvantage formerly colonized people, particularly women. Postcolonial feminists concern themselves primarily with economic and political issues, stressing that women's oppression as members of formerly colonized peoples often exceeds their oppression as women per se.

Women: The World's Proletariat

Robin Morgan and Rosemary Radforth Ruether

As Robin Morgan, whom we can view as either a global, postcolonial, or transnational feminist, noted, "Women are the world's proletariat." Despite constituting 60 to 80 percent of most countries' economies, housework continues to suffer from "gross national product invisibility."[30] To deny that women work, stressed Morgan, is absurd. Women constitute almost the totality of the world's food producers and undertake most of the world's hand portage of water and fuel. In most countries, handicrafts are largely or solely the products of female labor, and women constitute a large portion of workers in the tourist industry, including the questionable sex-tourism industry, which caters to businessmen who pay for the sexual services of women in the countries they visit.[31]

In addition, Morgan says, women are migrant and seasonal workers in agrarian countries and part-time laborers in industrialized countries. Women from developing countries do a significant percentage of the elder-care, child-care, and domestic work in Western countries, having left their own families back home to make money abroad to support them. There is, said Arlie Hochschild, a "global heart transplant" at work in the exportation of care from poor, developing countries to wealthy, developed countries.[32] Moreover, a double bind gets created. Rich women tend to pay their helpers low wages, and helpers tend to accept a range of abuse so long as their wages are high enough that they can send needed remittances back home to their families.

Also of particular significance in developing countries is the large number of women who work in factories owned by Western multinational companies. Most of these women (and men) labor under sweatshop conditions, which Rosemary Radford Ruether characterized as follows: "Workers receive less than a living wage, are forced to work long hours (ten to twelve hours a day) without overtime pay, work in unsafe conditions, are harassed on the job, physically and verbally abused, and are prevented from organizing unions and bargaining for better conditions."[33] According to Shawn Meghan Burn, countries where the global market is at work include Indonesia, where female factory workers receive about $1.25 a day for ten or more hours of work, and Vietnam, where they get about six cents an hour to assemble the promotional toys US children find in their McDonald's Happy Meal boxes.[34] Furthermore, in Mexico, female workers laboring in factories on the Mexican side of the United States–Mexico border receive far lower wages than their counterparts on the US side.[35]

Postcolonial feminists debate whether women should work under sweatshop conditions. On the one hand, "such work has made some women better off as members of families who rely on their support, as mothers who want a better standard of living for their children, as young unmarried women who want the status that economic independence sometimes brings."[36] On the other hand, such work has made other women compliant and docile, unwilling to defend their human rights for fear of losing their jobs. Protest seems in order, said Ruether, as long as a Nike worker in Asia earns less than two dollars a day and Nike CEO Phil Knight owns $4.5 billion in Nike stock.[37]

Adding to women's total workload is the unrecognized labor (housework, child care, elder care, sick care) they perform every day. Governmental and business responses, if any, to women's complaints about their "double day" (eight or more hours of recognized work outside the home and eight or more hours of unrecognized work inside the home) generally do not substantially improve women's situations. States or businesses tell women to work part-time or get on a "mommy track." But such strategies are not feasible for women supporting their families single-handedly. Moreover, they are not desirable for women who want to improve their status and wages at work. Some states and businesses fail to understand women's complaints about their "double day" at all, recommending sexist solutions. For example, said Morgan, Cuba's Fidel Castro once proposed that "hairdressers remain open during the evening to ease the burden of the woman who is employed during the day but needs to be attractive in her housewifing role at night."[38]

Reflecting on how hard women work and how little states and industry have done to ameliorate their lot, Morgan concluded that this state of affairs obtains because providing women the same work and economic security enjoyed by men does not serve "Big Brother's" interests. Whether Big Brother lives in the First or Third World, "a marginal female labor force is a highly convenient asset: cheap, always available, easily and callously disposed of."[39]

Postcolonial feminists are somewhat critical of developed countries' efforts to improve developing countries' economies in general and women's lot in particular. After World War II, said philosopher Alison Jaggar, most colonizers pulled out of the lands they had exploited, viewing these territories as an increasing cost burden. Largely because of what the colonizing countries had done to them by draining them of their natural resources, including talented individuals, many Asian, African, and South American states found themselves incredibly poor. They then had to borrow money from their former colonizers. In the 1960s, interest rates were relatively low, and many formerly colonized countries borrowed large amounts from the West, assuming that they could boost their economies relatively quickly and pay back their debts swiftly. Unfortunately, most found it extraordinarily difficult to do so. By the time they realized that development is a slow process, interest rates had risen steeply, and they were unable to pay the interest on their loans.[40]

To prevent the world economic system from crashing, the International Monetary Fund and the World Bank rescheduled the debts of many formerly colonized countries. As part of this plan, they required the affected countries to adjust their economic structures to ease their integration into the global economic system. According to Ruether, the formula for so-called structural adjustment was harsh. Among other things, it required "devaluation of local currency . . . the removal of trade barriers that protected local industries and agriculture . . . the privatization of public sector enterprises, such as transportation, energy, telephones, and electricity . . . and the removal of minimum wage laws and state subsidies for basic foods, education, and health services for the poor."[41]

Moreover, to earn enough foreign currency to finance their rescheduled external debts, formerly colonized countries had to export as many inexpensive goods as possible to Western countries or work inexpensively for large transnational companies located within their boundaries, or both. As a result, most formerly colonized countries could not produce their own consumer goods and had to import them from the West. These goods not only proved costly but also bore the cultural imprint of the West: Nike sneakers, Camel cigarettes, Coca-Cola, Ford automobiles, Calvin Klein blue jeans, and Apple computers. Many view this so-called McDonaldization of the world as an effective recolonization of formerly colonized countries.[42]

Maria Mies

Postcolonial feminists claim that women in formerly colonized countries bear the brunt of what Jaggar termed the "Southern debt."[43] Detailing how Western you-can-catch-up-to-us policies serve the interests of former colonizers rather than those of the formerly colonized, Maria Mies, for example, noted that Western economists make unrealistic promises to formerly colonized peoples, telling them that they can attain the same standard of living as people in the West, all the time doubting the truth of their predictions about limitless growth.[44] Observing that the world's population will swell to 11 billion after 2050, Mies stated, "If of these eleven billion people the per capita energy consumption was similar to that of Americans in the mid-1970s, conventional oil resource would be exhausted in 34–74 years."[45]

Because developed countries find it difficult to maintain ever-higher standards of living, Mies speculated that whatever the West gives to developing countries in the way of benefits, it extracts in the way of costs. Specifically, she said, industrialized countries pass on to their "partners" in developing nations the economic, social, and ecological costs they cannot pay without dropping from their privileged status to something more akin to that of developing countries: "The relationship between colonized and colonizer is based not on any measure of partnership, but rather on the latter's coercion and violence in its dealings with the former. This relationship is in fact the secret of unlimited growth in the centers of accumulation. If externalization of all the costs of industrial production were not possible, if they had to be borne by the industrialized countries themselves, that is if they were internalized, an immediate end to unlimited growth would be inevitable."[46] In sum, stressed Mies, "catching-up development" is not feasible for two reasons: (1) there are only so many resources to divide among humankind, and they are currently inequitably distributed and consumed; and (2) to maintain its present power, the existing "colonial world order" needs to maintain the economic gap it promises to eliminate. For example, the overall affluence of women in developed countries depends to some extent on the overall poverty of women in developing countries. Said Mies, "Only when women in Asia, Africa, or Latin America can be forced to work for much lower wages than those in affluent countries—and that is made possible through the debt trap—can enough capital be accumulated in the rich countries so that even unemployed women are guaranteed a minimum income; but all unemployed women in the world cannot expect this. Within a world system based on exploitation 'some are more equal than others.'"[47]

In addition to claiming that "catching-up development" schemes are not feasible, Mies noted that, in her estimation, nor are they desirable. She observed that the West's good life is actually a very bad life insofar as human relationships are concerned. People in the West are too busy making money to spend time with one another. They are so strained and stressed they have little sense of ultimate meaning. People in the West run the rat race, day after day, until they die, said Mies. Their children inherit their considerable material goods, and the cycle repeats itself.

By stressing in her critique of the West that poor people in developing countries have enviable relationships and a more appropriate set of life values than those typically displayed by hard-core Western materialists, Mies was not stating that the poor should stay dirt poor. Rather, she was making the point that because money and power are limited goods, a relentless and single-minded pursuit of them inevitably leads to discord. In this connection, Mies offered an example that focused on Western women and women in developing countries as competitors:

> It may be in the interest of Third World women working in the exporting garment industry in the global South to get higher wages, but if they get these better wages, then women in the North might stop buying their wares on the grounds that they are priced too high. Hence the interests of these two sets of women who are linked through the world market are antagonistic. These diverging interests are a major problem for feminists who view themselves as working for the good of all women. Seemingly, rich women must have less, so that poor women can have more. Not surprisingly, this is not a popular message with the "haves" of this world.[48]

Human Trafficking

Sally J. Scholtz and Shawn Meghan Burn on Human Trafficking

So far, we have been talking about work and trade involving mere commodities—that is, things. According to philosopher Sally J. Scholtz, however, other kinds of work and trade between countries involve people—mostly women and children. In *Feminism: A Beginner's Guide*, Scholtz pointed out, "Women are targeted for trafficking so that they may be used for prostitution, mail order brides, or domestic slavery. Children are targeted for these same purposes but also for illegal adoption and child soldiers."[49] Reflecting on the fact that the global market now trades in people as well as natural resources and manufactured goods, Scholtz claimed, "When some human beings are bought and sold for their sexual services, bodies or body parts, then all humans are degraded. Moreover, the growing prevalence of human trafficking means that we are all culpable for it in some way. While we may not directly partake in the activities of trafficking, we might implicitly condone it by not working to end it."[50]

Shawn Meghan Burn has also protested against human trafficking, particularly prostitution and so-called sex tourism. She claimed that to boost tourism and their economies, governments overlook the effect of prostitution on women, as do some military leaders who see "sexual recreation" as vital to the well-being and morale of their troops.[51] As mentioned in Chapter 2, some feminists find the prostitution problem particularly worrisome because many women trapped into sex work think they are being recruited as domestic workers. When they get to their destination country, they are treated as slaves. They either can't go home because their earnings are a mere pittance, scarcely enough to buy them an airline ticket, or won't because they have been impregnated against their will. Ashamed, these women often stay where they are because they think the men in their countries will treat them as undesirable for marriage or, worse, as "whores" and "bitches" deserving of bad treatment.[52]

Like Scholtz, Burn singled out Thailand for special comment. She noted that Thailand makes about $3 billion a year off the work of women who don't have the wherewithal to escape the lives they have found themselves in. Burn also pointed out that 75 percent of Thai men make use of prostitutes' services, seeking the youngest on the theory that they have the best chance of being HIV free.[53] But even though Thailand has the largest population of sex workers for its small size, Burn stressed that may other countries are also responsible for the plight of some prostitutes: "sex tourists come . . . from Australia, Canada, France, Germany, Japan, Kuwait, New Zealand, Norway, Qatar, Saudi Arabia, Sweden, the United Kingdom and the United States (Seagar 1997). Their main destinations are Brazil, Cambodia, Costa Rica, Cuba, the Dominic Republic, India, Indonesia, Hungary, Kenya, Morocco, the Philippines, and, [of course], Thailand."[54]

Transnational Feminism in General

Although transnational feminism shares many features with global and postcolonial feminisms, according to Parekh and Wilcox, at least three differences distinguish it from the other two. First, transnational feminism is sensitive to the myriad differences among women. It does not claim that a "global sisterhood" now exists that is strong enough to present "a unified front against global patriarchy." Rather, the kind of "solidarity" transnational feminists posit requires the methodology of intersectionality discussed in Chapter 4, as well as "sensitivity to concrete specificity" and "self-reflexivity."[55] For example, women in developed countries might be happy that they can hire a foreign-born, female elder-care worker for low wages, while that woman must endure separation from her own children and loss of the comforts of her own home.

Perhaps the most noteworthy feature of transnational feminism is its preference for engaging in specific activist movements. Parekh and Wilcox highlighted the power of women working together in worker-owned corporations, allying in labor unions, building fair trade organizations, and furthering land reform movements. Such activities allow women from the North and the South to come together as needed, usually to separate when their work is done.[56]

Chandra Talpade Mohanty

Transnational feminists focus on connections between nationhood, race, gender, sexuality, and economic exploitation in the context of capitalism's worldwide spread. They work to organize resistance to capitalist hegemonies as they interrogate the relationship between these hegemonies and the nation-state. For example, they challenge global feminists' usage and implementation of the concept of the "Third World Woman," as if all women in this category share the same cultural experiences or have the same experience of oppression. Chandra Talpade Mohanty wrote specifically that Western feminism tends to use language to colonize the material and historical heterogeneities of the lives of women in developing countries, thereby producing/re-presenting a composite, singular "Third World Woman"—an image that, however arbitrarily constructed, nonetheless carries with it the authorizing signature of Western humanist discourse.[57]

Mohanty continued this line of thought in a very personal way: "I argue that assumptions of privilege and ethnocentric universality on the one hand, and inadequate self-consciousness about the effect of Western scholarship on the 'third world' in the context of a world system dominated by the West on the other, characterize a sizable extent of Western feminist work on women in the third world. . . . It is in this process of homogenization and systemization of the oppression of women in the third world that power is exercised in much of recent Western feminist discourse, and this power needs to be defined and named."[58] From the perspective of many transnational feminists, then, while well intentioned in their attempts to extend to non-Western women what they take to be insights about women's general needs and rights, global and postcolonial feminists are limited in their efforts.

Transnational feminism works to build between women the kinds of worldwide alliances that global feminism purportedly seeks. But rather than pursuing the utopian ideal of global sisterhood, it has less ambitious aims.

Sally J. Scholtz, who can be viewed as either a global, postcolonial, or transnational feminist, gave the example of women in one developed country (Norway) working with women in one developing country (Thailand) to curb human trafficking. The Norwegian women funded grants for women's centers at Thai universities, offered loans to put money in Thai women's pockets, and funded educational programs about the intentions of some "recruiters." In return, the Thai women educated the Norwegian women about the "cultural traditions and practices that make some women more vulnerable to trafficking than others and describe[d] what sorts of alternatives will make a difference in the lives of poor women."[59] They also asked the Norwegian women to eliminate the sex trade in Norway, which the Norwegian women decided to do (see Chapter 2). Norway is among the European countries that have increased criminal penalties for prostitution, targeting buyers of sex and the recruiting agencies that import sex workers from developing countries.

Critiques of Global, Postcolonial, and Transnational Feminisms

Critique One: Global Feminism Relies Too Much on Rights Talk

Interestingly, unlike global feminists, who tend to use the language of women's rights as human rights found in international documents such as the "United Nations Universal Declaration of Human Rights," the "Convention on the Elimination of All Forms of Discrimination Against Women," and the "United Nations Declaration on the Elimination of Violence Against Women,"[60] many other feminists have doubts about a rights approach to women's problems. As they see it, this approach has a lingering tendency to privilege first-generation civil and political rights over second-generation economic and social rights. Typical first-generation rights include freedom from oppression and from governmental interference with liberty of thought and action, whereas typical second-generation rights include the right to food, clothing, shelter, education, health care, work, rest, and reasonable payment. If women's first-generation rights are honored without equal attention to their second-generation rights, many women will remain at a real disadvantage, say these feminists. For example, a poor woman's right to have an abortion does not mean much if it simply prevents others from interfering with her decision to abort her fetus. She also needs the funds to pay for the procedure. And even if funding is available, her right to have an abortion will mean little if, as a result of her decision, she ends up ostracized from her community or rejected, abused, or divorced by a husband on whom she is financially and socially dependent.

Other feminists reject the rights language of certain global feminists not so much for the reason just given but because they think some of the rights privileged as universal primarily reflect the values and interests that people in such countries as the United States favor. Anne Phillips pointed out that the high value placed on autonomy in statements of universal human rights may be "a central preoccupation of Western cultures" and that many women do not value "personal autonomy and mobility over the ties of family or community."[61] The latter women do not want to be liberated from either the constraints of tradition or the obligations and limitations that go with belonging to a community. Australian feminist Chilla Bulbeck reinforced this perspective in describing her reaction to a 1980s pro-choice rally she attended in Washington, DC:

> I was struck by the anger of many of the speakers and participants. A black and white women's vocal group from Manhattan . . . shouted out the slogan "We are fierce, we are feminist, and we are in your face." Robin Morgan urged us to buy T-shirts proclaiming, "Rage plus women equals power." One placard read "Abort Bush Before His Second Term." Angry arguments erupted between the pro-choice women and the pro-life women who had erected a "cemetery of innocents" nearby (representing aborted fetuses . . .). I went to the United States believing I knew it intimately from the flood of films, television programs, and academic books that pervade Australian popular and intellectual culture. Yet I felt battered and cut adrift by the assertiveness and anger, by the incessant refrain of rights and freedoms. This fashion of feminism was unfamiliar to me.[62]

Still other feminists raise even more basic objections to rights talk. They deem it mistaken to invoke as normative the concept of rights instead of the concept of responsibilities or duties. As they see it, one person's right to at least a subsistence amount of food depends on someone else's responsibility to provide it. Indeed, feminist political theorist Diane Elson presented human rights as claims "to a set of social arrangements—to norms, institutions, laws and an enabling economic environment—that can best secure the enjoyment of these [purported] rights."[63]

Critique Two: Global Feminism Neglects the Particularity of Women's Experiences

As global feminism is arguably based in a kind of Kantian ethics that takes for granted the reliability and legitimacy of such things as reason, autonomy, freedom, and universal moral truth, some critics understand it as problematically neglectful of the particularity of women's experiences. There is no one "women's experience," they charge, but a multiplicity of women's experiences. In their pursuit of sweeping solutions to the problems faced by the women of the world, these critics charge, well-meaning global feminists unwittingly engage in acts of cultural imperialism and ego-based paternalism. Wanting women in developing countries to be as "free" and "autonomous" as they are, some global feminists in developed countries fail to reflect on the extent to which what counts as "freedom" is culturally determined or how "autonomy" is a fiction created by the wealthy to justify a failure to consider the effects of their actions on the poor. Similarly, all discussion of the "best interests," "needs," or "functional human capabilities" of women in non-Western countries is limited by a lack of firsthand experience with the problems faced by particular women in particular countries. The solutions posed by global feminists cannot help but be ineffectual at a minimum and harmful in the worst-case scenario, say critics.

Critique Three: Postcolonial Feminism Fails to Address the Real Concerns of Women in Formerly Colonized Countries

Many critics of postcolonial feminism see little difference between it and global feminism in terms of the regard given to the unique problems faced by women of color. The primary concern of postcolonial feminism, these critics charge, is combatting capitalist exploitation of the proletariat rather than addressing the specific problems of women of color in developing nations or facilitating the agency of women of color.

Another critique of postcolonial feminism holds that its inclusion of texts written by persons of color merely operates as a new and exotic means to make the research of postcolonial feminists (most of them white) stand out. Writing in a jargon that ordinary women cannot understand, they fail to address the everyday concerns of women-of-color worldwide.

Critique Four: Transnational Feminism Is Not Strong Enough to Ground Feminism's Future

According to Sara Salem, the question is, "How can a strong transnational feminism movement be created, and how can it avoid the mistakes Western feminists made in articulating what feminism is and how patriarchy can be dismantled?"[64] All too often, said Salem, would-be transnational feminism gets separated from its grassroots activist base and starts importing neoliberal concepts into its thinking. Although Salem applauded the concept of "intersectionality," she did not think it was strong enough to fight alone against entrenched gender relations.[65]

In her view, it is naive for any feminist, no matter how enlightened, to believe that the "subject" can totally be erased, uncovering some mythological "universal and objective knowledge."[66] Feminists need to eradicate this ontological "truism" from their thinking and replace it with "critical border thinking"—the kind of thinking that is strong enough to eliminate vestiges of Western imperialism.[67] Salem specifically commented, "Constructing 'culture' as a barrier to women's personal freedom reveals a liberal conception of the human subject, where liberty—at a personal, individual level—is framed as especially important and as the direct result of the elimination of culture practices [say, suttee or clitorectomy] without taking into account the political, economic and social factors that are affected by both local and global factors."[68]

In an attempt to provide her readers with an example of a truly transnational approach to thinking, Salem focused on the issue of education for women. She said that such an approach would press us to question what we mean by education, which types of knowledge this understanding privileges, and how providing education and employment to women in the Global South "also has multiple structural effects that often remain understudied, most notably that it ties them into a global capitalist economy of production and consumption in which they face a new sort of oppressive relations."[69] In Salem's thinking, transnational, global, and postcolonial feminisms are all on the right track but have a long, sometimes hard walk to take.

Conclusion

Eager to forge bonds among all the women of the world, Robin Morgan stressed in *Sisterhood Is Global* that, in the end, women are not really so very different. Provided they ask each other "*sincere* questions about difference," said Morgan, they will see each other as searching for the same thing—namely, a self ("self-identity," "an articulation of self-hood," "self-realization," "self-image," "the right to be oneself").[70]

Furthering Morgan's point, Elizabeth Spelman itemized the kinds of sincere questions global, postcolonial, and transnational feminists might ask each other, including the following: "What do I and can I know about women from whom I differ in terms of race, culture, class ethnicity?" "What happens when oppressors want to undo racism or other oppression?" "How do they go about acquiring knowledge about others, knowledge whose absence is now regretted?"[71]

Among the many ways to find answers to these questions, said Spelman, is to "read books, take classes, open your eyes and ears to whatever instruments of awareness you might be blessed with, go to conferences planned and produced by the people about whom you wish to learn and manage not to be intrusive."[72] Other ways include trying to imagine what other women's lives are like and being tolerant of differences, including the off-putting and threatening ones.

Interestingly, Spelman later refined her thought with some subtle distinctions. She said that there is a difference between merely imagining another woman's life and actually perceiving it.

> When I am perceiving someone, I must be prepared to receive new information all the time, to adapt my actions accordingly, and to have my feelings develop in response to what the person is doing, whether I like what she is doing or not. When simply imagining her, I can escape from the demands her reality puts on me and instead construct her in my mind in such a way that I can possess her, make her into someone or something who never talks back, who poses no difficulties for me, who conforms to my desires much more than the real person does.[73]

In addition to specifying the difference between acts of imagination and acts of perception, Spelman elucidated a second important distinction between tolerating and welcoming someone's opinion. She claimed that merely to tolerate a viewpoint is to fail to seek it out actively as a serious critique of one's own viewpoint. If I am just tolerating you, I am not open to really changing myself. I am not prepared to be your friend; I am simply willing not to be your enemy. In contrast, if I am welcoming you into me, I am exposing myself to the possibility of real change. I am expressing willingness to view my present self as a self in need of improvement, indeed transformation.

In the dialogical essay with Maria Lugones mentioned in Chapter 4, Spelman stressed that to develop an adequate (i.e., multicultural, global, and postcolonial) feminist theory, a wide variety of women would have to formulate it together. Lugones reacted to Spelman's proposal with some challenging points. She wondered whether women previously marginalized by the recognized authorities in feminist thought would now want to join them to create a better feminist theory. Perhaps these once marginalized women would prefer to do their own theory, in their own voices, without shouldering the burdens that generally accompany collaborative projects.

Lugones was concerned about the motives behind reigning feminist authorities' sudden interest in the views of "others." Was the motive a self-interested one, in the sense of "self-growth or self expansion, feeding off the rich 'difference' of the other?" Or, just as bad, was it a mere sense of duty, understood as an act of noblesse oblige or an anemic substitute for true love?[74] Lugones then continued that such motives, if present, would make it impossible for white women/First World women to fully partner with women of color/Third World women in theory making. She stressed that a desire to be friends is the only motive capable of bringing women together to weave a feminist theory strong enough to withstand the challenges of the twenty-first century. Unless one woman wants to be another woman's friend, she will be unable to summon the psychic energy to travel to that woman's world to imagine or see the other woman living her life there as a self rather than an "other." Therefore, according to Lugones as well as Spelman and Morgan, the chief task of global, postcolonial, and transnational feminists is to help women learn how to be each other's friends.

A variety of thinkers, including bell hooks, Audre Lorde, Iris Marion Young, and Nancy Caraway, have voiced disagreement with Morgan's, Spelman's, and Lugones's views on the essential goal of multicultural and global feminism. Although hooks and Lorde sometimes employed the language of sisterhood in their writings, for them the concept is political rather than personal. Women can be sisters in the sense of being political comrades, but only if they are willing to truly confront their differences. Imagining, perceiving, tolerating, and welcoming are fine, insofar as they go, but confronting differences requires far more painful activities, like being enraged and being shamed. There is a difference, hooks emphasized, between "bourgeois-women's-liberation" sisterhood and postcolonial, global, and transnational feminist sisterhood. The former focuses on women's "supporting" each other, where support serves "as a prop or a foundation for a weak structure" and women, emphasizing their "shared victimization," give each other "unqualified approval."[75] The latter rejects this sentimental brand of sisterhood and offers instead a type that begins with women's confronting and combating each other's differences and ends with their using these very same differences to "accelerate their positive advance" toward the goals they share. As hooks explained, "Women do not need to eradicate difference to feel solidarity. We do not need to share common oppression to fight equally to end oppression. . . . We can be sisters united by shared interests and beliefs, united in our appreciation for diversity, united in our struggle to end sexist oppression, united in political solidarity."[76] Lorde also stressed the importance of maintaining women's differences rather than trying to transcend them. She claimed, for example, that feminists don't have to love each other to work with each other.[77] In the same vein, Young observed that although women should not be enemies, they should not expect to be friends. They should be content to remain respectful "strangers."[78]

Rejecting the homogenizing, conformist tendencies of the language of community and family, Young argued that feminists should not try to be "sisters" and "friends" with women whose worlds are radically different from their own. As Nancy Caraway noted, for Young, the "insistence on the ideal of shared subjectivity . . . leads to undesirable political implications."[79] Young repeatedly urged feminists to distrust the desire "for reciprocal recognition and identification with others . . . because it denies differences in the concrete sense of making it difficult for people to respect those with whom they do not identify."[80] She claimed, said Caraway, that global, postcolonial, and transnational feminists should not want to be sisters or friends because such desires "thwart our principled calls for heterogeneity of feminism."[81]

The choice between the sisterhood of friendship and the sisterhood of political solidarity is an important one. Global, postcolonial, and transnational feminists might need to make this choice once and for all in the future, but for now the consensus seems to be a combined approach in which political alliances become opportunities for women to form personal friendships. In this connection, Aristotle had some surprisingly good advice for feminists. According to the ancient Greek philosopher, there are three kinds of friendship: friendship between people who are useful to each other (e.g., professional colleagues and business partners); friendship between people who enjoy the same sorts of pleasures (e.g., drinking buddies and dance partners); and friendship between people who share meaningful goals and tasks (e.g., famine relief workers and women fighting oppression). Of these three types of friendships, the last is most central to feminists attaining their goals of freedom and equality for women in all their diversity.[82]

Questions for Discussion

1. Is it likely that white feminists will ever forsake "white privilege" for the sake of solidarity with women of color? Why or why not?
2. How might women work together to cherish non-Western women and their vantage points and include them in the larger sociopolitical context?
3. Explain the notion that some women are more equal than others. Is it possible for some women to remain affluent—at the expense of other, marginalized women (or men, for that matter)—and still consider themselves true feminists? Why or why not?

4. How might the language of universal human rights not actually benefit women universally? In your estimation, is there a better approach to ensure that all women enjoy equal dignity?
5. How aware are you of women's status and struggles outside the United States? Explain the origins of your awareness or unawareness.

6

Psychoanalytic Feminism

Liberal, radical (libertarian and cultural), Marxist/socialist, and women-of-color feminists here and abroad have offered explanations for women's oppression rooted in society's political and economic structures and/or sexual and reproductive relationships, roles, and practices. Liberal feminists claimed that providing women with the same rights and opportunities men enjoy may be enough to eliminate gender inequity. Radical feminists thought otherwise and insisted that if gender equity is the goal, men's and women's sexual and reproductive rights and responsibilities must first be examined. Radical-libertarian feminists claimed that women need to be liberated not only from the burdens of natural reproduction and biological motherhood but also from the restrictions of a sexual double standard that gives men sexual freedoms typically denied women. Radical-cultural feminists disagreed, claiming that women's power is rooted in their unique reproductive role. All children are born of women; without women, no children would be born. Radical-cultural feminists also stressed that male sexual behavior is not worthy of women's emulation because men frequently use sex as an instrument of control and domination rather than of love and bonding. In addition, Marxist and socialist feminists hypothesized that unless capitalist economic structures are destroyed, people will remain divided into two oppositional classes—the haves and the have-nots, with women, more than men, finding themselves in the ranks of the have-nots. Finally, women-of-color feminists, be they in the United States or elsewhere in the world, emphasized the intersecting lines of multiple oppressions, a field that contemporary feminists need to map skillfully to show every group of women equal respect and consideration.

In contrast to all the feminist thinkers already considered, psychoanalytic feminists maintained that the fundamental explanation for women's way of acting stems from deep within their psyche, specifically, from their way of thinking about themselves as women. Relying on Freudian constructs such as the pre-Oedipal and Oedipal stages (discussed on page 6) and/or on Lacanian constructs, such as the Symbolic order (discussed on pages 172–174), psychoanalytic feminists claim that gender identity, hence gender inequity, is rooted in a series of infantile and early childhood experiences. These experiences, most of them accessible only through psychoanalysis, are, in the estimation of psychoanalytic feminists, the cause of individuals' viewing themselves in masculine or feminine terms, of thinking of themselves as boys or girls. Moreover, these same experiences are the cause of society's privileging things "masculine" over things "feminine." Hypothesizing that a nonpatriarchal society would construct and value masculinity and femininity differently, psychoanalytic feminists recommend that we alter our early infantile childhood experiences or, more radically, transform the linguistic structures that cause us to describe ourselves in terms of our respective gender(s).

Classical Psychoanalytic Thought: Focus on Sigmund Freud

Although Sigmund Freud was not a feminist, many psychoanalytic feminists have found in his writings clues about how to better understand the causes and consequences of women's oppression. Freud's theories about psychosexual development disturbed his late-nineteenth-century Viennese contemporaries not so much because he addressed traditionally taboo topics (e.g., homosexuality, sadism, masochism, and oral and anal sex) but because he theorized that all sexual "aberrations," "variations," and "perversions" are simply stages in the development of normal human sexuality.[1] According to Freud, children go through distinct psychosexual developmental stages, and their gender identity as adults reflects how well or badly they have weathered this process. Masculinity and femininity are, in other words, the product of sexual maturation. If boys and girls develop "normally," they will end up as men and women who display, respectively, expected masculine and feminine traits.

We find the theoretical bases for Freud's views on the relationship between sex and gender in *Three Contributions to the Theory of Sexuality.*[2] In this work, Freud laid out his theory of psychosexual development in detail. Because adults in Freud's time equated sexual activity with reproductive genital sexuality (heterosexual intercourse), they thought children were asexual. Dismissing this view as naive, Freud argued that far from being without sexual interests, children engage in all sorts of sexual behavior. He claimed that children's sexuality is "polymorphous perverse"—that insofar as the infant is concerned, the entire body, especially its orifices and appendages, is sexual terrain. The infant moves from this type of "perverse" sexuality to "normal" heterosexual genital sexuality by passing through several developmental stages. During the oral stage, the infant receives pleasure from sucking its mother's breast or its own thumb. During the anal stage, the two- or three-year-old enjoys the sensations associated with controlling the expulsion of feces. During the phallic stage, the three- or four-year-old discovers that the genitals are a source of pleasure and either resolves or fails to resolve the so-called Oedipus complex. Around age six, the child ceases to display overt sexuality and begins a period of latency that ends at around puberty, when the young person enters the genital stage, characterized by a resurgence of sexual impulses. If all goes normally during this stage, the young person's libido (defined by Freud as undifferentiated sexual energy) will be directed outward, away from autoerotic and homoerotic stimulation and toward a member of the opposite sex.

Freud stressed that the critical moment in the psychosexual drama here described occurs when the child tries to successfully resolve the Oedipus complex. The fact that only boys have penises, he claimed, fundamentally affects the way in which boys and girls undergo psychosexual development. The boy's Oedipus complex stems from his natural attachment to his mother, for it is she who nurtures him. Because of the boy's feelings toward his mother, he wants to possess her—to have sexual intercourse with her—and to kill his father, the rival for his mother's attentions. Freud added, however, that the boy's hatred of his father is modulated by his coexisting love for him. Because the boy wants his father to love him, he competes with his mother for his father's affections, experiencing increased antagonism toward her. Nevertheless, the boy still wishes to possess her and would attempt to take her from his father were it not for his fear of punishment by him. Supposedly, having seen either his mother or some other female naked, the boy speculates that these creatures without penises must have been castrated, by his father, no less. Shaken by this thought, the boy fears his father will castrate him, too, should he dare to act on his desire for his mother. Therefore, the boy distances himself from his mother, a painful process that propels him into sexual latency.[3]

During this period of sexual latency, the boy begins to develop what Freud called a superego. To the degree the superego is the son's internalization of his father's values, it is a patriarchal social conscience. The boy who successfully resolves the Oedipus complex develops a particularly strong superego. In the course of giving up mother love (albeit out of fear of castration), he learns how to defer to the authority of his father. The boy waits his turn for his own woman, temporarily subordinating his id (instincts) to his superego (the voice of social constraints). Were it not for the trauma of the Oedipus complex and his fear of castration, the boy would fail to mature into a man ready, willing, and able at the appropriate time to claim the torch of civilization from his father.

The female experience of the Oedipus complex differs dramatically from the male experience in Freud's estimation. As is the case with boys, the girl's first love object is her mother. But unlike the typical boy, whose love object will supposedly remain a woman throughout his life, the typical girl must switch from desiring a woman to desiring a man—at first her father and, later, other men who take his place. According to Freud, the transition from a female to a male love object begins when the girl realizes she does not have a penis, that she is castrated: "They [girls] notice the penis of a brother or playmate, strikingly visible and of large proportions, at once recognize it as the superior counterpart of their own small and inconspicuous organ (the clitoris), and from that time forward they fall a victim to envy for the penis."[4]

Supposedly preoccupied by her deficiency, the girl somehow discovers her mother also lacks a penis. Distraught by the sight of her mother, the girl looks to her father to make good the deficiency she shares with her mother. She does not turn away from her mother without feeling an incredible sense of loss, however. Freud claimed that like any person who loses a love object, the girl will somehow try to become the abandoned love object. Thus, the girl tries to take her mother's place with her father. As a result she comes to hate her mother not only because of her mother's supposedly inferior state of being but also because her mother is a rival for the father's affections. At first the girl desires to have her father's penis, but gradually she begins to desire something even more precious—a baby, which for her is the ultimate penis substitute.[5]

Freud theorized that it is much more difficult for the girl than the boy to achieve normal adult sexuality, precisely because the girl must stop loving a woman (her mother)[6] and start loving a man (her father). This total switch in love object requires the girl to derive sexual pleasure from the "feminine" vagina instead of the "masculine" clitoris.[7] Freud further theorized that before the phallic stage, the girl has active sexual aims. Like the boy, she wants to take sexual possession of her mother, but with her clitoris. If the girl goes through the phallic stage successfully, said Freud, she will enter the stage of latency without this desire, and when genital sensitivity reappears at puberty, she will no longer long to use her clitoris actively. Instead, the girl will be content to use it passively for autoerotic masturbation or as a part of foreplay preparatory to heterosexual intercourse. But because the clitoris is not easy to desensitize, continued Freud, there is always the possibility the girl will either regress into the active clitoral stage by becoming a lesbian or, exhausted from suppressing her clitoris, give up on sexuality altogether.

The long-term negative consequences of penis envy and rejection of the mother go beyond possible frigidity for the girl. Freud thought the girl's difficult passage through the Oedipus complex scars her with several undesirable gender traits as she grows toward womanhood. First, she becomes narcissistic as she switches from active to passive sexual aims. Girls, said Freud, seek not so much to love as to be loved; the more beautiful a girl is, the more she expects and demands as much. Second, she becomes vain. As a compensation for her original lack of a penis, the girl focuses on her total physical appearance, as if her general good looks could somehow make up for her penile deficiency. Finally, the girl becomes a victim of an exaggerated sense of shame. It is, said Freud, not uncommon for girls to be so embarrassed by the sight of their "castrated" bodies that they insist on dressing and undressing under their bedsheets.[8]

As bad as female narcissism, vanity, and shame are, Freud suggested that these character flaws in women are small in comparison to those that most account for women's inferiority as a sex. As discussed earlier, the boy's fear of castration enables him to resolve his Oedipus complex successfully, to submit himself fully to the father's law. In contrast, because the girl has no such fear—since she literally has nothing to lose—she moves through the Oedipus complex slowly, resisting the father's laws indefinitely.[9] That the girl is spared the threat of castration is, said Freud, a mixed blessing, for only by being pushed to fully internalize the father's values can a girl develop a strong superego, which holds in check the animalistic urges of the id, the force that rules one's unconscious. As women remain resistant to the father's laws, they are supposedly less obedient than men to the civilizing forces of the superego. Ultimately, female moral inferiority is traceable to girls' lack of a penis. Because they do not have to worry about being castrated, girls are not nearly as motivated as boys to become obedient rule followers whose heads control their hearts.

Anglo-American Critiques and Appropriations of Freud: Focus on Dorothy Dinnerstein, Nancy Chodorow, and Juliet Mitchell

Because penis envy and related ideas paint such an unflattering portrait of women, many feminists were and remain angered by traditional Freudian theory. In the 1970s, feminists with otherwise widely different agendas—for example, Betty Friedan,[10] Shulamith Firestone,[11] and Kate Millett[12]—made

Freud a common target. They argued that women's social position and powerlessness relative to men had little to do with female biology and much to do with the social construction of femininity. They also noted that even if it were correct, Freud's theory of sexuality would apply only to bourgeois, heterosexual, Eurocentric people. In contrast, during the 1970s other feminists, including Dorothy Dinnerstein and Nancy Chodorow, strove to reinterpret Freud's texts. Dinnerstein and Chodorow in particular maintained that by focusing less on the Oedipal stage and more on the pre-Oedipal stage of psychosexual development, they could provide a better account of sexuality and gender than Freud did. Many of society's views about women's inferiority and men's superiority, said Dinnerstein and Chodorow, are traceable to women's doing all or most of the mothering work in society. Were men to mother just as much as women do, boys and girls would grow up differently. They would realize that neither sex is inferior or superior to the other and that both sexes merit equal respect.

Dorothy Dinnerstein

According to Dinnerstein, our society's gender arrangements strongly influence how men and women conceive of themselves and each other, and the resulting portrait is not pretty. It depicts women as "mermaids" and men as "minotaurs." Dinnerstein wrote, "The treacherous mermaid, seductive and impenetrable female representative of the dark and magic underwater world from which our life comes and in which we cannot live, lures voyagers to their doom. The fearsome minotaur, gigantic and eternally infantile offspring of a mother's unnatural lust, male representative of mindless, greedy power, insatiably devours live human flesh."[13] Because she found it ugly, Dinnerstein sought to explain why this portrait gets painted over and over again, albeit in different hues. The answer to our pathological need to make monsters of ourselves is buried, she speculated, deep in our psychosexual development, in the pre-Oedipal stage. The infant's relationship with its mother is profoundly symbiotic because the infant is initially incapable of distinguishing between itself and her. Because the maternal body is the infant's first encounter with the material or physical world, the infant experiences it as a symbol of an unreliable and unpredictable universe. The mother is the source of pleasure but also of pain for the infant, who is never certain whether she will meet its physical and psychological needs. As a result, the infant grows up feeling very ambivalent toward mother figures (women) and what they represent (the material/physical universe, or nature). Not wanting to reexperience utter dependence on an all-powerful force, men seek to control both women and nature, to exert power over them. Fearing the power of the mother within themselves, women concomitantly seek control by men. Men's need to control women and women's need to be controlled by them tragically lead, said Dinnerstein, to a misshapen set of gender arrangements, which together constitute a paradigm for destructive human relations in general.

Dinnerstein pointed to men's greater sexual possessiveness as the first characteristic of currently skewed gender relationships. Men hope to overcome their past inability to totally control their mothers by trying to dominate their wives or girlfriends. Given men's intense desire to control women, when a woman is unfaithful to a man, he feels the same despair he felt upon realizing his mother had a self separate from his own, whose will often conflicted with his. This refelt sense of despair, said Dinnerstein, explains men's violent reactions to their wives' or girlfriends' infidelities, ranging from extramarital affairs with male lovers to pajama parties with female friends.

Curiously, although many women accept men's sexual possessiveness of women as a sort of right, they do not generally claim the same right for themselves. According to Dinnerstein, because a woman fears the power of the mother within herself, she is always in search of a man who can control her. But because a man does not represent "mother" to her in the way she represents "mother" to him, she needs him less than he needs her. No matter how deep the symbiosis she achieves with him, it will not equal that which she had with her mother in the past or could have with another woman/mother now or in the future. Consequently, if a man leaves a woman, she will not feel the same intensity of grief she felt when she left her original mother.[14]

Muted female erotic impulsivity is the second mark of current gender arrangements, according to Dinnerstein. A muted female eroticism is one oriented exclusively toward male pleasure. Through sexual intercourse, the woman seeks to satisfy the man and experiences any pleasure vicariously as delight in his satisfaction. Her own sexual wants and needs must go unattended, for were she to insist on their fulfillment, she and the man would be in for a shock. They would both reexperience the rage they felt as infants on first recognizing their mothers as independent selves with lives and interests of their own. Moreover, were she to let her partner totally satisfy her, the woman would feel enormous guilt for having abandoned her primary love object (mother and women) for a secondary love object (father and men). Better to deprive herself of sexual pleasure than to suffer the pangs of conscience.[15]

This guilt on the part of women contributes to the third feature of current gender relations identified by Dinnerstein: the idea that sexual excitement and personal sentiment are tied together for women but not for men.

Because of her guilt over abandoning her mother, a woman refuses to allow herself even vicarious pleasure in sex unless the relationship is infused with the same type of all-encompassing love that existed between her and her mother. To feel good about a sexual liaison, a woman must believe the relationship underlying it is like the one she initially had with her mother: deep, binding, and strong. Only such a sexual liaison can possibly justify her rejection of her mother. To forsake total symbiosis with her mother for a one-night stand with a man, for example, is to settle for a superficial intimacy that cannot approximate the deep intimacy of the mother-child relationship.

In contrast to women, men are notorious for their ability to separate sex from intense emotional commitment, according to Dinnerstein. This ability is also rooted in the mother-infant relationship, especially in the infant's loss of the illusion of omnipotence. In the male-female sexual relationship, the man feels especially vulnerable because a woman "can reinvoke in him the unqualified, boundless, helpless passion of infancy."[16] Depending on how much a man needs to be in charge of his destiny, he will feel threatened by the overwhelming powers of sexual passion. Once again, he will fear being overwhelmed by a woman able to shatter his ego by withdrawing herself from him. Thus, he will seek to remain in control of the sexual act, distancing himself from the woman with whom he is being intimate.

Dinnerstein claimed the fourth hallmark of current gender arrangements is that a woman is viewed as an "it," whereas a man is seen as an "I." Because the child encounters a woman before being able to distinguish an "I" (center of self-interested sentience and perception) from an "it" (an impersonal force of nature), Dinnerstein speculated that the child initially perceives its mother not as a person but as an object. In contrast, because the father usually plays a small role in an infant's upbringing, taking on a larger part in his child's life only after the child has made the I-it distinction, the child has less difficulty recognizing him as an "I." Apparently, children perceive their fathers, but not their mothers, as persons with lives of their own. Dinnerstein also hypothesized that human beings fear the power of an "it" more than that of an "I." In her estimation, this explains why both men and women ultimately find "it-like" female power, in the private or public realm, more threatening than male power. Thus, not only do men feel a need to control women, but women also feel a need to be controlled by men.[17]

The fifth characteristic of current gender arrangements is rooted in our general ambivalence toward the flesh, according to Dinnerstein. We hate the flesh because it limits our control and because we know it will ultimately die; yet we love it because it gives us pleasure. Our general ambivalence toward the body is, however, intensified in the case of women. On the one hand, women's bodies are powerful because they represent the forces of life; on the other hand, they are disgusting because they bleed and ooze. Because men's bodies do not carry as much symbolic baggage as women's do, men can imagine their own bodies to be largely free of the impurities and problems associated with women's bodies. Rather unfairly, men dispel any remaining ambivalence they may have about the male body by displacing their fears of the flesh onto the female body. The denigration of the female body as dirty, foul, and sinful causes women to deny their bodily core of self-respect, which then deprives them of the ability to reject confidently the negative feelings projected onto their bodies. As a result, many women come to hate their bodies and to punish them in many ways.[18] We can attribute bulimia, anorexia, and overeating at least in part to women's "flesh" problems.

Dinnerstein observed that the final characteristic of current gender arrangements is the tacit agreement between men and women that men should go out into the public sphere and women should stay behind within the private sphere. Women funnel their energies into symbiosis and personal relationships, eschewing enterprise for fear of putting power back into the hands of women, while men make enterprise their be all and end all, avoiding symbiosis and personal relationships for fear of losing control. Regrettably, the terms of this bargain permit both men and women to remain perpetual children, said Dinnerstein. Rather than taking responsibility for themselves and their world, men and women continue to play the kind of sex and gender games they should have stopped playing generations ago.

As Dinnerstein saw it, our destructive gender arrangements stem directly from women's nearly exclusive role in child rearing and our subsequent tendency to blame them for everything wrong about ourselves, especially that we are limited beings destined to err, decay, and die. We fault mother/woman for our limitations, speculated Dinnerstein, because she most likely presides when we skin our knees, break our toys, get the flu, or flunk our exams. Dinnerstein insisted we must stop blaming mother/women for the human condition if we want to overcome our destructive gender arrangements—a set of relationships symptomatic of our increasing inability to deal with one another and our world.

Ultimately, Dinnerstein's solution to the scapegoating of women was to propose a dual-parenting system, which she believed would, for example, help us overcome our ambivalence about enterprise. All people, but especially men, tend to use world building as a defense against death, said Dinnerstein. Indeed, the wonders of civilization can be read as the tragic testimony of a species that strives to achieve the good, the true, and the beautiful, knowing full well everyone and everything is doomed to disintegration. Given man's traditional role as world builder, society has not permitted him to express reservations about the ultimate worth of his worldly projects. But because of her traditional role as mother goddess—the "wise one" not easily deceived by the pomp and circumstance of civilization—society has given woman some license to articulate her misgivings about civilization. Indeed, said Dinnerstein, women often play the role of court jester, poking fun at the games men play; women's irreverence serves to release the tension that ripples through the world of enterprise. As a result, things never seem bad enough for us to change the course of history dramatically. But, observed Dinnerstein, dual world building and dual child rearing would enable all of us to see just how bad the world situation is. Because men and women would have an equal role in world building as well as child rearing, women would no longer be able to play the role of court jester. With nowhere to hide, not even in laughter, both sexes would have to put aside their games to reshape a fundamentally misshapen world.[19]

Nancy Chodorow

Less interested in sexual relationships than Dinnerstein, Nancy Chodorow wondered why women want to mother even when they do not have to do so.[20] Rejecting Freud's idea that for women, babies are substitutes for penises (the phallus), Chodorow found the answer to her question in a reconsideration of the pre-Oedipal stage of human psychosexual development. She pointed to the different "object-relational" experiences infants have with their mothers. According to Chodorow, the infant boy's pre-Oedipal relationship with his mother is sexually charged in a way that it is not for the infant girl. Feeling a sexual current between himself and his mother, the infant boy senses his mother's body is not like his. As he enters the Oedipal stage, the growing boy senses how much of a problem his mother's otherness is. He cannot remain attached to her (i.e., overwhelmingly in love with her) without risking his father's wrath. Not willing to take this risk, the son separates from his mother. The dawning realization that power and prestige are to be had through identification with men—in this case, the father—makes this process of separation less painful for the son than it might otherwise be. The boy's increasing contempt for women supposedly helps him define himself in opposition to the female sex his mother represents.[21]

In contrast to that between the mother and son, the mother-daughter pre-Oedipal relationship is characterized by what Chodorow termed "prolonged symbiosis" and "narcissistic overidentification." Because both the daughter and the mother are female, the infant girl's sense of gender and self is continuous with that of her mother. During the Oedipal stage, however, the mother-daughter symbiosis is weakened as the growing girl begins to desire what her father symbolizes: the autonomy and independence that characterizes a subjectivity, or an "I," on the one hand and the ability to sexually satisfy a woman—in this case her mother—on the other. Thus, as Chodorow interpreted it, penis envy arises for the girl both because the penis symbolizes male power and because it is the sexual organ that apparently satisfies her mother: "Every step of the way . . . a girl develops her relationship to her father while looking back at her mother—to see if her mother is envious, to make sure she is in fact separate, to see if she is really independent. Her turn to her father is both an attack on her mother and an expression of love for her."[22]

Although most girls do finally transfer their primary love from a female to a male object, Chodorow suggested this transfer is never complete. Whether a girl develops into a heterosexual woman or not, she will probably find her strongest emotional connections with other women. Thus the pre-Oedipal mother-daughter relationship provides a reference point for female friendships and lesbian relationships: the original mother-daughter symbiosis is never totally severed.[23]

Chodorow theorized that the psychosexual development of boys and girls has several social implications. The boy's separateness from his mother causes a limited ability to relate deeply to others; this emotional deficiency, however, prepares him well for work in the public sphere, which values single-minded efficiency, a survival-of-the-fittest mentality, and the ability to distance oneself from others so as to assess them objectively and dispassionately.[24] In contrast, the girl's connectedness to her mother causes an ability to relate to others, to weave intimate and intricate human connections—the kind of relationships that hold the private sphere together. Unfortunately, this very ability also makes it difficult for a girl to create a place for herself in the public world. Precisely because women develop permeable ego boundaries, they will tend to merge their own interests with those of others, making the identification and pursuit of any independent interests discomfiting.

Because of her view that women's capacity for relatedness is overdeveloped, whereas men's is underdeveloped, and that men's capacity for separateness is overdeveloped, whereas women's is underdeveloped, Chodorow, like Dinnerstein, hypothesized that a dual-parenting system would eliminate these asymmetries. Were children reared by both their mother and their father, boys and girls would grow up equally capable of merging and separating, of valuing their relationships with others and taking pride in their autonomy. More specifically, dual-parented children would realize both men and women are self-interested as well as other-directed.[25] Finally, dual-parented children would no longer view the home as women's domain and the workplace as men's domain. On the contrary, they would grow up thinking that all human beings should spend some of their time out in the world working and the rest of it at home with their families and friends.

Critiques of Dinnerstein and Chodorow

Critics challenged Dinnerstein and Chodorow on three grounds. First, they faulted these two theorists for claiming that the root causes of women's oppression are psychological rather than social.[26] According to Dinnerstein and Chodorow, our legal, political, economic, and cultural systems would be dramatically different if women did not want or need to mother. Women become mothers not because law, politics, economics, or culture force them to do so but because they want or need to be mothers. Critics of Dinnerstein and Chodorow countered that women's want or need to mother stems not from psychological states of mind but from material circumstances—that is, from specific social conditions, such as men's typically higher pay in the public labor force. In a society that gives far greater economic rewards to men than to women, it makes sense for women to convince themselves they like staying at home with their children. Women would stop wanting and needing to mother if social conditions were such that they earned as much as or more than men in the public labor force, for example.

Second, critics objected to what they perceived as both Dinnerstein's and Chodorow's failure to appreciate the diverse forms family structure takes—particularly, for explaining the pre-Oedipal and Oedipal stages solely in terms of the structures of the two-parent, white, bourgeois, heterosexual family and not considering families differentially constructed by race and/ or ethnicity. There are, after all, many sorts of family structures, ranging from single-parent to blended and extended families. Moreover, sometimes a child's parents are both of the same sex, as when a homosexual couple rears the child; sometimes a child has only one or no parents. If the Oedipus complex is indeed universal, we need richer accounts of how it plays out in different family structures. By focusing on the two-parent, heterosexual family structure, Dinnerstein and Chodorow missed an opportunity to formulate a fully feminist psychoanalytic theory.

Third, critics objected to Dinnerstein's and Chodorow's preferred solution for women's oppression, the creation and maintenance of a dual-parenting system. Jean Bethke Elshtain, for example, singled out Dinnerstein for especially strong words. Dinnerstein, said Elshtain, believed women have less need than men to control things and people. As a result of their special symbiotic relationships with their mothers, girls supposedly grow up to be nurturant, affectionate, and caring persons who are "less avid than men as hunters and killers, as penetrators of Mother Nature's secrets, plunderers of her treasure, outwitters of her constraints."[27] If this observation indeed applies to how women's psychology is shaped, asked Elshtain, what will happen to women's positive qualities when women spend as much time in the public realm as men currently do? Absolutely nothing, responded Dinnerstein. Women will remain caring, compassionate, and considerate, "even as they gain public roles, authority, power."[28] Not satisfied by Dinnerstein's response, Elshtain asked why we should assume that men are capable of developing good feminine qualities in the private realm but not that women are capable of developing bad masculine qualities in the public realm? If men can become more nurturant by taking care of their babies, then it seems women can become more aggressive by doing battle in boardrooms, courtrooms, and hospitals. In sum, observed Elshtain, Dinnerstein failed to ask herself what will be lost as well as gained for men and women in a dual-parenting/dual-working system.

Another critic, philosopher Janice Raymond, offered a critique of dual parenting that applied equally well to Dinnerstein and Chodorow. Raymond observed that dual parenting seems like a reasonable way to transform distorted gender relations. After all, if Dinnerstein is right that "male absence from child rearing" is leading the world to nuclear war and ecological chaos, then by all means let fathers spend as much time in the nursery as mothers do. However, warned Raymond, to insist dual parenting is the solution to human malaise is to elevate men again to the status of saviors. Men's rapid insertion into the nursery, unaccompanied by women's rapid promotion in the work world, threatens to give men even more power than they now have—personal and psychic power within the family as well as political and economic power outside the family. Additionally, to present dual parenting as the solution to all our gender woes is again to neglect "gyn-affection," or woman-to-woman attraction and interaction.[29] Specifically, dual parenting, as presented by Dinnerstein and Chodorow, does not compare and contrast lesbian households in which one woman stays at home and the other goes to work with lesbian households in which neither woman is the primary parent or worker.

As Raymond saw it, that women mainly mother is not the problem. Rather, the real problem is that women mother when, where, and how men want them to. Girls are taught to direct their love away from women and toward men. They see their mothers loving their fathers in a way so special that girls surmise men must be worthy of a love that women themselves do not deserve. Raymond speculated that were girls to see their mothers loving other women in an equally special way, they would grow up with more positive feelings about themselves and other women. Despite their mutual claim that female bonds are stronger and deeper than male bonds, observed Raymond, neither Dinnerstein nor Chodorow envisioned powerful and strong women joining together in communities of care—communities supportive enough to give women as well as children the kind of love they would not otherwise find.[30] Women do not need men to help them mother.

Adrienne Rich added force to Raymond's critique of Dinnerstein and Chodorow, observing that both accepted without question the assumption that men are the appropriate object of women's sexual love and emotional energy. Specifically, she commented that both Dinnerstein and Chodorow are "stuck . . . trying to reform a man-made institution—compulsory heterosexuality—as if, despite profound emotional impulses and complementarities drawing women toward women, there is a mystical/biological heterosexual inclination, a 'preference' or 'choice' that draws women toward men."[31] Rich found it particularly puzzling that neither Dinnerstein nor Chodorow, both of whom focused on the pre-Oedipal stage, where mother love reigns supreme, thought to reject the institution of compulsory heterosexuality. Lesbianism rather than heterosexuality would seem to be "normal" for women. Why on earth, then, do girls decide to trade the fulfilling intensity of pre-Oedipal mother love for Oedipal father love? That seems the appropriate question for feminists to ask, in Rich's estimation.

Juliet Mitchell

Although usually considered a socialist feminist (see Chapter 3), Juliet Mitchell can, at least in her later years, also be viewed as a psychoanalytic feminist. As such, Mitchell, like Dinnerstein and Chodorow, sought to use the feminist ideas buried in Freud's views on the unconscious.[32] In her understanding Freud's theory is not some simpleminded enunciation of the slogan "Biology is destiny." On the contrary, it demonstrates how social beings emerge from merely biological ones. Psychosexual development is a process of the "social interpretation" of biology, not the inexorable manifestation of biological destiny.[33] Although Freud studied psychosexual development among a specific group of people (the petite bourgeoisie of nineteenth-century Vienna), said Mitchell, his analysis is applicable to psychosexual development among any group. However, continued Mitchell, it is important to separate the particular emphases of Freud's analysis, its incidental features, from its general parameters, its essence. After all, certain things about nineteenth-century Viennese, bourgeois psychosexual development are unique to it and do not apply, for example, to twenty-first-century working-class Black/African American families or upper-class Chinese families. Still, most kinds of biological families seem to play out some version of the family drama Freud named the Oedipal situation.[34]

When Mitchell agreed with Freud that the Oedipal situation is universal, she meant that without some sort of prohibition on incest, human society is an impossibility. According to structuralist Claude Lévi-Strauss, on whose work Mitchell relied, if sexual relations are permitted within the biological family, it will have no impetus to form reproductive alliances with other biological families to create the expanded network we call "society"[35] and to build up the genetic diversity of humankind.

As Lévi-Strauss explained, the incest taboo, by forbidding sexual relations within the biological family, forces people to form other, larger social organizations. Of course, a mere ban on sexual intercourse within biological families is not enough. There must also be some way to facilitate sexual intercourse between biological families. Lévi-Strauss claimed this takes the form of an exchange system between biological families—specifically, the exchange of women from one group of men to another.[36] Because the incest taboo forbids a woman from marrying her brother or father, these men will encourage her to marry a man they select outside the biological family. According to Lévi-Strauss, this male-controlled exchange of women constitutes humans' "decisive break" with the beasts. Moreover, added Mitchell, the patriarchal character of human society explains men's exchange of women rather than vice versa.[37]

Critiques of Mitchell

Mitchell's feminist critics found much of her analysis of the basics of psychoanalysis useful but remained unconvinced by it. They asked Mitchell why women rather than men are exchanged and why the father rather than the mother has power over the family. Mitchell sought the answers to these questions in Freud's *Totem and Taboo*,[38] in which he described the primal murder of an original mythical father. The totem is the symbol of the father, and associated with it are two taboos, one against destruction of the totem and one against incest. In the myth, a group of brothers band together to kill the feared and envied father—feared for his power, envied for his harem of women. After their act of patricide, the brothers, feeling very guilty and not knowing quite what to substitute for the law of the father, eventually reestablish his two taboos. Freud commented that whereas the brothers' reinscription of the totem taboo is "founded wholly on emotional motives," their reinscription of the incest taboo has a practical as well as an emotional basis.

Sexual desires do not unite but divide men. Although the brothers had banded together to overcome their father, they were all one another's rivals regarding the women. Each of them would have wished, like his father, to have all the women to himself. The new organization would have collapsed in a struggle of all against all, for none of them was of such overmastering strength as to be able to take on his father's part with success. Thus the brothers had no alternative, if they were to live together, but to institute the law against incest, by which they all alike renounced the women whom they desired and who had been their chief motive for dispatching their father.[39] In sum, the brothers must refrain from incest; only then can patriarchy, in which they have a vested interest, thrive.

Although Mitchell's feminist critics dismissed the myth of the primal crime, Mitchell countered that it is extraordinarily powerful and speaks loudly to the collective human unconscious. The figure of the father stands for the desire of human beings to transcend, to assert their will, to somehow control their lives. The father (and here Mitchell borrowed from Jacques Lacan, discussed later in this chapter) is "he who is ultimately capable of saying 'I am who I am.'"[40] The father represents success in the so-called Symbolic order. Disentangled from confusions and struggles, he is clear thinking, far seeing, and powerful. Because he can say, "I am who I am," he can name things as he wishes. Yet, however seductive the image of the transcendent father and the omnipotent patriarch, the image is also the source of women's oppression, conceded Mitchell. Thus, to the degree that the successful resolution of the Oedipus complex leads to patriarchy as well as civilization, it requires reinterpretation. We must find some way to explain psychosexual development that does not purchase civilization at women's expense.[41]

Responding in part to Mitchell's challenge, noted feminist anthropologist and theorist Sherry Ortner observed, "The Oedipus complex is part of a theory of the development of the person. It is powerful, and significantly, an eminently dialectical theory: the person evolves through a process of struggle with and ultimate supersession . . . of symbolic figures of love, desire, and authority. As a general structure (without gender valences attached to the particular figures), there seems no need to dispose of (and . . . probably no possibility of disposing of) this process."[42] Ortner theorized that as historical accretions, gender valences can be changed, and their change can free the Oedipal process from its current patriarchal agenda.[43] In other words, according to Ortner, no law mandates that maleness and femaleness be understood in only one way or that maleness be privileged over femaleness.

In developing her argument, Ortner insisted that labeling authority, autonomy, and universalism as male and love, dependence, and particularism as female is not essential to the Oedipus complex. Gender valences are simply the consequences of a child's experiences with men and women. A society changes children's ideas about maleness and femaleness by changing their experiences with men and women. Does this mean, then, that the implementation of Dinnerstein's and Chodorow's system of dual parenting would, after all, be enough to effect a different telling of the Oedipal tale? Or must society undergo a more radical social transformation than this to eliminate the gender valences that favor one sex over the other? Must we, for example, enter Marge Piercy's Mattapoisett, a fictional world in which children are gestated ex utero and reared by three co-mothers (two men and one woman or two women and one man)?[44] The possibilities for social transformation in general and for family structure in particular would seem to be many, each requiring a different telling of the Oedipal tale, according to Mitchell.

With greater or lesser success, Chodorow, Dinnerstein, and Mitchell challenged a strict Freudian account of psychosocial development. They tried to provide explanations for psychosexual development that would help rather than hinder women's liberation. Still, this trio of psychoanalytic feminists did not go far enough, in critics' estimation. They did not emphasize, as some later psychoanalytic feminists would, that to understand why we construct men/maleness/masculinity and women/femaleness/femininity as we do, we may not simply take as gospel a general theory of the psyche. Commented Chris Weedon, "If we assume that subjectivity is discursively produced in social institutions and processes, there is no pre-given reason why we should privilege sexual relations above other forms of social relations as constitutive of identity. There may, of course, be historically specific reasons for doing this in a particular analysis, but they will not be universal. Furthermore, if we are concerned specifically with the question of sexual identity, then psychoanalysis itself must be looked at as one discourse among many which has been influential in constituting inherently patriarchal norms of sexuality."[45] Weedon's point is this: if we think that we can change current psychosocial identity by, for example, instituting a practice such as dual parenting, then we can also change it, albeit differently, by instituting an alternative practice such as single parenting. As Weedon put it, "Discourse constitutes rather than reflects meaning."[46] Everyday practice precedes the formulation of general theory.

Observations such as Weedon's partly explain why, in recent years, a new generation of psychoanalytic feminists, including Luce Irigaray and Julia Kristeva, have found French psychoanalyst Jacques Lacan's reinterpretation of Freud useful. For Lacan, anatomy is not destiny; language is. Therefore, to the degree that language can be changed, so can destiny.

Contemporary Psychoanalytic Thought: Focus on Jacques Lacan

Jacques Lacan on the Symbolic Order

Structural anthropologist Claude Lévi-Strauss contended that a series of interrelated signs, roles, and rituals regulates every society. Jacques Lacan termed this series the "Symbolic order."[47] To function adequately within society, a child must be incorporated into the Symbolic order by undergoing three stages of psychosexual development.[48] In the first, or pre-Oedipal, phase—termed the "Imaginary" by Lacan—an infant is completely unaware of its own ego boundaries. In fact, it has no sense of where the mother's body ends and its own begins. As far as the infant is concerned, it and the mother are one. Moreover, during this stage of development, the infant is neither feminine nor masculine but possibly either, because the infant has yet to acquire language.

In the second, or mirror, phase (also part of the Imaginary), the infant thinks the image of itself, as reflected through the "mirror" of the mother's gaze, is its real self. According to Lacan, this is a normal stage in self-development. Before the infant can see itself as a self, it must see itself as seen by the mother—that is, as another.[49] Lacan claimed that the process of infantile self-discovery serves as a paradigm for all subsequent relations; the self always discovers more about itself through the eyes of the other.

The third, or Oedipal phase, in Lacan's scheme of things includes a period of growing estrangement between the mother and the maturing child. Unlike the infant, the child does not view itself as a unity; rather, it regards the mother as the other—someone to whom the child must communicate its wishes and, therefore, someone who, due to the limitations of language, can never truly fulfill those wishes. During the Oedipal phase proper, the intervention of the father erodes the already weakened mother-child relationship.[50] Fearing symbolic castration, the child separates from the mother in return for a medium (language) through which to maintain some connection with the mother—the original, never-to-be-had-again source of total gratification.[51]

Like Freud, Lacan maintained that boys and girls experience the splitting from the mother differently. In the Oedipal phase, the boy rejects identification with his mother, eschewing the undifferentiated and silent state of the womb, and bonds with his anatomically similar father, who represents the Symbolic order, the word. Through identification with his father, the boy not only enters into subjecthood and individuality but also internalizes the dominant order, the rules of society. In contrast, because of her anatomy, the girl cannot wholly identify with her father in the psychosexual drama. Nor can she totally disidentify with her mother. As a result, the girl cannot fully accept and internalize the Symbolic order.

From this situation, we can draw one of two conclusions: on the one hand, that women are virtually excluded from the Symbolic order; on the other hand, that women are repressed within the Symbolic order, forced into it unwillingly. A man with a predilection for contradictions, Lacan seemed to draw both conclusions. He thought that because women cannot totally internalize the law of the father, this law must be imposed on them from the outside. Women are given the same words as men: masculine words. These words cannot express what women feel, however; masculine words can express only what men think women feel. Lacking feminine words, women must either babble outside the Symbolic order or remain silent within it.

Critique of Jacques Lacan

Thus far, it seems Lacan was no more able than Freud to find a comfortable place for women within his framework. Because women cannot completely resolve the Oedipal complex, they remain strangers in the Symbolic order, largely unknown because of their phallic wordlessness. Lacan speculated that were society to try to do the impossible—to know women—it would have to begin its inquiry at the pre-Oedipal level of women's sexual pleasure (jouissance). But like women themselves, their jouissance cannot be known, because it can be neither thought nor spoken in the phallic language of the fathers. It leads a repressed existence at the margins of the Symbolic order, seeking a nonphallic language capable of thinking and speaking it. Were women's jouissance to find the words to express itself, it would burst the Symbolic order and the order's major prop, patriarchy.

"French" Psychoanalytic Feminism: Focus on Luce Irigaray and Julia Kristeva

Luce Irigaray on the Feminine

Although French psychoanalyst Luce Irigaray found much of value in Lacanian (and, for that matter, Freudian) thought, she aimed overall to liberate, in her terms, "feminine" from "masculine" philosophical thought. We will recall that, in Lacan, the Imaginary is the prelinguistic, pre-Oedipal domain in which the child initially mistakes itself for its own mirror image. On realizing that the mirror image is distinct from its own real self, the child enters the Symbolic order. In this realm, the child can assert itself as an "I" in language, a distinct subjectivity, separate from other subjectivities. Like Lacan, Irigaray drew contrasts between the Imaginary and the Symbolic order, but unlike Lacan, she posited within the Imaginary a male/masculine and a female/feminine imaginary.[52] In other words, for Irigaray, the psyche is never bisexual but always either male/masculine or female/feminine.

For Lacan, the Imaginary is a prison within which the infant is captive to illusory images. After successfully completing the Oedipal phase, boys are liberated from the Imaginary and enter the Symbolic order, the realm of language and selfhood. Because they never completely resolve the Oedipal phase, however, girls either remain behind in the Imaginary or enter the Symbolic order mute. In opposition to Lacan, Irigaray refused to bemoan this state of affairs. Instead, she viewed women's total existence in the Imaginary or wordlessness in the Symbolic order as two situations full of untapped possibilities for both women and society.

Irigaray noted that, at present, anything we know about the Imaginary and women, including women's sexual desire, we know from a male point of view. In other words, the only kind of woman we know is the "masculine feminine," the phallic feminine, woman as man sees her. But, said Irigaray, there is another kind of woman to know, the "feminine feminine," woman as women see her.[53] This woman must not be defined, however, through any statement definitively asserting what the true feminine is. Defining woman in any one way will re-create the phallic feminine: "To claim that the feminine can be expressed in the form of a concept is to allow oneself to be caught up again in a system of 'masculine' representations, in which women are trapped in a system or meaning which serves the auto-affection of the (masculine) subject."[54] Obstructing the progression of women's thought out of the Imaginary is the concept of sameness, the thought product of masculine narcissism and singularity.

Irigaray adopted the word "speculum" (a cylindrical, hinged medical instrument used in vaginal examinations) to capture the nature and function of the idea of sameness in Western philosophy and psychoanalysis. "Specularization," commented Toril Moi, "suggests not only the mirror-image that comes from the visual penetration of the speculum inside the vagina" but also "the necessity of postulating a subject that is capable of reflecting on its own being."[55] Because of narcissistic philosophical "specularization"—epitomized in the medieval description of God as thought thinking thought—masculine discourse has never been able to understand woman, or the feminine, as anything other than a reflection of man, or the masculine. Therefore, it is impossible to think the "feminine feminine" within the structures of patriarchal thought. When men look at women, they see not women but reflections of the image and likeness of men.

In her study of Western philosophy and psychoanalysis, Irigaray found sameness everywhere. Her analysis of sameness in Freud's theory was particularly important because she used it to criticize his theory of female sexuality. Freud saw the little girl as a deficiency or negativity, as a "little man" without a penis. He suppressed the notion of difference, characterizing the feminine as a lack: Woman is a reflection of man, the same as a man except in her sexuality. Female sexuality, because it does not mirror male sexuality, is an absence, or lack, of the male's sexuality. Where woman does not reflect man, she does not exist and, stressed Irigaray, will never exist until the Oedipus complex is exploded.[56]

Irigaray claimed that if women want to experience themselves as something other than "waste" or "excess" in the structured margins of man's world, they should take three steps.[57] First, they should create a female language, eschewing gender-neutral language as forcefully as they eschew male language. The search for "neutrality" is not only pointless (because no one is really neutral about anything), claimed Irigaray, but also morally misguided. Trying to hide the identity of the speaker from the reader/listener is cowardly. Stressing that women will not find liberation in objectivity, Irigaray noted, "Neither *I* nor *you*, nor *we* appears in the language of science."[58] Science resists the "subjective," often because it wishes to mask the identities of its agents. Distressed by the unwillingness of science—and, for that matter, traditional Western philosophy and psychoanalysis—to take responsibility for its own words and deeds, Irigaray urged women to find the courage to speak in the active voice, avoiding at all costs the false security and ultimate inauthenticity of the passive voice.

Second, women should create a female sexuality. Irigaray contrasted the singularity implied by the male sexual organ with the multiplicity implied by the female sexual organs. In particular, she localized the feminine voice in the labia, "two lips" that reveal woman to be neither one nor two. Woman is not two, because the labia belong to a single woman's body, "which keeps woman in touch with herself, but without any possibility of distinguishing what is touching from what is touched."[59] However, woman is not one, either, because the labia represent a woman's multiple and diffuse (nonphallic) sexuality: "So woman does not have a sex organ? She has at least two of them, but they are not identifiable as ones. Indeed, she has many more. Her sexuality is always at least double, goes even further; it is plural."[60]

Irigaray did not simply contrast the plural, circular, and aimless vaginal/clitoral libidinal economy of women with the singular, linear, and teleological phallic libidinal economy of men. She also argued that the expression of these libidinal economies is not restricted to sexuality but instead extends to all forms of human expression, including social structures. Just as the penetration of the penis prevents the lips from touching, so the phallic unity of the Symbolic order represses the multiplicity of female sexuality. Thus, patriarchy is the social manifestation of masculine libidinal economy and will remain the order of the day until the repressed "feminine feminine" is set free. Women can unshackle this potentiality, however, only through lesbian and autoerotic practice. As women explore the multifaceted terrain of the female body, they can learn to think thoughts, speak words, and do deeds powerful enough to displace the phallus.

Third, in their efforts to be themselves, women should mime the mimes men have imposed on women. Women should take men's images of women and reflect them back to men in magnified proportions. Through miming, women can "*undo* the effects of phallocentric discourse simply by *overdoing* them."[61] For example, if men view women as sex objects, fetishizing women's breasts in particular, then women should pump up their breasts as big as possible and walk into church on Sunday, their breasts fully exposed in all their naked glory, as if to say, "Here, boys; we know what is on your minds. So look. See if we care." To be sure, conceded Irigaray, miming is not without its perils. The distinction between miming the patriarchal definition of woman so as to subvert it and merely fulfilling it is not clear. In their attempts to overdo the definition of woman, women may inadvertently be drawn back into it. Nevertheless, despite this risk, women should take every opportunity to raise a ruckus in the Symbolic order.

The preceding discussion reveals a clear tension between Irigaray's competing convictions that we must finally end the process of labeling and categorizing and that we cannot help but engage in this process.[62] Because Irigaray dared to express both of these convictions, sometimes in the same breath, her critics described her as self-contradictory. Rather than feeling embarrassed by the ambiguities and ambivalence in her writing, however, Irigaray took increasing pleasure in them. For Irigaray, self-contradiction is a form of rebellion against the logical consistency required by phallocentrism: "[Woman] is indefinitely other in herself. This is doubtless why she is said to be whimsical, incomprehensible, agitated, capricious . . . not to mention her language, in which 'she' sets off in all directions leaving 'him' unable to discern the coherence of any meaning. Hers are contradictory words, somewhat mad from the standpoint of reason, inaudible for whoever listens to them with ready-made grids, with a fully elaborated code in hand."[63] Refusing to be pinned down even by her own theory, Irigaray vowed to liberate her life

from the phallocentric concepts that would squeeze its multiple meanings—
its exciting differences—into boring sameness.

Julia Kristeva: Semiotic Versus Symbolic Language

Like Irigaray, psychoanalytic feminist Julia Kristeva relied on Lacan's work.
She largely accepted Lacan's identification of the pre-Oedipal stage with the
Imaginary (see page 172) and the Oedipal and post-Oedipal stages with the
Symbolic order. However, Kristeva added to Lacan's account a further complexity. She claimed that a certain modality of language, which she termed
the "semiotic," is the exclusive modality of language in the pre-Oedipal period, whereas another modality of language, the "symbolic," is the dominant
though not exclusive modality of language in the Oedipal and post-Oedipal
stages. Furthermore, she associated the semiotic with maternal/poetic language and the symbolic with paternal/logical language. As Kristeva saw it, on
entering the Symbolic order as described by Lacan, the child brings with it
some of the language of the Imaginary. However, most of that language remains behind, because it is fundamentally at odds with the Symbolic order.
Thus, for Kristeva, the semiotic exists both inside and outside the Symbolic
order, whereas for Lacan, it presumably exists only outside the Symbolic
order.[64]

Further explaining the semiotic-symbolic distinction, Kristeva claimed
that the symbolic modality of language is that aspect of meaning-making
that permits us to make rational arguments; it produces linear, rational, objective, and grammatical writing. In contrast to the symbolic modality of
language, the semiotic is that aspect of meaning-making that permits us to
express feelings. It is, as Kelly Oliver has noted, "the drives as they make
their way into signification."[65] The semiotic produces circular, emotional,
subjective, and rule-breaking writing. Kristeva believed that a liberated person is able to play not only in the space between the pre-Oedipal Imaginary
and the post-Oedipal Symbolic order but also in the space between the semiotic and symbolic aspects of meaning-making inside the Symbolic order.[66] In
other words, she claimed that the liberated person can move freely between
the feminine and the masculine, chaos and order, revolution and the status
quo.

Unlike Irigaray, Kristeva resisted identification of the "feminine" with
biological women and the "masculine" with biological men. She maintained
that when the child enters the Symbolic order, it may identify with either
the mother or the father. Depending on the choice it makes, the child will
be more or less "feminine" or "masculine." Thus, men can exist and write in

a "feminine" mode, and women can exist and write in a "masculine" mode. One of Kristeva's most controversial claims is that the "feminine" writings of men have more revolutionary potential than those of women. Culture is more upset when a man speaks like a woman than when a woman speaks like a man, said Kristeva. As Oliver put it, Kristeva thought that "whereas in males an identification with the maternal semiotic is revolutionary because it breaks with traditional conceptions of sexual difference, for females an identification with the maternal does not break traditional conceptions of sexual difference."[67]

Kristeva's main emphasis was on difference in general rather than sexual difference in particular. Rejecting traditional accounts of two binary sexes, of two opposed gender identities, Kristeva admitted that there are, nonetheless, male and female sexual differences. Like Dinnerstein and Chodorow, she located the beginnings of sexual difference in the child's relation to the mother; but in Kristeva's version of this relationship, a child's sexual identity is specifically formed through a struggle to separate from the mother's body. The male does this not by rejecting his mother's body but by "abjecting" it—that is, by reconceiving it as an object that represents everything that is disgusting about being a human being (excrement, blood, mucus).[68] In contrast, the more the female identifies with her mother's body, the more trouble she has rejecting or abjecting it. To the degree that the rejected or abjected maternal body is associated with women per se, women are grouped with society's "misfits"—Jews, Gypsies, homosexuals, deformed or diseased people—an identification that would, contrary to what Kristeva has said elsewhere, motivate women, far more than men, to be revolutionaries.

In Dorothy Leland's estimation, Kristeva's resolution of the Oedipal tale is particularly disturbing because it offers women only three "options"—none entirely good—to avoid psychosis.[69] The first option, which Kristeva considered undesirable for women, is total father identification. According to Kristeva, Electra, who had her mother, Clytemnestra, killed so as to "avenge her father," is the perfect example of a totally father-identified woman.[70] Clytemnestra must be punished, indeed eliminated, because she has dared to take a lover, thereby exposing to the world her jouissance (instinctual pleasure), a jouissance that the patriarchal order forbids. By having her mother killed, Electra expresses her hate not only of her mother's jouissance but also of her own jouissance. Electra's expression of mother-hate/self-hate "perpetuates the patriarchal social/symbolic order," said Leland.[71]

The second option for women, which Kristeva also considered undesirable, is total mother identification. Because she largely accepted Lacan's view that to become civilized, the child must repress both its jouissance and its symbiotic relation to the mother, Kristeva viewed total mother identification as condemning women to "forever remain in a sulk in the face of history, politics, and social affairs."[72] In other words, the price of total mother identification is not being permitted to be an adult.

The third option for women, which Kristeva considered desirable, is to avoid both total father identification and total mother identification:

> Let us refuse both extremes. Let us know that an ostensibly masculine, paternal identification . . . is necessary in order to have a voice in the chapter of politics and history . . . [But] let us right away be wary of the premium on narcissism that such an integration can carry; let us reject the development of a "homologous" woman [i.e., an Electra] who is finally capable and virile; and let us rather act on the socio-politico-historical stage as her negative: that is, act first with all those who refuse and "swim against the tide"—all who rebel against the existing relations of production and reproduction. But let us not take the role of Revolutionary either, whether male or female: let us on the contrary refuse all roles to summon [a] truth outside time, a truth that is neither true nor false, that cannot be fitted into the order of speech and social symbolism.[73]

By "truth," Kristeva meant the semiotic modality of language, said Leland.[74] Yet Kristeva did not view as desirable the total replacement of the symbolic modality of language in the Symbolic order with the semiotic modality. Any attempt to totally substitute the symbolic with the semiotic would, in her estimation, destroy the Symbolic order and, with it, civilization. Everyone would be propelled back into the pre-Oedipal stage, or the Imaginary. Permanent existence in this stage is nothing more or less than psychosis, according to Kristeva. Thus, according to Leland, Kristeva recommended specifically that women who did not want to go crazy engage in an "impossible dialectic," a "permanent alienation" between the semiotic ("maternal" jouissance) and the Symbolic ("paternal" power or law).[75]

Critiques of Freudian, Lacanian, and Psychoanalytic Feminist Thought

Although we have already provided critiques of Dinnerstein, Chodorow, Mitchell, Lacan, Irigaray, and Kristeva, here we add two more general critiques of psychoanalytic feminism. Readers may also wish to consult Simone de Beauvoir's critique of Freud in Chapter 9, for many of the criticisms directed at psychoanalytic feminism are better directed at Freud himself. Rightly or wrongly, he is often dismissed as a sexist who made men the normative representatives of humanity.

Critique One: Psychoanalytic Feminism Is Very White and Eurocentric—Indeed, Quite "French"

Some critics of psychoanalytic feminism view it as the product of mostly white French intellectuals.[76] This critique seems somewhat unfair because there exists a thriving community of Anglo-American psychoanalytic feminist thinkers, including Juliet Mitchell, Teresa Brennen, Elizabeth Gross, Jane Gallop, and Jacqueline Rose.[77] Still, it is an empirical fact that few women of color engage in psychoanalytic feminist thought. This is puzzling, given contemporary psychoanalytic feminists' insistence on stressing woman's/women's sexual multiplicities and identities. So long as race and ethnicity remain relatively invisible in psychoanalytic feminist thought, women of color are not likely to find it a welcoming way of viewing themselves or a helpful way of understanding others.

Critique Two: Psychoanalytic Feminists Are Too Beholden to Freud, Lacan, or Some Other Major Male Thinker

Although it is our opinion that most contemporary psychoanalytic feminists have gone beyond Freud or Lacan, it remains an open question whether it is possible to construct a totally nonpatriarchal psychoanalytic feminism. Specifically, are there more convincing stories to tell about human psychosexual development than some version of the Western Oedipal tale?[78] Such accounts may exist in non-Western traditions and are therefore an avenue for feminist speculation and exploration, as well as a possible corrective for some of what Lacan and Freud have written about sexuality and women.

Conclusion

Like all schools of feminist thought, psychoanalytic feminism remains a work in progress. In "Psychoanalytic Feminism," Emily Zakin praised psychoanalytic feminism for paying "attention to the core constituents of civilization [and] to the nuclei of sexual differences and communal affiliation."[79] She also insisted that psychoanalytic feminist thought helps "explain the perpetuation of masculine power and enables [other] feminist theorists to articulate possible correctives, challenges, routes of amelioration, or ethical interruptions that go to the roots of political life and to its beyond and do not simply operate on the given social terrain."[80]

All who engage in feminist thinking may not share Zakin's enthusiasm for psychoanalytic feminism. Still, it provides us with a way of accessing our "unconscious"—the place where our drives and nonrational powers reside.[81]

Psychoanalytic feminism reveals human opaqueness to self and others. The unconscious, said Zakin, "cannot be assumed to be inherently either a transgressive or a conservative force, but an unreliable one, promoting revolt or rebellion sometimes, intransigence and rigid border preservation at other times."[82] If this is the case, the more that psychoanalytic feminists take the lead in explaining the unconscious, the better off all people, particularly women, will be.

Questions for Discussion

1. Discuss how historic Freudian constructs such as "penis envy" and "rejection of the mother" contribute to a generally unflattering societal portrait of women.

2. Consider Dinnerstein's dual-parenting and dual-world-building solution to current skewed gender arrangements. How might such a solution repair such grievances as the imbalance within male-female sexual relationships, the objectification and control of women, and the disproportionate numbers of women in the private sphere and men in the public.

3. Provide examples of the Lacanian notion that because both men and women are provided with only a masculine vocabulary (lacking adequate avenues for feminine expression), women therefore either must remain silent within the symbolic order or "babble" outside it. Give illustrations from both public and private life. Can Irigaray's suggestion to create a female language help alleviate these situations?

4. In what way(s), if any, is Kristeva optimistic or pessimistic about women's social status and sexual development?

5. Is there a distinctly feminist way for a psychiatrist to do psychoanalysis?

7

Care-Focused Feminism

Like psychoanalytic feminists, care-focused feminists are interested in the differences that distinguish the female from the male psyche. However, unlike psychoanalytic feminists, care-focused feminists do not emphasize boys' and girls' psychosexual development. If they stress any aspect of children's development in particular, it is their psychomoral development. According to care-focused feminists, boys and girls grow up into men and women with gender-specific values and virtues that serve to empower men and disempower women in a patriarchal society. Thus, we must ask whether women's liberation will be best served by women adopting male values and virtues, by men adopting female values and virtues, or by everyone adopting a mix of both. If the answer to this crucial question is that men and women should share a morality encompassing an equal mix of female and male virtues and values, then how should we inculcate this morality in boys and girls? Is dual parenting the best means to achieve the end of gender equity in everything, including the practice of morality? Or do care-focused feminists propose another means to achieve this worthy goal?

The Roots of Care-Focused Feminism

Carol Gilligan

In her groundbreaking book *In a Different Voice*,[1] moral psychologist Carol Gilligan noted that men's emphasis on separation and autonomy leads them to develop a style of moral reasoning that focuses on justice, fairness, and rights. In contrast, women's emphasis on connections and relationships leads them to develop a style of moral reasoning that stresses the needs and re-sponsibilities of particular people. Gilligan also claimed that because most experts in moral development theory have used male as opposed to human norms to measure women's as well as men's moral development, they have mistakenly concluded that women are less morally developed than men. Deeply disturbed by this negative assessment of women, Gilligan set out to prove that not women, but the standards used to judge women's growth as moral persons, must be changed.[2]

In articulating her position that women are no less morally developed than men, Gilligan singled out her former mentor, Harvard's Lawrence Kohlberg, for particular criticism. According to Kohlberg, moral develop-ment consists of a six-stage process through which a child must pass to be-come a fully functioning moral agent. Stage one is "the punishment and obedience orientation." To avoid the stick of punishment or receive the car-rot of reward, the young child does as it is told. Stage two is "the instrumen-tal relativist orientation." Based on a limited principle of reciprocity ("you scratch my back, and I'll scratch yours"), the young child does what meets others' needs, but only if its own needs are thereby met. Stage three is "the interpersonal concordance or 'good boy–nice girl' orientation." The matur-ing child conforms to prevailing moral norms so as to secure the approbation of other people. Stage four is "the 'law and order' orientation." The maturing child begins to do its duty, show respect for authority, and maintain the given social order for its own sake. Stage five is "the social-contract legalistic orientation." The young adult adopts an essentially utilitarian moral point of view according to which individuals are permitted to do as they please, pro-vided they refrain from harming other people in the process. Stage six is "the universal ethical principle orientation." The adult adopts an essentially Kan-tian moral point of view that provides a moral perspective universal enough to serve as a critique of any conventional morality. The adult is now ruled not by self-interest, the opinion of others, or the force of legal convention but by self-legislated and self-imposed universal principles such as justice, reciprocity, and respect for the dignity of human persons.[3]

Gilligan took exception to Kohlberg's sixfold scale not because she re-garded it as entirely without merit but because girls and women tested on it rarely got past stage three, the "good boy–nice girl" stage. Fearing that people would interpret this test result as confirming Freud's view that women are less moral than men, Gilligan set out to prove that women's low scores on Kohlberg's test were undeserved. She hypothesized that women did poorly on Kohlberg's scale because of its flawed design. The test was, in her estimation, constructed to measure men's method of moral reasoning, as if it were the standard of human moral reasoning. Due to the scale's faulty construction, women who did not morally reason like men did poorly on it. Gilligan claimed the solution was not to construct a test to measure women's method of moral reasoning, as if that were the standard of human moral reasoning, but to develop a test that could accurately measure both men's and women's moral development. Neither men nor women should be viewed as the morally inferior sex.[4]

Importantly, in Gilligan's estimation, women's style of moral reasoning is no better or worse than men's; it is simply different. Moreover, stressed Gilligan, although a woman or a man might, as an individual or as a member of a group, typically engage in a certain style of moral reasoning, fully developed moral agents are likely to display a marked ability to speak the languages of care and justice equally well. Had Gilligan stopped her research on moral development with this observation, we could confidently conclude that, for her, the morally androgynous person is the paradigm moral agent. However, after writing *In a Different Voice*, Gilligan hinted that the ideal moral thinker might after all be more inclined to an ethics of care than an ethics of justice. In her anthology *Mapping the Moral Domain*, she expressed concern that a high percentage of today's adolescents "[tend] to characterize care-focused solutions or inclusive problem-solving strategies as utopian or outdated."[5] Gilligan worried that because our culture overvalues scientific, objective, and rational thinking, teachers urge students to use only their head and not also their heart in moral deliberation. Challenging the wisdom of this pedagogical approach, Gilligan claimed that in many ways, young children who have not been schooled to suppress their feelings seem more moral than adults. Precisely because of their strong attachments to family members and friends, young children seem not only to care about the feelings, wants, needs, and interests of those to whom they are related but also to act upon these sentiments. That girls are more likely than boys to grow into adults who continue to respond to other people's need to be loved and appreciated probably signals not women's moral weakness, then, but their moral strength.

Nel Noddings

Similarly to Gilligan, Nel Noddings observed that traditional ethics has favored theoretical as opposed to practical modes of reasoning and "masculine" as opposed to "feminine" values. Rather than using the interpretive style of reasoning that characterizes the humanities and social sciences, most traditional ethicists have instead used the deductive-nomological style of reasoning that characterizes math and the natural sciences. So focused have most traditional ethicists been on "principles and propositions" and "terms such as justification, fairness, and justice," said Noddings, that "human caring and the memory of caring and being cared for . . . have not received attention except as outcomes of ethical behavior."[6]

Noddings's assertion relates to one of Gilligan's tentative suggestions in *Mapping the Moral Domain*[7]—namely, that care is probably ethics' foundation and justice its supplement or corrective. Noddings underscored that, in its preoccupation with universals, traditional ethics has overlooked the particulars. Specifically, she commented that deontologists (especially Kantians) and utilitarians either neglect the kind of relationships that exist between intimates or analyze them in highly counterintuitive ways. For example, some utilitarians suggest that if parents can net more overall utility by depriving their child of a much-wanted birthday gift so that they can partially fund a much-needed operation for their disadvantaged neighbor's child, then it is their duty as utilitarians to do so. Perhaps this somewhat atypical course of action may be the morally preferable one. Yet it is not clear that parents have a duty to deprive their child of a much-wanted gift, especially if the child will interpret their act as a sign of parental coldness. Insofar as parents are concerned, not all children are created equal. Their own count for more, in Noddings's estimation.

Whatever quarrels Noddings had with rationalistic ethics, however, she did not seek to substitute "eros, the feminine spirit," for "logos," the masculine spirit.[8] She argued not that logos, understood as the logic of reasoning, has no role to play in ethics but that eros, understood as an attitude "rooted in receptivity, relatedness, and responsiveness,"[9] is an alternative and more basic approach to ethics than logos. As important as analyzing the concept of goodness is, Noddings suggests, ethics begins at the emotional level, with the desire to be a good person, rather than at the intellectual level, with a rational reconstruction of the concept of "goodness."

Among the features of traditional ethics that most disturbed Noddings is its tendency to undervalue caring, as if it were easy to truly care for people. Although Noddings conceded that women can speak the language of justice as well as men can, she insisted that this language is not their native tongue. Women enter the moral realm through a "different door" than men, and although women can construct hierarchies of principles and argue deductively, they are apt to regard such displays of reasoning as beside the point when it comes to a moral crisis like deciding whether to stop aggressive medical treatment for a dying child.[10]

Ethics, insisted Noddings, is about particular relations, where a "relation" means "a set of ordered pairs generated by some rule that describes the affect—or subjective experience—of the members."[11] There are two parties in any relation: the first is the "one-caring"; the second is the "cared-for." The one-caring is motivationally engrossed or "displaced" in the cared-for and makes it a point to attend to the cared-for in deeds as well as in thoughts. When all goes well, the cared-for actively receives the caring deeds of the one-caring, spontaneously sharing his or her aspirations, appraisals, and accomplishments with the one-caring. Caring is not simply a matter of feeling favorably disposed toward humankind in general, of being concerned about people with whom we have no concrete connections, said Noddings. There is a fundamental difference between the kind of care a mother has for her child and the kind of care a well-fed American woman has for a starving Ethiopian child she has never met. Real care requires actual encounters with specific individuals; it cannot be accomplished through good intentions alone, in Noddings's estimation.

Noddings realized that we will tend to care about our family members and friends more than anyone else. She nonetheless recommended that we move beyond our present circles of intimate connections by means of what she calls "chains." These chains, meant to deliver us from a regrettable ethical incestuousness, apparently function in one of two ways: one "personal" and the other "formal."[12] In the personal interpretation, we widen our circles by revealing ourselves to persons linked to individuals for whom we already care—for example, the spouse of a child or a friend of a friend. In the formal interpretation, we widen our relational circles by virtue of some role we play. Noddings claimed, for example, that teachers are linked to their students. Although we must be prepared to link even with strangers, according to Noddings, she admitted that this is difficult and we don't usually seek to do it. In fact, said Noddings, the one-caring would understandably "prefer that the stray cat not appear at the back door—or the strange teenager at the front."[13]

Unlike Gilligan, Noddings claimed that the ethics of care is not only different from but ultimately better than an ethics of justice. As Noddings saw it, we should reject rules and principles as major guides to ethical behavior and with them the accompanying notion of universalizability. For Noddings, relationships are about not universals but particulars—what makes each man or woman, boy or girl unique. Noddings qualified her rejection of universals and affirmation of particulars, however. She insisted that she did not espouse relativism, since something properly "universal" about the "caring attitude" underpins her ethics. A child's memories of caring are not peculiar to it only. On the contrary, virtually all human beings have access to these kinds of memories, according to Noddings: "I am claiming that the impulse to act in behalf of the present other is itself innate. It lies latent in each of us, awaiting gradual development in a succession of caring relations."[14]

As someone who believes that virtue can be taught, Noddings insisted that an ethics of caring can be communicated just as effectively as an ethics of rules and principles. Our initial experiences of care come easily, almost unconsciously; we act from a natural caring that impels us to help others because we want to: "The relation of natural caring will be identified as the human condition that we, consciously or unconsciously, perceive as 'good.' It is that condition toward which we long and strive, and it is our longing for caring—to be in that special relation—that provides the motivation for us to be moral. We want to be moral in order to remain in the caring relation and to enhance the ideal of ourselves as one-caring."[15]

Interestingly, Noddings did not describe moral development as the process of replacing natural caring with ethical caring. Although ethical caring requires efforts that natural caring does not, Noddings disagreed with Immanuel Kant's view that ethical caring is somehow better than natural caring. We will recall that for Kant an action is not morally worthy unless its agent does it out of duty and not merely out of inclination. Kant even suggested that to the degree an action goes against our grain, we can be confident that we are doing it because we ought to and not simply because we want to.[16]

In contrast to Kant, Noddings thought that our "oughts" build on our "wants." She said, "An ethic built on caring strives to maintain the caring attitude and is thus dependent upon, and not superior to, natural caring."[17] Morality is not about affirming others' needs through the process of denying one's own interests. Rather, it is about affirming one's own interests through the process of affirming others' needs. When we act morally (engage in ethical caring), we act to fulfill our "fundamental and natural desire to be and to remain related."[18] If we have any duty when our interests conflict with others' needs, it a duty not to these others but to ourselves to be moral—that is, to be and remain related. We meet other's needs not because our natural inclination toward caring impels us to do so, nor because our rationality instructs us that we must do so (Kant), but because, on reflection, we choose to do so.

Critiques of Care-Focused Feminism

Critique One: Caring Is a Two-Edged Moral Concept

A number of critics faulted Gilligan's methodology.[19] Some claimed that her empirical data was too thin to support the weighty generalizations she made about men's and women's supposedly different moral voices.[20] They emphasized that although most of the women in Gilligan's study made reference to their husbands, boyfriends, lovers, and fathers, Gilligan failed to ask these men about their views on moral quandaries. Had she chosen to interview men as well as women while writing *In a Different Voice*, said the critics,

Gilligan might have articulated a more convincing theory about men's and women's allegedly different styles of moral reasoning. Then again, continued the critics, she might have instead generated studies showing that men and women actually reason quite similarly about perplexing ethical issues. Such study results would have had dramatic consequences for Gilligan, however. Indeed, they would require her to rethink her views about women's supposed ethics of care and men's supposed ethics of justice.

Among the critics who worried about the negative consequences of associating women too closely with the values of care was Sandra Lee Bartky. In *Femininity and Domination*, Bartky sought to determine whether women's experience of feeding men's egos and tending their wounds ultimately disempowers or empowers women. By way of example, she noted that the kind of "emotional work" female flight attendants (and we may add male flight attendants) typically do often leads "to self-estrangement, an inability to identify one's own emotional states, even to drug abuse or alcoholism."[21] To pay a person to be "relentlessly cheerful"[22]—to smile at even the most verbally abusive and unreasonably demanding passengers—means paying a person to feign a certain set of emotions, said Bartky. A person can pretend to be happy only so many times before forgetting how it feels to be genuinely or authentically happy.

Admitting that the kind of emotional work female flight attendants typically do for passengers differs somewhat from the kind of emotional work wives typically do for their husbands, Bartky noted that many wives find the experience of caring for their husbands empowering. The better caregiver a wife is, the more she may regard herself as the pillar without whom her husband would crumble. But, cautioned Bartky, subjective feelings of empowerment are not the same as the objective reality of actually having power. Women's androcentric emotional work probably harms women far more than it benefits them in the long run. According to Bartky, caring women reinforce men's status through a variety of "bodily displays," including "the sympathetic cocking of the head; the forward inclination of the body; the frequent smiling; the urging, through appropriate vocalizations, that the man continue his recital, hence, that he may continue to commandeer the woman's time and attention."[23] Men do not accord women similar status, however, and because they do not, said Bartky, women's care of men amounts to "a collective genuflection by women to men, an affirmation of male importance that is unreciprocated."[24]

In Bartky's estimation, the epistemic and ethical consequences of women's unreciprocated care of men are most worrisome. The more emotional support a woman gives a man, the more she will tend to see things as he sees

them. She will participate in his projects, share his friends, rejoice in his successes, and feel badly about his failures. But women do not need yet another
reason to lose their sense of self or to doubt their own vision of reality and
version of the truth. Men's and women's interests are not identical in a patriarchal society, and it is important for women to realize this.

Critique Two: Justice, like Care, Is a Feminist Concept

Gilligan was criticized not only for overestimating the value of an ethics of
care but for underappreciating the value of an ethics of justice. For example,
philosopher Brian Barry dismissed Gilligan's ethics of care "as an invitation
to dispense with morality and replace it with nepotism, favoritism, and injustice."[25] Indeed, Barry went so far as to claim that care-focused women
"would have to be excluded from all public responsibilities [because] it would
be impossible to trust them to carry out public duties conscientiously."[26]

Less harsh than Barry's criticism of Gilligan's ethics of care were those
that faulted her simply for not better explaining the relationship between
care and justice.[27] For example, feminist philosopher Marilyn Friedman said
that justice is relevant to care in at least three ways. First, if we view a personal relationship as a "miniature social system which provides valued mutual intimacy, support, and concern for those who are involved,"[28] we will
fault relationships in which one person is the main giver and the other the
main taker. Regrettably, continued Friedman, many heterosexual relationships are deficient in just such a way. Women often serve men's physical
and psychological needs and wants with little or no reciprocation for their
caregiving acts. At some point, said Friedman, women must take men to task
and demand, as a matter of justice, reciprocation. It is not fair for one person
in a relationship to shoulder the lion's portion of the burden of care, while
the other lounges in the security of being well cared for.

Second, noted Friedman, personal relationships create "special vulnera-
bilities to harm."[29] When someone who supposedly cares about us harms us,
we may feel especially hurt or violated. An injustice perpetrated in the context of a caring relationship, said Friedman, is in many ways far worse than
an injustice perpetrated outside such a context. For example, rape by an ac-
quaintance may inflict deeper psychological wounds than rape by a stranger,
because a date rapist takes advantage of the victim's trust.

Third, stressed Friedman, if we focus on our closest relationships, especially our familial relationships, we will discover they are fraught with the
potential for myriad injustices. Should mom and dad give their son privileges they are not willing to give their daughter? Should Mr. and Mrs. Jones

pay for their parents' nursing home expenses, or should they instead pay for their children's college education? Should Mr. Smith give up an excellent job so that he can move with Ms. Chang, who has a mediocre job, to a city where she will have an excellent job but he will have only a mediocre one? Unassisted by notions of justice, care cannot adequately address these questions, insisted Friedman.

Despite Friedman's valid point about the interaction between justice and care, she should in fairness have properly credited Gilligan with exploring this interaction in several of her later writings. Initially, Gilligan offered a care-justice convergence theory. She claimed that, properly practiced, care and justice converge in the realization that just as inequality adversely affects both parties in an unequal relationship, violence is destructive for everyone involved.[30] Later, Gilligan replaced her care-justice convergence theory with a care-justice gestalt theory. Like an ambiguous drawing that may be seen as either a duck or a rabbit, a moral drama may be framed either in terms of justice or care, she said. Although these two perspectives never completely and finally converge, they are not usually diametrically opposed polarities. Most individuals can interpret a moral drama first from one of these perspectives and then from the other, even if a few individuals lack this perspectival skill. In the same way that some individuals can see only the duck or only the rabbit in an ambiguous "duck-rabbit" drawing, some individuals can view moral issues only through the lens of care or justice.[31]

Philosopher Claudia Card focused her objections to care theory on Noddings's distinction between feminine and masculine approaches to morality. Noddings characterized a "feminine approach" to morality as that of "one attached" and a "masculine approach" as that of "one detached,"[32] adding that ethics is ultimately a matter of close attachments. As Card saw it, however, we are closely attached only to a tiny fraction of the world's people, and yet, given advances in communication networks and technology, we invariably affect not only this small percentage but also a multiplicity of people from whom we seem profoundly detached. Therefore, said Card, we require "an ethic that applies to our relations with people with whom we are connected *only by relations of cause and effect* as well as to our relations with those with whom we are connected by personal and potential encounters."[33] Such an ethic need not view universal principles as masculine impediments to particular relationships. On the contrary, principles such as "Honor thy parents" help bridge many generational divides, and principles such as "Love thy neighbor as thyself" help bring people together rather than drive them apart.

As wonderful a virtue as caring is, Card concluded, it is not the only intrinsically valuable moral virtue. Justice is also an intrinsically valuable moral virtue, and even though ideas such as justice, impartiality, and objectivity can be misinterpreted in ways that encourage fathers, for example, to sacrifice their sons on the altar of some "higher" cause, properly interpreted, justice is necessary for our defense against the sexism, racism, ethnocentrism, homophobia, and xenophobia that plague our "poorly integrated, multicultural society."[34] Given the fact that so many social groups knowingly or negligently, willfully or unintentionally fail to care about those whose sex, race, ethnicity, religion, or even size and shape differ from their own, justice must be treasured. We cannot have a caring society, said Card, until we have a just society, and our society is anything but one in which all persons are equally well treated. Justice must not be dismissed simply as the abstract, alien tool of the fathers, for it can be used to protect the weak as well as the strong. Justice often is correctly blind to particulars in order to prevent details of sex, race, and creed from determining whether we care for someone or not.[35]

Critique Three: Unconditional Care Is a Contested Ethical Concept

Sarah Lucia Hoagland disputed Noddings's claim that breaking a relationship almost always results in some type of "ethical diminishment." She took particular exception to Noddings's view that a seriously abused woman who kills her husband while he sleeps may be morally at fault even if she and her children can escape her husband's tyranny only through her violent act. As Hoagland saw it, such a woman should be praised for having finally found the moral strength to exchange a disempowering and false ethical ideal for a true one. An ethics that keeps the one-caring in a destructive relationship is not a good ethics, said Hoagland. If told that ending a marriage with an abusive husband may damage their moral self-image, women might, due to guilt coupled with a fear of reprisal, stay in relationships that will ultimately destroy them. Unlike Noddings, Hoagland refused to say anything at all negative about women who end abusive relationships: "I must be able to assess any relationship for abuse/oppression and withdraw if I find it to be so. I feel no guilt, I have grown, I have learned something. I understand my part in the relationship. I separate. I will not be there again. Far from diminishing my ethical self, I am enhancing it."[36] There are times in life when ethics demands we not care, insisted Hoagland. For example, in an awful section of Fyodor Dostoyevsky's *The Brothers Karamazov*, Ivan shrieks that he does not want to dwell in a "heaven" in which a cruelly murdered child, his mother, and his murderer embrace in a hug of cosmic reconciliation. This scene illustrates Noddings's critics assertion that there is a final limit on caring. Some things are so evil that they must not be forgiven.

The Roots of Maternal Ethics

Despite critics' serious reservations about invoking the concepts, metaphors, and images associated with the mother-infant or parent-child relationship as the paradigm for caring human relationships, care-focused feminists nonetheless continued to claim that these are precisely the ones to use. Among these maternal thinkers are Sara Ruddick, Virginia Held, and Eva Kittay, all three of whom, interestingly, viewed caring not only as an other-directed psychological attitude of attentiveness but also as a practice, work, or labor. Caring is about having a certain sort of mind-set, but it is also about assisting those in need of care. Moreover, their insistence that caring practice, work, or labor should be performed in the public as well as the private domain further tied together Ruddick's, Held's, and Kittay's thought.

Sara Ruddick

Sara Ruddick identified mothering as both cultural and biological—that is, as an activity that both men and women can do, even though, because the role has largely fallen to women throughout human history, they now do it better. Ruddick observed that although biology destines women to bear children, it does not destine them to rear them. Nevertheless, a complex interaction between women's childbearing capacities on the one hand and patriarchal society's child-rearing needs on the other has made the latter women's work. As a result, most, though by no means all, women develop what Ruddick termed "maternal practice."[37] Society, in her view, should not trivialize maternal practice, which, like any human practice, requires special abilities and particular ways of thinking and acting: "The agents of maternal practice, acting in response to demands of their children, acquire a conceptual scheme—a vocabulary and logic of connections—through which they order and express the facts and values of their practice. . . . There is a unity of reflection, judgment, and emotion. This unity I call 'maternal thinking.'"[38] Ruddick rejected the notion of maternal thinking as merely an emotional, irrational display of love that comes naturally to women, instead presenting it as a type of learned thought. Like all modes of human thinking, maternal thinking has its own logic and interests, specifically, the preservation, growth, and acceptability of one's children.[39]

According to Ruddick, preserving the life of a child is the "constitutive maternal act"[40] and the first dimension of maternal practice. Infants are totally vulnerable. They simply will not survive unless their caretakers feed, clothe, and shelter them. Ruddick gave the example of Julie, an exhausted young mother with a very demanding infant. Having reached her physical and psychological limits, Julie pictures herself killing her baby daughter. Horrified by her thought, Julie spends the night riding a city bus, her baby in her arms, reasoning that as long as they remain in public view, her baby will be safe.[41]

Ruddick told Julie's story to stress how difficult it is for some mothers to meet their children's basic needs. Not every mother grows so rundown and desperate that she must take steps to ensure that she will not kill her child. But even under relatively ideal circumstances, most mothers do have days when they find mothering extraordinarily difficult. To preserve their children on these bad days, said Ruddick, mothers need to cultivate the intellectual virtue of scrutiny and the moral virtues of humility and cheerfulness.[42]

The second dimension of Ruddick's maternal practice is fostering children's growth. A good mother does not impose an already-written script on her children. She does not insist they meet unrealistic standards of abstract perfection. Instead, she tells her children "maternal stories"—that is, realistic, compassionate, and "delightful" stories that help them reflect on the persons they have been, are, and might someday be. Faced with a stubborn daughter, for example, a mother should help the girl understand why stubbornness is a character defect and how she might transform her stubbornness into the virtue of proper self-determination.[43] A mother should help her children grow not only in physical size and mental intelligence but also in virtue, said Ruddick. People become stubborn for reasons. They get tired of having to do things as others dictate. Therefore, when they get the opportunity to resist, they fight back by digging in their heels and doing things their own way, no matter how potentially disastrous the consequences. Self-awareness of this human tendency can help children understand why a modus operandi of perpetual stubbornness does not make good sense and why it may be best to do things other people's way from time to time.

The third and final dimension of Ruddick's maternal practice is training. Mothers work hard to socialize their children, to transform them into law-abiding citizens who adhere to societal norms. But good mothers do not want their children to become mindless conformists. Mothers may, for example, refuse to fit their children's vulnerable bodies into military uniforms, or diet them into designer jeans, or dress them for success in the so-called dog-eat-dog world. In a patriarchal—that is, overly competitive, hierarchical, and individualistic—society, mothers may find themselves caught between the demands of patriarchy and their own inner conviction that many of these demands are dehumanizing. If a mother trains her son to be a winner, he may become both the chief executive officer of a large firm and a very mean-spirited human being. In contrast, if she refuses to teach him the ways of the world, he may become both a very nice guy and someone labeled a loser. On almost a daily basis mothers must decide, said Ruddick, when and when not to let their personal values guide their child-rearing practices. Ruddick added that mothers should make these decisions not by themselves but, ideally, together with their children. If children adopt their mothers' values unquestioningly, their "training" will never be completed.[44] External compliance with others' values is an inadequate substitute for learning how to choose and live in conformity with one's own values.

Clearly, maternal practice is a complex activity. Overall, it is guided by what Ruddick termed the metavirtue of "attentive love." This metavirtue, at once cognitive and affective, rational and emotional, enables mothers to "really look" at their children and not be shocked, horrified, or appalled by what they see.[45] Among the several characteristics that distinguish maternal from nonmaternal thinkers is the formers' utter realism, emphasized Ruddick. A mother who loves her children inattentively lets her fantasies blind her. She sees them not as they are but as some sort of fulfillment of her dreams. In contrast, mothers who love their children attentively accept who they are and work within their physical and psychological limits.

Virginia Held

Like Ruddick in some ways but not others, philosopher Virginia Held maintained that there are multiple moral approaches designed to fit certain sets of relationships and activities in the public and private realms. Some of these moral approaches, closely related to the value of justice, are likely to be of particular use in the legal and economic realms. Others are tightly linked to the value of care and likely to be of special help in the realms of child care, health care, and education. Held insisted that each of these two types of moral approaches should recognize the other as particularly valuable in its respective sphere of influence and generally necessary in the other. Society should recognize that the moral approaches designed to govern family disputes are just as socially necessary as those fashioned to negotiate international treaties.[46]

Held's observation about multiple moral approaches merits careful consideration. At least in the Western world, moral approaches generated in, from, and for private relations have not usually been recognized as fully moral. Rather, they have been viewed as merely relational matters not warranting serious moral scrutiny. Held pointed out that all too often traditional ethicists have assumed that bona fide moral issues take root in one sphere only, the public sphere. She claimed this assumption was misguided. Experiences need not unfold in a bustling marketplace or a contentious courtroom to merit moral analysis. On the contrary, they may just as easily arise in a nursery or around the dinner table. In other words, Held maintained that what makes an experience worthy of moral analysis is not where but how it occurs. If moral experience is "the experience of consciously choosing, of voluntarily accepting or rejecting, of willingly approving or disapproving, of living with these choices, and above all of acting and of living with these actions and their outcomes,"[47] then it can as easily occur in one's bedroom as in one's office. Therefore, any adequate moral theory must address filial, parental, spousal, and friendship relations as well as physician-patient, lawyer-client, and seller-buyer relations. In the grand scheme of moral concerns, women's struggles and striving in the private realm count as much as men's struggles in the public realm.

Held stressed that traditional ethicists view contractual relations as the primary model for human interaction, justifying a human relationship as moral to the degree that it serves the separate interests of individual rational contractors. Yet life is about more than conflict, competition, and controversy—about getting what one wants. It is, as mothering persons know, also about cooperation, consensus, and community—about meeting other people's needs. Held speculated that were the relationship between a mothering person and a child, rather than that between two rational contractors, the paradigm for good human relationships, society might look very differently. She commented, "Instead of seeing law and the states or the economy as the central and appropriate determinants of society, an ethics of care might see bringing up children and fostering trust between members of society as the most important concerns of all. Other arrangements might then be evaluated in terms of how well or badly they contribute to the flourishing of children and the health of social relations. Just imagine how restructured our society might become if the salaries of business executives and childcare workers were reversed."[48]

Held conceded, however, that the kinds of relationships that exist between mothering persons and children can be just as oppressive—indeed, more so—than the relationships that exist between two rational contractors. For example, it is sometimes harder to recognize and handle abuses of power in a parent-child relationship than in an employer-employee relationship.[49] Moreover, it takes greater moral skill to address questions of justice and rights in the domain of the family than it does in the workplace. People cannot quit their families as easily as they quit a job; nor should they if their families have "more good dimensions than bad aspects."[50]

Like principles, relationships can be evaluated as good, bad, or somewhere in between. We should quit entirely bad relationships but at least allow relationships with more good than bad aspects a chance to survive. Premature or unreflective severance of mixed good/bad ones is not warranted, in Held's estimation.[51]

Held maintained that we must, as a society, cultivate our emotions, particularly sensitivity to the feelings of others, because doing so is essential to the practice of care and mothering/parenting. She emphasized that going through the motions of a caring activity without feeling anything in the way of love, affection, compassion, or sympathy is not actually engaging in the practice of care. People who "are thoroughly unaware of what others are feeling and thinking, and grossly unable to read the moods and intentions of others"[52] cannot truly care, said Held. They must be taught to care. Thus, it is not enough for schools to develop students' rational capacities—their powers of critical thinking. Schools must also develop students' emotional capacities—their powers of sympathy, empathy, and imagination.

Eva Feder Kittay

One of the latest additions to the ranks of care-focused feminists who emphasize the mother-child and similar relationships, Eva Feder Kittay has described herself as among those feminist thinkers who "have begun to formulate a moral theory and a politics grounded in the maternal relation, the paradigm of a relation of care."[53] Yet, to avoid accusations of bolstering either the essentialist view that women are by nature mothers or the mythical view that all mothers are good mothers, Kittay used the idea of "dependency relations" and "dependency workers" instead of "maternal relations" and "mothers" in her work.

For Kittay, the paradigmatic dependency worker is a close relative or friend who assumes daily responsibility for a dependent's survival. A dependency worker can be either male or female, according to Kittay, but due to a variety of socioeconomic, cultural, and biological factors, most societies have assigned dependency work to their female members. Kittay theorized that intimate and caring connections to the dependent characterize the dependency worker's labor. She also speculated that, typically, dependency workers suffer negative personal or professional consequences, or both, as a result of doing their essential work.

Closely related to the paradigmatic case of a dependency worker, said Kittay, is the worker who is paid, often quite modestly, to care for an unrelated person but who views her vocation as much more than a mere job. Kittay provided an example of such a dependency worker from her own life: Peggy, who has cared for her severely developmentally disabled daughter, Sesha, for over a quarter century and to whom Kittay has delegated many of her motherly tasks. Without Peggy's help, said Kittay, Sesha would not have done nearly as well as she has, and Kittay and her husband would not have been able to pursue full-time careers vigorously. On the contrary, most of their energies, particularly Kittay's, would have gone to caring for Sesha.[54]

Unlike the subject of traditional equality theory, Kittay's dependency worker is not an independent, self-interested, and fully autonomous agent. On the contrary, she is, in Kittay's estimation, a transparent self, that is, "a self through whom the needs of another are discerned, a self that, when it looks to its own needs, it first sees the needs of another."[55] As Kittay saw it, the dependency worker is ordinarily obligated to the dependent person to the degree that he or she needs the dependency worker's help.

Kittay's explanation for the dependency worker's obligations to the dependent person resembles that offered by Robert Goodin in *Protecting the Vulnerable*: "The moral basis of special relations between individuals arises from the vulnerability of one party to the actions of another."[56] For example, a mother has an obligation to care for her infant because she is "*the* individual best situated, or exclusively situated to meet the needs of the dependent."[57] The source of a mother's moral obligation to her infant is not the rights of the dependent as a person but the relationship that exists between one in need and one situated to meet that need. The defining characteristic of this largely socially constructed relationship is that it is not usually chosen but already given in the ties of family, the dynamics of friendship, or the obligations of employment.

The fact that a relationship is given to the dependency worker, however, does not mean that he or she is necessarily wrong to break it. Kittay disagreed with Goodin when he refused to absolve a slave from his obligations to a master who becomes so ill that he cannot survive without the slave's help. The master's fragile condition is the slave's one chance for freedom. Is the slave obligated to stay and take care of his master? Goodin argued yes. As he saw it, if a vulnerability arises in a relationship, the moral worth of the relationship is not relevant to the existence of the obligation. Kittay argued no. As she saw it, the relationship given to the slave was one that society should not have constructed. Its coerciveness cancels out the obligations that human vulnerability ordinarily creates.[58]

For Kittay, a theory of justice not infused with a theory of care will never produce equality. People in philosopher John Rawls's hypothetical world subscribe to two principles of justice. The first claims that each person is to have an equal right to the most extensive total system of equal basic liberties compatible with a similar system of liberty for all. The second argues that social and economic inequalities are to be arranged so that they are both (1) to the greatest benefit of the least advantaged, and (2) attached to offices and positions open to all under conditions of fair and equal opportunity.[59] But people in Kittay's actual world subscribe to more than these two principles of justice. They also call for a third principle of social responsibility for care that Kittay articulates as follows: "To each according to his or her need for care, from each according to his or her capacity for care, and such support from social institutions as to make available resources and opportunities to those providing care, so that all be adequately attended in relations that are sustaining."[60]

Critiques of Maternal Ethics

Critique One: Maternal Ethics Are Unbalanced

Although Kittay escapes many of the criticisms directed against maternal ethics since she uses dependency workers rather than mothers as her fundamental unit of moral analysis, some of philosopher Sarah Lucia Hoagland's subtler criticisms of maternal ethics may yet apply to her as well as to Ruddick and Held. As Hoagland saw it, if maternal thinkers aim to develop an ethics that will elucidate the necessary and sufficient conditions for a morally good relationship, then they should not use unequal relationships as the focus of their inquiry for at least four reasons. First, the goal of practices such as parenting, teaching, and providing therapy "is to wean the cared-for of dependency."[61] The parent-child, teacher-student, and therapist-client relationships are meant to be transcended. As personified by the child, student, or client, the cared-for submits to the parent, teacher, or therapist, trusting that there is really a method in the "madness" of these authorities (drink this nasty penicillin, read this boring book, dredge up all your phobias). Repeatedly, Hoagland noted that dependency relationships are ethically problematic. To achieve full moral development, the cared-for must break these dependency relationships, a fact that makes them an unviable paradigm for fully morally good relationships.

Second, Hoagland does not accept the assumption that it is always morally required for the one-caring to control the relationship with the cared-for. After all, the one-caring does not necessarily know what is best for the cared-for. Sometimes the cared-for is in fact the best judge of his or her own good. Similarly, the cared-for is not the only one who should expect to be nurtured. The one-caring should also receive love and attention. Morally good relationships are not about the one-caring always playing the role of giver and the cared-for always playing the role of taker. As long as this sort of role playing occurs, says Hoagland, we can be sure that the relationship being described is less than morally good.

Third, Hoagland rejects the assumption that inequalities in ability make a relationship unequal. What makes our friendship relationships equal is not the fact that our friends have precisely the same skills that we have—that they are as linguistically or mathematically talented as we are, for example. Rather, it is the fact that our friends have approximately the same amount of power as we have. A relationship is unequal to the extent that one of its members controls its dynamics. When we choose unequal relationships as the paradigm for an ethical system, said Hoagland, we propagate rather than overcome problems of power since "we live in a society premised on dominance and subordination, and oppression emerges in many forms—from parental all the way to colonial relationships—when decisions are made 'for another's own good.'"[62] Any ethics based on the powerful helping the powerless is rooted in some people telling others what to do and how.

Fourth, and finally, Hoagland thought that children, students, and clients should not be encouraged to blindly trust parents, teachers, and therapists. Teachers and therapists often join with parents to decide about a child's various abilities, aptitudes, and prospects. The cared-for learns to trust a presumedly beneficent authority figure whose true motives are opaque to her. Such a model of "blind trust" makes the cared-for vulnerable in a hierarchical society where most people feel a need to maintain the upper hand in their relationships. A fully moral ethics, said Hoagland, must challenge the hierarchical ways of being, thinking, and acting that make some people but not others vulnerable.[63]

Taking unequal relationships as paradigmatic for ethics leaves open the risk of abuse. Insofar as relationships are unequal, they may become invitations for one person to dominate the other. This is particularly true of parent-child relationships, observed Hoagland. According to one study, in nearly one-third of American households, fathers (or stepfathers) sexually abuse their female children,[64] and mothers are just as likely to feel "resentment" as tenderness toward their children.[65] The parent-child relationship is far from totally innocent and purely good. The people with the power—that is, the ones-caring—may be tempted to wield their power arbitrarily when it suits their purposes.

Critique Two: The Mother-Child Relationship Is a Shaky Basis for Developing a Mature Ethics

The claim that something like the mother-child relationship is an inappropriate paradigm for ethical relationships is the most serious challenge to maternal ethics. Critic Jean Grimshaw argued that at least three factors weaken the paradigmatic strength of the mother-child relationship. First, parents are responsible for their children's physical and psychological well-being, but children are not responsible for their parents' physical and psychological well-being—at least minor children have no such filial duty. Second, parents are permitted—indeed sometimes required—to tell their children what to do, but not vice versa except in certain circumstances (think of an elderly parent with advanced Alzheimer's disease). Third, parents are expected to behave better than their children. Indeed, mom and dad are expected to "tolerate, accept, and try not to be hurt by behavior that would be quite intolerable or a cause for anger in most adult relationships."[66]

Given these three asymmetries, modeling adult relationships on the mother-child relationship seems like a prescription for disaster. Precisely the features that tend to make a mother-child relationship work will quite likely damage or destroy a relationship between two adults, in Grimshaw's and most probably also in Hoagland's estimation.[67] For an adult relationship to work, both parties must be responsible for each other; neither must presume to know the other's good better than the other knows it; and both must behave equally well, since one adult will not accept from another the small manipulations, name calling, and temper tantrums parents accept from children.

According to Grimshaw, women in particular think maternally for bad as well as good reasons. Some women develop such virtues as care, responsiveness, attentive love, and resilient good humor to create and maintain strong female friendships from which they derive support. Other women develop these same virtues simply to please the men on whom they depend or to cater to their children, on whom they pin their own identities. Rather than looking to unequal mother-child relationships to decide whether their maternal virtues are really virtues, women should compare and contrast their equal and unequal relationships. Women will discover, in Grimshaw's estimation, that relationships between equals are more fully satisfying than those between unequals.

Critique Three: White Women Predominantly Voice Care Ethics and Maternal Ethics

A serious critique of the field of care ethics/maternal ethics is that it does not, as a rule, discuss the caring relationships that exist between women of color and their children, especially their daughters. This is disappointing because many women of color have written most perceptively about the mother-daughter relationship in particular. We think here of Patricia Hill Collins, who, in *Black Feminist Thought*, presented an ethics of care that relied on "personal expressiveness, emotions, and empathy" to achieve self-realization.[68] Collins's ethics of care had three components. First, she emphasized the kind of "individual uniqueness" novelist Alice Walker expressed when she said she "never doubted her powers of judgment because her mother assumed they were sound."[69] Black/African American women, said Collins, are known for making quilts that "place strong color and patterns next to one another . . . to see the individual differences not as detracting from each piece but as enriching the whole quilt."[70] Ethics is founded on a strong and vibrant self-consciousness of the value of a human person.

A second component of any ethic of care, said Collins, is the realization that ethics consists mostly not in rational arguments but in the expression of powerful emotions. Collins insisted that singer Aretha Franklin's 1967 plea in her well-known song "Respect" would be "virtually meaningless" without emotion.[71] Morality and neutrality are not generally a good mix. Ethics requires some sort of passion, in Collins's estimation.

In addition to a proper show of emotion, an ethics of care also requires developing one's powers of empathy, claimed Collins. The moral person can think like another person thinks and see that person's self-interests as his or her own. Empathy takes more moral energy than sympathy because it requires us to move beyond the limits of our own possibly biased psyches.

Having identified the three components of her ethics of care, Collins pointed to the call-and-response tradition in which the minister's message melds with the congregation's feeling as a prime example of ethical discourse. She also said that "certain dimensions of women's ways of knowing bear striking resemblance to Afrocentric expressions of the ethic of caring"[72] and that the mother-daughter relationship in the Black/African American community is one of caring. Mothers express their true moral sentiments to their daughters as they raise them to be special. Collins expressed the nuances of an ethic of care using author Willi Coleman's description of a mother who cared for her daughters more than anyone else: "Except for special occasions mama came home from work early on Saturdays. She spent six days a week mopping, waxing and dusting other women's houses and keeping out of reach of other women's husbands. Saturday nights were reserved for 'taking care of them girls' hair and the telling of stories. Some of which included a recitation of what she had endured and how she had triumphed over 'Folks that were lower than dirt' and 'no-good snakes in the grass.' She combed, patted, twisted and talked, saying things which would have embarrassed or shamed her at other times."[73]

Care is very basic in the Black/African American community, according to Collins. When the character of a daughter in a novel asks her demanding mother if she really loves and cares for her, the mother simply states, "What you talkin' 'bout did I love you girl, I stayed alive for you."[74] Collins's ethics of care is ferocious and in no way sentimental. It is a handbook for survival in a larger and sometimes uncaring white society.

Conclusion

The writings of care-focused feminists are appealing in how they mesh with many ordinary intuitions about sexual behavior, mothering, and moral conduct. To be sure, "gender identity" explanations for women's oppression are problematic. In expressing concern about the dangers of care, Gilligan's critics echo Elizabeth Cady Stanton's nineteenth-century admonition that given society's tendency to take advantage of women, it is vital that they prioritize self-development over other-directed self-sacrifice.[75] Still, it is important not to overemphasize the problems of patriarchy. Whatever the weaknesses of care-focused feminisms, there are serious problems with women's abandoning all their nurturant activities. The world would be a much worse place tomorrow than it is today were women suddenly to stop meeting the physical and psychological needs of those who depend on them. Just because men and children have more or less routinely taken advantage of some women's willingness to serve them does not mean we should dismiss every woman's caring actions as yet another instance of women's "pathological masochism" or "passivity."[76] Many defenders of maternal ethics say that we can rescue care from the patriarchal structures that would misuse or abuse it.

These defenders point to the differences between what Sheila Mullett terms "distortions of caring" and "undistorted caring."[77] Mullett said a person cannot truly care for someone else if economically, socially, or psychologically forced to do so. Thus, authentic caring cannot occur under patriarchal conditions characterized by male domination and female subordination. Only under conditions of sexual equality and freedom can women care for men without men in any way diminishing, disempowering, or disregarding women. Until such conditions are achieved, women must care cautiously, asking themselves whether the kind of caring in which they are engaged

1. fulfills the one-caring;
2. calls upon the unique and particular individuality of the one-caring;
3. is not produced by a person in a role because of gender, with one gender engaging in nurturing behavior and the other in instrumental behavior;
4. is reciprocated with caring and not merely with the satisfaction of seeing the cared-for flourishing and pursuing other projects;[78]
5. takes place with the framework of consciousness-raising practice and conversation.[79]

Care can be freely given only when the one-caring is not taken for granted. As long as men demand and expect caring from women as their right, both sexes will fail to actualize their moral potential. Neither men nor women will be able to care authentically.

Questions for Discussion

1. Do you support or reject Gilligan's and/or Noddings's ethics? Explain and/or justify the reasons for your position.
2. How are care and justice complementary? In what ways are an ethics of care and an ethics of justice at odds?
3. Give an example of a care-based ethics that is not feminist. What are its comparative weaknesses and strengths?
4. What conditions should be present within healthy caretaking/dependency relationships? Assess both personal and paid relationships. If the caretaker is receiving monetary remuneration for the role, does this lessen society's obligation to protect the caretaker's psychological and emotional well-being?
5. In what ways does/doesn't Ruddick's, Held's, and Kittay's thinking escape Hoagland's criticisms?

8

Ecofeminism

Ecofeminists, who include many global, postcolonial, and transnational feminists as well as mainstream, generally privileged, white feminists, focus on human beings' domination of the nonhuman world, or nature. Because women are culturally tied to nature, ecofeminists argue that there are conceptual, symbolic, and linguistic connections between feminist and ecological issues. According to Karen J. Warren, an oppressive patriarchal conceptual framework, whose purpose is to explain, justify, and maintain relationships of domination and subordination in general and men's domination of women in particular, has shaped the Western world's basic beliefs, values, attitudes, and assumptions about itself and its inhabitants. She laid out the following as the most significant features of this framework:

- Value-hierarchical thinking: "up-down" thinking, which gives higher value, status, or prestige to what is "up" rather than what is "down"
- Value dualisms: disjunctive pairs in which the disjuncts are seen as oppositional (rather than complementary) and exclusive (rather than inclusive), with higher value (status, prestige) placed on one disjunct than on the other (e.g., dualisms that give higher value or status to that historically identified as "mind," "reason," and "male" than to that historically identified as "body," "emotion," and "female")
- Logic of domination: a structure of argumentation that leads to a justification of subordination[1]

Patriarchy's hierarchical, dualistic, and oppressive mode of thinking has harmed both women and nature, in Warren's opinion. Indeed, because women have been "naturalized" and nature has been "feminized," it is difficult to know where the oppression of one ends and that of the other begins. Warren emphasized that women are naturalized when they are described in animal terms—for instance, as "cows, foxes, chicks, serpents, bitches, beavers, old bats, pussycats, cats, bird-brains, hare-brains."[2] Similarly, nature is feminized when "she" is raped, mastered, conquered, controlled, penetrated, subdued, and mined by men. If man is the lord of nature, if he has been given dominion over it, then he has control not only over nature but also over nature's human analog, woman. Whatever man may do to nature, he may also do to woman.

Much as radical-cultural and radical-libertarian feminists disagree about whether women's association with the work of childbearing and child rearing is ultimately a source of power or disempowerment, ecofeminists debate about the wisdom of stressing women's association with nature.[3] Despite their sometimes divergent views on women's particular responsibilities to the environment (should we live as simply as possible?), to animals (should we be vegetarians and antivivisectionists?), and to future generations (should we be pacifists and strict population controllers?), all ecofeminists agree with Rosemary Radford Ruether that women's and nature's liberation is a joint project: "Women must see that there can be no liberation for them and no solution to the ecological crisis within a society whose fundamental model of relationships continues to be one of domination. They must unite the demands of the women's movement with those of the ecological movement to envision a radical reshaping of the basic socioeconomic relations and the underlying values of this [modern industrial] society."[4]

Some Roots of Ecofeminism

In *Silent Spring* (1962), Rachel Carson warned Americans that unless they began to take care of their environment, "all man's assaults upon the environment [including] the contamination of air, earth, rivers, and sea with dangerous and even lethal materials . . . [will undoubtedly] shatter or alter the very material . . . upon which the shape of the future depends."[5] As ecological concerns about global warming, ozone depletion, waste disposal, factory farming, endangered species, energy conservation, and wilderness preservation grew, an environmental movement took hold in the United States and throughout the world. Although all environmentalists believed human beings should respect nature, "human-centered" environmentalists provided reasons for doing so based on furthering human interests, whereas "earth-centered" environmentalists provided reasons based on the supposedly intrinsic value of the planet itself.

Human-centered environmentalists emphasized that people harm themselves when they harm the environment. If people exhaust their natural resources or pollute their skies and water, not only they but their progeny will suffer. If people want to have the material goods and lifestyles that industrialization makes possible, they must devise some means to handle the toxic wastes it produces as a by-product. If people desire the benefit of bountiful and inexpensive energy, they must harness new energy sources, such as the sun and wind, lest they use up the entire supply of oil and natural gas currently fueling our economy. If people want to experience the wilderness and see uncultivated vegetation and undomesticated animals, they must prevent commercial enterprises from transforming every piece of wild land into a Disneyland or Club Med. And if people want to preserve the rich diversity of nature and the treasures it might still hold for them, they must safeguard all life-forms, refusing to imperil their existence.

Viewing themselves as realistic or pragmatic about environmental concerns, human-centered environmentalists conceded that from time to time, we may have to sacrifice the environment to serve our interests. In other words, sometimes we must cut down a forest so people can use the trees to build homes; sometimes we must pollute the air so people can continue to drive their automobiles; sometimes we must hunt a predatory species of wild animals so that domesticated animals like cows and sheep can graze safely. In short, the environment's value is instrumental; its meaning, significance, and purpose depend on people's needs or wants. The environment exists not for itself but for human beings.

Critics of human-centered environmentalism condemned it as "arrogant anthropocentrism," generally faulting the Judeo-Christian tradition as a main player in the devaluation of the environment. They pointed to the biblical mandate instructing men to "subdue" the earth and "have dominion over the fish of the sea and over the birds of the air and every living thing that moves upon the earth" as promoting the view that nature has instrumental value only.[6] These same critics also stressed how the metaphors and models of mechanistic science, which gained sway during the pre-Enlightenment and Enlightenment periods, reinforced the Bible's anthropomorphic view of nature. They claimed that prior to the seventeenth century, people thought of nature organically, as a benevolent female or nurturing mother, as someone who gave freely and generously of her bounty to them, her children. After the scientific revolution, however, people reconceived nature mechanistically, as an inert, lifeless machine. As a result of this paradigm shift, people found it easier to justify not only the use but also the misuse and abuse of nature. They reasoned that there is nothing morally wrong with treating a mere object in whatever way we wish.

René Descartes's philosophy, which privileged mind over matter, further bolstered the mechanistic conception of nature, according to critics of human-centered environmentalism. His belief that human beings' ability to think ("I think, therefore I am") makes them special led to the view that things that think (*res cogitans*, or human beings) are meant to control things that do not think (animals [as was then believed], trees, and rocks). Gradually, human beings convinced themselves that they were indeed the highest life-form: the center of the universe. Due to their exalted self-conception, human beings took it upon themselves to decide not only when to protect and preserve the environment for their use but also when to sacrifice it for their greater glory and good.

Human-centered, or anthropomorphic environmentalism, sometimes termed "shallow ecology," remained the order of the day until the late 1940s, when a new generation of environmentalists forwarded an earth-centered environmentalism they termed "deep ecology." This post-Enlightenment view of nature repudiated the modern conception of nature as a machine, reverting to medieval and even ancient conceptions of it as an organism with intrinsic as well as instrumental value.

In his much-anthologized essay "The Land Ethic," Aldo Leopold wrote that we should think about the land as "a fountain of energy flowing through a circuit of soils, plants, and animals."[7] Leopold believed the earth is a life system, an intricately interwoven and interdependent intersection of elements that functions as a whole organism. If one element of this system becomes diseased, the whole system becomes sick, and the only way to heal the system is to treat or cure the diseased part, be it an excessively flooded plain, a severely overpopulated herd of deer (or human beings), or a heavily polluted river. To be sure, a treatment or cure for the diseased element will not always be found, but that is to be expected. In fact, the ecosystem's laws of death and decay require that its old elements be extinguished: the patterns of regeneration and life continually provide the space necessary for new elements of the ecosystem. It is important not for each particular part to persist, said Leopold, but only for the whole to continue.

From nature's perspective, as opposed to what Leopold called man's perspective, flows an environmental ethics best termed "biocentric" or "ecocentric." He claimed that "a thing is right when it tends to preserve the integrity, stability, and beauty of the biotic community. It is wrong when it tends to do otherwise."[8] Leopold's thinking was at the forefront of the conceptual revolution that replaced the anthropomorphism of shallow ecology with the biocentrism of deep ecology. Arne Naess and George Sessions articulated the principal tenets of deep ecology as follows:

1. The well-being and flourishing of human and non-human life on earth have value in themselves (synonyms: intrinsic value, inherent value). These values are independent of the usefulness of the non-human world for human purposes.

2. Richness and diversity of life forms contribute to the realization of these values and are also values in themselves.

3. Humans have no right to reduce this richness and diversity except to satisfy vital needs.

4. The flourishing of human life and cultures is compatible with a substantial decrease of the human population. The flourishing of non-human life requires such a decrease.

5. Present human interference with the non-human world is excessive, and the situation is rapidly worsening.

6. Policies must therefore be changed. These policies affect basic economic, technological, and ideological structures. The resulting state of affairs will be deeply different from the present.

7. The ideological change is mainly that of appreciating life quality (dwelling in situations of inherent value) rather than adhering to an increasingly higher standard of living. There will be a profound awareness of the difference between big and great.

8. Those who subscribe to the foregoing points have an obligation directly or indirectly to try to implement the necessary changes.[9]

Critics of deep ecology faulted both its underlying theory and some of its tactics. They demanded to know the source of nature's intrinsic value, rejecting the mere fact of nature's "is-ness" as an inadequate answer to their question. Just because something exists, they said, does not make it intrinsically valuable.

Early Conceptions of Ecofeminism

Ecofeminism is a relatively new variant of ecological ethics. In fact, the term "ecofeminism" first appeared only in 1974 in Françoise d'Eaubonne's *Le féminisme ou la mort*. In this work d'Eaubonne expressed the view that there exists a direct link between the oppression of women and the oppression of nature. She claimed the liberation of one cannot be effected apart from the liberation of the other.[10] A decade or so after d'Eaubonne coined the term,

Karen J. Warren further specified four core assumptions of ecofeminism: "(1) There are important connections between the oppression of women and the oppression of nature; (2) understanding the nature of these connections is necessary to any adequate understanding of the oppression of women and the oppression of nature; (3) feminist theory and practice must include an ecological perspective; and (4) solutions to ecological problems must include a feminist perspective."[11] In many ways, ecofeminism resembles deep ecology; yet ecofeminists generally fault deep ecologists for mistakenly opposing only anthropocentrism when the main problem is not so much or only the Western world's human centeredness but its male centeredness. Androcentrism, not anthropocentrism, is the chief enemy of nature, said many ecofeminists.[12]

Although she praised deep ecologists' "concerted effort . . . to rethink Western metaphysics, epistemology, and ethics," ecofeminist Ariel Kay Salleh nonetheless found their rethinking "deficient."[13] Noting that most of deep ecology's spokespeople are men, she accused them of being afraid to confront the sexism as well as naturism causing our current environmental crisis. The "deep ecology movement will not truly happen," she said, "until men are brave enough to rediscover and to love the woman inside themselves."[14] Salleh's thesis, shared by many ecofeminists, is "that the hatred of women, which ipso facto brings about that of nature, is one of the principal mechanisms governing the actions of men (of 'males') and, thus, the whole of Western/patriarchal culture."[15]

Carol Adams perhaps most significantly reshaped the debate between shallow and deep ecology with the publication of *The Sexual Politics of Meat*,[16] in which she established a link between patriarchal culture's oppression of both women and animals. She pointed to the Greek myth in which Zeus ("patriarch of patriarchs") lusts after Metis (goddess of knowledge and prudence), pursuing, raping, and ultimately swallowing her alive. Zeus seeks to justify these monstrous deeds by observing that Metis will always remain in his belly, providing him with counsel. According to Adams, this myth demonstrates how "sexual violence and meat eating are collapsed" into each other.[17] Adams stressed that "an essential component of androcentric culture has been built upon these activities of Zeus: viewing the sexually desired object as consumable."[18] Animals, like women, are consumed as objects of pleasure in a cycle of objectification (animals equal food), fragmentation (animal carcasses are dismembered so as to be turned into food), and finally consumption (on our dinner plates). Likewise, women are objectified (female body equals sexual plaything), fragmented (into fetishized parts, such as breasts, buttocks, and vaginas), and consumed (via conquest, rape, pornography, and so forth). In Adams's estimation, the rights of women and animals are inextricably joined, placing vegetarian ecofeminists firmly in the corner of deep ecology.

Women, Nature, and Culture: Some Tensions

Although ecofeminists agreed that the association of women with nature is the root cause of both sexism and naturism, they disagreed about whether women's connections to nature are primarily biological and psychological or social and cultural. They also disagreed about whether women should de-emphasize, emphasize, or reconceive their connections with nature. According to Ynestra King, "The recognition of the connections between women and nature and of women's bridge-like position between nature and culture poses three possible directions of feminism."[19] The first is to sever the woman-nature connection by totally integrating women into culture and the realm of production. The second is to reaffirm the woman-nature connection, proposing that female nature is not only different from but also somehow better than male culture. The third is to transform the woman-nature connection by using it to create "a different kind of culture and politics that would integrate intuitive, spiritual, and rational forms of knowledge . . . and create a free, ecological society."[20] Implicit in King's understanding of transformative ecofeminism (discussed later) is the postmodern feminist belief that ultimately all forms of human oppression are rooted in dichotomous conceptual schemes that privilege one member of a dyad over another (e.g., male over female, nature over culture, science over spirituality).

Sherry B. Ortner

Among the feminist thinkers who reflected on women's relation to nature was cultural ecofeminist Sherry B. Ortner. She said it will not be easy for women to disassociate themselves from nature because virtually all societies believe women are closer to it than men. This belief is nearly universal, she said, for three reasons. First, women's physiology is "more involved more of the time with the 'species of life'; it is woman's body that nurtures humanity's future." Second, women's primary place remains the domestic sphere, where "animal-like infants" are slowly transformed into cultural beings and where plant and animal products are shaped into food, clothing, and shelter. Third, women's psyche, "appropriately molded to mothering functions by [their] own socialization," tends more than men's toward relational, concrete, and particular modes of thinking.[21]

In Ortner's opinion, virtually every society's view of women as somehow existing between nature and culture has several consequences, each of which invites a different interpretation of the term "intermediate." First, the term can simply mean that women have a middle status, lower than men's but higher than nature's. Second, it can mean that women "mediate," or perform some set of synthesizing or converting functions, between nature and culture—for example, the socialization of children. Unless children are properly socialized, no society can survive; it needs its members to conform to its rules and regulations. For this reason, hypothesized Ortner, societies seek to restrict women's sexual, reproductive, educational, and occupational choices. The more conservative women are, the more they and their children will follow the rules. Third, and finally, the term "intermediate" can mean "of greater symbolic ambiguity." Because society cannot quite understand the nature of women, it is not certain whether to associate women with life or death, good or evil, order or chaos.[22] Do women hold society together, or do they chip away at its margins?

Society's view that women are intermediaries between culture and nature, said Ortner, stems from women's "social actuality"—that is, women's physiology, domestic role, and feminine psyche. Thus, the way to alter this view of women is to change women's social actuality so that they, as well as men, are viewed as fully cultural persons capable of determining the course of history. Unfortunately, continued Ortner, women's social actuality cannot change unless society's view of women as intermediaries between culture and nature changes. Women will never escape this circular trap unless their situation is simultaneously attacked from both sides: from the social actuality side (women's reproductively special physiology, domestic role, and feminine psyche) and the conceptual or ideological side (women as occupying middle status, performing mediating functions between nature and culture, and carrying ambiguous symbolic baggage).[23] Ortner believed that the effect of this two-pronged attack on women's situation would be to involve both men and women equally "in projects of creativity and transcendence." At last women as well as men would be seen as cultural, and women no less than men would participate "in culture's ongoing dialectic with nature."[24]

Nature Ecofeminism

Mary Daly

In general, ecofeminists with a radical-cultural feminist background sought to strengthen rather than weaken women's connections to nature. Unlike Ortner, nature ecofeminists such as Mary Daly believed the traits traditionally associated with women—for example, caring, nurturing, and intuitiveness—stem not so much from their social construction as from their actual biological and psychological experiences. The problem is not that women have a closer relationship with nature than men but that this relationship is undervalued. Nature ecofeminists rejected the assumed inferiority of both women and nature as well as the assumed superiority of both men and culture. Instead, they insisted nature/woman is at least equal to, and perhaps even better than, culture/man, implying that traditional female virtues, not traditional male virtues, can foster improved social relations and less aggressive, more sustainable ways of life.

As noted in Chapter 2, when Daly moved toward a lesbian separatist feminist perspective, she began to reject male culture as evil and to embrace female culture as good. She speculated that before the establishment of patriarchy, there existed an original matriarchy. In this gynocentric world, women flourished. They controlled their own lives, bonded with one another and with the nonhuman world of animals and nature, and lived both freely and happily. Thus, Daly saw the process of women's liberation as putting women back in touch with their original "wild" and "lusty" natural world and freeing them from men's "domesticating" and "dispiriting" cultural world.[25]

Daly contrasted women's life-giving powers with men's death-dealing powers. She claimed that women can have fully human lives, lived vigorously in dynamic communion with animals, the earth, and the stars. Men, she maintained, lack this capacity. They are, she said, parasites who feed off women's energy to fuel their destructive activities and constricting thoughts. Because they cannot bring life into the world and are incapable of bonding with nature, men substitute artificial life for flesh-and-blood life and, in acts of envious rage directed against women, seek to control and destroy not only them but all that is natural. Male culture is everything female nature is not; it is about disease and death rather than health and life, said Daly.[26]

Daly linked men's pollution of nature with men's pollution of women, contrasting men's gynecology with women's "gyn/ecology." Men's gynecology is about segmenting and specializing reproduction as if it were just another mode of production; it is about substituting the fake for the real, the artificial for the natural; it is about cutting the whole into parts. In contrast, women's gyn/ecology is about "discovering, developing the complex web of living/loving relationships *of our own kind.* It is about *women* living, loving, creating our Selves, our cosmos."[27] Whereas men's gynecology depends upon "fixation and dismemberment," women's gyn/ecology affirms that everything is connected.[28] According to Daly, women must work hard to stop the patriarchal forces of necrophilia—that is, of death. Most women, she claimed, have been seduced into cooperating with the "phallocentric" system of "necrophilia"; they have become men's "fembots," permitting themselves to be drained of their life forces.[29] In the days of matriarchy, Daly said, women reproduced through parthenogenesis, their eggs dividing and developing independently of sperm. Now, in the days of patriarchy, men have persuaded women to exchange natural reproduction for artificial reproduction. With this supposed advance in science, said Daly, men move closer to achieving what they really seek—death—and unless women refuse to become men's "fembots," men will consume them together with nature.[30]

Susan Griffin

Although Susan Griffin did not claim biological connections between women and nature, she did posit ontological connections between them.[31] "We know ourselves to be made from this earth. We know this earth is made from our bodies. For we see ourselves. And we are nature. We are nature seeing nature. We are nature with a concept of nature. Nature weeping. Nature speaking of nature to nature."[32] In addition to implying women have a special way of knowing and perceiving reality because of their special connections to nature, Griffin suggested that women must help human beings escape the false and destructive dualistic world into which men, particularly male Western philosophers, have led us.

Griffin sought to overcome dualism by providing a cure for what she regarded as ancient philosopher Plato's harmful "epistemological hierarchy."[33] In his *Republic*, Plato led Western man out of what the philosopher regarded as an inferior sensory realm, the world of appearances, into what he regarded as a superior intellectual realm, the world of forms. In this latter world supposedly reside such ideas as beauty, truth, and goodness. However, in the first book of *Woman and Nature*, Griffin suggested that Plato had led us astray by incorrectly insisting that spirit is superior to matter and prompting us to view man as mind and woman as body. Plato's dualistic hierarchy, stressed Griffin, is behind Western society's view that women are men's inferiors.[34]

Emphasizing the links between men's ideas about nature and their attitudes toward women, Griffin saw similarities between their domestication of animals on the one hand and their "domestication" of women on the other. She also noted ways in which women have either actively participated in or passively accepted their own "taming."[35] Asked why she chose to describe women in terms of domestic rather than wild animals, Griffin responded that her two-year experience as a housebound wife and mother caused her to identify with domestic animals, whom she viewed as well cared for but decidedly unfree.[36]

Griffin viewed Western thought's privileging of culture (man) over nature (woman) as wrongheaded. In the second book of *Woman and Nature*, she identified the main conceptual rifts generated by Platonic philosophy: mind-body, intellect-emotion, city-wilderness, knower-known. She also critiqued scientific knowledge and its reduction of everything to a number, a statistic, a cost-benefit ratio. Horrified by the thought of a world ruled by and reduced to numbers, Griffin urged women to journey out of culture— the labyrinth of dualistic thinking—back into nature, the cave where matter and spirit merge into one, the true habitat of human beings who are more than mere ideas.

Finally, in the third and fourth books of *Woman and Nature*, Griffin claimed we can overcome the kind of thinking that belittles nature, materiality, the body, and women, but only if women learn to speak for themselves and for the natural world. She insisted we need to replace "his certainty"— quantity, probability, and gravity—with "her possibility," his "land" and "timber" with "this earth" and "the forest," and his reason with her emotion. Nature has a value irreducible to its usefulness to culture, and woman has a value irreducible to her usefulness to man.[37]

In some of her later work, Griffin revisited the nature-culture dichotomy, depicting pornography as culture's revenge against nature as well as men's revenge against women. "We will see," said Griffin, "that the bodies of women in pornography, mastered, bound, silenced, beaten, even murdered, are symbols for natural feeling and the powers of nature which the pornographic mind hates and fears."[38] Just as women's violated bodies are used to sell all sorts of commodities such as cars, boats, and designer jeans, nature's violated "body" is used to sell all sorts of exotic tours, Antarctica being one of the most highly sought destinations. Women, insisted Griffin, must refuse to permit the exploitation of themselves and nature in such ways. Reform, indeed revolution, begins with saying no to what is and instead seeks what might be.[39]

Spiritual Ecofeminism

Closely allied to radical-cultural ecofeminists and inspired by Daly's *Gyn/Ecology* and Rosemary Radford Ruether's *New Woman, New Earth*,[40] so-called spiritual ecofeminists insisted that no matter which theology, religion, or spirituality women adopt, it must be an embodied rather than a disembodied way of relating to the ultimate source or deepest wellspring of meaning. Most spiritual ecofeminists implied that unless patriarchal religions, especially Christianity, can purge themselves of the idea of an omnipotent, disembodied male spirit, women should abandon the oppressive confines of their synagogues, mosques, and churches and run to the open spaces of nature, where they can practice any one of several earth-based spiritualities.

Although spiritual ecofeminists drew strength from a variety of earth-based spiritualities, these thinkers tended to gravitate toward ancient goddess worship and nature-oriented Native American Indian ritual. They believed cultures that view the female body as sacred also view nature as sacred, honoring its cycles and rhythms. Spiritual ecofeminists often drew an analogy between the role of women in biological production and that of an archetypal "Earth Mother" or "birth-mother" (usually referred to as "Gaia") in giving life to and creating all that exists.[41] Because women's role is analogous to Gaia's, women's relationship to nature is privileged over men's, according to spiritual ecofeminists.

Starhawk

Among the best-known spiritual ecofeminists is Starhawk, a Wiccan priestess, social activist, and psychotherapist. In her poems, she frequently wrote that nature's and women's work are one and the same.[42] Through their uniquely female bodily experiences—their monthly menses, the demanding symbiosis of pregnancy, the pain of childbirth, and the pleasure of breast-feeding their infants—women supposedly come to know, in a way men cannot, that human beings are one with nature.

Starhawk claimed that the kind of earth-based spirituality she practices as a witch—that is, a woman charged with the task and possessing the skill to "bend" and "reshape" Western culture—provides a good deal of the energy in the feminist movement.[43] In her estimation, earth-based spirituality has three core concepts. The first is immanence. The Goddess is in the living world, in the human, animal, plant, and mineral communities. Therefore, each being has value, and each conscious being also has power. Understood not as power over but as power from within, it is "the inherent ability . . . to become what we are meant to be—as a seed has within it the inherent power to root, grow, flower, and fruit."[44] We grow in this kind of creative power, claimed Starhawk, when we take on responsibility for everyone and everything to which we are related and also when we strive to achieve personal integrity by viewing our needs as no more important than those of others in our relational network. Spirituality is not an "opiate"; it is an energizer and stimulus to action. Starhawk explained, "When what's going on is the poisoning and destruction of the earth, our own personal development requires that we grapple with that and do something to stop it, to turn the tide and heal the planet."[45]

The second feature of earth-based spirituality is interconnection and the expanded view of self it encourages. Not only are our bodies natural, but so, too, are our minds. Starhawk stressed, "Our human capacities of loyalty and love, rage and humor, lust, intuition, intellect, and compassion are as much a part of nature as the lizards and the redwood forests."[46] The more we understand that we are nature, she wrote, the more we will understand our oneness with all that exists: human beings, natural cycles and processes, animals, and plants.[47]

The third and probably most important feature of earth-based spirituality is the leading of a compassionate life. Starhawk claimed that unless all people adopt this type of lifestyle, which requires them to care for one another, we can forget about "reweaving the world" or "healing the wounds." Thus, she faulted deep ecologist Daniel Conner for suggesting that "the AIDS virus may be Gaia's tailor-made answer to human overpopulation," as well as deep ecologist Dave Foreman for opposing the provision of famine relief to starving African countries: "When environmentalists applaud the demise of Africans and homosexuals, they ally themselves with the same interests that are killing people of color, gay people, women, and other vulnerable groups. Those same interests are destroying the earth's ecosystems and raping the wilderness."[48] According to Starhawk, spiritual ecofeminists—especially those who regard themselves as witches—bring to the environmental movement a compassionate perspective that permits them "to identify powerlessness and the structures that perpetuate it as the root cause of famine, of overpopulation, of the callous destruction of the natural environment."[49]

We must dissolve the nature-culture dichotomy, indeed all dichotomies, so that we can appreciate the oneness of reality. Starhawk implied, however, that it is not a matter of indifference how we achieve this oneness. Nature ought to subsume culture rather than vice versa, for unless we all live more simply, masses of people will not be able to live at all. Like Ruether, Starhawk viewed the present distribution of the world's wealth among people as shockingly unjust.[50] She urged people committed to world justice and ecological sustainability to engage in direct action movements such as the massive anti–World Trade Organization protests that started in Seattle in November 1999 and have continued to this day. She also recommended that social justice activists use communications media, in particular the Internet and cell phones, to make visible and audible to people the sights and sounds of human poverty.

Starhawk admitted that, initially, it would be difficult for people to forsake the creature comforts and luxuries of today's high-end, unsustainable economies. Still, she believed that as people started to lead simpler existences, they would discover there is more to life than possessing things. Starhawk urged women to take the lead in the save-the-earth movement, bringing as many men into it as possible.[51]

Carol Christ

Like Starhawk, Carol Christ is a pagan spiritual ecofeminist. She consistently sought to replace the God of patriarchy (omniscient, omnipotent, and immutable) with a Goddess of humanity (learning, fallible, and constantly changing). She wanted people to practice Goddess religion—that is, the effort to imaginatively reconstruct the egalitarian harmony between humans and nature that existed in supposedly nonhierarchical, prepatriarchal times. For Christ, hierarchical thinking and its alienating dualisms have been our undoing. By tapping into the power of the Goddess in ourselves—which she defined as the lure to goodness—we can help one another overcome the alienated and hostile relations that characterize our power-hungry world.

Interestingly, Christ did not guarantee us success in our efforts to become more egalitarian and loving. She saw the web of good human relationships, including those with nature, as fragile and in continual need of repair. But rather than despairing at the thought of people endlessly trying to fix relationships, Christ embraced it as providing us with our meaning and purpose. She suggested that we rise each morning with the following greeting to the sun: "As this day dawns in beauty, we pledge ourselves to repair the web."[52]

Transformative Ecofeminism

Unlike nature and spiritual ecofeminists, transformative or social-constructionist ecofeminists sought to transform the nature-woman connection. They claimed that women's connection to nature is socially constructed and ideologically reinforced. Because this is so, women can help transform the meaning of their connection to both nature and culture.

Dorothy Dinnerstein

We need to explode Western dichotomous thought, said Dorothy Dinnerstein (see Chapter 6), if we hope to end the oppression of everyone and everything currently devalued. This explosion must begin with the deconstruction of the male-female dichotomy, for it is the fundamental source of "the silent hatred of Mother Earth which breathes side by side with our love for her, and which, like the hate we feel for our human mothers, poisons our attachment to life."[53] Dinnerstein asserted, however, that the attempt to exclude women and nature from men and culture has caused society (she includes women as complicit in this psychopathological arrangement) not only to "*maim and exploit women, and stunt and deform men*" but also to proceed "*toward the final matricide—the rageful, greedy murder of the planet that spawned us.*"[54] Borrowing an idea from Lewis Mumford, she observed that most of us are firm believers in the "megamachine" myth according to which human beings can use their minds and tools not only to extend control over nature and everything identified with it—woman, the body, life, death, and so on—but also to make huge monetary profits in doing so. Dinnerstein said that this myth will continue to rule our thoughts and actions unless we end the present division of the world into male and female (culture and nature) and the assignments of women to nature (child rearing and childbearing) and men to culture (world building).

Women must bring nature into culture (by entering the public world), and men must bring culture into nature (by entering the private world). Then and only then will we see that men and women (culture and nature) are one and that it is counterproductive for half of reality to try to dominate the other half. A reality, divided and at war with itself, cannot and will not survive. Thus, Dinnerstein proclaimed, "the core meaning of feminism . . . lies, at this point, in its relations to earthly life's survival."[55]

Karen J. Warren

Like Dinnerstein, Karen J. Warren emphasized that the dualisms threatening to destroy us are social constructions. In a capitalist, patriarchal society, women and nature, men and culture have certain meanings, but these meanings are far from necessary. They would be very different in the kind of socialist, nonpatriarchal society Marge Piercy posited in *Woman on the Edge of Time*—a society in which people rejected all dualisms, beginning with the male-female dichotomy (see Chapter 2). People are both masculine and feminine; society is both natural and cultural.[56]

Aiming to reconceptualize nature and culture as well as man and woman, Warren claimed that feminists must be ecofeminists—without insisting, as Piercy did, that women must forsake their special role in biological reproduction.[57] Warren argued that, logically, feminism is just as much a movement to end naturism as it is a movement to end sexism:

(C1) Feminism is a movement to end sexism.
(C2) But sexism is conceptually linked with naturism (through an oppressive conceptual framework characterized by a logic of domination).
(C3) Thus, feminism is (also) a movement to end naturism.[58]

All forms of oppression are interlocked and intertwined. Oppression is a many-headed beast that will continue to exist and regenerate itself until human beings manage completely to behead it.

Focusing on the kind of ethics currently informing environmentalism, Warren noted within it many sexist elements, or male biases, that undermine its ability to save the earth. Only an ecofeminist ethics—an ethics free of androcentric as well as anthropocentric distortions—can overcome naturism once and for all. Such an ethics, said Warren, must be "care-sensitive."[59]

Warren claimed that her preferred ecofeminist ethics has eight "necessary" or "boundary" conditions. First, it is a theory in process that evolves together with people. Second, it is entirely "opposed to any 'ism' that presupposes or advances a logic of domination."[60] No thread of sexism, racism, classism, naturism, or other ism may be woven into the ecofeminist quilt. Third, and very importantly, an ecofeminist ethics is a contextualist ethics that invites people to narrate their relationships: to specify how they relate to humans, nonhuman animals, and nature. Fourth, said Warren, it is, if anything, an inclusivist ethics that acknowledges, respects, and welcomes difference. It passes the "R-4 test" for good generalizations (i.e., representative, random, the right size, replicable).[61] Fifth, it does not aim to be "objective," even though, as we just noted, it does aim to be unbiased.[62] To be unbiased is not to be neutral; it is to incorporate all perspectives, particularly those that might otherwise not get voiced. Sixth, an ecofeminist ethics views the values of care, love, friendship, and appropriate trust as the core of all ethics. Seventh, it aims to redefine what it means to be a truly human person and to make a decision ethically. Eighth, and most importantly for Warren, an ecofeminist ethics is not based on reason to the exclusion of emotion but on an intelligence that requires reason and emotion to work together and to be recognized as equally valuable in ethical decision making.[63]

In an example of ecofeminist ethics at work, Warren told the story of a young Sioux boy sent by his father to learn "the old Indian ways" from his grandfather. Among other things, the boy's grandfather taught him how to hunt, instructing him to shoot a deer in his hind area, slowing it down but not killing it.

> Then, take the four-legged's head in your hands, and look into his eyes. The eyes are where all the suffering is. Look into your brother's eyes and feel his pain. Then, take your knife and cut the four-legged under his chin, here, on his neck, so that he dies quickly. And as you do, ask your brother, the four-legged, for forgiveness for what you do. Offer also a prayer of thanks to your four-legged kin for offering his body to you just now, when you need food to eat and clothing to wear. And promise the four-legged that you will put yourself back into the earth when you die, to become nourishment for the earth, and for the sister flowers, and for the brother deer. It is appropriate that you should offer this blessing for

the four-legged and, in due time, reciprocate in turn with your body in this way, as the four-legged gives life to you for your survival.[64]

The lesson the Sioux grandfather taught his grandson about hunting is clearly far more ecofeminist than the lesson the typical "great white hunter" would teach his grandson about hunting for the pleasure of the kill. The Sioux hunting lesson informs us how people whose conceptual schemes are not oppositional see themselves in relation to nonhuman nature.

Global Ecofeminism

Ecofeminists who have adopted a global perspective include Maria Mies, a sociologist known for her work on development economics, and Vandana Shiva, a physicist known for her interests in spirituality. Mies and Shiva stressed that because women, more than men, engage in the work of sustaining daily life, they, more than men, are concerned about the elements: air, water, earth, fire. To bear and rear healthy children and provide their families with nourishing food, adequate clothing, and sturdy housing, women need fertile soil, lush plant life, fresh water, and clean air. In addition, Mies and Shiva lamented Western culture's obsession with the idea of "sameness"—the universal "I," the overarching "one." Capitalism and patriarchy, they observed, are systems that stamp out difference, doggedly cloning themselves, their ideas, and their salable goods wherever they go. Finally, like many Marxist and socialist feminists, Mies and Shiva observed how people in capitalist patriarchies tend to be alienated from everything: the products of their labor, nature, each other, and even themselves. As a result, human beings in capitalist patriarchies often engage in some fairly bizarre behavior to reduce their alienation.

In "White Man's Dilemma: His Search for What He Has Destroyed," Mies described in detail some of the mind-boggling ways all people, but particularly white men in capitalist patriarchies, aim to connect with nature—the very nature that their lifestyles and patterns of consumption threaten to destroy. First, she said, the white man attempts to run away from the confines of his urban office "into 'Nature,' the 'wilderness,' the 'underdeveloped' countries of the South, to areas where the white man has not yet 'penetrated.'"[65] Tourist agents in developed countries promote excursions into developing countries with safari-like descriptions: "European tourists can live in villages in close contact with the 'natives' in African-style huts with minimum comfort, African food, no running water and where European and African children play together. The 'real' Africa to be touched!"[66] Second, continued Mies, rather than trying to unite with the mundane nature right in his backyard, the white man seeks to experience a more "exotic" type of nature: nature as "colony, backward, exotic, distant and dangerous, the nature of Asia, Africa, South America."[67] Those who yearn for this kind of nature desire not to relate to it productively by working on it or tending to it but to absorb or consume it by locking it in the chambers of their cameras or marketing it to others through souvenirs. Third, she said, the white man longs for yet another kind of nature, the space known as a woman's body. It, too, is wild terrain, the "dark continent," so the white man relates to a woman's body as he relates to nature: as object of his gaze, as commodity, as a form of play to liberate him, if only for a moment, from his relentless workday.

If life is a theme for socialist-transformative ecofeminists like Mies and Shiva, so, too, is freedom. The freedom to which Mies and Shiva referred does not require man to master nature and therefore woman's body. Rather, it asks all of us to recognize and accept our naturalness, our physicality and materiality, our carnality and mortality. Because nature is an exhaustible good, we must learn to conserve it by living as simply as possible and by consuming as little as possible. If we care about our descendants' lives, we must develop a so-called subsistence perspective as the key to dissolving all the practices and systems that threaten to destroy the earth. All people should have a materially equal share in the world's resources.[68]

Vegetarian Ecofeminism

The relationship between vegetarianism and ecofeminism, mentioned briefly above, deserves more consideration because of not only the large role that animals play in nature but also the amount of suffering and pain inflicted upon them worldwide. According to Carol Adams, "From the leather in our shoes, the soap we use to cleanse our face, the down in the comforter, the meat we eat, and the dairy products we rely on, our world as we now know it is structured around a dependence on the death of the other animals."[69]

Many ecofeminists are vegetarians or vegans. Vegetarians do not eat meat but use animal by-products. For vegans, the abstention from animal flesh is insufficient, because animals used for by-products are also reduced to their instrumental value and are subjects of extreme suffering within, for example, dairy farms, egg hatcheries, and experimentation laboratories. Vegetarian and vegan ecofeminists tend not to be absolutist in their moral stances; rather, they are often contextual as opposed to universal moral vegetarians. In general, contextual moral vegetarians concede that there are societies in which using animal flesh or bodily products is necessary for human survival. One such society may be the Native American tribe Karen J. Warren described above, which could not survive unless it hunted. Such societies are exceptional, however. According to many contextual vegetarian feminists, eating meat or even eggs and dairy products is not necessary for survival for most people living in developed countries. On the contrary, developed countries have readily available a surplus of protein and calcium options, such as beans, whole grains, nut milks, and soy-based cheese and meat alternatives, as well as a variety of synthetic materials for clothing and other commodity needs.

Traditional philosophers Peter Singer (*Animal Liberation,* 1975)[70] and Tom Regan (*The Case for Animal Rights,* 1983) took the moral standing of animals seriously.[71] According to Singer, utilitarianism demands that the interests of each sentient being (that is, any creature able to feel pleasure and pain) be taken into account in moral decision making. Reasoning differently, Regan posited that we must not kill any sentient being because all sentient beings have the capacity and/or actuality of some form of thinking, calculating, reasoning, and consciousness. Many nonhuman animals—especially large mammals, such as whales, dolphins, elephants, and great apes—seem self-aware and able to engage in some form of thinking and communication. Therefore, human beings must not violate these animals' most basic rights by abusing or killing them. Singer and Regan proclaimed as "speciesist"—that is, unfairly biased toward members of their own species—those critics who protested that the interests of nonhuman animals are not as important as those of human beings or their thinking not as advanced.

Going beyond Singer's and Regan's arguments on behalf of animal interests, vegetarian ecofeminist Greta Gaard stressed the importance of sympathy for nonhuman animals, which we should view as individuals with the capacity to feel.[72] Although some feminists may be persuaded to become vegetarian ecofeminists through rational argument alone, many do so because they can't stand to see an animal suffer.[73]

An ethics of care toward animals is an extension of the sympathy argument in favor of vegetarian ecofeminism, according to Grace Kao.[74] A good way to understand Kao's point here is to reflect on how much some people care about their pet dogs and cats. Many people view these companion animals as members of the family: they feed them, enjoy recreation with them, tend to their health-care needs, and suffer immense distress on losing them. Moreover, most people cringe at animal cruelty if it involves dogs, cats, horses, great apes, dolphins, or other large, culturally familiar animals. So, the argument goes, if we can and should sympathize with a beaten and starving dog, then why can't or shouldn't we sympathize with a hen stuffed into a battery cage (unable to spread her wings or enjoy the sunlight) or a sickly piglet lying forgotten on the concrete floor of a factory farm? It is worth considering that something like Adams's "absent referent" must be at work here. Adams explained, "We live in a culture that has institution-alized the oppression of animals on at least two levels: in formal structures such as slaughterhouses, meatmarkets, zoos, laboratories, and circuses, and through our language. That we refer to meat eating rather than to corpse eating is a central example of how our language transmits the dominant cul-ture's approval of this activity."[75] When we are singing "Old MacDonald Had a Farm" or reading *Charlotte's Web*, we block from our consciousness the individual pigs, cows, chickens, lambs, and so forth that wind up as so-called meat on our platters; these animals, according to Adams, are "absent referents." In this view, the word "meat" hides from us the fact that we are eating the cow or pig we saw last week in a feed lot. If we focus on the indi-vidual animal, we become conscious that we are eating a sentient being and not an object.

Environmental Ecofeminism

In *Scared Gaia*, Anne Primavesi constructed what we might call a feminist environmentalism. She focused on how people in the North use fossil fu-els to the detriment of people in the South: "In today's consumerist cul-ture, over extraction and overconsumption of energy can be seen to harm the most vulnerable members of society and other life forms on the planet. The harm lies not only in the gross inequities between one group's access to energy sources compared with that of another, but also in the fact that the extraction and processing of raw materials has been advanced to a stage where the scale and pace of their extraction far outstrips the scale and pace of their replacement."[76] Primavesi sought to answer Willi Brandt's 1978 ques-tion: "Are we to leave our successors a scorched planet of advancing deserts, impoverished landscapes and an ailing environment?"[77] The Brandt Report took as its framework the now familiar North-South divide, which distin-guishes between rich and developed "Northern" countries and poor and de-veloping "Southern" countries.[78] Whereas the life expectancy, number of calories consumed, and access to water are high in the former, they are low in the latter. For example, people in Somalia consume only 1,505 calories per day,[79] the number allowed in many US weight-loss plans.

Primavesi argued that it is very unfair for people in the North to use three times more of the world's resources than people in the South. The North's "ecological footprint"[80] is huge, using much more than the hemisphere's fair share of nature's bounty.[81] The South does so much of the North's work and produces so much of its goods and services that it scarcely has enough time to generate a subsistence level of products for itself. Primavesi expressed en-thusiasm for the "environmental space" analyses developed by a variety of

Northern economists in the last decade or so. The best of these analyses, she said, rests on three principles: "First, that environmental space is limited, and that its limits are sufficiently quantifiable to provide valuable policy guidance. Second, that there is a need for equitable global development, which means that all countries should have equal access to the world's resources, and equal responsibility for their management. Third, that production and consumption should serve to enhance the quality of life rather than degrade it."[82]

According to Primavesi, feminists should take the lead in programs that downsize the North's "ecological feet" and refuse to buy into the kind of consumerism that causes people to overconsume and then, frantically, to overproduce in a sort of bulimic cycle. Equality is impossible unless all the earth's people learn to live with less so that no one is without enough.[83]

Critiques of Ecofeminism

Critique One: Nature Ecofeminism Reduces Women to Mere Bodies

The critiques raised against nature ecofeminism resembled those raised against radical-cultural feminism. Janet Biehl asserted that nature ecofeminists err when they "biologize women as presumably uniquely ecological beings" who can relate to and understand nature, and who care and nurture, in ways that men, try as they might, simply cannot.[84] There is, said Biehl, too much willingness among nature ecofeminists either to reduce women to mere bodies or to limit their potentialities and abilities to those associated with their supposedly caring nature. Biehl saw nature ecofeminism as reactionary rather than revolutionary. Quoting Simone de Beauvoir, from whom many nature ecofeminists borrow their basic concept of women's and nature's otherness, she stressed that women who celebrate the nature-woman connection do so at their own peril, for "that's the formula used to try and keep women quiet."[85] Biehl insisted that nature ecofeminists, such as Mary Daly, misled women by suggesting women can by fiat reclaim the meaning of the nature-woman connection as entirely positive. In reality, Biehl pointed out, the nature-woman connection has been "enormously debasing to women," and passionate "reclaiming" alone cannot cast off centuries of negative cultural baggage.[86]

Critique Two: Spiritual Ecofeminism Is Not Secular Enough

Critics faulted spiritual ecofeminists for substituting religion for politics and for spending too much time dancing in the moonlight, weaving magic spells, chanting mantras, doing yoga, mindfully meditating, and giving one another massages. Defenders of spiritual ecofeminism conceded that some spiritual ecofeminists may have mistaken New Age or "spa" spirituality for genuine ecofeminism, but they insisted such mistakes are the exception, not the rule. Goddess worship is not, according to Mies and Shiva, "luxury spirituality," "the idealist icing on top of the material cake of the West's standard of living."[87] It is not about turning the East's spiritual and cultural treasures into commodities for sale as exotica to privileged and pampered Western people who lack meaning. Rather, Goddess worship is an attempt to break the culturally constructed dichotomy between spirituality and materiality and to recognize everything and everyone as worthy and deserving of respect. Spiritual ecofeminists, observed Ynestra King, are not otherworldly dreamers; they are this-worldly activists. They use such "community-building techniques" as performance art, kinesthetic observations (dancing and chanting), and ritual to enable people "to establish and maintain community with one another in contentious and difficult situations of political engagement in the public world."[88]

Critique Three: Transformative Ecofeminism Requires Too Much Commitment to Environmental Causes

Despite finding the perspective of transformative ecofeminism compelling, critics suspected its demands might be too challenging for relatively affluent people to accept. In particular, they thought comfortable and complacent citizens would be unlikely to embrace the degree of activism and lifestyle change required by transformative-socialist ecofeminism. Most people, including most feminists, do not want to radically change the way they live. For example, they do not want to become card-carrying vegetarians or pacifists.

In response to this objection, some transformative-socialist ecofeminists simply commented that people's reluctance to make lifestyle changes is not a moral justification for their not doing so. Altruism requires a certain measure of self-sacrifice. Other socialist and transformative-socialist ecofeminists softened this response by conceding that moral progress is often incremental. Even if not willing to forsake eating meat altogether, a person can at least refuse to eat factory-farmed animals or those raised under extremely cruel conditions. Likewise, even those who are unwilling to devote the bulk of their time to environmental causes or who feel overwhelmed by them can always make some positive difference, however small. For example, one can take a reusable tote bag to the grocery store, thereby lessening the use of paper and/or plastic bags.

Critique Four: Global Ecofeminism Is a Self-Contradictory Theory

Critics of global ecofeminism, such as Janet Biehl, found the counterpositioning of women and nature against Western culture at large regressive for the interests of women. Biehl found the following of particular concern: (1) the association of the feminine with the irrational, (2) the location of Western women outside of the purview of Western culture, (3) the implication that women have a dominant role in developing a sensibility of "caring" and "nurturing," and (4) the claim that women are unique in their ability to appreciate humanity's "interconnectedness" with the natural world.[89] In addition, critics of global ecofeminist faulted it for offering a theory full of contradictions: "Some assert that 'All is One,' while others argue for particularism and multiplicity. Some are influenced by social ecology, while others have ties with deep ecology. Some regard ecofeminism as a liberatory concept of nearly unprecedented proportions, while others reject the name 'ecofeminism' altogether as insulting to feminist activists."[90] Most worrisome, said Biehl, global ecofeminism's "sweeping but highly confused cosmology introduces magic, goddesses, witchcraft, privileged quasi-biological traits, irrationalities, Neolithic atavisms, and mysticism into a movement that once tried to gain the best benefits of the Enlightenment and the most valuable features of [Western] civilization for women."[91]

Critique Five: Vegetarian Ecofeminism Is Too Restrictive

As stated above, most vegetarian ecofeminists are contextual as opposed to universal moral vegetarians; that is, they concede exceptions to the rule of not using or killing animals, whereas universal moral vegetarians do not. Karen J. Warren, however, faulted champions of animal welfare for raising animals "to the status of full-fledged members of the moral club to which humans belong," challenging the traditionally accepted ethical hierarchy.[92] Some feminists also found comparison of the plight of animals to that of women both degrading and distracting from women's interests. These critics thought that linking women's rights to the rights of nonhuman animals suggests a demeaning commonality with so-called lower species. Additionally, animal welfarists elevate sentient individuals (humans and animals) "over and against the rest of nature," while the "ecological 'wholes' (e.g., populations, communities, species, and ecosystems) are inappropriately omitted from moral consideration."[93] In other words, Warren said, animals and humans are viewed without any "historical, social, and material contexts and independent of any relationships to other moral subjects."[94] Likewise, she said, universal moral vegetarianism problematically rests on a "male physiological norm" that presupposes everyone can easily and safely abstain from animal products, when in fact some populations would find the lifestyle quite challenging (e.g., "some infants, children, adolescents, gestating and lactating women, Inuit, [and] primal peoples").[95]

Critique Six: Environmental Ecofeminism Is Just Environmentalism

Because it is difficult to argue against using the world's resources prudently so that future generations have adequate food, clothing, shelter, and so forth, critics of feminist environmentalism said that it is simply good environmentalism for everyone. As such, the label "feminist" unnecessarily limits the scope of environmentalism.

Conclusion

No matter their differences, nature, spiritual, transformative, and environmental ecofeminists all believe human beings are connected to the nonhuman world: animal, plant, and inert. Unfortunately, because we do not always acknowledge our relationship to the nonhuman world, we do violence to one another and to nature, congratulating ourselves on protecting our self-interests. In reality, each day we kill ourselves by laying waste to the earth from which we originate and to which we will return.

Given the state of human affairs just described, ecofeminists wonder what it will take for humanity to realize how irrational as well as unfeeling human systems of oppression and domination are. These systems bring in their wake hate, anger, destruction, and death; yet we cling to our social constructs. Is the solution to this pathological state of affairs to create a culture in which we honor women and nature as saviors of sorts? Or should we instead follow Dinnerstein's instructions and insist that men and women alike assume equal responsibility for both child rearing and world building? What will it take for us to stop thinking dichotomously and to recognize that we are our own worst enemy? Are we wasting time waiting for the saving grace of some Godot when we should instead be using our own heads and hearts to stop destroying what we in fact are: an interdependent whole, a unity that exists in and through, not despite, its diversity? Ecofeminists have already made their decision. They stopped waiting for the revolution, the transformation, the miracle to happen a long time ago. They urge all people to do what they can to eliminate the blights that brown the earth and kill the human spirit.[96]

Questions for Discussion

1. Provide examples in which both women and nature are devalued, and consider under what religious reasoning such devaluation might have occurred.

2. Do you believe women can be liberated without simultaneously liberating nature? Or do you believe we must topple a larger culture of oppression to emancipate all within the grip of injustice?

3. Reflect on connections among the commodification of women, the "sexual politics of meat," and "earth pornography." Consider examples from advertising, entertainment, and recreation. How does the "pornographic mind" convey that women, animals, and nature are only useful in so far as they are useful to man and to culture writ large?

4. In what ways does Warren's suggestion to erase the nature-culture dichotomy work to liberate both women and men, as well as animals and nature? How does inclusivist ethics provide a voice to the historically voiceless among us (both sentient and nonsentient)?

5. Are ecofeminists (and other sorts of feminists, for that matter) morally obligated to adopt some form of vegetarian lifestyle? Why or why not?

9

Existentialist, Poststructural, and Postmodern Feminisms

Shortly before Simone de Beauvoir died, Margaret A. Simons and Jessica Benjamin interviewed her for the journal *Feminist Studies*. In their background commentary, Simons and Benjamin commented on the significance of de Beauvoir's major theoretical work, *The Second Sex*.[1] Written in 1958, yet still sounding contemporary, *The Second Sex* has clearly achieved the status of a classic in feminist thought. Thus, no introduction to feminist thought would be nearly complete without a discussion of this work, which has elucidated the significance of woman's otherness in existentialist terms.

Over the years questions have arisen about the precise relationship between de Beauvoir's *Second Sex* and Jean-Paul Sartre's *Being and Nothingness*. The first and ultimately mistaken view holds that *The Second Sex* merely applies *Being and Nothingness* to women's specific situation. To be sure, Sartre and de Beauvoir were on-and-off lovers for many years and, initially, Sartre was de Beauvoir's teacher. However, by the time they both became well-known authors, de Beauvoir was anything but Sartre's student; she was his intellectual companion and at times his teacher.[2] Still, there are enough existentialist links between de Beauvoir and Sartre to warrant a brief overview of Sartre's thought.

Existentialism: Focus on Jean-Paul Sartre

In *Being and Nothingness* Sartre made a fundamental distinction between the observer and the observed by dividing being into two parts: being-in-itself (*en-soi*) and being-for-itself (*pour-soi*). Being-in-itself refers to the repetitive,

231

material existence humans share with animals, vegetables, and minerals; being-for-itself refers to the moving, conscious existence human beings share with one another.[3]

The distinction between being-in-itself and being-for-itself is useful in an analysis of the human person to the degree we associate being-in-itself with the body. The body has constant and objective being. As it can be seen, touched, heard, smelled, and tasted; the body is the perceived. In contrast, the perceiver—the entity that does the seeing, touching, hearing, smelling, and tasting—is not itself a perceptible object but, according to Sartre, still has a certain kind of being: being-for-itself. To appreciate being-for-itself fully, picture someone who is momentarily conscious of the fingers on her hand. Her "I" is identified with her fingers because they are, after all, her fingers, not anyone else's. However, her "I" is also distinct from her fingers because she is at the same time more, or other, than her fingers. According to Sartre, paradoxically, nothing (literally, no-thing, or nothingness) separates one's "I"—one's consciousness or mind—from one's body.

To the first two kinds of being, Sartre added a third, being-for-others. He sometimes described this mode of being positively as *Mitsein*, a communal "being-with." More frequently, however, he described it negatively, as involving "a personal conflict as each For-itself seeks to recover its own Being by directly or indirectly making an object out of the other."[4] Because each being-for-itself establishes itself as a subject, as a self, precisely by defining other beings as objects, as others, the action of consciousness sets up a system of fundamentally conflictual social relations. Thus, the process of self-definition is one of seeking power over other beings: "While I attempt to free myself from the hold of the Other, the Other is trying to free himself from mine; while I seek to enslave the Other, the Other seeks to enslave me. . . . Descriptions of concrete behavior must be seen within the perspective of conflict."[5] In establishing itself as a self, each self describes and prescribes roles for the other. Moreover, each subject conceives of itself as transcendent and free and views the other as immanent and enslaved.

Of Sartre's three categories, being-for-others is probably the most suited for a feminist analysis. According to Sartre, human relations are variations on two basic themes of conflict between rival consciousnesses, between the self and the other: love, which is essentially masochistic, and indifference, desire, and hate, which are essentially sadistic.[6]

Fools that we are, most of us start out with very grand ideas about love, about harmonizing the self and the other, said Sartre. The quest for love, we believe, is our attempt to be one with the other. This attempt is similar to Christian "mystics'" effort to become one with God without forsaking their unique personal identities. Mystical union, we believe, is a very mysterious state. Mystics are at one and the same time themselves and God. We wish to create this mysterious state for ourselves. But according to Sartre, union without absorption is an impossible dream. We live in a very nonmystical world. There is no possibility of harmony, or union, between the self and the other; the self's need for total freedom is too absolute. Our attempts at true love—at union without absorption—will always deteriorate into mutual possession or mutual objectification. Exhausted by the struggle to maintain our subjectivity and freedom, but still desiring a relationship (albeit one that is literally self-destructive) with the other, we may be led to masochism, the prospect of losing our subjectivity altogether in that of the other, who is now invited to treat us as a mere object.

Masochism is, for Sartre, not the perversion of love but its essential consequence. Through pain and humiliation, we hope to erase our subjectivity, to actually become the object that the other, the torturer, perceives as us. Our suffering may seem to testify that we have no choice in the matter; however, as Sartre explained, this is a delusion. To be masochists, we must choose to apprehend ourselves as objects. Thus, as a flight from subjectivity, masochism is a dead end. The more we try to reduce ourselves to mere objects, the more we became aware of ourselves as subjectivities attempting this reduction.[7]

Defeated in our attempt to exist either as lovers or as failed lovers (masochists), we may be driven to indifference-desire or sadism-hate, the attempt to defy the freedom of the other. Our defiance begins quietly with indifference, a form of what Sartre called "blindness," or the nonrecognition of the subjectivity of others. Blind, we make no attempt to apprehend the other as anything but an object: "I scarcely notice [others]; I act as if I were alone in the world."[8] This solipsism is ego building, for it allows us to overlook that we are determined by others, shaped by the look of those others among whom we strut. When we are indifferent to others, we pretend they do not exist, that they cannot define us or pigeonhole us. But our pretense fails. Others exist whether we acknowledge them or not, and in their eyes we are only objects. Nevertheless, what occurs without our acknowledgment still, in fact, occurs: there exist others in whose eyes we are objects. What we refuse to recognize, then, may at any moment intrude upon us. The other may at any moment direct at us an altogether human look: "Brief and terrifying flashes of illumination," said Sartre, may rip through the shroud of our indifference, forcing us to recognize the subjectivity and freedom of the other.[9]

Receiving the look of the other ruins our attempt at total indifference, at times so much so that we come to desire the other sexually. To desire the other sexually is to want the other as mere flesh, as total object. There is, said

Sartre, something sadistic about this desire. But no sooner do we possess the other as body than we discover it was not the other as body but the other as self we desired: "To be sure, I can grasp the Other, grab hold of him, knock him down. I can, providing I have the power, compel him to perform this or that act, to say certain words. But everything happens as if I wished to get hold of a man who runs away and leaves only his coat in my hands. It is the coat, it is the outer shell which I possess. I shall never get hold of more than a body, a psychic object in the midst of the world."[10] Just when we think we are about to triumph over the other—just when the other's consciousness as well as its flesh seems ready to yield to us—the other may look us in the eye and make of us an object. By reestablishing itself as a subject, insisted Sartre, the other frustrates our attempt at sadism.

Unable to eliminate the threat or independence of the other even through sadism, our only recourse is hate—the wish for the death of the other. We want to wipe out forever the self who has, by looking at us as the other, threatened our freedom. If we feel we have been ridiculous or evil or cowardly in the other's consciousness, we may wish to wipe out the embarrassment by destroying that consciousness. Sartre pointed out that hatred of a particular other is, in reality, hatred of all others. If we wish not to be a self-for-others, logically we must annihilate all others. But hate is also futile, for even if all others ceased to exist, the memory of their looks would live on forever in our consciousness, inseparable from whatever ideas we might try to form about ourselves. So even our last recourse does not suffice: "Hate does not enable us to get out of the circle. It simply represents the final attempt, the attempt of despair. After the failure of this attempt nothing remains for the for-itself except to re-enter the circle and allow itself to be infinitely tossed."[11]

Existentialist Feminism: Focus on Simone de Beauvoir

In adopting the ontological and ethical language of existentialism, de Beauvoir observed that men named "man" the self and "woman" the other. If the other is a threat to the self, then woman is a threat to man. Therefore, if man wishes to remain free, he must subordinate woman to him. To be sure, gender oppression is not the only form of oppression. Far from it. People of color know oppression by whites, and the poor know oppression by the rich. Nonetheless, insisted Dorothy Kaufmann McCall, women's oppression by men is unique for two reasons: First, unlike the oppression of race and class, it is not a contingent historical fact, an event in time that has sometimes been contested or reversed. Woman has always been subordinate to man. Second, women have internalized the alien point of view that man is the essential, woman the inessential.[12]

Destiny and History of Women

A good way to test de Beauvoir's characterization of woman's oppression as unique is to examine her analysis of how woman became the other. In the first three chapters of *The Second Sex*, respectively titled "The Data of Biology," "The Psychoanalytic Point of View," and "The Point of View of Historical Materialism," de Beauvoir discussed how woman became not only different and separate from man but also inferior to him. She claimed that although biologists, Freudian psychoanalysts, and Marxist economists helped illuminate the reasons for woman's otherness, existentialist philosophers provided the best explanation for it.

De Beauvoir noted that biology provides society with facts, which society then interprets to suit its own ends. For example, biology describes the respective reproductive roles of males and females: "The sperm, through which the life of the male is transcended in another, at the same instant becomes a stranger to him and separates from his body, so that the male recovers his individuality intact at the moment when he transcends it. The egg, on the contrary, begins to separate from the female body when, fully matured, it emerges from the follicle and falls into the oviduct; but if fertilized by a gamete from outside, it becomes attached again through implantation in the uterus. First violated, the female is then alienated—she becomes, in part, another than herself."[13] Although these reproductive "facts" might explain why a woman oftentimes finds it harder to become and remain a self, especially if she has a child, in de Beauvoir's estimation they in no way prove the societal myth that women's capacity for selfhood is somehow intrinsically less than men's.

De Beauvoir repeatedly observed that although biological and physiological facts about woman—such as her primary role in reproduction relative to man's secondary role, her physical weakness relative to man's physical strength, and her inactive role in heterosexual intercourse relative to man's active role—are true enough, how much value we attach to these facts is up to us as social beings. She wrote, "The enslavement of the female to the species and the limitations of her various powers are extremely important facts; the body of woman is one of the essential elements in her situation in the world. But that body is not enough to define her as woman; there is no true living reality except as manifested by the conscious individual through activities and in the bosom of a society. Biology is not enough to give an answer to the question that is before us: why is woman the Other?"[14] In other words, because woman is being-for-herself as well as being-in-itself, we must look for causes and reasons beyond those suggested by female biology and physiology to fully explain why society has selected woman to play the role of the other.

When de Beauvoir looked beyond biology to psychology, especially psychoanalysis, for a better explanation of woman's otherness, she was disappointed. According to de Beauvoir, traditional Freudians all tell essentially the same story about woman: She is a creature who must struggle between her "viriloid" and her "feminine" tendencies, the first expressed through clitoral eroticism, the second through vaginal eroticism. To win this battle—to become "normal"—woman must overcome her "viriloid" tendencies and transfer her love from a woman to a man. Although de Beauvoir conceded Freud's genius—which, for her, consisted in his having forwarded the bold idea that sexuality is the ultimate explanation for the human condition—she nevertheless rejected this notion as simplistic. In other words, civilization cannot be explained merely as the product of repressed or sublimated sexual impulses. Civilization is more complicated than this, and so are the relations between men and women.

In particular, de Beauvoir viewed Freud's explanation for woman's otherness as incomplete. She faulted Freudians for teaching that women's low social status relative to men stems simply from their lack of a penis. Anticipating by decades a central tenet of the US woman's movement, de Beauvoir refused to concede that women's anatomy consigns them to second-class personhood and citizenship. Women envy those who possess a penis, said de Beauvoir, not because they want a penis per se but because they desire the material and psychological privileges society accords to penis possessors. The social status of men is not to be traced to certain features of the male anatomy; rather, the "prestige of the penis" is to be explained "by the sovereignty of the father." Women are the other not because they lack penises but because they lack power.[15]

Finally, de Beauvoir considered the Marxist explanation for why woman is the other and found it as unsatisfying as Freud's. Friedrich Engels contended that from the beginning of time women performed *en-soi*–like tasks, such as cooking, cleaning, and child rearing, whereas men performed *pour-soi*–like tasks, such as hunting and fighting, most of which involve the use of tools to subdue the world. As a result of this particular division of labor, men seized the means of production; they became the "bourgeoisie" and women became the "proletariat." Capitalism favors this state of affairs as it does not have to pay women for the work they do in the home. The system gets women's housework for free. Thus, men will remain the bourgeoisie and women the proletariat until capitalism is overthrown and the means of production are owned equally by men and women. Then and only then, said Engels, will work be divided based not on gender but on individuals' ability, readiness, and willingness to perform certain jobs.

Disagreeing with Engels, de Beauvoir insisted a move from capitalism to socialism would not automatically change the relations between men and women. Women are just as likely to remain the other in a socialist society as in a capitalist society, for the roots of women's oppression are more than economic; they are ontological. "If the human consciousness had not included . . . an original aspiration to dominate the Other," de Beauvoir stressed, "the invention of the bronze tool could not have caused the oppression of woman."[16] Women's liberation requires far more than the elimination of the institution of private property; it requires nothing less than the elimination of men's desire to control women—a very radical feminist notion.

Unsatisfied by the traditional biological, psychological, and economic explanations of women's oppression, de Beauvoir sought a deeper account of why men named man the self and woman the other. She speculated that in perceiving themselves as subjects capable of risking their lives in combat, men perceived women as objects, capable only of giving life. "It is not in giving life but risking life," said de Beauvoir, "that man is raised above the animal; that is why superiority has been accorded in humanity not to the sex that brings forth but to that which kills."[17] In addition, de Beauvoir surmised there was probably another, even more basic explanation for men's relegation of woman to the sphere of otherness. She observed that as soon as man asserted himself "as subject and free being, the idea of the Other [arose]"[18]—specifically, the idea of woman as the other. Woman became for man everything man was not, an alien power that man had best control, lest woman become the self and man the other.

Woman's Lived Experience

Unlike Sartre, de Beauvoir specified social roles as the primary mechanisms the self, or subject, uses to control the other, or object. She labeled woman's tragic acceptance of her own otherness the feminine "mystery," which passes from generation to generation through the socialization of girls. De Beauvoir spoke from her own experience—that of a bourgeois French girl growing up between two world wars. She claimed girls recognize their bodily differences from boys very early on. With puberty, with the swelling of their breasts, and with the beginning of their menstrual flow, girls accept and internalize as shameful and inferior their otherness. This otherness is cemented, said de Beauvoir, in the institutions of marriage and motherhood.

As de Beauvoir saw it, the role of wife blocks women's freedom. Although de Beauvoir believed men and women capable of deep love, she claimed the institution of marriage ruins couples' relationships. It transforms freely given feelings into mandatory duties and shrilly asserted rights. Marriage is a form of slavery, said de Beauvoir. It gives women (at least French bourgeois women) little more than "gilded mediocrity lacking ambition and passion, aimless days indefinitely repeated, life that slips away gently toward death without questioning its purpose."[19] Marriage offers women contentment, tranquility, and security but also robs them of the chance to be great. In return for their freedom, women receive "happiness." Gradually, they learn how to settle for less.

> It is not without some regret that she shuts behind her the doors of her new home; when she was a girl, the whole countryside was her homeland; the forests were hers. Now she is confined to a restricted space; Nature is reduced to the dimensions of a potted geranium; walls cut off the horizon. But she is going to set about overcoming these limitations. In the form of more or less expensive bric-a-brac she has exotic countries and past time; she has her husband representing human society; and she has her child, who gives her the entire future in portable form.[20]

If the role of wife limits women's self-development, the role of mother does so even more.[21] Although de Beauvoir conceded that rearing a child to adulthood can be existentially engaging, she insisted that bearing a child is not an action but a mere event. She stressed the ways in which pregnancy alienates a woman from herself, making it difficult for her to chart, unencumbered, the course of her destiny. Like radical-libertarian feminist Shulamith Firestone, de Beauvoir questioned the supposed joys of pregnancy, observing that even women who want to have children seem to have a tough time of it. Also like Firestone, de Beauvoir worried about how the mother-child relationship is so easily distorted. At first the child seems to liberate the mother from her object status because she "obtains in her child what man seeks in woman: an other, combining nature and mind, who is to be both prey and *double*."[22] As time goes on, however, the child becomes a demanding tyrant—a toddler, an adolescent, an adult, a conscious subject who, by looking at "mother," can turn her into an object, into a machine for cooking, cleaning, caring, giving, and especially sacrificing. Reduced to an object, the mother, not unexpectedly, begins to view and to use her child as an object, as something that can make up for her lacks.

Wifing and mothering are clearly, in de Beauvoir's estimation, two feminine roles that limit woman's freedom, but so, too, is the role of "career" woman, as Betty Friedan discussed in the *Second Stage* (see Chapter 1). De Beauvoir stressed that a career woman can no more escape the trap of femininity than a wife and mother can. Indeed, in some ways, the career woman is in a worse situation than the stay-at-home wife and mother because she is at all times and places expected to be and act like a woman. In other words, a career woman must add to her professional duties those implied by her femininity, by which society seems to mean a certain sort of pleasing appearance.[23]

Although all women engage in feminine role playing, said de Beauvoir, three kinds of women play the role of woman to the hilt: the prostitute, the narcissist, and the mystic. De Beauvoir's complex analysis of the prostitute fits with our analysis of that role in Chapter 2. On the one hand, the prostitute is a paradigm for woman as the other, as object, as the exploited one; on the other hand, the prostitute, like the man who purchases her services, is a self, a subject, an exploiter. She prostitutes herself, suggested de Beauvoir, not simply for the money but for the homage men pay to her otherness. Unlike men's wives and girlfriends, prostitutes get something for yielding their bodies to men's dreams: "wealth, and fame."[24]

Conceding that the so-called streetwalker most likely sells her body because it is the only thing she has to sell, de Beauvoir stressed that, in contrast, the so-called call girl, the hetaera, who regards her whole self as capital, usually has the upper hand in a relationship.[25] Men need her more than she needs them. De Beauvoir's point seems to be that even if the hetaera, like the wife and the mother, cannot escape being the other, at least she can use her otherness to her own personal advantage by wrapping men around her finger.

A feminine role even more problematic than the prostitute is the narcissist. De Beauvoir claimed that woman's narcissism results from her otherness. Woman is frustrated as a subject because she is not allowed to engage in self-defining activity and because her feminine activities are not fulfilling.[26] Woman then becomes her own object of importance. Believing herself an object—a belief confirmed by most everyone around her—she is fascinated by, and perhaps even fixated on, her own image: face, body, clothes. The sense of being a subject and object simultaneously is, of course, illusory. Nevertheless, the narcissist somehow believes that she is the impossible synthesis of being-for-itself and being-in-itself.[27]

The most objectifying feminine role, according to de Beauvoir, is arguably the mystic, who seeks to be the supreme object of a supreme subject. The mystic confuses God with man and man with God. She speaks of divine beings as if they were human beings, and she speaks of men as if they were gods. In divine love, said de Beauvoir, the mystic seeks "first of all what the *amoureuse* seeks in that of man: the exaltation of her narcissism: this sovereign gaze fixed attentively, amorously, upon her is a miraculous godsend."[28]

The mystic does not pursue transcendence through God. Instead, she seeks supreme possession by a God who would have no other woman before him. The mystic wants from God the exaltation of her objecthood.

There are, of course, no easy ways for female prostitutes, narcissists, and mystics to escape what de Beauvoir repeatedly described as woman's immanence—the limits, definitions, and roles that society, propriety, and men have imposed on her. Nevertheless, if a woman wants to cease being the second sex, the other, she must overcome the forces of circumstances; she must have her say and her way as much as man does. On the way to transcendence, said de Beauvoir, women can employ four strategies.

First, in accord with Marxist and socialist feminists (see Chapter 3), women can go to work. To be sure, de Beauvoir recognized that work in a capitalist patriarchy can be oppressive and exploitative, particularly when it results in women's working a double day: one shift in the office or factory and another at home. Nonetheless, de Beauvoir insisted that no matter how taxing or tiring, a woman's job still opens up possibilities for her that she would otherwise lack. By working outside the home alongside men, woman "regains her transcendence"; she "concretely affirms her status as subject, as someone who is actively charting the course of her destiny."[29]

Second, women can become intellectuals, members of the vanguard of change for women. Intellectual activity is, after all, the activity of one who thinks, looks, and defines, not the nonactivity of one who is thought about, looked at, and defined. De Beauvoir encouraged women to study writers such as Emily Brontë, Virginia Woolf, and Katherine Mansfield, who took themselves seriously enough as writers to probe death, life, and suffering.[30]

Third, women can work toward a socialist transformation of society. Like Sartre, de Beauvoir held out hope for an end to the subject-object, self-other conflict among human beings in general and between men and women in particular. In *Being and Nothingness*, Sartre added a footnote to his conclusion that all attempts at love or union are bound to lapse into either masochism or sadism. He explained that his "considerations do not exclude the possibility of an ethics of deliverance and salvation. But this can be achieved only after a radical conversion which we cannot discuss here."[31]

Like Sartre, de Beauvoir believed one key to women's liberation is economic, a point she emphasized in her discussion of the independent woman. De Beauvoir reminded women that their circumstances will, of course, limit their efforts to define themselves. Just as the marble block at hand limits a sculptor's creativity, the size of a woman's bank account limits her freedom, for example. If a woman wants to be all that she can possibly be, she must help create the kind of society that will provide her with the material support to transcend her present limits.

Finally, women can refuse to internalize their otherness—that is, to identify themselves through the eyes of the dominant group in society. To accept the role of the other, said de Beauvoir, is to accept being an object. It is, as Josephine Donovan wrote, "to deny the subject-self that is autonomous and creative" and risk the kind of "madness and schizophrenia" that results from "engaging in a perpetual lie."[32] On the one hand, woman's inauthentic self lives as the "object-self" seen by the male world; on the other hand, woman's authentic self lives as a "withdrawn-invisible self—invisible at times even to oneself."[33] As a result, woman's person is split.

Donovan found Meredith Tax's analysis of women's splitness particularly insightful. Tax described a woman who is forced to put up with men's catcalls and whistles as she walks down a public street. In such a situation, the woman has but two choices: "Either she remains sensitive and vulnerable to the pain; or she shuts it out by saying, 'It's only my body they are talking about. It doesn't affect me. They know nothing about me.' Whatever the process, the solution is a split between the mind and the body."[34]

To further elucidate how the "gaze of the Other" petrifies women's self into an object, Sandra Lee Bartky speculated that in our society the other internalized in women takes a particular form; it is the other created by the "fashion-beauty complex." "Women are," she said, "presented everywhere with images of perfect female beauty—at the drugstore cosmetics display, the supermarket magazine counter, on television";[35] women internalize these images, mercilessly measuring their imperfect bodies against the supposedly perfect bodies of high fashion. Women in our society—indeed, in any society where cosmetics and fashion exist—fail to realize, said Bartky, something de Beauvoir knew only too well: that "costumes and styles are often devoted to cutting off the feminine body from any possible transcendence."[36] The mobility of the foot-bound or high-heeled woman is limited; the dexterity of the long-fingernailed or bejeweled woman is impeded. Women are so busy attending to their deficient bodies that they have no time to improve their minds. Thus, the only way for a woman to become a self in a society such as ours is to free her self from her body, to refuse to make her appearance the "be all and end all," when she could be engaged in some sort of creative or service-oriented project.

Critiques of Existentialist Feminism

Critique One: De Beauvoir Presents a Negative View of the Female Body

A wide variety of critics faulted de Beauvoir for writing primarily for the European intelligentsia, and communitarian critic Jean Bethke Elshtain censured her for failing to speak to ordinary women, especially women of color and working-class women. "Immanence" and "transcendence," "essence" and "existence," "being-for-itself" and "being-in-itself" are ideas that do not arise directly out of ordinary women's lived experience. Rather they are abstractions that emerge from the philosopher's armchair speculations. De Beauvoir's technical words, said Elshtain, are more likely to "pummel" less formally educated women into agreeing with her than to persuade them they are indeed the second sex.[37]

Elshtain strongly objected to de Beauvoir's treatment of the body, especially the female body. She claimed de Beauvoir presents all bodies, but particularly female bodies, as negative: unfortunate, insignificant, dirty, shameful, burdensome, inherently alienating. Elshtain speculated that de Beauvoir's general distrust of the body was rooted in her existentialist anxieties about the carnality and mortality of the flesh. The body is a problem within the existentialist framework insofar as it is a stubborn and unavoidable object limiting the freedom of each conscious subject. De Beauvoir recorded in her memoirs her own war against the flesh: her squashed sexual urges, her attempts to do without sleep, her sense of horror as she relentlessly aged.[38] Because the slow disintegration of the body signals the coming of death—the end of consciousness, of freedom, of subjectivity—existentialists such as de Beauvoir have little desire to celebrate a body that represents to them the forces of death.

De Beauvoir's general distrust of the body, claimed Elshtain, morphed into a very particular mistrust of the female body. According to de Beauvoir, woman's reproductive capacities rob her of her personhood. In contrast, a man's reproductive capacities do not threaten his personhood. After sexual intercourse, the man remains exactly as he was before. But if fertilization takes place, a woman is no longer the same person she was: "Ensnared by nature, the pregnant woman is plant and animal, a stock-pile of colloids, an incubator, an egg; she scares children proud of their young, straight bodies and makes young people titter contemptuously because she is a human being, a conscious and free individual, who has become life's passing instrument."[39] In focusing on this passage and others like it, Elshtain commented that de Beauvoir's description of pregnancy is profoundly alienating to the majority of pregnant women, most of whom view their swelling with child positively. One does not win many converts to feminism by claiming pregnant women are just incubators.

Critique Two: De Beauvoir Celebrates "Male" Values

Elshtain also criticized de Beauvoir for celebrating largely male norms. All de Beauvoir's complaints about woman's character as passive, submissive, and immanent translate into a valorization of man's character as active, dominant, and transcendent. The denigration of woman's body arises from the elevation of man's mind. Thus, de Beauvoir urged women to be like men, rejecting their own embodiment and connections to nature to achieve freedom. But, said Elshtain, de Beauvoir's prescription for women's liberation is extraordinarily shortsighted. Asking women to give up their female identity without considering the ramifications of trading in sisterhood for brotherhood or even personhood is irresponsible.[40] Women have something to lose in not being the "other"; namely, their ability to criticize so-called culture.

Poststructuralism: Focus on Michel Foucault

Many a critic has observed that French intellectuals are particularly competitive with respect to generating new ideas. For over a decade, Sartre and de Beauvoir remained the "king" and "queen" of French intellectual talk. Their books and essays were widely read and debated not only in France but throughout the Western world. Then existentialism became passé. In the late 1960s a number of theorists, among them Claude Lévi-Strauss, Roland Barthes, Jacques Derrida, Jacques Lacan, Luce Irigaray, Hélène Cixous, Julia Kristeva, and Judith Butler, vied for first place among the world's idea makers. Depending on critics' theories, members of this distinguished group were alternately labeled poststructuralists, psychoanalysts, postmodernists, or deconstructionists. Realizing that we cannot brand these thinkers infallibly, we have chosen to identify Michel Foucault and Judith Butler as representative poststructuralists and Jacques Derrida and Hélène Cixous as representative postmodernists. Labeling our selected intellectuals in this way lets us discuss two important modes of earlier philosophical thought: structuralism and modernism. Understanding these earlier schools of thought enables us to make better sense of newer modes of thought, especially feminist thought.

Michel Foucault

To understand poststructuralism, one must first understand structuralism as presented by Swiss linguist Ferdinand de Saussure. According to critic Jim Powell, as Saussure saw it, language is not a collection of sounds and letters that correspond to concepts and things. For example, the word "horse" does not have a direct connection to the horse that is now racing down the track or some kind of universal idea or concept of the horse. Why? For the simple reason that depending on where one lives, one will have a different word for "horse." English-speaking people use the word "horse" for an actual horse, but Germans use the word "Pferd," and Spaniards use the word "caballo." In other words, the word "horse" gains its meaning only in relationship to all the other words in the language one speaks. Powell explained Saussure's essential point in a particularly clear way. He said that, for Saussure, "language is a system of differences, something like the red, yellow and green lights in traffic signals. . . . The red, yellow and green lights gain their meanings only in relationship to each other. A system of purple, blue and gold lights would work just as well."[41]

In other words, said another thinker, Lydia Alix Fillingham, "Saussure looked at language as a whole, to see how it worked, rather than focusing on the details of individual languages."[42] Building on Saussure's thoughts, Lévi-Strauss said that within an entire culture, like a language, "certain overarching rules" govern all of society (e.g., rules for proper sex, rules for normal behavior, and so on).[43] There is no one order to all human civilization; rather, there are orders specific to a particular time and place. Fillingham quoted from *The Order of Things*, in which Foucault refers to an amusing passage in a Chinese encyclopedia that divides animals into the following groups: "(a) belonging to the Emperor, (b) embalmed, (c) tame, (d) suckling pigs, (e) sirens, (f) fabulous, (g) stray dogs, (h) included in the present classification, (i) frenzied, (j) innumerable, (k) drawn with a very fine camelhair brush, (l) et cetera, (m) having just broken the water pitcher, (n) that from a long way off look like flies."[44] Analyzed from the perspective of a twenty-first century, Harvard-educated etymologist or biologist, this list of animals is not only disorderly but ridiculous. Motivated by a desire to explain what it is that "I" mean when "I" communicate, Foucault claimed, "We should not view the subject as the knowing, willing, autonomous, self-critical or 'transcendental' subject of Kantian discourse."[45] Rather, we should understand the subject—that is, the individual person—as the product or effect of a variety of power relations manifested through a plurality of discourses.

Understanding what Foucault means by power and power relations is no easy task, however. He said, "Power is not an institution, and not a structure; neither is it a certain strength we are endowed with; [rather] it is the name that one attributes to a complex strategical situation in a particular society."[46] Seeking to elucidate Foucault's understanding of power, Philip Barker claimed that, according to Foucault, power has the following features:

1. Power is coextensive with the social body;
2. Relations of power are interwoven with other kinds of relations: production, kinship, family, sexuality;
3. Power does not take the sole form of prohibition and punishment, but is multiple in form;

4. Interconnections of power delineate general conditions of domination organized in a more or less coherent and unitary strategy;

5. Power relations serve because they are capable of being utilized in a wide range of strategies;

6. There are no relations of power without possible resistances.[47]

We find ourselves the objects of multiple power relations and social discourses about sanity, sexuality, and violence, for example, and we experience ourselves as being controlled by these relations and discourses, as having to be obedient to them.

Discourse about sexuality is a primary site of power in contemporary society, according to Foucault. What society says about legitimate and taboo types of sexuality shapes the sexual behavior of individual persons.[48] We are, said Foucault, literally policed by society's discourse about sexuality.[49] I confess my sexual fantasies and hang-ups to my psychiatrist; I expose my sexual sins to my priest in search of forgiveness; I report my comings and goings to my parole officer if I bear the label "sexual predator"; I reveal my sexual fantasies to my lover. In turn, these people judge me in one way or another. I take their judgments to heart, internalize them, and then regulate myself in terms of them. Madan Sarup commented that, in Foucault's view, "complex differential power relationships extend to every aspect of our social, cultural, and political lives, involving all manner of (often contradictory) 'subject-positions,' and securing our assent not so much by the threat of punitive measures as by persuading us to internalize the norms and values that prevail within the social order."[50]

Foucault frequently claimed that as sexual subjects, we are the objects of a set of intersecting power relations and discourses that inscribe themselves on our bodies and cause us to recognize ourselves in certain ways. Often we are unaware of the social forces that have constituted our sexual subjectivity. For this reason, we operate on the unquestioning assumption that our subjectivity is really our own. Thus, it is the role of critical thinkers to help us challenge the ways in which power relations and discourses constitute our subjectivity, particularly our sexual subjectivity, so that we can somehow understand it.[51] Foucault maintained that he did not conduct his analyses "to say: this is how things are, look how trapped you are."[52] He conducted them to permit others to help us transform our realities.

To better appreciate how power relations and discourses shape our subjectivities, sexualities, and bodies, we may look at a specific example. A variety of feminist thinkers have expressed disapproval of cosmetic surgery for the purpose of women's beautification. In particular, Kathryn Pauly

Morgan, Naomi Wolf, and Debra Gimlin argued that cosmetic surgery is a negative and harmful aspect of Western culture and generally runs counter to the feminist stance on the female body. For Morgan, cosmetic surgery is "primarily self-imposed surveillance of the body under patriarchal power . . . a form of colonization of women's bodies."[53] She claimed that cosmetic surgery is required for women in ways that it is not for men:

> As cosmetic surgery becomes increasingly normalized through the con-
> cept of female "make overs" and/or "success stories" ("I used to be an
> ugly duckling but now I'm a beautiful Swan"), women who refuse to sub-
> mit to the knives and to the needles, to the anesthetics and the bandages,
> come to be seen as deviant in one way or another. Indeed women who re-
> fuse to use these technologies are already stigmatized as not caring about
> their appearance (a sign of disturbed gender identity and low self-esteem
> according to some health-care professionals), as refusing to be all that
> they could be or as "granola-heads."[54]

Like Morgan, Wolf claimed that cosmetic surgery is an example of "institutionalized forms of power working in concert to force women into extreme
beauty practices."[55] Wolf postulated that women's desire to be beautiful
(and the forms that this desire takes) is "the result of nothing more exalted
than the need in today's power structure, economy, and culture to mount a
counter-offensive against women."[56] Women's beauty, said Wolf, serves as
the foundation of women's identity and leaves them prey to the eyes of critics. Regarding cosmetic surgery in particular, Wolf claimed that a market for
it has been created for surgeons to make money, but, more generally, for the
powers-that-be to keep women politically, economically, and socially stag-
nated. Because women are forced to focus on their perceived flaws, their supposed ugliness, they have little time to focus on far more important issues.

Adding yet more force to Morgan's and Wolf's Foucaultian analysis of
cosmetic surgery, Debra Gimlin observed that "cosmetic surgery is not about
controlling one's own body but is instead an activity so extreme, so invasive
that it can only be interpreted as subjugation."[57] On a more general note,
discussing women's overall beauty regime in the United States, Sandra Lee
Bartky made these observations:

> Women are no longer required to be chaste or modest, to restrict their
> sphere of activity to the home, or even to realize their properly feminine
> destiny in maternity. Normative femininity [that is, the rules for being
> a good woman] is coming more and more to be centered on women's
> body—not its duties and obligations or even its capacity to bear children,

but its sexuality, more precisely, its presumed heterosexuality and its appearance. . . . The woman who checks her makeup half a dozen times a day to see if her foundation has caked or her mascara has run, who worries that the wind or the rain may spoil her hairdo, who looks frequently to see if her stockings have bagged at the ankle, or who, feeling fat, monitors everything she eats, has become, just as surely as the inmate of Panopticon, a self-policing subject, a self committed to a relentless self-surveillance. This self-surveillance is a form of obedience to patriarchy.[58]

The question then becomes one of resistance. How can women disobey the "rule of the Father"? By refusing to submit to the knife? Or, instead, by using cosmetic surgery to deliberately make themselves ugly rather than beautiful?

Poststructural Feminism: Focus on Judith Butler

Although influenced by many thinkers, Judith Butler definitely took inspiration from Foucault, and poststructuralist theory in general, in some of her work. In *Gender Trouble*, Butler challenged the general view that sex, gender, and sexuality constitute a seamless web such that if a person is biologically female (having two X chromosomes), she will display feminine traits and desire men as her sexual partners. Instead, Butler claimed that there is no necessary connection between a person's sex and a person's gender. Indeed, she went further, saying that "sex, by definition, will be shown to have been gender all along."[59] She agreed with Simone de Beauvoir that one is not born a woman; one becomes a woman.[60]

But what does it mean to become a woman? Do I choose to become a woman? Or do the kinds of discursive powers about which Foucault spoke determine that I become a woman? Butler claimed that no preexisting "I" chooses its gender. Rather, in Foucaultian fashion, she stated that "to choose a gender is to interpret received gender norms in a way that organizes them anew. Less a radical act of creation, gender is a tacit project to renew one's cultural history in one's own terms. This is not a prescriptive task we must endeavor to do, but one in which we have been endeavoring all along."[61] Within the discursive territory of heterosexuality, homosexuality, or transexuality, said Butler, not only is gender constructed through our actions, but so, too, is sex.

Although most contemporary feminists have always considered gender (masculine/feminine) a constructed category, until relatively recently, they did not think sex (male/female) to be one as well. But then Butler, among others, started to reflect on the identities of intersexed persons. Their sex is ambiguous and may be oriented in either the male or female direction.

Gender and sex, said Butler, are more like verbs than nouns. But my actions are limited; I am not permitted to construct my gender and sex willy-nilly, according to Butler. I am controlled by the scripts society writes about people's sex and gender. It takes considerable imagination and fortitude to alter these scripts.

In an attempt to rewrite the scripts that control them, many readers of Butler focused on her discussion of gender and sex as identities one chooses to perform. They mistakenly understood her to mean that gender and sex are wide-open categories and that individual subjects are free to enact any sex or gender they choose. These readers, said Sara Salem, failed to realize the limitedness of their options to self-create:

> In Butler's scheme of things, if you decided to ignore the expectations and the constraints imposed by your peers, colleagues, etc. by "putting on a gender," which for some reason would upset those people who have authority over you or whose approval you require, you could not simply reinvent your metaphorical gender wardrobe or acquire an entirely new one (and even if you could do that, you would obviously be limited by what was available in the shops). Rather, you would have to alter the clothes you already have in order to signal that you are not wearing them in a "conventional" way—by ripping them or sewing sequins on them or wearing them back to front or upside-down. In other words, your choice of gender is constrained, as is your choice of subversion—which might make it seem as though, what you are doing is not "choosing" or "subverting" your gender at all. I can cross-dress, I can undergo a sex change operation, I can act on my primary homosexual desire. But I remain in society's boy-girl grid.[62]

Realizing that many of her readers were not understanding the nuances of her thought, Butler sought to distinguish between the concepts of performance and performativity. She relied on the work of analytic philosopher John Austin to help her articulate her position. Austin distinguished between constative utterances or perlocutionary acts, on the one hand, and performative utterances or illuctionary acts, on the other.[63]

According to Salem, constative utterances or perlocutionary acts simply report and describe something, whereas performative utterances or illuctionary acts actually make what is being said happen. For example, a perlocutionary statement or act is an observational statement, such as "Today is a windy day" or "My dress is blue." In contrast, an illuctionary statement or act is a power statement, such as "I take you to be my wife" in the context of a wedding ceremony. Saying these words literally makes you a husband. Similarly, commented Salem, in Butler's scheme of things, "When the doctor or nurse declares 'It's a girl/boy,' they are not simply reporting on what they see . . . , they are actually assigning a sex and a gender to a body that can have no existence outside discourse."[64] In other words, to be in this world, one must fit into one of these categories. There would need to be a whole other way of classifying individuals to get out of the girl-boy game entirely. To get her point across, Butler referred to a cartoon strip in which an infant is proclaimed to be neither a boy nor a girl but a lesbian. She did this, said Salem, to introduce the idea that it might "be possible to designate or confer identity on the basis of an alternative set of discursively constituted attributes."[65] But a possibility is just that. Many interpreters of Butler think that her bottom line is pessimistic: that, at least in our lifetime, it is highly unlikely that we will be liberated from the gender games that preoccupy us and the hierarchical systems that entrap us.

Critiques of Poststructural Feminism

Critique One: Poststructural Feminism Is Too Full of Jargon

Butler's seeming pessimism about transforming society prompted philosopher Martha Nussbaum to fault her as a thinker. Nussbaum complained, "Thus the one place for agency in a world constrained by hierarchy is in the small opportunities we have to oppose gender roles every time they take shape. When I find myself doing femaleness, I can turn it around, poke fun at it, do it a little bit differently. Such reactive and parodic performances, in Butler's view, never destabilize the larger system. . . . Just as actors with a bad script can subvert it by delivering the bad lines oddly, so too with gender: the script remains bad, but the actors have a tiny bit of freedom."[66] Convinced that Butler's thought, and thought like it, is no more than jargon for an elite group of feminists and other social critics, Nussbaum criticized Butler's ideas about resistance. She claimed that Butler's advice to feminists—namely, that the best they can do is to make fun of the institution of sex-gender that constrains women (and men)—is akin to someone's advising abolitionists that the best they can do is to roll their eyes at the master-slave hierarchy that weakens slaves' bodies and crushes their spirits.[67] But, continued Nussbaum, in the nineteenth century, US abolitionists did far more than roll their eyes at slavery. They fought with every ounce of their energy to achieve freedom for the enslaved. Resistance to injustice is not a matter of personal sniping; it is a matter of public outrage.

Critique Two: Gender Identity Is Not the Central Concern of Women Worldwide

Nussbaum also disagreed with Butler's seeming reduction of resistance to "jabbing" at one's oppressors. Indeed, in Nussbaum's estimation, Butler delights in the role of being oppressed. Specifically, Nussbaum claimed that the central thesis of Butler's *The Psychic Life of Power* is that "we all eroticize the power structures that oppress us, and can thus find sexual pleasure only within their confines."[68] In other words, real social change "would so uproot our psyches that it would make sexual satisfaction impossible."[69] We would be forced to give up our sexual pacifiers if we were to engage in bona fide social revolution, and, above all, we do not want to lose what personally "turns us on." Nussbaum found this conclusion about ourselves truly sad. She asserted that personal sexual pleasure is not our raison d'être. Rather, doing good for others is the purpose of our lives: "Life . . . offers many scripts for resistance that do not focus narcissistically on personal self-preservation. Such scripts involve feminists (and others of course) in building laws and institutions without much concern for how a woman displays her own body and its gendered nature: in short, they involve working for others who are suffering."[70]

Written in 1999, Nussbaum's critique was quite stern and conceivably based on some misunderstanding of Butler's full views on matters related to social resistance and personal satisfaction. In *Undoing Gender* (2004), Butler insisted that she does not think "theory is sufficient for social and political transformation."[71] In fact, she claimed, something "besides theory must take place, such as interventions at social and political levels that involve actions, sustained labor, and institutionalized practice, which are not quite the same as exercise of theory. I would add, however, that in all of these practices, theory is presupposed. We are all, in the very act of social transformation, lay philosophers, presupposing a vision of the world, of what is right, of what is just, of what is abhorrent, of what human action is and can be, of what constitutes the necessary and sufficient conditions of life."[72] Butler may have indeed believed this all along, but perhaps the strong words of such critics as Nussbaum prompted her to develop her thought in more applied and accessible directions. Such developments in Butler's thinking are a testimony to the resilience of feminist thought, an encouraging sign that it is very much present and evolving.

Postmodernism: Focus on Jacques Derrida

Jacques Derrida focused much of his work on the mechanisms of the Symbolic order (see Chapter 6)—that is, the series of interrelated signs, roles, and rituals a child must internalize to function adequately in society. The more a child submits to society's linguistic rules, the more those rules will be inscribed in his or her unconscious. In other words, the Symbolic order regulates society through the regulation of individuals. As long as individuals speak the language of the Symbolic order—internalizing its gender, race, and class norms—society will reproduce itself in fairly constant forms.

Derrida sought to liberate thinking from the assumption of singularity— that is, the view that one single truth or essence, a "transcendental signifier," exists, in and of itself, as a giver of meaning. He did this using the techniques of a philosophical method often referred to as deconstruction. Deconstruction is a deliberate attempt to open or subject a literary, philosophical, or political text to several interpretations, some of which may contradict each other. According to Derrida (as well as Saussure), our understanding of any word—say, "cat"—does not depend on the "metaphysical presence" (existence/reality) of either any particular cat or the idea of cat/catness in general. Rather it depends on other words—on a very long chain of "signifiers" that refer to nothing over and beyond themselves.[73]

In an attempt to explain Derrida's deconstructionist views, most commentators focus on his concept of difference (which he spells *différance* instead of *différence*, the ordinary spelling of the French word for "difference"). Prior to the emergence of postmodern thought, structuralists insisted that so-called binary oppositions produce meaning in language. In other words, structuralists claimed our understanding of the term "masculine," for example, depends on our understanding of the term "feminine," and vice versa. Derrida disagreed. As he saw it, we achieve language through the free play of myriad signifiers and must resist bipolar thought whenever it manifests itself.

Toril Moi clarified Derrida's understanding of "playful" signifiers by pointing to structuralist Ferdinand de Saussure's concept of the phoneme, "defined as the smallest differential—and therefore signifying—unit in language."[74] No one phoneme—say, *b*—has any meaning in and of itself, said Moi. On the contrary, *b* only signifies anything because it differs from *h* and numerous other phonemes. Likewise, word "bat" only means anything in English because it can be contrasted with such words as "cat," "hat," and the myriad other words that constitute the English language. The word "bat" achieves its meaning by continually deferring that meaning to other English words. It never gets to rest safe and secure in the comfort of an actual bat or the idea of batness-in-itself. Nor does it come into permanent existence by virtue of the intent of some particular author who defines its meaning once and for all. Rather, the word "bat" becomes temporarily meaningful only when an author lets it come to the fore by suppressing other words that other authors might select over it. No phoneme, word, sentence, paragraph, article, or book has a final meaning. Thus, thinking is nothing more than continually producing new readings of texts, said Moi.[75] Language and reality are variable and shifting, missing each other in an ever-flowing flux of words, according to Derrida. Words do not stand for things, for pieces of reality. Rather, reality eludes language, and language refuses to be pinned down or limited by reality.

Postmodern Feminism: Focus on Hélène Cixous

Unlike some feminists who found Derrida's ideas opaque, writer Hélène Cixous found useful his concept of *différance* (defined by Moi as the "open-ended play between the presence of one signifier and the absence of others")[76] and his rejection of binary thought. In applying Derrida's notion of *différance* to writing, Cixous, primarily a novelist experimenting with literary style, contrasted feminine writing (*l'écriture feminine*) with masculine writing (*literature*). Viewed within a psychoanalytic framework, masculine writing is rooted in a man's genital and libidinal economy, emblemized by the phallus. For a variety of sociocultural reasons, masculine writing has reigned supreme over feminine writing. In the words of Ann Rosalind Jones, man (white, Eurocentric, and ruling class) has claimed, "I am the unified, self-controlled center of the universe. The rest of the world, which I define as the Other, has meaning only in relation to me, as man/father, possessor of the phallus."[77]

Cixous objected to masculine writing and thinking as cast in binary oppositions. Traditional society has unnecessarily segmented reality by coupling concepts and terms in pairs of polar opposites, one always privileged over the other. In "Sorties," Cixous listed some of these dichotomous pairs:

> Activity/Passivity
> Sun/Moon
> Culture/Nature
> Day/Night
> Thought has always worked through opposition.
> Speaking/Writing
> Parole/Ecriture
> High/Low
> Through dual, hierarchical oppositions.[78]

According to Cixous, each of these dichotomies finds its inspiration in the dyad man-woman. Man is associated with all that is active, cultural, light, high, or generally positive, whereas woman is associated with all that is passive, natural, dark, low, or generally negative. Moreover, the first term in the dyad man-woman is that from which the second departs or deviates. Man is the self; woman is the other. Thus, woman exists in man's world on his terms. She is either the other of man, or she is unthought. After man is done thinking about woman, "what is left of her is unthinkable, unthought," said Cixous.[79]

Cixous challenged women to write themselves out of the world men constructed for women. She urged women to put themselves—the unthinkable/unthought—into words. The kind of writing Cixous identified as woman's own—marking, scratching, scribbling, jotting—connotes movements that, once again, bring to mind Heraclitus's ever-changing river. In contrast, the kind of writing Cixous associated with man composes the bulk of the so-called accumulated wisdom of humankind. Stamped with the official seal of social approval, masculine writing is too weighted down to move or change.

For Cixous, feminine writing is not merely a new style of writing; it is "the very possibility of change, the space that can serve as a springboard for subversive thought, the precursory movement of a transformation of social and cultural standards."[80] By developing feminine writing, women can, she insisted, change the way the Western world thinks, speaks, and acts. This is no easy task, however. Trying to write the nonexistent into existence, to "foresee the unforeseeable," may, after all, strain women writers to the breaking point.[81]

In further distinguishing woman's writing from man's, Cixous drew many connections between male sexuality and masculine writing on the one hand and female sexuality and feminine writing, on the other. Male sexuality, which centers on what Cixous called the "big dick," is ultimately boring in its pointedness and singularity.[82] Like male sexuality, masculine writing, which Cixous usually termed "phallogocentric writing," is also ultimately boring. Men write the same old things with their "little pocket signifier"—the trio of penis/phallus/pen.[83] Fearing the multiplicity and chaos that exist outside their Symbolic order, men always write in black ink, carefully containing their thoughts in a sharply defined and rigidly imposed structure, said Cixous.

In contrast, female sexuality is anything but boring. Cixous wrote, in no uncertain terms, "Almost everything is yet to be written by women about femininity: about their sexuality, that is, its infinite and mobile complexity; about their eroticization, sudden turn-ons of a certain minuscule-immense area of their bodies; not about destiny, but about the adventure of such and such a drive, about trips, crossings, trudges, abrupt and gradual awakenings, discoveries of a zone at once timorous and soon to be forthright."[84] Like female sexuality, feminine writing is open and multiple, varied and rhythmic, full of pleasures and, more importantly, possibilities. When a woman writes, said Cixous, she writes in "white ink," letting her words flow freely where she wishes them to go: "Her writing can only keep going, without ever inscribing or discerning contours. . . . She lets the other language speak—the language of 1,000 tongues which knows neither enclosure nor death. . . . Her language does not contain, it carries; it does not hold back, it makes possible."[85]

Running through Cixous's writing are an optimism and joy that seem lacking in Derrida, for whom logocentrism is inevitable. Cixous insisted that women writers can lead the Western world out of the dichotomous conceptual order that causes it to think, speak, and act in terms of someone who is dominant and someone else who is submissive. If woman explores her body "with its thousand and one thresholds of order," said Cixous, she "will make the old single-grooved mother tongue reverberate with more than one language."[86] The id, implied Cixous, is the source of all desires: "Oral drive, anal drive, vocal drive—all these drives are our strengths, and among them in the gestation drive—just like the desire to write: a desire to live self from within, a desire for the swollen body, for language, for blood."[87]

Critiques of Postmodern Feminism

Critique One: Postmodern Feminists Are Essentialists

Clearly, there is dispute about how illuminating or opaque postmodern feminist writers are. Still, many critics of postmodern feminism are not that concerned about its opacity. Rather, they fault postmodern feminists for taking the wrong side not only in the so-called sameness-difference debate—are women essentially the same as or fundamentally different from men?—but also in the so-called antiessentialism-essentialism debate: is woman's nature "plastic" (mutable, ever changing, always becoming something different, in Heraclitean flux) or "fixed" (immutable, unchangeable, always remaining the same, in Parmidean status)? Is gender ("femininity") an organic outgrowth of sex ("femaleness"), an arbitrary cultural imposition on sex, or, more radically, a determinant of sex?

In "Sexual Difference and the Problem of Essentialism," Elizabeth Grosz noted that in the 1960s and 1970s egalitarian (liberal) feminists insisted on men and women's equality in the sense of sameness. They promulgated the view that there is nothing distinct about woman's nature. Women's subordinate status stems not from biological nature but from cultural construction and can, therefore, be changed. In other words, stressed Grosz, egalitarian (liberal) feminists maintained that "the 'raw materials' of socialization are fundamentally the same for both sexes: each has analogous biological or natural potential, which is unequally developed because the social roles imposed on the two sexes are unequal. If social roles could be readjusted or radically restructured, if the two sexes could be resocialized, they could be rendered equal. The differences between the sexes would be no more significant than the differences between the individuals."[88] Women can be masculine; men can be feminine. The decision is up to them.

In their attempts to delink sex and gender, claimed Grosz, egalitarian (liberal) feminists made several mistakes. First, they took "male achievements, values and standards as the norms to which women should aspire."[89] In the name of equality, they urged women to become men but not vice versa, signaling that women's ways are not as valuable as men's. Second, they minimized women's specific needs and interests, including those that arise from "women's corporeality and sexuality."[90] In erasing women's bodies—women's reproductive and sexual identities—said Grosz, egalitarian (liberal) feminists also erased the visible signs of women's oppression as women and therefore women's concrete rallying points for justice between the sexes. As a result, women's struggle for gender justice became a mere moment in the struggle for human justice, and feminism receded into the bowels of humanism.

Sketching the contrast between egalitarian (liberal) feminists on the one hand and so-called difference or postmodern feminists on the other, Grosz implied that the latter feminists are to be commended for preventing feminism's devolution into humanism and woman's (re)absorption into man. Difference or postmodern feminists celebrated women's bodies, reproductive rhythms, and sexual organs. Women and men are different, and women have no interest in forsaking their differences, they said. Women do not want the right to be the same as men. Rather, women want the right to be as free as men—to construct themselves apart from, not in opposition to, men; to be opposite of men yet to be themselves.[91] Thus, Grosz claimed that, in her understanding, the postmodern feminist idea of difference, among other things, "resists the homogenization of separate political struggles—insofar as it implies not only women's differences from men, and from each other; but also women's differences from other oppressed groups. It is not at all clear that, for example, struggles against racism will necessarily be politically allied with women's struggles or, conversely, that feminism will overcome forms of racist domination. This, of course, does not preclude the existence of common interests shared by various oppressed groups, and thus the possibility of alliances over specific issues; it simply means that these alliances have no prior necessity."[92] Woman is not to be subsumed into man or vice versa, and feminism is not to be viewed as humanism dressed in a skirt.

Grosz's interpretation of the postmodern feminist understanding of difference is far more sympathetic than that of other readers, however. Whereas Grosz argued that postmodern feminists see difference "not as difference from a pre-given norm but as pure difference, difference itself, difference with no identity,"[93] critics of postmodern feminism claimed that, truth be told, difference feminists use the term "difference" in an "essentialist" way. To say that difference feminists are "essentialist," however, is to imply that unlike more "enlightened" or "politically correct" feminists, difference feminists are incapable of "carefully holding apart the poles of sex and gender,"[94] of femaleness and femininity.

Defending themselves from the "essentialist" label, most postmodern feminists maintained, in the estimation of Margaret Whitford, that in their writings they do attempt to distinguish between "(1) women as biological and social entities and (2) the 'female,' 'feminine' or 'other,' where 'female' stands metaphorically for the genuinely other in a relation of difference (as in the system consciousness/unconscious-ness) rather than opposition."[95] In other words, postmodern feminists insisted that they describe woman's nature "not as some sort of 'thing-in-itself' to which all the 'sensible properties' of 'woman's nature' actually cling but as the 'totality of the properties, constituent elements,'"[96] and so on, without which it would be impossible to refer consistently and coherently to woman's nature at all.

Critique Two: Postmodern Feminists Deny Gender/Sex Is a Category of Analysis

Explaining that difference feminists are nominalists as opposed to realists, Teresa de Lauretis agreed with most difference or postmodern feminists' defense of themselves. She said that indeed, for most difference or postmodern feminists,

> the essence of woman is more like the essence of the triangle than the essence of the thing-in-itself: it is the specific properties of (e.g., a female-sexed body), qualities (a disposition to nurturance, a certain relation to the body, etc.), or necessary attributes (e.g., the experience of femaleness, of living in the world as female) that women have developed or have been bound to historically, in their differently patriarchal sociocultural contexts, which makes them women, and not men. One may prefer one triangle, one definition of women and/or feminism, to another and, within her particular conditions and possibilities of existence, struggle to define the triangle's existence, struggle to define the triangle she wants or wants to be—feminists do want differently.[97]

Just as we have no access to a triangle as it exists in itself but only to the enormous variety of particular triangles we can conceive of, we have no access to woman as she exists in herself. Yet in the same way we can recognize a triangle, we know a woman when we see one.

Unlike most difference or postmodern feminists, however, de Lauretis claimed that like feminist realism/essentialism, feminist nominalism/postmodernism is problematic. Whereas the former implies that all women must be the same, the latter suggests that women have nothing in common and therefore no basis for collaborative political action. In de Lauretis's estimation, the pitfalls of nominalism must be avoided just as much as the pitfalls of essentialism. She claimed that it is best to understand "woman as position,"[98] as neither exclusively "One" nor exclusively "Many."

In becoming feminists, said de Lauretis, women should assume a position, a point of view or perspective termed "gender," from which "to interpret or (re)construct values and meanings."[99] Proceeding from their specific sociohistorical locations—their concrete interests—feminist women can, said de Lauretis, consciously use the category of gender to forge political alliances aimed at increasing each other's freedom and well-being at particular places and times. For de Lauretis, the (female) sex/(feminine) gender relationship is such that gender is neither an unproblematic procession from biologically determined sex nor a purely arbitrary imaginary construct. Rather, gender is the "product and process of a number of social technologies" that "create a matrix of differences and cross any number of languages."[100] Gender points to a conception of women as neither already unified nor inseparably divided but as multiple and therefore capable of unifying and dividing at will. Furthermore, said de Lauretis, if postmodern feminists wish to remain feminist, they must in some way privilege the category of gender so that women have some sort of common launching pad for political action to improve the condition of women everywhere.[101]

Conclusion

Despite all the criticisms raised against existentialist, poststructuralist, and postmodern feminisms, they remain three of the most galvanizing developments in contemporary feminist thought. Despite having distinct agendas, these three kinds of feminists share certain tendencies, such as an appreciation for the possibilities latent in nothingness, absence, the marginal, the peripheral, the repressed, the other, the second sex. Moreover, they share a common desire to rethink woman/women as the relationship between sex and difference, identity, power, and meaning. Still, existentialist and postmodern feminists part ways at a deeply conceptual level. For de Beauvoir, binary and oppositional thinking is the way to go: self/other, man/woman, transcendence/immanence. In contrast, poststructuralist feminist Butler and postmodern feminist Cixous totally resist binary thinking as impeding free thought.

Moreover, poststructuralist and postmodern feminists desire to think nonbinary, nonoppositional thoughts, the kind that may have existed before the God of Christianity gave Adam (the first human being) the power to name the animals, to determine the beginning and ends of things: "And out of the ground the Lord God formed every beast of the field, and every fowl of the air; and brought them unto Adam to see what he would call them—and whatsoever Adam called every living creature, that was the name thereof."[102] We can imagine this original state prior to Adam's purported intrusion either as a Taoist undifferentiated "uncarved block,"[103] as a Lacanian imaginary, as a Kristevan abject, or as any number of disordered conditions—the point being that there was, in the beginning, no word but only myriad voices waiting for time and space to interpret their meaning.

Yet, as Christine Di Stefano emphasized, women may also have something to lose in their embrace of multiplicity, of the enriching differences of race, class, sexual preference, ethnicity, culture, age, religion, and so on. They may lose themselves as women.[104] Therefore, whatever their differences, for now, women should recognize that "gender is basic in ways that we have yet to fully understand, . . . [that] it functions as 'a difference that makes a difference,' even as it can no longer claim the legitimating mantle of *the* difference. The figure of the shrinking woman may perhaps be best appreciated and utilized as an aporia within contemporary theory: as a recurring paradox, question, dead end, or blind spot to which we must repeatedly return, because to ignore her altogether is to risk forgetting and thereby losing what is left of her."[105] Women exist as women; at least each of us knows she exists as a woman. We are comfortable with this label. The admission that one is, after all, a woman may be the condition of the possibility of women speaking out on issues that matter to them and human beings in general.

Questions for Discussion

1. Analyze past and current examples of women internalizing "the myth of women." Consider incidences relevant to men's concept of the "ideal woman," ambivalence about women's nature, and the resulting subjugation of women throughout various spheres of life.

2. Is being "the other" always a negative thing? Reflect upon postmodern feminism's proposition that otherness is much more than simply an oppressed condition. Do you agree or disagree?

3. Who are some female writers using what Cixous calls "white ink"? Research such feminine authors online. Compare and contrast their "white ink" writing style with the "black ink" style of their masculine counterparts. What characteristics of "white ink" stand out in particular?
4. Butler says society writes to control sex and gender. Cite examples of the gender scripts society constructs for people. Can we ever escape the boy-girl grid? How?
5. Do you think, contra Nussbaum, that postmodern feminism (*a lá* Butler) has a significant political agenda? If so, articulate that agenda in your own words.

Third-Wave and Queer Feminisms

Third-Wave Feminism

Most scholars think that third-wave feminism officially started with the coining of the term in 1992 by Rebecca Walker[1] and the activism of feminist/womanist women of color. The 1980s and 1990s saw "white feminism" fade as women of color voiced the matters of most concern to them. According to R. Claire Snyder, third-wave feminists made two significant "tactical moves that responded to a series of theoretical problems within the second wave [of feminism]."[2] First, in response to the collapse of the essentialist concept of woman, they brought to the fore "personal narratives that illustrate[d] an intersectional and multiperspectival version of feminism;[3] second, "in response to the ascendance of postmodernism, third-wave feminists embraced multivocality over synthesis and action over theoretical justification."[4]

Third-wave feminism resists simple description. Its writers have produced numerous varied and multifaceted works in a short period, a phenomenon that makes the approach difficult to thematize. Nonetheless, if third-wave feminists share any single characteristic, it is their willingness to accommodate diversity and change. They are fairly characterized as feminist sponges, able and ready to absorb some aspects of all the modes of feminist thought that preceded the third wave's emergence. They are particularly eager to understand how various forms or axes of oppression cocreate and comaintain each other. The term they use for this phenomenon is "intersectionality" (see Chapter 4).

Broadly speaking, for third-wave feminists, difference is the way things are. Moreover, they expect and even welcome contradiction, including

self-contradiction, as well as conflict. In fact, two leading third-wave feminists, Leslie Heywood and Jennifer Drake, commented, "Even as different
strains of feminism and activism sometimes directly contradict each other,
they are all part of our third-wave lives, our thinking, and our praxes: we are
products of all the contradictory definitions of and differences within feminism, beasts of such a hybrid kind that perhaps we need a different name
altogether."[5]

Intersectionality, as mentioned in previous chapters, is the overriding principle for third-wave feminists. Originating in Black/African American feminist thought[6] and standing for the proposition that race, gender, class, ability
status, sexuality, and other identity markers overlap and generate distinct
forms of oppression in the lives of the oppressed, intersectionality has many
facets.[7] For different feminists it operates as a research program, a description
of personal identity, a counterhegemonic political agenda, a symbolic antidote to mainstream legal theory, a critique of the methods and practices of
mainstream philosophy, and, most centrally, a theory of oppression.

As a research program, the concept of intersectionality stands for the
proposition that no phenomenon is adequately researched or understood
without factoring in how race, gender, sexuality, ability status, and class interact and affect the topic under investigation.[8] As a description of personal
identity, it stands for the idea that personal identity cannot be described
in terms of neat, monolinear, timeless categories.[9] As a counterhegemonic
political agenda, it is a call to remember the oppositionality that originally
motivated intersectional analysis,[10] as well as the concept's roots in radical
women-of-color feminism.[11] As a symbolic antidote to mainstream (liberal)
legal theory, it is a practical recognition of the complex legal and social needs
of the oppressed, including a suspicion that mainstream jurisprudence cannot meet those needs adequately.[12] As a critique of the methods and practices
of mainstream philosophy, it calls the discipline of philosophy to take account of its European, androcentric, and white biases as a rudimentary first
step toward opening its curricular and conceptual vista to the myriad ways of
knowing and being that the discipline currently systematically excludes from
the realm of legitimate knowledge and reality claims.[13] And finally, as a theory of oppression, it holds that axes of oppression (such as race, gender, class,
sexuality, and ability status) overlap and fuse in the lives of the oppressed.[14]

As part of their study of intersectionality, third-wave feminists engage
in research and writing that attends to the lives and problems of specific
groups of women. Like women-of-color, global, postcolonial, and transnational feminists, they stress that women and feminists come in many colors,
with numerous ethnicities, nationalities, religions, and cultural backgrounds.

Thus, a typical third-wave feminist text will include articles representing a wide variety of perspectives held by feminists of color: Latin American/Latina/Chicana, Black/African American, Mixed Race, Asian American, Indigenous, and so on.

For fear of misrepresenting the identities and issues of particular groups, however, third-wave feminists take pains to hear what very different groups of women are actually saying. More than other feminists so far, they have brought more different kinds of women, particularly women of color, to the feminist table. A hopeful sign that feminism is well on its way to finally overcoming its "whiteness" is the publication of books like Daisy Hernández and Bushra Rehman's *Colonize This! Young Women of Color on Today's Feminism*.[15] Hernández and Rehman claimed they aimed primarily to "introduce some of the ideas of women of color feminists to women who have thought that feminism is just a philosophy about white men and women and has nothing to do with our communities."[16] They viewed their book as enabling women of color to forge their own unique brands of feminism by directly addressing their differences.

Hernández and Rehman's book, among others, has gone a long way to correct in part what women of color, global, postcolonial, and transnational feminists identified as the foremost failing of the second-wave women's movement—namely, the imposed invisibility of women of color (see Chapters 4 and 5). Third-wave feminists let women of color speak for themselves about their experiences of intersectional oppression. For example, being a woman per se is not necessarily a Black/African American woman's worst problem. Her blackness, as it intersects with her womanness, may constitute her paramount liability.

Third-wave feminists emphasize that soon not white people but people of color will constitute the majority of the US population. Significantly, third-wave feminists note that, in general, US society is already increasingly comfortable with mixed-race and multiethnic people—individuals who have transcended the boundaries of any one race or one ethnicity. They also observe that parents of children with mixed race or ethnicity are starting to report that their children find white/nonwhite oppositions of little meaning or concern. In a *New York Times* article, for example, one mother of three mixed-race and diversely ethnic sons commented, "Race takes a backseat to what they listen to on their CD players, what movies they see. . . . One is into Japanese anime. Another is immersed in rap. Basically it's a ghetto culture, but ghetto doesn't mean poor or deprived, but hip."[17] The same mother noted that one of her sons has a "hip-hop persona" and friends whose skin color ranges from very white to very black.

Being a third-wave feminist in a society where a growing number of young people choose their racial or ethnic classification differs from being a feminist in second-wave feminist days, when racial and ethnic identities were largely neglected. Doing third-wave feminism is very challenging in a global context, where women in developing and developed countries interact. According to third-wave feminist Chilla Bulbeck, women in developing countries lead a particularly complex life because their world, the "Third World," is "double valenced." In other words, the "Third World" can be understood either negatively, as a backward, poor, and bad place to live, or positively, as "a subversive, immense, repressed voice about to burst into centre stage of the globe."[18]

Oftentimes, in addition to being open to women's different racioethnic, social, economic, political, and cultural differences, third-wave feminists are open to women's sexual differences. In contrast to most second-wave feminists, they are less prescriptive about what counts as good sex for women. They are also more comfortable with women enhancing their bodies to suit social norms and cultural expectations about what counts as beautiful. If a woman wants to put on makeup, have cosmetic surgery, wear sexually provocative clothes, or sell her sexual services, then, as far as many third-wave feminists are concerned, she should do so, provided she feels empowered by her actions and not somehow demeaned, diminished, or otherwise objectified by them. Unlike their second-wave predecessors, third-wave feminists do not think, for example, that a woman's choice to work as a porn model or prostitute necessarily stems from economic desperation, a history of past sexual abuse, or some sort of false consciousness that makes her think she likes using her body to make money when she really does not. On the contrary, many third-wave feminists maintain that a woman can be both a feminist and a porn star, call girl, or lap dancer, so long as she likes her job and thinks she is good at it (see discussion of prostitution in Chapter 2).

For these reasons and others, third-wave feminists are shaping a new kind of feminism interested not so much in getting women to want what they should want as in responding to what women say they want and not second-guessing or judging whether their wants are authentic or inauthentic. Third-wave feminists describe the context in which they practice feminism as one of "lived messiness."[19] According to Leslie Heywood and Jennifer Drake, part of this messiness includes "girls who want to be boys, boys who want to be girls . . . blacks who . . . refuse to be white, people who are white and black, gay and straight, masculine and feminine."[20] Similarly, Rebecca Walker speculated that because many third-wave feminists grew up both "transgender, bisexual, interracial, [and] knowing and loving people who are racist, sexist, and otherwise afflicted,"[21] they are not as judgmental about people's sexual lives as their second-wave counterparts were. Walker stressed that because "the lines between Us and Them are often blurred," third-wave feminists seek to create identities that "accommodate ambiguity" and "multiple positionalities."[22]

Amy Richards further explained the nonjudgmental, nonprescriptive stance of third-wave feminism: "I don't think these women are saying, 'I'm going to be female, going to be objectified, going to wear sexy clothes and so on and be part of the backlash against feminism.' I think they're saying, 'I'm going to do all these things because I want to embrace my 'femininity.'"[23] Although many second-wave feminists take issue with third-wave feminists playing up their femininity, some do not. For example, second-wave feminist Anne Braithwaite reacted to third-wave feminists' overt sexiness more sympathetically, commenting that this is 2017, not 1967: "An engagement with . . . practices of seemingly traditional femininity does not necessarily carry the same meanings for young women today or for the culture they live in [that it] might have to earlier feminists periods, and thus cannot be the point upon which to write off specific cultural practices as somehow apolitical and therefore 'post'—or 'anti' feminist."[24] For second-wave feminist Cathryn Bailey, the fact that younger feminists are focusing on their femininity is "a wake-up call for older feminists that what appears, from one perspective, to be conformist, may from another perspective have subversive potential."[25]

An icon of third-wave feminism is probably Donna Haraway, whose "A Cyborg Manifesto: Science, Technology, and Socialist Feminism in the Late Twentieth Century"[26] is a feminist classic. In this essay, Haraway argued that contemporary people have replaced the image of the simple machine with that of the Man-machine—the hybrid of man and machine, the so-called cyborg. According to Jim Powell, Haraway says that the old myths about what makes a human being a person are being replaced by new myths about what makes a cyborg a person. Old myths go back to some primeval place of unity and innocence, like the Judeo-Christian Garden of Eden in which Adam and Eve were whole and unified until they ate from the forbidden Tree of Knowledge and were banished from paradise to bear children in pain and toil. The cyborg myth is very different, in Powell's estimation: "a cyborg is always a split, a hybrid identity, a cybernetic organism: a human computer."[27] From a feminist point of view, if women can think of themselves as cyborgs, they can come to terms with the fact that feminists have "always already fractured identities, never just one."[28] Feminism takes on a new dynamic in which we cannot tell where the computer stops and the human organism begins, suggested Powell.[29]

Of course, wherever there are cyborgs, said Powell, there are "hip," "anti-authoritarian," and rebellious people who use "big data" to identify their own desires and states of mind even before they are self-consciously aware of them.[30] The hacker becomes an "ethical hero" who gets maximum information to the people through his or her mastery over computer systems. This state of affairs is mind-exploding, in Powell's estimation, because "information" exists in a space where "TV, telex, tape recorder, VCR, laser disk, camcorder, teledildo [for the purpose of a kind of computer sex game between people], audio animatronic paparazzi [sound-activated robotic photographers that snap your photo as if you were a celebrity], nanorover [a very small robot that sends back pixel images from the planet Mars], and telephone"[31] are all wired together like a kudzu plant gone wild. In a wired world, feminists need to ask some new questions about women's situation. They can do so through so-called cyberpunk—that is, the use of computers "to fight against the technological powers of giant international mega-corporations."[32]

Third-wave feminists often use the Internet to engage in micropolitics. They are generally against constituting organizations, networks, and institutions that have a life of their own as well as a relatively set agenda. An exception to this rule might be a network like the International Network for Feminist Approaches to Bioethics, whose members can meet on the spur of the moment, addressing issues such as female genital mutilation or hyperstimulation of egg donors with potentially harmful hormones. Supposedly, third-wave feminists can define and confidently espouse their own brands of feminism. They believe that even if not individual in nature, feminism is at least generational in form and content. Jennifer Baumgardner and Amy Richards voiced this view in *Manifesta*:

> The fact that feminism is no longer limited to arenas where we expect to see it—NOW, *Ms.*, women's studies, and redsuited congress women—perhaps means that young women today have really reaped what feminism has sown. Raised after Title VII and *William Wants a Doll* [*sic*], young women emerged from college or high school or two years of marriage or their first job and began challenging some of the received wisdom of the past ten or twenty years of feminism. We're not doing feminism the same way that seventies feminists did it; being liberated doesn't mean copying what came before but finding one's own way—a way that is genuine to one's own generation.[33]

Worried about imposing labels on their own behavior and subscribing to any sort of sex-gender binary that suggests one's biology is one's cultural destiny, third-wave feminists reject both the "feminist" and the "womanist" labels. Rather they prefer to call themselves "grrls" (girls), at one and the same time both seriously and playfully coalescing with whomever they must to achieve their immediate ends or goals. Sally J. Scholtz stated in *Feminism: A Beginner's Guide*, "Girl power celebrates the power of youth culture" and deliberately chooses a name for itself that many second-wave feminists would call "demeaning or infantilizing."[34] Scholtz also said, "The double r of girl also indicates anger and aggression. Girl power is 'a movement to claim agency and effectiveness in spite of a culture that devalues contributions from young people.'"[35] In Scholtz's opinion, "'Third-wave' feminism works to bring girls and women to feminism by breaking feminism out of the ranks of upper- and middle-class educated women." As third-wave feminists see it, working-class, homeless women and women in the so-called sex industry can be just as feminist as women who belong to the National Organization for Women or subscribe to *Ms.*

To get a better appreciation of the popularity of the grrl movement, it is important to note it's nationwide with strong bases on the West Coast (Olympia, Washington) and the East Coast (Washington, DC). Third-wave feminists make considerable use of social media, particularly blogging, tweeting, and e-zines, according to Powell. No longer does a woman deliver her message just to her immediate family or, at most, her neighborhood. Instead she delivers it to the world and can expect a response nearly immediately. Part of delivering one's message, for many third-wave feminists, includes patronizing only "politically correct" stores. Rather than purchasing their clothes from a name-brand manufacturer who exploits child labor, they shop at thrift, second-hand, and consignment shops or at stores known for their progressive policies, said Powell.[36]

Third-wave feminists also use music to disseminate their message as widely as possible. To do this, they reappropriate rap and hip-hop, giving new meanings to the misogynistic messages those genres usually contain. All-girl bands give young feminists the opportunity to voice "woman" as they see her: feisty, resilient, and bold enough to cause mini riots. Finally, many third-wave feminists are becoming savvy computer programmers and hackers, eager to subvert causes and companies that show scant regard for people's, especially women's, rights. They use the Internet to write "fan fiction" or to further liberatory movements like the so-called Arab Spring.

Third-wave feminists borrow second-wave feminist Mary Daly's technique of substituting positive meanings for negative terms used to hurt women. A case in point is the notorious word "bitch." Third-wave feminist Elizabeth Wurtzel said, "I intend to scream, shout, race the engine, all when

I feel like it, throw tantrums in Bloomingdale's if I feel like it and confess intimate details about my life to complete strangers. I intend to do what I want to do and be whom I want to be and answer only to myself: that is, quite simply, the bitch philosophy."[37]

Another dramatic reappropriation of a negative term involves the word "slut." In 2011, a Toronto police officer said, "Women should avoid dressing like sluts in order not to be victimized."[38] Angered by this all too familiar tendency to blame the victim, many feminists in North America started to stage Slutwalks in which women wore any clothes they wished.

Critiques of Third-Wave Feminism

Critique One: Grrls Fail to Address Everyday Socioeconomic Problems

Although much about third-wave feminism is liberatory, its second-wave critics questioned the feminist value of "girlie culture" and its emphasis on female self-empowerment as exhibited in shows like *Buffy the Vampire Slayer*, performances by activist groups like Riot Grrrl, and books like Elizabeth Wurtzel's *Bitch*. Equating dressing like a slut with female empowerment, however clever or ironic, may distract from the accomplishments of second-wave feminists who demanded they be taken seriously as women and not dismissed as lightweight girls.

The question to ask third-wave feminism, said Tamara Strauss, is "Can a Third Wave that tries to push forward urgent feminist issues—such as national health care and child care as well as the passage of the Equal Rights Amendment—also champion girlie power with its penchant for adolescent role playing?"[39] Baumgardner and Richards say yes because, as they see it, women who dress to the hilt are simply saying, "I'm going to be female, and being female is just as valuable as being male." They are not saying, "I'm going to be female, going to be objectified, going to wear sexy clothes and so on and be part of the backlash against feminism."[40] Critics of third-wave feminism also faulted its subscribers for avoiding the term "feminist" in articulating their identity. But, say third-wavers, there are good reasons not to identify as a feminist in a society that makes jokes about being feminist. In addition, there are, says feminist Martha Rampton, good reasons to develop "a 'rhetoric of mimicry,' which reappropriates derogatory terms like 'slut' and 'bitch' in order to subvert sexist culture and deprive it of verbal weapons."[41] Particularly empowering is women's ability to use social media to make a special space for themselves, where they can hide as much of their identity, including gender and sex, as they wish.

In response to the critique that third-wave feminists are just "airhead" girls out to have fun, Walker and Shannon Liss pointed out that the coalition they started, the Third Wave Direct Action Corporation, aims to get young men as well as women to be more socially and politically involved in their immediate communities. By 1995, the corporation was raising funds to support women's initiatives, a much-needed activity because of a lack of research funds for gynocentric socioeconomic projects.[42] Unlike many foundations, the corporation is extremely dynamic, refusing to pin itself down to only certain causes and operating mainly online. Indeed, according to Kira Cochraine, the online feminist movement is huge. It is about people saying, "Here is something that doesn't make sense to me, I thought women were equal, I'm going to do something about it."[43] Action can range from protesting misogynist pages on Facebook to demonstrating against racist immigration laws and propaganda.

Critique Two: Third-Wave Feminism Is Too Individualistic

On the surface, third-wave feminists seem better equipped than second-wave feminists to deal with women's differences. On a deeper level, however, this may not be the whole story. Critics say that the "kitchen" of third-wave feminists seems so "messy" that it may not have enough clean pots and pans to cook a satisfying feminist meal. Sometimes third-wave feminists seem just a collection of strongly individual women expressing their differing feelings to one another and leaving it at that. As Alison Howry and Julia Wood put it, "Many young women today wear their feminism lightly."[44]

Critics also say that third-wave feminists need some sort of unitary goal—an agenda that rallies women to go beyond just being themselves, doing what they want, or being someone whose identity is almost overwhelmingly hyphenated. Whereas the challenge of second-wave feminism was to learn to recognize how all women are necessarily oppressed in the same sort of way, the challenge for today's feminists is to recognize that no matter how different certain groups of women are, they need to coalesce from time to time to serve common goals and interests. Just because some women are empowered does not mean all women are, stress critics of third-wave feminism.[45]

Critique Three: Third-Wave Feminism Shares Too Many Characteristics with So-Called Power Feminism

Particularly concerning to some second-wave feminists is the tendency of some third-wavers to dismiss them as "victim feminists" and to identify themselves as "power feminists." In the writings of such third-wave feminists as Heywood, Drake, and Walker, so-called power feminism seems fairly benign, but in the hands of other thinkers, best labeled "postfeminists," power feminism can get mean-spirited. For example, by insisting that nowadays women are free to be whomever they want and to do whatever they want,[46] postfeminists writers such as Katie Roiphe, Camille Paglia, and Rene Denfeld implied that women's only enemy today is themselves.

But the facts do not support these assertions. Women in the United States and many other developed countries may be more equal with men and freer than they were fifty or even twenty-five years ago, but, as noted in Chapter 3, in the United States they earn only about seventy-seven cents for every dollar men earn, they still do a disproportionate amount of the housework, child care, and elder care, and the "glass ceiling" still limits their full potential. Moreover, violence against women is still a worldwide problem that transcends race, class, and socioeconomic status, as evidenced by the recognition that domestic violence is today the leading cause of injury to women. In addition, women of color in the United States continue to suffer the consequences of institutionalized and intersectional oppression and marginalization, and women worldwide—particularly women of color in developing countries—live in conditions more oppressive than even those that challenged first-wave US feminists at the turn of the nineteenth century.

Feminist Queer Theory

One of the most dynamic developments in contemporary feminist thought is the ascendancy of queer theory. Although the term "queer" originally had a negative connotation, as in "weird," "odd," "peculiar," it has a positive, even celebratory connotation among those who use it currently. Queer theory has in some ways displaced/replaced gay and lesbian studies. Scholars who do queer studies interrogate gender, sexuality, and human desire strenuously, shredding to pieces old norms about heterosexuality being the only acceptable sexual behavior between human beings.

Clearly, queer theory puts into question everything traditionally assumed about the "rightness" of heterosexual behavior and the "wrongness" of homosexual desire. A quick survey of queer terminology reveals it to be the antithesis of a stable identity politics. Tongue in cheek, some queer theorists say that the old acronym LGBT should be replaced by the new "quilt bag" acronym LGBTQQIA (lesbian, gay, bisexual, transsexual, queer, questioning, intersex, and asexual). Teresa de Lauretis coined the term "queer" in 1991 in a special issue of *Signs: Journal of Women in Culture and Society.*

According to Annamarie Jagose, when de Lauretis used the term "queer" in her article "Queer Theory: Lesbian and Gay Sexualities," she meant to make three points: (1) heterosexuality is not the norm, either descriptively or prescriptively, for all of human sexuality; (2) all gay and lesbian studies do not boil down to the same set of narrow assumptions and/or questions; and (3) race "crucially" shapes "sexual subjectivities."[47]

Queerness draws its power from "its opposition to whatever happens to be normative," said Jagose. It is a concept that "evokes endless possibilities of self-understanding," in her opinion.[48] Moreover, queer theory makes problematic issues even more complex and complicated. Sally J. Scholtz offered the issue of transsex marriages to make this point emphatically. If marriage is between one man and one woman, then what do we say, said Scholtz, "if a woman who has only the top surgery, keeping the genitals of a female wants to marry an 'ordinary woman.' Does s(he) count as a man who wants to marry a woman? Or a woman who wants to marry a woman?"[49]

At its deepest levels, the main teachings of queer theory are, as Ralph R. Smith stated, fivefold: "(1) all categories are falsifications, especially if they are binary and descriptive of sexuality; (2) all assertions about reality are socially constructed; (3) all human behavior can be read as textual significations; (4) texts form discourses that are exercises in power/knowledge and which properly analyzed, reveal revelations of dominance within historically-situated systems of regulation; (5) and deconstruction of all categories of normality *and* deviance can best be accomplished by queer readings of performative texts ranging from literature . . . to other cultural expressions."[50] Reflecting on Smith's observations leads to one conclusion—namely, that what makes the category queer so powerful is its continual deviance from whatever society views as normal. It is everything that family situation comedies like *Leave It to Beaver* and *Eight Is Enough* are not. Largely in sync with Smith, J. Jack Halberstam said he is a queer person, assigned female at birth but living his life as a queer male. A forgiving person, Halberstam maintained that he does not mind being called Jude by his sister and Judith by many other people with whom he has cordial relations. Best known for his work on "the bathroom problem" (transsexual people's use of bathrooms that correspond to their chosen gender rather than their gender at birth), Halberstam refuses to be "policed" when it comes to the bathroom he uses. He is also known for using Lady Gaga as a symbol of aspects of sexual and gender expression in the twenty-first century. According to Halberstam, there are five tenets of "Gaga Feminism": "(1) wisdom lies in the unexpected and the unanticipated; (2) transformation is inevitable, but don't look for the evidence of change in the everyday—look around, look on the peripheries, the margins, and there you will see its impact; (3) think counteractively, act accordingly; (4) practice creative nonbeliefs; and (5) Gaga Feminism is outrageous, impolite, abrupt, abrasive and bold."[51]

In a succinct online queer theory timeline, shmoop.com chronologically itemized the main steps in the development of queer theory. Arguably, it began in 1895 with the trials of Oscar Wilde, who was the Victorian "poster boy" for the stereotypical homosexual: a male person who is "nonchalant, witty, intellectual, fancily dressed, and long-haired."[52]

A decade after the trials of Oscar Wilde, observed shmoop.com, Sigmund Freud published *Three Essays on the Theory of Sexuality*, which forced European society to rethink the stages of "normal" human sexuality as described in Chapter 6, with boys developing love for women other than their mothers and girls forsaking love of their mothers in order to attain a man, more specifically, a penis/phallus and all the power it represents, as well as a new life—a baby.[53]

The next stop on shmoop.com's timeline was the 1950 founding of the Mattachine Society in Los Angeles, which provided gay men and women with private spaces in which to gather quietly and feel at home with each other's "deviance." Gaining comfort from each other, gay people produced works of literature and poetry like the 1955 poem "Howl," in which Allen Ginsberg unleashed his own homosexual identity and ranted against all that the very straight man in the grey flannel suit represented—namely, the respectable, "all-American," heterosexual family.[54]

According to shmoop.com, Ginsberg's howl was loud enough to prompt gay people to become more conspicuous in American society, as they did during the 1969 Stonewall Riots in Manhattan. Provoked by police officers (arguably emblematic of society's repressive forces), the patrons of gay bars started to resist the "men in blue," who seemingly enjoyed disrupting gatherings of gay people.[55]

Also, according to shmoop.com, homosexuality became not only more visible but more acceptable in 1973 when the American Psychiatric Association removed it from the list of mental disorders. Only three years after this historic development did Michel Foucault publish *The History of Sexuality*, where he argued that in order to confront human sexuality truthfully and honestly, society must look through the lenses of those living at society's margins rather than at its center.[56]

More than any other book of its kind, Foucault's served to disempower "old, rich, straight, white" men. However, said shoomp.com, it took the 1980s AIDS epidemic to make homosexuals fully visible in American society. By the time it had peaked, a sizable number of gay men and lesbians had come out of their closets, a movement that continued into 1990 with the publication of *Queer Nation* and the emergence of the group ACT UP, which, according to shmoop.com, "took the term *queer* away from homophobic people and turned it into a fierce symbol of resistance."[57] To be queer was to be proud of one's (non)identity.[58]

Another important moment for queers, said shmoop.com, was the 1990 publication of Judith Butler's *Gender Trouble* (see Chapter 9). Over the years Butler established a preeminent presence in the queer community. She has put into question everybody's professed gender and sexuality; so too has Eve Kosofsky Sedgwick. In *Epistemology of the Closet*, she argues, "Queer theory . . . is about talking about what people have often kept hidden."[59] According to shmoop.com, Sedgwick believes that "there is a language of silence. This occurs when one speaks in codes, or tries to suggest something in what one wears, or in how one reacts to questions of identity. And the longer closet doors are shut, the more vivid and outlandish the stories become of what's inside."[60]

Critiques of Feminist Queer Theory

Critique One: Queer Theory Is Divisive

One critique of queer theory is that by celebrating difference, queer policies leads to "individualism" and "fragmentation." This critique, said commentator David Gauntlet, is all too reminiscent of "what white feminists said to black women to keep them quiet."[61] Attention to the sexual, socioeconomic, political, and legal problem of all kinds of queer people, especially transpeople, is well over due. More than most other people, said Gauntlet, they experience discrimination, be it through threats to parental rights, fewer work and school opportunities, or enforcement of bathroom etiquette.[62]

Critique Two: Queer Theory Is Too Easily Institutionalized and Normalized

Interestingly, Sedgwick, a heterosexual woman who does queer theory brilliantly nonetheless, expressed reservations about its future. She said, "Queer politics may, by now, have outlived its political usefulness"[63]—that is to say, it may have been "institutionalized" and "normalized" in queer studies programs. Sedgwick said that queer theory is only useful "so long as it holds open non-referentiality as a political strategy for thinking about a future that will be nonterritorial, domestic, and provisional but that remains for the present unimaginable."[64]

In other words, queer theory must always ask questions like shmoop.com formulates. Examples include "Are males of a species always really tough or really handsome, and are females always coy and homely and patient? Where do native American history . . . and transgendered people fit into our society's cultural narratives? Why do Western ethnic groups stigmatize what the Native American peoples called 'two-spirited' individuals"[65]—that is, people said to have both a masculine spirit and a feminine spirit living in their bodies at the same time and who wear the clothing and do the work of both men and women.

Critique Three: Queer Theory Has a Shaky Relationship to Feminist Thought

In the estimation of sociologist Suzanna Walters, some queer theorists seek to distance themselves from gay men and lesbians on the grounds that they are too conformist, too anxious to show that down deep they are like straight people—eager to get legally married, for example. Walters found queer people's distancing themselves from gay and lesbian people disconcerting because it seemed to flow from some amorphous ideal of "queer," floating above the real lives of actually marginalized people. As Walters saw it, talk about "camp," "drag," and "cross-dressing" is well and good, but it is not the raison d'être[66] of feminist thought. Although Walters affirmed queer theory's desire to interrogate gender more vigorously than anyone had before, she also said, "Destabilizing gender (or rendering its artifice apparent) is not the same as overthrowing it. Indeed in a culture in which drag queens can become the hottest fashion, commodification of resistance is an omnipresent threat. Moreover, a queer theory that posits feminism (or lesbian theory) as the transcended enemy is a queer theory that will really be a drag."[67]

Conclusion

Third-wave feminism and queer theory have much in common. They are intersectional ways of thinking about personal identity, the human experience, sexuality, knowledge, and politics. Both third-wave feminism and queer theory transcend traditional male-female dichotomies. Their interrogation of the concept of gender is thoroughgoing. Gender is more of a "choice" now than it has been. Because gender is an open-ended classification, with room for heterosexual people, bisexual people, gay people, transsexual people, and queer people, we think it is important to reflect on how it shapes our particular identities.

Questions for Discussion

1. Do you identify with third-wave feminism? If so, why?
2. Do you think "slut walks" really empower women?
3. Should transsexual people be allowed to use facilities and access services originally meant for one or the other of the traditional genders (male/female)?
4. Do all feminists regard a transgender woman as a "real" woman? Why or why not?
5. Is a "fourth wave" of feminism in the making, or has feminism gone just about as far as it can go? What would a "fourth wave" of feminism look like?

Conclusion

Feminist Thought has grown and developed in the years since its first edition in 1989. At that time, the goal was to capture the full spectrum of feminist thought without judging any of its facets or insisting that feminists accept or appreciate every aspect of every approach. While the general program remains, in this edition we have sought to highlight contemporary feminism's focus on rejecting the universalist, essentialist, neoliberal, Eurocentric thinking that characterized much of second-wave feminist thought. While feminism retains its focus on women and women's oppression (sexism), women-of-color feminists and third-wave feminists in particular are intentionally inclusive of those who suffer from the world's many other violences: heterosexism, racism, classism, colonialism, ableism, speciesism, and so forth. As we see it, then, contemporary feminism is fundamentally about addressing intersectional oppression across boundaries of race, class, ability, status, gender identity, sexuality, and other marginalized, oppressed, and subjugated identity markers.

There was a time in the 1960s and 1970s when some feminists thought that Marxist/socialist feminism was the most inclusive form of feminism because it showed how the forces of sexism and classism interlock in a capitalist patriarchy and how "women's estate" is determined by both her reproductive and productive role. Recently, some feminists believed that ecofeminism was the most inclusive form of feminism, embracing all of nature, including nonhuman animals. Contemporary feminists, however, do not see inclusiveness per se as the primary objective of feminist thought. Rather, for them feminism's main work is to continue to address the problem of human oppression, especially as manifested in the ideas, actions, and lives of women historically excluded from consideration by systemic and institutional power structures.

For contemporary feminists, it is important to focus on the problems faced by women of all demographics. Undoubtedly, as these problems change worldwide, feminist concerns will also change. Indeed, this demographic shift is already occurring as women of color insist more and more on speaking for themselves and bringing their issues to the forefront.

Although women's status and equality with men has increased in a wide variety of societies, we do not think it is time for humanism or postfeminism to supplant further feminist thought. While women as a whole in the United States and many other developed countries may be more equal and free than they were fifty or even twenty-five years ago, the data available indicate that they still earn about seventy-nine cents for every dollar men earn; they still do a disproportionate amount of the homework, child care, and elder care, and they still face the glass ceiling. Moreover, violence against women is still a worldwide problem that transcends race, class, and socioeconomic status, as evidenced by the fact that domestic violence is now recognized as the leading cause of injury to women.[1] In addition, women of color in the United States continue to suffer the consequences of institutionalized and intersectional oppression and marginalization, and women worldwide—particularly women of color in developing nations—live in conditions far more oppressive than even those that challenged first-wave US feminists at the turn of the nineteenth century.

So, in our estimation, feminist Christine Di Stefano, who has done much to mediate between second- and third-wave feminists, is on to something when she points out that to solve these problems feminists must hold on to the belief that, for women, "gender is basic in ways that we have yet to fully understand. . . . [I]t functions as 'a difference that makes a difference,' even as it can no longer claim the legitimating mantle of the difference. The figure of the shrinking woman may perhaps be best appreciated and utilized as an aporia within contemporary theory: as a recurring paradox, question, dead end, or blind spot to which we must repeatedly return, because to ignore her altogether is to risk forgetting and thereby losing what is left of her."[2]

From our point of view, women exist as *women*. And this knowledge requires us to ask contemporary feminists to see in women's differences—especially their differences in privilege—a call to judgment and for judgment. It "just ain't fair" (and violates the basic feminist call for equality) that some women are so powerful while others remain so powerless. Understood from this perspective, third-wave feminists have a lot of work to do—so much so that we are looking forward to the fourth-wave of feminism. Collectively rethinking what has already been thought about women is one task for us, but our major challenge is to conceive distinctively new thoughts about women in all their diversity.

Notes

Introduction

1. Mary Wollstonecraft, *A Vindication of the Rights of Woman*, ed. Carol H. Poston (New York: W. W. Norton, 1975).

2. John Stuart Mill, "The Subjection of Women," in *Essays on Sex Equality*, ed. Alice S. Rossi (Chicago: University of Chicago Press, 1970), 184–185.

3. Catharine A. MacKinnon elaborated upon the sex/gender system in "Feminism, Marxism, Method, and the State: An Agenda for Theory," *Signs: Journal of Women in Culture and Society* 7, no. 3 (spring 1982): 515–516.

4. Linda Alcoff, "Cultural Feminism Versus Poststructuralism: The Identity Crisis in Feminist Theory," *Signs: Journal of Women in Culture and Society* 13, no. 3 (spring 1988): 408; Ann Ferguson, "The Sex Debate in the Women's Movement: A Socialist-Feminist View," *Against the Current* (September/October 1983): 10–16; Alice Echols, "The New Feminism of Yin and Yang," in *Powers of Desire: The Politics of Sexuality*, ed. Ann Snitow, Christine Stansell, and Sharon Thompson (New York: Monthly Review Press, 1983), 445.

5. Carole S. Vance, ed., *Pleasure and Danger: Exploring Female Sexuality* (Boston: Routledge & Kegan Paul, 1984).

6. Rosemarie Tong, *Women, Sex, and the Law* (Totowa, NJ: Rowman & Littlefield, 1984).

7. Mary Daly, *Gyn/Ecology: The Metaethics of Radical Feminism* (Boston: Beacon Press, 1978).

8. Charlotte Bunch, "Lesbians in Revolt," in *Women and Values*, ed. Marilyn Pearsall (Belmont, CA: Wadsworth, 1986), 128–132.

9. Shulamith Firestone, *The Dialectic of Sex* (New York: Bantam Books, 1970).

10. Adrienne Rich, *Of Woman Born* (New York: W. W. Norton, 1979); Sara Ruddick, "Maternal Thinking," in *Mothering: Essays in Feminist Theory*, ed. Joyce Trebilcot (Totowa, NJ: Rowman & Allanheld, 1984).

11. See, for example, Gena Corea, *The Mother Machine: Reproductive Technologies from Artificial Insemination to Artificial Wombs* (New York: Harper & Row, 1985).

12. Friedrich Engels, *The Origin of the Family, Private Property, and the State* (New York: International Publishers, 1972), 103.

13. Juliet Mitchell, *Woman's Estate* (New York: Pantheon Books, 1971).

14. Alison M. Jaggar, *Feminist Politics and Human Nature* (Totowa, NJ: Rowman & Allanheld, 1983), 316–317.

15. Iris Marion Young, "Socialist Feminism and the Limits of Dual Systems Theory," *Social Review* 10, nos. 2–3 (March–June 1980): 174.

16. Heidi I. Hartmann, "The Unhappy Marriage of Marxism and Feminism: Towards a More Progressive Union," in *Women and Revolution: A Discussion of the Unhappy Marriage of Marxism and Feminism*, ed. Lydia Sergeant (Boston: South End Press, 1981), 1–14.

17. Ella Shohat, "Area Studies, Transnationalism, and the Feminist Production of Knowledge," *Signs: Journal of Women in Culture and Society* 26, no. 4 (2001): 1269–1272.

18. Sigmund Freud, "Femininity," in *The Complete Introductory Lectures on Psychoanalysis*, ed. and trans. James Strachey (New York: W. W. Norton, 1966), 542.

19. Sherry B. Ortner, "Oedipal Father, Mother's Brother, and the Penis: A Review of Juliet Mitchell's *Psychoanalysis and Feminism*," *Feminist Studies* 2, nos. 2–3 (1975): 179.

20. Nancy Chodorow, *The Reproduction of Mothering: Psychoanalysis and the Sociology of Gender* (Berkeley: University of California Press, 1978); Dorothy Dinnerstein, *The Mermaid and the Minotaur: Sexual Arrangements and Human Malaise* (New York: Harper Colophon Books, 1977).

21. Jacques Lacan, *Écrits: A Selection*, trans. Alan Sheridan (New York: W. W. Norton, 1977).

22. Luce Irigaray, *This Sex Which Is Not One*, trans. Catherine Porter (Ithaca, NY: Cornell University Press, 1985), 28.

23. Julia Kristeva, *Desire in Language*, trans. Leon Roudiez (New York: Columbia University Press, 1982), 205–206.

24. Carol Gilligan, *In a Different Voice* (Cambridge, MA: Harvard University Press, 1982).

25. Nel Noddings, *Caring: A Feminine Approach to Ethics and Moral Education* (Berkeley: University of California Press, 1984).

26. Virginia Held, *The Ethics of Care: Personal, Political, and Global* (New York: Oxford University Press, 2006).

27. Ynestra King, "Healing the Wounds: Feminism, Ecology, and Nature/Culture Dualism," in *Feminism and Philosophy*, ed. Nancy Tuana and Rosemarie Tong (Boulder, CO: Westview Press, 1995).

28. Carol J. Adams, *The Sexual Politics of Meat: A Feminist Vegetarian Critical Theory*, 3rd. ed. (New York: Continuum International Publishing Group, 2010).

29. Simone de Beauvoir, *The Second Sex*, ed. and trans. H. M. Parshley (New York: Vintage Books, 1974).

30. Judith Butler, *Gender Trouble: Feminism and the Subversion of Identity* (New York: Routledge, 1990).

31. Rebecca Walker, ed., *To Be Real: Telling the Truth and Changing the Face of Feminism* (New York: Anchor Books, 1995).

Chapter 1: Liberal Feminism

1. Alison M. Jaggar, *Feminist Politics and Human Nature* (Totowa, NJ: Rowman & Allanheld, 1983).

2. Ibid., 33.

3. According to Carole Pateman, in *The Problem of Political Obligation: A Critique of Liberal Theory* (Berkeley: University of California Press, 1979), 190, the private world is one "of particularism, subjection, inequality, nature, emotion, love and partiality."

4. Ibid., 198. According to Pateman, the public world is one "of the individual, or universalism, of impartial rules and laws, of freedom, equality, rights, property, contract, self-interest, justice—and political obligation" (ibid.).

5. Sandel employed this terminology in Michael J. Sandel, ed., *Liberalism and Its Critics* (New York: New York University Press, 1984), 4. We owe this distinction to Michael Weber.

6. Susan Wendell, "A (Qualified) Defense of Liberal Feminism," *Hypatia* 2, no. 2 (summer 1987): 65–94.

7. Martha Nussbaum, *Sex and Social Justice* (New York: Oxford University Press, 2000), 62.

8. Zillah R. Eisenstein, *The Radical Future of Liberal Feminism* (Boston: Northeastern University Press, 1986), 96–99.

9. Mary Wollstonecraft, *A Vindication of the Rights of Woman*, ed. Carol H. Poston (New York: W. W. Norton, 1975).

10. Ibid., 56.

11. Ibid., 23.

12. Jean-Jacques Rousseau, *Emile*, trans. Allan Bloom (New York: Basic Books, 1979).

13. Allan Bloom advanced a contemporary argument in support of sexual dimorphism. See Allan Bloom, *The Closing of the American Mind* (New York: Simon & Schuster, 1987), 97.

14. Wollstonecraft, *A Vindication of the Rights of Woman*, 61.

15. Ibid.

16. Immanuel Kant, *Groundwork of the Metaphysics of Morals*, trans. H. J. Paton (New York: Harper Torchbooks, 1958).

17. Jane Roland Martin, *Reclaiming a Conversation: The Ideal of the Educated Woman* (New Haven, CT: Yale University Press, 1985), 76.

18. Judith A. Sabrosky, *From Rationality to Liberation* (Westport, CT: Greenwood Press, 1979), 31.

19. Wollstonecraft, *A Vindication of the Rights of Woman*, 147.

20. Ironically, emotion drove Wollstonecraft's personal life. As Eisenstein, saw it, Wollstonecraft "tried unsuccessfully to live the life of independence." See Eisenstein, *The Radical Future of Liberal Feminism*, 106.

21. Wollstonecraft, *A Vindication of the Rights of Woman*, 147.

22. Kant, *Groundwork of the Metaphysics of Morals*.

23. Alice S. Rossi, "Sentiment and Intellect: The Story of John Stuart Mill and Harriet Taylor Mill," in *Essays on Sex Equality*, ed. Alice S. Rossi (Chicago: University of Chicago Press, 1970).

24. John Stuart Mill and Harriet Taylor Mill, "Early Essays on Marriage and Divorce," in Rossi, *Essays on Sex Equality*, 75, 81, and 86.

25. Ibid., 75.

26. Harriet Taylor Mill, "Enfranchisement of Women," in Rossi, *Essays on Sex Equality*, 95.

27. Ibid., 104.

28. Ibid., 105.

29. Ibid.

30. Richard Krouse, "Mill and Marx on Marriage, Divorce, and the Family," *Social Concept* 1, no. 2 (September 1983): 48.

31. Eisenstein, *The Radical Future of Liberal Feminism*, 131.

32. John Stuart Mill, "The Subjection of Women," in Rossi, *Essays on Sex Equality*, 221.

33. Susan Moller Okin, *Women in Western Political Thought* (Princeton, NJ: Princeton University Press, 1979), 197–232.

34. Wollstonecraft, *A Vindication of the Rights of Woman*, 77.

35. Mill, "The Subjection of Women," 186.

36. Ibid., 154.

37. Ibid., 213.

38. Wollstonecraft, *A Vindication of the Rights of Woman*, 39.

39. See Mill's description of Harriet Taylor in John Stuart Mill, *Autobiography* (London: Oxford University Press, 1924), 156–160.

40. Mill, "The Subjection of Women," 177.

41. Angela Y. Davis, *Women, Race, and Class* (New York: Random House, 1981), 42.

42. Judith Hole and Ellen Levine, *Rebirth of Feminism* (New York: Quadrangle Books, 1971), 3.

43. Donald R. Kennon, "An Apple of Discord: The Woman Question at the World's Anti-Slavery Convention of 1840," *Slavery and Abolition* 5 (1984): 244–266.

44. Hole and Levine, *Rebirth of Feminism*, 434.

45. Ibid.

46. Ibid., 435.

47. Quoted in Elizabeth Cady Stanton, Susan B. Anthony, and Matilda Joslyn Gage, eds., *History of Woman Suffrage*, vol. 1: *1848–1861* (New York: Fowler and Wells, 1881), 115.

48. Davis, *Women, Race, and Class*, 75.

49. Quoted in ibid., 76.

50. Hole and Levine, *Rebirth of Feminism*, 14.

51. Maren Lockwood Carden, *The New Feminist Movement* (New York: Russell Sage Foundation, 1974), 3.

52. Ibid., 16.

53. Caroline Bird, *Born Female* (New York: David McKay Company, 1968), 1.

54. Betty Friedan, "N.O.W.: How It Began," *Women Speaking* (April 1967): 4.

55. See Pauli Murray, *Song in a Weary Throat: An American Pilgrimage* (New York: Harper & Row, 1987); also see Shirley Chisholm, *Unbought and Unbossed* (Boston: Houghton Mifflin, 1970).

56. Pauli Murray, *States' Laws on Race and Color, and Appendices* (Cincinnati, OH: Women's Division of Christian Service, Board of Missions and Church Extension, Methodist Church, 1951).

57. See Barbara Winslow, *Shirley Chisholm: Catalyst for Change* (Boulder, CO: Westview Press, 2014).

58. "NOW (National Organization for Women) Bill of Rights (Adopted at NOW's First National Conference, Washington, D.C., 1967)," in *Sisterhood Is Powerful*, ed. Robin Morgan (New York: Random House, 1970), 513–514.

59. All these issues are addressed in Patricia Tjadens and Nancy Thoenes, *Full Report of the Prevalence, Incidence and Consequences of Violence Against Women* (Washington, DC: National Institute of Justice and Centers for Disease Prevention, 2000).

60. Report of the President, Second National Conference of NOW, Washington, DC, November 18, 1967, cited in Hole and Levine, *Rebirth of Feminism*, 6.

61. Betty Friedan, *National Organization for Women, Memorandum*, September 22, 1969.

62. Quoted in Carden, *The New Feminist Movement*, 113.

63. Alice Echols, *Daring to Be Bad: Radical Feminism in America, 1967–1975* (Minneapolis: University of Minnesota Press, 1987), 215.

64. For more on the radical feminist critique of liberal feminism, including the charge that it excluded the concerns of women of color, please see Chapter 2, "Radical Feminism," and Chapter 4, "Women-of-Color Feminism(s) in the United States."

65. Betty Friedan, *The Feminine Mystique* (New York: Dell, 1974).

66. Ibid., 69–70.

67. Ibid., 22–27.

68. Betty Friedan, *The Second Stage* (New York: Summit Books, 1981).

69. Ibid., 20–21.

70. Ibid., 27.

71. Friedan, *The Feminine Mystique*, 362–363.

72. See Judith Stacey, "The New Conservative Feminism," *Feminist Studies* 9, no. 3 (fall 1983): 562.

73. Friedan, *The Second Stage*, 248–249.

74. Betty Friedan, *The Fountain of Age* (New York: Simon & Schuster, 1993), 157.

75. Ibid., 638.

76. Friedan, *The Second Stage*, 342.

77. Ibid., 41.

78. Catharine MacKinnon, "Difference and Dominance: On Sex Discrimination," in *Toward a Feminist Theory of the State* (Cambridge, MA: Harvard University Press, 1989).

79. Ibid. Also see Iris Marion Young, "Five Faces of Oppression," *Philosophical Forum* 19, no. 4 (summer 1988).

80. Louise August, "It Isn't Over: The Continuing Under-Representation of Female Faculty" (paper presented at the Association for Institutional Research, Chicago, Illinois, May 2006), 15.

81. Not all liberal feminists agree that women and minority male candidates should be viewed as equally disadvantaged. The more liberal a liberal feminist is, the more likely she is to view gender and race or ethnic disadvantages as being on par. The more feminist a liberal feminist is, the more likely she is to focus her attention exclusively on women.

82. See Elizabeth S. Anderson, "What Is the Point of Equality?," *Ethics* 109 (January 1999): 287–337.

83. Ibid.

84. Ibid.

85. See Martha Nussbaum, "Women and Cultural Universals," in *Sex and Social Justice* (Oxford: Oxford University Press, 1999).

86. National Organization for Women, "1998 Declaration of Sentiments of the National Organization for Women," accessed January 2016, http://www.now.org/organization/conference/1998/vision98.html.

87. Jaggar, *Feminist Politics and Human Nature*, 28.

88. Ibid., 40–42.

89. Ibid., 41.

90. Naomi Scheman, "Individualism and the Objects of Psychology," in *Discovering Reality: Feminist Perspectives on Epistemology, Metaphysics, Methodology, and the Philosophy of Science*, ed. Sandra Harding and Merrill B. Hintikka (Dordrecht, Netherlands: D. Reidel, 1983), 225–244.

91. Ibid., 232.

92. Jean Bethke Elshtain, "Feminism, Family and Community," *Dissent* 29 (fall 1982): 442.

93. Jean Bethke Elshtain, *Public Man, Private Woman: Women in Social and Political Thought* (Princeton, NJ: Princeton University Press, 1981), 252.

94. Ibid., 251.

95. Ibid., 336.

96. Ibid., 237.

97. Barbara Arneil, *Politics and Feminism* (Oxford: Blackwell Press, 1999), 147.

98. Angela Y. Davis, "Reflections on the Black Woman's Role in the Community of Slaves," *Black Scholar* 3 (1971): 7.

99. Elizabeth Erlich, "Do the Sunset Years Have to Be Gloomy?," Bloomberg.com, October 13, 1993, https://www.bloomberg.com/news/articles/1993-10-31/do-the-sunset-years-have-to-be-gloomy.

100. Ibid.

101. Ellen Willis, "The Conservatism of *Ms.*," in *Feminist Revolution*, ed. Redstockings (New York: Random House, 1975), 170–171.

102. See, for example, Gaiutra Bahadur, "Should My People Need Me," *Ms.* 22, no. 1 (winter 2012): 40–42. Bahadur interviews Burmese (Myanmar) political leader Aung San Suu Kyi.

103. Cited in Anne Phillips, "Feminism and Liberalism Revisited: Has Martha Nussbaum Got It Right?," *Constellations* 8, no. 2 (2001): 250.

104. Ibid., 62 (Nussbaum's emphasis).

Chapter 2: Radical Feminism

1. See, for example, Dale Smith, *Poets Beyond the Barricade: Rhetoric, Citizenship, and Dissent After1960* (Tuscaloosa: University of Alabama Press, 2012).

2. Linda Napikoski, "New York Radical Women," Women's History, http://womenshistory.about.com/od/feminism/a/new_york_radical_women.htm (accessed March 24, 2016).

3. Ibid.

4. Tasha N. Dubriwny, "Consciousness-Raising as Collective Rhetoric: The Articulation of Experience in the Redstockings' Abortion Speak-Out of 1969," *Quarterly Journal of Speech* 91, no. 4 (November 2005): 395–422.

5. Valerie Bryson, *Feminist Debates: Issues of Theory and Political Practice* (New York: New York University Press, 1999), 27.

6. Joreen Freeman, as quoted in Anne Koedt, Ellen Levine, and Anita Rapone, eds., *Radical Feminism* (New York: Quadrangle, 1973), 52.

7. Alice Echols, "The New Feminism of Yin and Yang," in *Powers of Desire: The Politics of Sexuality*, ed. Ann Snitow, Christine Stansell, and Sharon Thompson (New York: Monthly Review Press, 1983), 445.

8. Gayle Rubin, "The Traffic in Women," in *Toward an Anthropology of Women*, ed. Rayna R. Reiter (New York: Monthly Review Press, 1975), 159.

9. Kate Millett, *Sexual Politics* (Garden City, NY: Doubleday, 1970), 25.

10. Ibid., 43–46.

11. Ibid., 178.

12. Herbert Barry III, Margaret K. Bacon, and Irwin L. Child, "A Cross-Cultural Survey of Some Sex Differences in Socialization," in *Selected Studies in Marriage and the Family*, ed. Robert F. Winch, Robert McGinnis, and Herbert R. Barringer (New York: Holt, Rinehart and Winston, 1962), 267.

13. In the 1970s, Millett asserted that society needs a single standard of "sex freedom" for boys and girls and a single standard of parental responsibility for fathers and mothers. Without a unitary standard for sexual and parental behavior, equality between men and women would remain ephemeral (Millett, *Sexual Politics*, 62).

14. Shulamith Firestone, *The Dialectic of Sex* (New York: Bantam Books, 1970), 59.

15. Ibid., 175.

16. Ibid.

17. Ibid., 190.

18. Ibid., 191, 242.

19. Echols, "The New Feminism of Yin and Yang," 440.

20. Alison M. Jaggar, "Feminist Ethics," in *Encyclopedia of Ethics*, ed. Lawrence Becker, with Charlotte Becker (New York: Garland, 1992), 364.

21. Linda Alcoff, "Cultural Feminism Versus Poststructuralism: The Identity Crisis in Feminist Theory," *Signs: Journal of Women in Culture and Society* 13, no. 3 (1988): 408.

22. Mary Daly, *Beyond God the Father: Toward a Philosophy of Women's Liberation* (Boston: Beacon Press, 1973).

23. Perhaps Daly meant that an imminent God infuses women with the power-to-grow into their own image rather than be molded into that of a transcendent God interested only in expressing his power over others.

24. Mary Daly, *Gyn/Ecology: The Metaethics of Radical Feminism* (Boston: Beacon Press, 1978).

25. Ibid., 59.

26. Ibid., 107–312. Note: "African female circumcision" is a contested term. Some commentators instead refer to this practice as "female genital mutilation" or, less pejoratively, as "female genital cutting." In the main, feminists oppose this practice, whatever it is called.

27. Ibid., xi.

28. Ibid., 68.

29. See Ann-Janine Morey-Gaines, "Metaphor and Radical Feminism: Some Cautionary Comments on Mary Daly's *Gyn/Ecology*," *Soundings* 65, no. 3 (fall 1982): 347–348.

30. Mary Daly, *Pure Lust: Elemental Feminist Philosophy* (London: Women's Press Ltd., 2001).

31. Ibid., 2.

32. Ibid., 2–3.

33. Ibid., 35.

34. Ann Ferguson, "Sex War: The Debate Between Radical and Liberal Feminists," *Signs: Journal of Women in Culture and Society* 10, no. 1 (autumn 1984): 109.

35. Ibid., 108.

36. See the debate between Christina Hoff Sommers and Marilyn Friedman in Marilyn Friedman and Jan Narveson, eds., *Political Correctness: For and Against* (Lanham, MD: Rowman & Littlefield, 1995), 36–37.

37. Catharine A. MacKinnon, "Francis Biddle's Sister: Pornography, Civil Rights, and Speech," in *Feminism Unmodified: Disclosures on Life and Law* (Cambridge, MA: Harvard University Press, 1987), 176.

38. Catharine A. MacKinnon, "Feminism, Marxism, Method, and the State: An Agenda for Theory," *Signs: Journal of Women in Culture and Society* 7, no. 3 (spring 1982): 533.

39. Appendix I, Minneapolis, Minnesota, Code of Ordinances, title 7, chap. 139, 1, amending 39.10.

40. Stuart Taylor Jr., "Pornography Foes Lose New Weapons in Supreme Court," *New York Times*, February 25, 1986, 1.

41. Nan D. Hunter and Sylvia A. Law, Brief Amici Curiae of Feminist Anticensorship Task Force et al. to U.S. Court of Appeals for the Seventh Circuit, *American Booksellers Association, Inc. et al. v. William H. Hudnut III et al.* (April 18, 1985): 9–18.

42. MacKinnon, "Feminism, Marxism, Method, and the State," 533.

43. KaeLyn, "Feminist Porn: Sex, Consent, and Getting Off," *Feministe*, July 23, 2008, http://www.feministe.us/blog/archives/2008/07/23/feminist-porn-sex-consent-and-getting-off.

44. Ibid.

45. Ibid.

46. Emily Bazelon, "Should Prostitution Be a Crime?," *New York Times Magazine*, May 8, 2016, 38.

47. Ibid., 39.

48. Ibid., 40.

49. Ibid.

50. Ibid.

51. Ibid., 42.

52. Ibid.

53. Cited in ibid., 43.

54. Ibid.

55. Ibid., 57.

56. Friedrich Engels, *Socialism: Utopian or Scientific*, quoted in Firestone, *The Dialectic of Sex*, 11–12.

57. Firestone, *The Dialectic of Sex*, 12.

58. Because the claim that biology is the cause of women's oppression sounds like the claim that women's biology is their destiny, it is important to stress the difference between the two. Whereas conservatives believe that the constraints of nature

exist necessarily, radical-libertarian feminists insist that it is within women's power to overcome them. For some conservative views, see George Gilder, *Sexual Suicide* (New York: Quadrangle, 1973); Lionel Tiger, *Men in Groups* (New York: Random House, 1969). For a feminist view, see Mary Vetterling-Braggin, ed., *"Femininity," "Masculinity," and "Androgyny"* (Totowa, NJ: Rowman & Littlefield, 1982).

59. Firestone, *The Dialectic of Sex*, 12.

60. Ibid., 198–199.

61. Marge Piercy, *Woman on the Edge of Time* (New York: Fawcett Crest Books, 1976).

62. Ibid., 102.

63. Ibid., 105–106.

64. Ibid., 183.

65. Azizah al-Hibri, article in *Research in Philosophy and Technology*, ed. Paul T. Durbin (London: JAL Press, 1984), 7:266.

66. Anne Donchin, "The Future of Mothering: Reproductive Technology and Feminist Theory," *Hypatia* 1, no. 2 (fall 1986): 131.

67. Mary O'Brien, *The Politics of Reproduction* (Boston: Routledge & Kegan Paul, 1981), 8, 20ff, 35–36. See also Sara Ann Ketchum, "New Reproductive Technologies and the Definition of Parenthood: A Feminist Perspective" (paper given at the Feminism and Legal Theory Conference at the University of Wisconsin, Madison, summer 1987, photocopy dated June 18, 1987). Note: now that assisted reproduction is available, a woman may give birth to a child that is not hers genetically. Embryos can be switched in the lab, so that the embryo a woman gestates is not from her ovum but from another woman's.

68. Adrienne Rich, *Of Woman Born* (New York: W. W. Norton, 1979), 111.

69. Ibid., 111.

70. Ibid., 38–39.

71. Quoted in Firestone, *The Dialectic of Sex*, 199.

72. Margaret Atwood, *The Handmaid's Tale* (New York: Fawcett Crest Books, 1985).

73. Ibid., 164.

74. Gena Corea, "Egg Snatchers," in *Test-Tube Women: What Future for Motherhood?*, eds. Rita Arditti, Renate Duelli Klein, and Shelley Minden (London: Pandora Press, 1984), 45.

75. Jennifer Parks, "Rethinking Radical Politics in the Context of Assisted Reproductive Technology," *Bioethics* 23, no. 1 (2009): 20–27.

76. Christine Overall, "Access to In Vitro Fertilization: Costs, Care and Consent," *Dialogue* 30 (1991): 383–398.

77. Jennifer Ludden, "Egg Freezing Puts the Biological Clock on Hold," NPR, May 31, 2011, http://www.npr.org/2011/05/31/136363039/egg-freezing-puts-the-biological-clock-on-hold.

78. Ibid.

79. Alison M. Jaggar, *Feminist Politics and Human Nature* (Totowa, NJ: Rowman & Allanheld, 1983), 256.

80. Ann Oakley, *Woman's Work: The Housewife, Past and Present* (New York: Pantheon Books, 1974), 186.

81. Ibid., 187, 199.

82. Ibid., 201.

83. Ibid., 203.

84. Firestone, *The Dialectic of Sex*, 229.

85. Ibid., 228–230.

86. Rich, *Of Woman Born*, 174.

87. Ibid., 13 (our emphasis).

88. Ibid., 57.

89. Ibid., 13.

90. Ibid., 57.

91. Because the term "surrogate mother" suggests that such a woman is not a real mother but a substitute mother, many feminists prefer the term "contracted mother" or "gestational carrier."

92. Gena Corea, *The Mother Machine: Reproduction Technologies from Artificial Insemination to Artificial Wombs* (New York: Harper & Row, 1985), 213–249.

93. "A Surrogate's Story of Loving and Losing," *U.S. News & World Report*, June 6, 1983, 12.

94. Susan Sherwin, *No Longer Patient: Feminist Ethics and Health Care* (Philadelphia: Temple University Press, 1993), 107.

95. Ibid., 41.

96. Anne Koedt, "The Myth of the Vaginal Orgasm," *Notes from the Second Year: Women's Liberation—Major Writings of the Radical Feminists* (April 1970): 41.

97. Adrienne Rich, "Compulsory Heterosexuality and Lesbian Existence," in *Living with Contradictions: Controversies in Feminist Social Ethics*, ed. Alison M. Jaggar (Boulder, CO: Westview Press, 1994), 488.

98. Deirdre English, quoted in Hole and Levine, *Rebirth of Feminism*, 221.

99. Amber Hollibaugh, Deirdre English, and Gayle Rubin, "Talking Sex: A Conversation on Sexuality and Feminism," *Feminist Review* 11 (June 1982): 49.

100. Nancy Myron and Charlotte Bunch, eds., *Lesbianism and the Women's Movement* (Baltimore: Diana, 1975), 36.

101. Bat-Ami Bar On, "The Feminist Sexuality Debates and the Transformation of the Political," *Hypatia* 7, no. 4 (fall 1992): 49.

102. See "Redstockings Manifesto," in *Sisterhood Is Powerful*, ed. Robin Morgan (New York: Random House, 1970), 534.

103. English, Hollibaugh, and Rubin, "Talking Sex," 50.

104. "Redstockings Manifesto," 534.

105. "New York Covens' Leaflet," in Morgan, *Sisterhood Is Powerful*, 539–540.

106. Rich, "Compulsory Heterosexuality and Lesbian Existence," 488–489.

107. Jean Bethke Elshtain, *Public Man, Private Woman: Women in Social and Political Thought* (Princeton, NJ: Princeton University Press, 1981), 226.

108. Ibid., 213.

109. Audre Lorde, "An Open Letter to Mary Daly," in *This Bridge Called My Back*, ed. Cherríe Moraga and Gloria Anzaldúa (Watertown, MA: Persephone Press, 1987), 94–97.

110. Elshtain, *Public Man, Private Woman*, 213.

111. Ibid., 225.

112. R. A. Hatcher, et al., *Contraceptive Technology: 1990–1992* (New York: Irvington Publishers, 1990).

113. N. C. Lee et al., "Type of Intrauterine Device and the Risk of Pelvic Inflammatory Disease," *Obstetrics and Gynecology* 62, no. 1 (1983): 1–10.

114. J. Shiver Jr., "Dalkon Shield Company Files for Bankruptcy," *Los Angeles Times*, August 22, 1985, section 1, 20.

115. Sherwin, *No Longer Patient*, 128.

116. Anita Petra Hardon, "The Needs of Women Versus the Interests of Family Planning Personnel, Policy-Makers and Researchers: Conflicting Views on Safety and Acceptability of Contraceptives," *Social Science and Medicine* 35, no. 6 (1992): 762.

117. Adele Clark, "Subtle Forms of Sterilization Abuse: A Reproductive Rights Analysis," in Arditti, Klein, and Minden, *Test-Tube Women*, 198.

118. Ann Ferguson, "The Sex Debate in the Women's Movement: A Socialist-Feminist View," *Against the Current* (September/October, 1983): 12.

119. Ibid.

120. Ibid.

121. Ibid., 13.

122. Ibid.

123. Ibid.

124. Denise Thompson, *Radical Feminism Today* (London: Sage Publishing, 2001), 146.

Chapter 3: Marxist and Social Feminisms

1. Karl Marx, *Capital* (New York: International Publishers, 1967), 3:791.

2. Nancy Holmstrom, "The Socialist Feminist Project," *Monthly Review Press* 54, no. 10 (2002): 1.

3. Richard Schmitt, *Introduction to Marx and Engels* (Boulder, CO: Westview Press, 1987), 7–8.

4. Karl Marx, *A Contribution to the Critique of Political Economy* (New York: International Publishers, 1972), 20–21.

5. Schmitt, *Introduction to Marx and Engels*, 14 (our emphasis).

6. Nancy Holmstrom, "A Marxist Theory of Women's Nature," *Ethics* 94, no. 1 (April 1984): 464.

7. Robert L. Heilbroner, *Marxism: For and Against* (New York: W. W. Norton, 1980), 107.

8. Henry Burrows Acton, *What Marx Really Said* (London: MacDonald, 1967), 41.

9. Ernest Mandel, *An Introduction to Marxist Economic Theory* (New York: Pathfinder Press, 1970), 25.

10. For Marx's discussion of surplus value and exploitation, see his three-volume work *Capital*, particularly volumes 1 and 2. For a more detailed introduction to these concepts, see Wallis Arthur Suchting, *Marx: An Introduction* (New York: New York University Press, 1983).

11. Schmitt, *Introduction to Marx and Engels*, 96–97.

12. For an elaboration of these points, see Mandel, *An Introduction to Marxist Economic Theory.*

13. Karl Marx, *The 18th Brumaire of Louis Bonaparte* (New York: International Publishers, 1968), 608.

14. Here the term "class" does not follow the technical Marxist sense. As we shall see, it is very debatable that women form a true class. For an excellent discussion of the phrase "bourgeois feminism," see Marilyn J. Boxer, "Rethinking the Socialist Construction and International Career of the Concept 'Bourgeois Feminism,'" *American Historical Review* 112, no. 1 (February 2007): 131–158.

15. Allen W. Wood, *Karl Marx* (London: Routledge & Kegan Paul, 1981), 8.

16. Heilbroner, *Marxism: For and Against*, 72.

17. Ibid.

18. Ibid.

19. Karl Marx, "Economic and Philosophic Manuscripts," in *Early Writings*, ed. and trans. T. B. Bottomore (New York: McGraw-Hill, 1964), 122. We owe this reference, as well as several good analyses of alienation, to Michael Weber.

20. Ann Foreman, *Femininity as Alienation: Women and the Family in Marxism and Psychoanalysis* (London: Pluto Press, 1977), 65.

21. Ibid., 101–102.

22. Quoted in David McLellan, *Karl Marx* (New York: Penguin Books, 1975), 33.

23. Karl Marx and Friedrich Engels, *The German Ideology*, in *The Marx-Engels Reader*, ed. and trans. Robert C. Tucker (New York: W. W. Norton, 1978), 199.

24. Schmitt, *Introduction to Marx and Engels*, 202.

25. Friedrich Engels, *The Origin of the Family, Private Property, and the State* (New York: International Publishers, 1972), 103.

26. Ibid.

27. Notions of hunting and gathering as popularized by anthropological studies are often oversimplified. We should be aware, therefore, of the danger of attributing a rigid sexual division of labor to "hunting and gathering" societies, past and present. Women and children may contribute meat to the diet, just as men may contribute root or grain foods. Noticing Engels's dependence on stereotypical ideas of women's and men's work should lead readers to view Engels's account as less-than-accurate history.

28. Engels quoted approvingly the controversial thesis of a now largely discredited anthropologist. The thesis was that women in pairing societies wielded considerable political as well as economic power: "The women were the great power among the clans, [*gentes*], as everywhere else. They did not hesitate, when occasion required 'to knock off the horns,' as it was technically called, from the head of a chief, and send him back to the ranks of the warriors" (Engels, *Origin of the Family*, 113). Apparently, it did not strike Engels as odd that a powerful matriarch would let herself be forcibly seized as a wife by a man whose "horns" she could have "knocked off."

29. Ibid.

30. Lise Vogel, *Marxism and the Oppression of Women: Towards a Unitary Theory* (New Brunswick, NJ: Rutgers University Press, 1983), 82.

31. Engels, *Origin of the Family*, 117.

32. Jane Flax asked why a group of matriarchs would have let men control the tribe's animals or use the fact of their control to gain power over women. See Jane Flax, "Do Feminists Need Marxism?," in *Building Feminist Theory: Essays from "Quest," a Feminist Quarterly* (New York: Longman, 1981): 176.

33. Engels, *Origin of the Family*, 117.

34. Marx and Engels, *The German Ideology*, 201.

35. Engels, *Origin of the Family*, 118–119.

36. Ibid., 120.

37. Ibid., 121.

38. Ibid., 137.

39. Ibid., 128.

40. Ibid., 137–139.

41. Ibid., 79.

42. Michèle Barrett, *Women's Oppression Today: Problems in Marxist Feminist Analysis* (London: Verso, 1980), 49.

43. Evelyn Reed, "Women: Caste, Class, or Oppressed Sex?," *International Socialist Review* 31, no. 3 (September 1970): 15–17, 40–41.

44. Ibid., 17.

45. Ibid.

46. Ibid.

47. Ibid., 40.

48. Ibid.

49. Ibid., 41.

50. Ibid.

51. Margaret Benston, "The Political Economy of Women's Liberation," *Monthly Review* 21, no. 4 (September 1969): 16.

52. Ibid., 21.

53. Mariarosa Dalla Costa and Selma James, "Women and the Subversion of the Community," in *The Power of Women and the Subversion of Community* (Bristol, UK: Falling Wall Press, 1972), 34.

54. In the final analysis, Dalla Costa and James viewed men as the dupes of capital rather than as the wily oppressors of women. Men, they said, appear to be the sole recipients of domestic services, but in fact "the figure of the boss is concealed behind that of the husband" (ibid., 35–36).

55. Wendy Edmond and Suzie Fleming expressed the same conviction in even more forceful terms: "Housewives keep their families in the cheapest way; they nurse the children under the worst circumstances and all the toiling of thousands of housewives enables the possessing classes to increase their riches, and to get the labor-power of men and children in the most profitable way." See Wendy Edmond and Suzie Fleming, "If Women Were Paid for All They Do," in *All Work and No Pay*, eds. Wendy Edmond and Suzie Fleming (London: Power of Women Collective and Falling Wall Press, 1975), 8.

56. See Ann Crittenden Scott, "The Value of Housework for Love or Money?," *Ms.*, June 1972, 56–58.

57. Ibid.

58. "Median Weekly Earnings of Full-Time Wage and Salary Workers by Selected Characteristics, 2015," Bureau of Labor Statistics, Current Population Survey, http://www.bis.gov/cps/cpsaat37.htm (assessed March 2012).

59. Ibid.

60. Carol Lopate, "Pay for Housework?," *Social Policy* 5, no. 3 (September/October 1974): 28.

61. Ibid., 29–31.

62. Observed in Stevi Jackson, "Marxism and Feminism," in *Marxism and Social Science*, eds. Andrew Gamble, David Marsh, and Tony Tant (Champaign: University of Illinois Press, 1999), 17.

63. Chris Beasley, *What Is Feminism?* (London: Sage Publications, 1999), 62–64.

64. Juliet Mitchell, *Woman's Estate* (New York: Pantheon Books, 1971).

65. Ibid., 100–101 (our emphasis).

66. Mitchell was convinced that women's supposed physical weakness cannot explain, solely or even primarily, their limited role in production. In the first place, men have forced women to do "women's work," and "women's work in all its varieties requires much physical strength. Second, even if women are not as physically strong as men, and even if their original, limited role in production can be attributed to their gap in strength, this same gap cannot explain women's current, limited role in production" (ibid., 104).

67. Ibid., 107.

68. Ibid.

69. Alison M. Jaggar, *Feminist Politics and Human Nature* (Totowa, NJ: Rowman & Allanheld, 1983), 114–115, 308.

70. Ibid., 309–310.

71. Ibid., 310–311.

72. Although Jaggar did not make specific points about in vitro fertilization, the points raised here seem to fit her analysis.

73. "The percentage of women leading medical research studies rises, but still lags behind men." See news release, Massachusetts General Hospital, July 19, 2006, http://www2.massgeneral.org/news/releases/071906jagsi.html (accessed March 2012).

74. Jaggar, *Feminist Politics and Human Nature*, 315.

75. Ibid.

76. Ibid., 316.

77. Iris Marion Young, "Beyond the Unhappy Marriage: A Critique of Dual Systems Theory," in *Women and Revolution: A Discussion of the Unhappy Marriage of Marxism and Feminism*, ed. Lydia Sargent (Boston: South End Press, 1981), 58 (emphasis in original).

78. Heidi I. Hartmann, "The Unhappy Marriage of Marxism and Feminism: Towards a More Progressive Union," in Sargent, *Women and Revolution*, 428.

79. Ibid., 428–431.

80. Human Development Report Team 2010, "The Real Wealth of Nations: Pathways to Human Development," United Nations Development Programme, 2010, http://hdr.undp.org/en/media/HDR_2010 _EN_Complete_reprint.pdf, 113.

81. Ibid.

82. "Caregiving in the U.S. 2009," National Alliance for Caregiving, 2009, http://www.caregiving.org/ data/Caregiving_in_the_US_2009_full_report.pdf, 22.

83. "Gender at Work: A Companion to the World Development Report on Jobs," Washington, DC: World Bank, February 20, 2014.

84. Ibid.

85. Ibid.

86. Ibid.

87. Aki Ito and Toru Fujioka, "Women Beat Men to Jobs as Japan 'Mancession' Spurs Deflation," *Bloomberg Businessweek*, January 5, 2012, http://www.business week.com/news/2012-01-05/women-beat-men-to-jobs-as-japan-mancession-spurs -deflation.html (accessed March 2012).

88. Geoff Meade, "Gender Pay Gap Across Europe Condemned," *Independent*, March 5, 2010, http://www.independent.co.uk/news/world/europe/gender-pay-gap -across-europe-condemned-1916862.html.

89. "The Simple Truth About the Gender Pay Gap," American Association of University Women, spring 2015, http://www.aauw.org/research/the-simple-truth -about-the-gender-pay-gap.

90. Ibid.

91. Christina Huffington, "Women and Equal Pay: Wage Gap Still Intact, Study Shows," *Huffington Post*, April 9, 2013, http://www.huffingtonpost.com/2013/04/09 /women-and-equal-pay-wage-gap_n_3038806.html.

92. "The Simple Truth About the Gender Pay Gap."

93. Annie-Rose Strasser, "Despite Growing Number of Female Doctors and Lawyers, Women's Pay Still Lags Behind," ThinkProgress, December 5, 2012, http:// thinkprogress.org/economy/2012/12/05/1284131/women-pay-gap-persists.

94. Valerie Bryson, *Feminist Debates: Issues of Theory and Political Practice* (New York: New York University Press, 1999), 137.

95. Colleen Leahey and Caroline Fairchild, "Women CEOs in the Fortune 500," *Fortune*, January 6, 2015.

96. See "Employed Persons by Detailed Occupation, Sex, Race, and Hispanic or Latino Ethnicity," US Department of Labor, Bureau of Labor Statistics, September 2011, http://www.blg.gov/eps/cpsaat11.pdf (accessed March 2012).

97. Ibid., 4.

98. Ibid.

99. Ibid., 3.

100. Ibid., 2.

101. For example, a 2010 Bureau of Labor Statistics report found that 26 percent of women wage earners work part-time, while 13 percent of men wage earners work part-time. See "Highlights of Women's Earnings in 2009," US Department of Labor, Bureau of Labor Statistics, June 2010, http://www.bls.gov/cps/cpswom2009.pdf (accessed March 2013).

102. A provocative article suggests that women do not "choose" to leave the paid workforce in droves but are ambivalent at best about this decision or necessity: E. J. Graff, "The Opt-Out Myth," *Columbia Journalism Review* (March–April 2007), http://www.cjr.org/issues/2007/2/Graff.asp.

103. "Despite Growing Number of Female Doctors and Lawyers, Women's Pay Still Lags Behind."

104. Equal Pay Act of 1963 (Pub. L. 88-93) (EPA), as amended, as it appears in volume 29 of the United States Code, at section 206(d).

105. Amy Joyce, "Unusual Job Titles a Sign of the Times," *Merced (California) Sun-Star*, December 23, 2006, 1.

106. Roslyn L. Feldberg, "Comparable Worth: Toward Theory and Practice in the United States," *Signs: Journal of Women in Culture and Society* 10, no. 2 (winter 1984): 311–313.

107. "Gender Pay Gap Statistics," Workplace Gender Equality Agency in Australia, March 2014, https://www.wgea.gov.au/sites/default/files/2014_03_04_Gender_Pay_Gap_factsheet, 1–9 (accessed March 2012).

108. Ibid.

109. Helen Remick, "Major Issues in A Priori Applications," in *Comparable Worth and Wage Discrimination: Technical Possibilities and Political Realities*, ed. Helen Remick (Philadelphia: Temple University Press, 1984), 102.

110. Jake Lamar, "A Worthy but Knotty Question," *Time*, February 6, 1984, 30.

111. Teresa Amott and Julie Matthaei, "Comparable Worth, Incomparable Pay," *Radical America* 18, no. 5 (September/October 1984): 25.

112. Amott and Matthaei, "Comparable Worth, Incomparable Pay," 25.

113. "Globalization," World Bank Group, January 20, 2015, http://go.worldbank.org/V7BJE9FD30.

114. Shawn Meghan Burn, *Women Across Cultures: A Global Perspective* (Mountain View, CA: Mayfield Publishing, 2000), 120.

115. Ibid.

116. Ibid.

117. Ricardo Alonso-Zaldivar, "Care Homes Hiring More Foreigners," *Los Angeles Times*, October 20, 2005, http://articles.latimes.com/2005/oct/20/nation/na-immig20.

118. Alessio Cangiano et al., "Migrant Care Workers in Ageing Societies: Research Findings in the United Kingdom," Report, COMPAS: ESRC Centre on Migration, Policy, and Society, University of Oxford, June 2009, 182.

119. Pei-Chia Lan, "Among Women: Migrant Domestics and Their Taiwanese Employers Across Generations," in *Global Woman: Nannies, Maids, and Sex Workers in the New Economy*, ed. Barbara Ehrenreich and Arlie Russell Hochshild (New York: Holt Paperbacks, 2002), 184.

120. Ibid., 171.

121. Ibid., 188.

122. Ibid., 171.

123. Ibid., 172.

124. Matt McAllester, "America Is Stealing the World's Doctors," *New York Times Magazine*, March 11, 2012, http://www.nytimes.com/2012/03/11/magazine/america-is-stealing-foreign-doctors.html.

125. Olga Voronina, "Soviet Patriarchy: Past and Present," *Hypatia* 8, no. 4 (fall 1993): 107.

126. Juliet Mitchell, *Psychoanalysis and Feminism* (New York: Vintage Books, 1974), 416.

127. Jackson, "Marxism and Feminism," 33.

128. Nancy Holmstrom, introduction to *The Socialist Feminist Project: A Contemporary Reader in Theory and Politics*, ed. Nancy Holmstrom (New York: Monthly Review Press, 2002), 3 (our emphasis).

129. Barbara Ehrenreich, *Nickeled and Dimed: On (Not) Getting By in America* (New York: Metropolitan Books, 2001).

130. Ann Ferguson, *Stanford Encyclopedia of Philosophy* (Stanford, CA: Stanford University Press, 2010).

Chapter 4: Women-of-Color Feminism(s) in the United States

1. Naomi Zack indicated that her preference for the term "nonwhite" over "of color" to describe the organizing quality that defines the groups of people these phrases mean to reference on the theory that "of color" implies the existence of biological races, which she famously and appropriately rejects. See Naomi Zack, *Women of Color and Philosophy: A Critical Reader* (Oxford: Blackwell Publishers, 2000), 2.

2. For a definition of "double consciousness," see note 21.

3. For a good discussion of "white privilege," see Peggy McIntosh, "White Privilege and Male Privilege: A Personal Account of Coming to See Correspondences Through Work in Women's Studies," in *Critical White Studies: Looking Behind the Mirror*, eds. Richard Delgado and Jean Stefanic (Philadelphia: Temple University Press, 1997).

4. In this chapter, we capitalize the word "Black" unless an author uses a lowercase *b*.

5. Tisa M. Anders, "Combahee River Collective (1974–1980)," *Online Encyclopedia of Significant People and Places in African American History*, http://www.blackpast.org/aah/combahee-river-collective-1974-1980.

6. Ibid.

7. Ibid.

8. For general information about the Comisión Femenil Mexicana Nacional, see "Comision Femenil Mexicana Nacional, Inc," UC Santa Barbara Library, http://www.library.ucsb.edu/special-collections/cema/cfmn (accessed March 5, 2016).

9. Kristin Olsen, *Chronology of Women's History* (Westport, CT: Greenwood Press, 1994).

10. Anders, "Combahee River Collective (1974–1980)."

11. Ibid.

12. Ibid.

13. Ibid.

14. Ibid.

15. Kimberlé Crenshaw, "Mapping the Margins: Intersectionality, Identity, Politics, and Violence Against Women of Color," in *Critical Race Theory: The Key Writings That Formed the Movement*, eds. Kimberlé Crenshaw et al. (New York: New Press, 1995), 357–383.

16. Ibid, 360.

17. Anna Julia Cooper, *A Voice from the South: By a Woman from the South* (New York: Oxford University Press, 1988).

18. Ibid.

19. From a speech delivered at the Women's Rights Convention in Akron, Ohio, in 1851. For Sojourner Truth's dictated autobiography, see *The Narrative of Sojourner Truth: A Northern Slave* (Boston: J. B. Yerrinton & Son, 1850).

20. Ibid.

21. In the realm of race theory, "double consciousness," a term originated by W. E. B. DuBois in *The Souls of Black Folk* (New York: Gramercy Books, 1994), refers to the idea that Black persons in the United States (regardless of gender) have (at least) two different phenomenological identity experiences. DuBois describes the experience of "double-consciousness" as a constant feeling of two-ness—an American, a person of color.

22. Quoted in Harriet Beecher Stowe, "Sojourner Truth," *Rochester Evening Express*, December 13, 1866.

23. The perception of woman as powerful later gets reflected, for example, in Alice Walker's definition of "womanism" (her substitute term for Black/African American feminism). See Alice Walker, *In Search of Our Mothers' Gardens: Womanist Prose* (Orlando, FL: Harcourt Books, 1983).

24. For example, during the formative years of the United States, white men enacted laws whereby white women who married men of color would lose their citizenship rights. See Nancy Leong, "Judicial Erasure of Mixed Race Discrimination," *American University Law Review* 59, no. 3 (February 2010): 469.

25. See, for example, Aida Hurtado, *The Color of Privilege: Three Blasphemies on Race and Feminism* (Ann Arbor: University of Michigan Press, 1996).

26. Ibid., 58.

27. See, for example, Kimberlé Crenshaw, "Mapping the Margins: Intersectionality, Identity Politics, and Violence Against Women of Color," *Stanford Law Review* 43, no. 6 (1991): 1242–1243. Crenshaw said, "Feminist efforts to politicize experiences of women and antiracist efforts to politicize experiences of people of color have frequently proceeded as though the issues and experiences they each detail occur on mutually exclusive terrains. . . . Contemporary feminist and antiracist discourses have failed to consider intersectional identities such as women of color."

28. Audre Lorde, "The Master's Tools Will Never Dismantle the Master's House," in *This Bridge Called My Back: Writings by Radical Women of Color*, eds. Cherríe Moraga and Gloria E. Anzaldúa (New York: Kitchen Table/Women of Color Press, 1984), 112.

29. Ibid.

30. Ibid.

31. Joan Martin, "The Unicorn Is Black: Audre Lorde in Retrospect," in *Black Women Writers (1950–1980): A Critical Examination*, ed. Mari Evans (Garden City, NY: Doubleday, 1984), 277–291.

32. Audre Lorde, *Coal* (New York: W. W. Norton and Company, 1976).

33. Audre Lorde, "Poetry Is Not a Luxury," in *Sister Outsider: Essays and Speeches* (Berkeley, CA: Crossing Press 1984), 36–39.

34. Ibid., 39.

35. Ibid., 59.

36. Audre Lorde, *The Cancer Journals* (San Francisco, CA: Aunt Lute Books, 1980), 59–60.

37. Carla M. Hammond, "Audre Lorde: Interview," *Denver Quarterly* 16, no.1 (1981): 10–27.

38. bell hooks, *Feminist Theory: From Margin to Center* (Boston: South End Press, 1984).

39. bell hooks, *Feminism Is for Everybody: Passionate Politics* (Boston: South End Press, 2000), 97–99.

40. Ibid., 87.

41. bell hooks, *Ain't I a Woman: Black Women and Feminism* (New York: Routledge, 1987).

42. Sheryl Sandberg, *Lean In: Women, Work, and the Will to Lead* (New York: Knopf, 2013).

43. "I wanted to come up with an everyday metaphor that anyone could use," said Kimberlé Crenshaw in an April 12, 2014, interview on intersectionality with Bim Adewunmi. See http://www.newstatesman.com/lifestyle/2014/04/kimberl-crenshaw-intersectionality-i-wanted-come-everyday-metaphor-anyone-could?

44. Ibid., 7.

45. Kimberlé Crenshaw, "The Girls Obama Forgot," *New York Times*, July 29, 2014, 1.

46. Ibid., 3.

47. Patricia Hill Collins, *Black Feminist Thought: Knowledge, Consciousness, and the Politics of Empowerment* (Boston: Unwin Hyman, 1990), 6.

48. Ibid., 7.

49. Ibid., 67.

50. Ibid., 218.

51. Eve Browning Cole, *Philosophy and Feminist Criticism: An Introduction* (New York: Paragon House, 1913), 260.

52. Quoted in Collins, *Black Feminist Thought*, 234.

53. Cole, *Philosophy and Feminist Criticism*, 29–30.

54. Quoted in Collins, *Black Feminist Thought*, 236.

55. Collins, *Black Feminist Thought*, 237.

56. Cole, *Philosophy and Feminist Criticism*, 29–30.

57. Patricia Hill Collins, *Fighting Words: Black Women and the Search for Justice* (Minneapolis: University of Minnesota Press, 1998), xvii.

58. K. Leon, "La Hermandad and Chicanas Organizing: The Community Rhetoric of the Comisión Femenil Mexicana Nacional," *Community Literacy Journal* 7, no. 2 (1973): 1–20.

59. Gloria Anzaldúa and Cherríe Moraga, eds., *This Bridge Called My Back: Writings by Radical Women of Color* (San Francisco: Aunt Lute Books, 1999).

60. Tania Modleski, "This Bridge Called My Back: Writings by Radical Women of Color," *Minnesota Review* (New Series) 23 (fall 1984): 199–200.

61. Gloria Anzaldúa, *Borderlands/La Frontera: The New Mestiza* (San Francisco: Aunt Lute Books, 1999).

62. Ibid.

63. Sandra L. Colby and Jennifer M. Norten, "Projections of the Size and Composition of the U.S. Population: 2014–2060," US Census Bureau, March 2015, https://www.census.gov/content/dam/Census/library/publications/2015/demo/p25-1143.pdf.

64. Cristina Herrera, *Contemporary Chicana Literature: (Re)writing the Maternal Script* (Amherst, MA: Cambria Press, 2014).

65. Ibid.

66. Ofelia Schutte, "Cultural Alterity," in *Women and Color and Philosophy*, ed. Naomi Zack (Malden, MA: Blackwell Publishers, Ltd., 2000), 46.

67. Ibid., 49.

68. Chela Sandoval, "U.S. Third World Feminism: The Theory and Method of Oppositional Consciousness in the Postmodern World," *Genders* 10 (spring 1991): 2–3, 10.

69. Ibid.

70. Maria Lugones and Elizabeth Spelman, "Have We Got a Theory for You! Feminist Theory, Cultural Imperialism, and the Demand for the Woman's Voice," in *Feminist Philosophies*, eds. Janet A. Kourany, James Sterba, and Rosemarie Tong (Englewood Cliffs, NJ: Prentice Hall, 1992), 388.

71. Chen Chao-ju, "The Difference That Differences Make: Asian Feminism and the Politics of Difference," *Asian Journal of Women's Studies* 13, no. 3 (2007): 7–36, 146.

72. Ibid.

73. Grace Lee, dir., *American Revolutionary: The Evolution of Grace Lee Boggs* (Lee Lee Films, 2013).

74. Robert D. McFadden, "Grace Lee Boggs, Human Rights Advocate for 7 Decades, Dies at 100," *New York Times*, October 5, 2015, http://www.nytimes.com /2015/10/06/us/grace-lee-boggs-detroit-activist-dies-at-100.html.

75. "Bill Moyers Talks with Grace Lee Boggs, Bill Moyers Journal, June 15, 2007, http://www.pbs.org/moyers/journal/06152007/watch3.html.

76. Hansi Lo Wang, "Yuri Kochiyama, Activist and Former World War II Internee, Dies at 93," NPR, June 2, 2014, http://www.npr.org/sections/codeswitch/2014 /06/02/318072652/japanese-american-activist-and-malcolm-x-ally-dies-at-93.

77. Ibid.

78. Diane Fujino, *Heartbeat of Struggle: The Revolutionary Life of Yuri Kochiyama* (Minneapolis: University of Minnesota Press, 2005).

79. Wang, "Yuri Kochiyama, Activist and Former World War II Internee, Dies at 93."

80. Leslie Bow, *Partly Colored: Asian Americans and Racial Anxiety in the Segregated South* (New York: New York University Press, 2010).

81. Leslie Bow, "Racial Interstitiality and the Anomalies of the 'Partly Colored': Representations of Asians Under Jim Crow," *Journal of Asian American Studies* 10, no. 1 (February 2007): 1.

82. Ibid., 4.

83. Ibid.

84. Ibid.

85. Ibid., 3.

86. Ibid., 4. See James W. Loewen, *The Mississippi Chinese: Between Black and White* (Long Grove, IL: Waveland Press, 1988).

87. Bow, "Racial Interstitiality and the Anomalies of the 'Partly Colored,'" 26.

88. Mitsuye Yamada, "Asian Pacific American Women and Feminism," in *Feminist Theory: A Reader*, eds. Wendy K. Kolmar and Frances Bartkowski (Boston: McGraw-Hill Higher Education, 2013), 366.

89. Ibid.

90. Ibid., 367.

91. Ibid.

92. Ibid.

93. Ibid.

94. Ibid.

95. Ibid.

96. See Luana Ross, "From the 'F' Word to Indigenous/Feminisms." *Wicazo Sa Review* 24, no. 2 (2009): 39–52.

97. See "Decolonizing Feminism: Challenging Connections Between Settler Colonialism and Heteropatriarchy," *Feminist Formations* 25, no. 1 (spring 2013): 8–34, 10.

98. Ibid.

99. Ibid.

100. Donna Hightower Langston, *The Native American World* (Hoboken, NJ: John Wiley & Sons, 2003), 430.

101. Ibid.

102. Paula Gunn Allen, "Kochinnenako in Academe: Three Approaches to Interpreting a Keres Indian Tale," in *Feminist Theory: A Reader*, eds. Wendy K. Kolmar and Frances Bartkowski (New York: McGraw-Hill, 2013), 395–404.

103. Ibid.

104. Ibid.

105. Ibid., 401.

106. Ibid.

107. Ibid., 402.

108. Ibid.

109. Ross, "From the 'F' Word to Indigenous/Feminisms."

110. Ibid. (our emphasis).

111. Ibid.

112. Ibid., citing Paula Gunn Allen, "Who Is Your Mother? Red Roots of White Feminism," *Sinister Wisdom* 25 (winter 1984): 34–46.

113. Walker, *In Search of Our Mothers' Gardens.*

114. Ibid.

Chapter 5: Women-of-Color Feminism(s) on the World Stage: Global, Postcolonial, and Transnational Feminisms

1. "Why Population Aging Matters: A Global Perspective," National Institute on Aging, National Institutes of Health, March 2007, https://www.nia.nih.gov/research/publication/why-population-aging-matters-global-perspective, 14.

2. R. Shorto, "¿No hay beb'es? Keine Kinder? Nessum Bambino? No Babies?," *New York Times Magazine*, June 29, 2008, 34, 41.

3. Serena Parekh and Shelley Wilcox, "Feminist Perspectives on Globalization," in *Stanford Encyclopedia of Philosophy* (Stanford, CA: Stanford University, 2013), 1.

4. Charlotte Bunch, "Prospects for Global Feminism," in *Feminist Frameworks*, eds. Alison M. Jaggar and Paula S. Rothenberg, 3rd ed. (New York: McGraw-Hill, 1993), 249.

5. Bunch, "Prospects for Global Feminism," 249.

6. Ibid., 250.

7. Shawn Meghan Burn, *Women Across Cultures: A Global Perspective* (Mountain View, CA: Mayfield Publishing, 2000), 73.

8. Noemi Ehrenfeld Lenkiewicz, "Women's Control over Their Bodies," in *Women in the Third World: An Encyclopedia of Contemporary Issues*, ed. Nelly Stromquist (New York: Garland Publishing, 1998), 197–199.

9. Burn, *Women Across Cultures*, 53.

10. David Warwick, "Ethics and Population Control in Developing Countries," *Hastings Center Report* 4, no. 3 (June 1974): 3.

11. Barbara Hartmann, *Reproductive Rights and Wrongs: The Global Politics of Population Control* (Boston: South End Press, 1995).

12. David A. Grimes et al., "Unsafe Abortion: The Preventable Pandemic," *World Health Organization* (Geneva: Department of Reproductive Health and Research, 2006), 4.

13. Ibid., 2.

14. Friday E. Okonofua, "Abortion and Maternal Mortality in the Developing World," *Journal of Obstetrics and Gynecology Canada* 28, no. 11 (November 2006): 974–979.

15. Patricia H. David et al., "Women's Reproductive Health Needs in Russia: What Can We Learn from an Intervention to Improve Post-abortion Care?," *Health Policy and Planning* 22, no. 2 (February 2007): 83–94.

16. "The World Factbook: Sex Ratio," Central Intelligence Agency, https://www.cia.gov/library/publications/the-world-factbook/fields/2018.html.

17. Judith Banister, "Shortage of Girls in China Today: Causes, Consequences, International Comparisons, and Solutions," *Journal of Population Research*, May 2004, http://www.prb.org/presentations/ShortageofGirlsinChina.ppt.

18. "The World Factbook: Sex Ratio."

19. Ibid.

20. Swapan Seth, "Sex Selective Feticide in India," *Journal of Assisted Reproduction and Genetics* 24, no. 5 (May 2007): 153–154.

21. Maria Mies, "New Reproductive Technologies: Sexist and Racist Implications," in *Ecofeminism*, eds. Maria Mies and Vandana Shiva (London: Zed, 1993), 194 (Mies's emphasis).

22. Nancy Holmstrom, "Human Nature," in *A Companion to Feminist Philosophy*, eds. Alison M. Jaggar and Iris Marion Young (Oxford: Blackwell Publishers, 1998), 288.

23. Susan Moller Okin, "Inequalities Between Sexes in Different Cultural Contexts," in *Women, Culture, and Development*, eds. Martha Nussbaum and Jonathan Glover (Oxford, UK: Clarendon Press, 1995), 294.

24. Susan Moller Okin, "Feminism, Women's Human Rights, and Cultural Differences," *Hypatia* 13, no. 2 (1998): 42.

25. Martha Nussbaum, "Women's Capabilities and Social Justice," in *Gender Justice, Development, and Rights*, eds. Maxine Molyneux and Shahra Razavi (Oxford: Oxford University Press, 2002), 60–62.

26. Daniel Engster, "Rethinking Care Theory: The Practice of Caring and the Obligation to Care," *Hypatia* 20, no. 3 (summer 2005): 52.

27. Martha Nussbaum, *Sex and Social Justice* (New York: Oxford University Press, 1999). Note: the woman was really widowed at seven—the age she was married off to a rather old man.

28. Quoted in Vivienne Jabri, "Feminist Ethics and Hegemonic Global Politics," *Alternatives* 29 (2004): 275.

29. See Gayatri Chakravorty Spivak, "Can the Subaltern Speak?," in *Marxism and the Interpretation of Culture*, eds. Gary Nelson and Lawrence Grossberg (London: Macmillan, 1988), 280–287.

30. Robin Morgan, *Sisterhood Is Global* (Garden City, NY: Crossing Press, 1984), 5.

31. Ibid., 765.

32. Arlie Russell Hochschild, "Love and Gold," in *Global Economy*, ed. Arlie Russell Hochschild (New York: Henry Holt and Company, 2002).

33. Rosemary Radford Ruether, *Integrating Ecofeminism, Globalization, and World Religions* (Lanham, MD: Rowman & Littlefield, 2005), 146.

34. See Burn, *Women Across Cultures*; Joann Lim, "Sweatshops Are Us," in *Rethinking Globalization: Teaching for Justice in an Unjust World*, eds. Bill Bigelow and Bob Peterson (Milwaukee: Rethinking Schools Press, 2002), 158–159.

35. See Burn, *Women Across Cultures*; Aurelie Charles, "Fairness and Wages in Mexico's Maquiladora Industry: An Empirical Analysis of Labor Demand and the Gender Wage Gap," *Review of Social Economy* 69, no. 1 (March 2011): 1–28.

36. See Burn, *Women Across Cultures*; Fauzia Erfan Ahmed, "The Rise of the Bangladesh Garment Industry: Globalization, Women Workers, and Voice," *NWSA Journal* 16, no. 2 (summer 2002): 34–45.

37. Ruether, *Integrating Ecofeminism, Globalization, and World Religions*, 146.

38. Morgan, *Sisterhood Is Global*, 16.

39. Ibid.

40. Alison Jaggar, "Globalizing Feminist Ethics," *Hypatia* 13 (1998): 7–31.

41. Ruether, *Integrating Ecofeminism, Globalization, and World Religions*, 4.

42. See George Ritzer, *The McDonaldization of Society* (Thousand Oaks, CA: Pine Forge Press, 2004).

43. Jaggar, "Globalizing Feminist Ethics."

44. Maria Mies, "The Myths of Catching-Up Development," in Mies and Shiva, *Ecofeminism*, 58.

45. Ibid., 60.

46. Ibid., 59.

47. Ibid., 66.

48. Ibid., 67.

49. Sally J. Scholtz, *Feminism: A Beginner's Guide* (Oxford, UK: Oneworld Publications, 2010), 147.

50. Ibid.

51. Burn, *Women Across Cultures*, 23.

52. Ibid., 20.

53. Ibid., 23.

54. Ibid.

55. Parekh and Wilcox, "Feminist Perspectives on Globalization," 5.

56. Ibid.

57. Chandra Talpade Mohanty, "Under Western Eyes," in *Colonial Discourse and Postcolonial Theory*, eds. Patrick Williams and Laura Chrisman (New York: Columbia University Press, 1994), 334–335.

58. Ibid., 335.

59. Scholtz, *Feminism*, 136.

60. For the first two documents, see Susan Moller Okin, "Recognizing Women's Rights as Human Rights," *APA Newsletters* 97, no. 2 (spring 1998). For the last document, see "Declaration on the Elimination of Violence Against Women," United Nations General Assembly, 85th Plenary Meeting, December 20, 1993, A/RES/48/104, http://www.un.org/documents/ga/res/48/a48r104.htm.

61. Anne Phillips, "Multiculturalism, Universalism, and the Claims of Democracy," in Molyneux and Razavi, *Gender Justice, Development, and Rights*, 125.

62. Chilla Bulbeck, *Re-Orienting Western Feminisms: Women's Diversity in a Postcolonial World* (Cambridge: Cambridge University Press, 1998), 5.

63. Quoted in the introduction to Maxine Molyneux and Shahra Razavi, eds., *Gender Justice, Development, and Rights* (Oxford: Oxford University Press, 2002), 13.

64. Sara Salem, "Decolonial Intersectionality and a Transnational Feminist Movement," *Feminist Wire*, April 17, 2014, http://www.thefeministwire.com/2014/04/decolonial-intersectionality.

65. Ibid.

66. Ibid.

67. Ibid.

68. Ibid.

69. Ibid.

70. Morgan, *Sisterhood Is Global*, 5 (Morgan's emphasis).

71. Elizabeth V. Spelman, *Inessential Woman: Problems of Exclusion in Feminist Thought* (Boston: Beacon Press, 1998), 178.

72. Ibid., 178–179.

73. Ibid., 181.

74. Maria Lugones and Elizabeth Spelman, "Have We Got a Theory for You! Feminist Theory, Cultural Imperialism, and the Demand for the Woman's Voice,"

in *Feminist Philosophies*, eds. Janet A. Kourany, James Sterba, and Rosemarie Tong (Englewood Cliffs, NJ: Prentice Hall, 1992), 333–389.

75. bell hooks, *Feminist Theory: From Margin to Center* (Boston: South End Press, 1984), 404.

76. Ibid.

77. Audre Lorde, *Sister Outsider: Essays and Speeches* (Freedom, CA: Crossing Press 1984), 11.

78. Iris Marion Young, "The Ideal of Community and the Politics of Difference," in *Feminism/Postmodernism*, ed. Linda J. Nicholson (New York: Routledge, 1990), 308.

79. Nancie Caraway, *Segregated Sisterhood: Racism and the Politics of American Feminism* (Knoxville: University of Tennessee Press, 1991).

80. Young, "The Ideal of Community and the Politics of Difference," 311.

81. Caraway, *Segregated Sisterhood*, 206.

82. W. D. Ross, *Nichomechean Ethics*, revised by J. D. Urmson, in *The Complete Works of Aristotle: The Revised Oxford Translation*, ed. Jonathan Barnes (Princeton, NJ: Princeton University Press, 1984), Vol. 2, Books 8 and 9.

Chapter 6: Psychoanalytic Feminism

1. Sigmund Freud, *Sexuality and the Psychology of Love* (New York: Collier Books, 1968).

2. Sigmund Freud, *Three Contributions to the Sexual Theory*, trans. A. A. Brill (New York: The Journal of Nervous and Mental Disease Publishing Company, 1910; New York, Bartleby.com. 2010), http://www.bartleby.com/278.

3. Ibid., 192.

4. Ibid., 187–188.

5. Sigmund Freud, "Femininity," in *The Complete Introductory Lectures on Psychoanalysis*, ed. and trans. James Strachey (New York: W. W. Norton, 1966), 542.

6. Ibid., 593–596.

7. Ibid., 580.

8. Ibid., 596.

9. Freud, *Sexuality and the Psychology of Love*, 191.

10. Betty Friedan, *The Feminine Mystique* (New York: Dell, 1974).

11. Shulamith Firestone, *The Dialectic of Sex* (New York: Bantam Books, 1970).

12. Kate Millett, *Sexual Politics* (Garden City, NY: Doubleday, 1970).

13. Dorothy Dinnerstein, *The Mermaid and the Minotaur: Sexual Arrangements and Human Malaise* (New York: Harper Colophon Books, 1977), 5.

14. Ibid., 40–54.

15. Ibid., 59–66.

16. Ibid., 66.

17. Given that a man cannot enter a symbiotic relationship with a woman without reinvoking painful memories of his total helplessness before the infinite power

of the mother, he will use his power, Dinnerstein theorized, to fulfill his basic needs for security, love, and self-esteem. This bid for omnipotence extends to an attempt to control both nature and women, two forces that must be kept in check lest their own considerable powers be unleashed. In contrast to a man, a woman can safely seek symbiosis with a man as a means to attain the ends of security, love, and self-esteem. She can do this because, for her, symbiosis with a man does not conjure up the specter of the omnipotent mother. However, the idea of being or becoming an omnipotent mother does terrify her, and this specter explains some women's discomfort with female power (Ibid., 61).

18. Ibid., 124–134.

19. Ibid.

20. Nancy Chodorow, *The Reproduction of Mothering: Psychoanalysis and the Sociology of Gender* (Berkeley: University of California Press, 1978), 32.

21. Ibid., 107.

22. Ibid., 126.

23. Ibid., 200.

24. Ibid., 135, 187.

25. Ibid., 218.

26. Judith Lorber, "On *The Reproduction of Mothering*: A Methodological Debate," *Signs: Journal of Women in Culture and Society* 6, no. 3 (spring 1981): 482–486.

27. Jean Bethke Elshtain, *Public Man, Private Woman: Women in Social and Political Thought* (Princeton, NJ: Princeton University Press, 1981), 288.

28. Ibid., 290.

29. Janice Raymond, "Female Friendship: Contra Chodorow and Dinnerstein," *Hypatia* 1, no. 2 (fall 1986): 44–45.

30. Ibid., 37.

31. Adrienne Rich, "Compulsory Heterosexuality and Lesbian Existence," in *The Signs Reader: Women, Gender, and Scholarship*, eds. E. Abel and E. K. Abel (Chicago: University of Chicago Press, 1983), 182.

32. Juliet Mitchell, *Woman's Estate* (New York: Pantheon Books, 1971), 164–165.

33. Ibid.

34. Ibid., 170.

35. Juliet Mitchell, *Psychoanalysis and Feminism* (New York: Vintage Books, 1974), 370.

36. Ibid., 373.

37. Ibid., 375.

38. Sigmund Freud, "Totem and Taboo," in *The Standard Edition of the Complete Psychological Works of Sigmund Freud*, ed. and trans. James Strachey (New York: W. W. Norton, 1966), 144.

39. Ibid., 144.

40. Jacques Lacan, *The Language of the Self* (Baltimore: Johns Hopkins University Press, 1968), 271.

41. Mitchell, *Psychoanalysis and Feminism*, 415.

42. Sherry B. Ortner, "Oedipal Father, Mother's Brother, and the Penis: A Review of Juliet Mitchell's *Psychoanalysis and Feminism*," *Feminist Studies* 2, nos. 2–3 (1975): 179.

43. Ibid.

44. Marge Piercy, *Woman on the Edge of Time* (New York: Fawcett Crest Books, 1976).

45. Chris Weedon, *Feminist Practice and Poststructuralist Theory* (New York: Basil Blackwell, 1987), 50.

46. Ibid., 51.

47. Jacques Lacan, *Écrits: A Selection*, trans. Alan Sheridan (New York: W. W. Norton, 1977), 64–66.

48. Claire Duchen, *Feminism in France: From May '68 to Mitterrand* (London: Routledge & Kegan Paul, 1986), 78.

49. Lacan, *Écrits*, 2.

50. According to Lacan, the original mother-child unity is in some way a metaphor for truth—for an isomorphic relationship between word and object. Ideally, both mother and child and word and object would remain united, but society will not stand for such unity. As a result of the castration complex brought on by the arrival of the father, who represents social power symbolized by the phallus, not only mother and child but also word and object must be split.

51. Lacan, *Écrits*, 1–7.

52. Luce Irigaray, *This Sex Which Is Not One*, trans. Catherine Porter (Ithaca, NY: Cornell University Press, 1985), 28.

53. According to Claire Duchen, Irigaray believed that "before a 'feminine feminine,' a non-phallic feminine, can even be *thought,* women need to examine the male philosophical and psychoanalytical texts which have contributed to the construction of the 'masculine feminine,' the phallic feminine, in order to locate and identify it" (Duchen, *Feminism in France*, 87–88) (Irigaray's emphasis).

54. Irigaray, *This Sex Which Is Not One*, 32.

55. Toril Moi, *Sexual/Textual Politics: Feminist Literary Theory* (New York: Methuen, 1985), 132.

56. Irigaray, *This Sex Which Is Not One*, 74.

57. Ibid.

58. Luce Irigaray, "Is the Subject of Science Sexed?," trans. Carol Mastrangelo Bové, *Hypatia* 2, no. 3 (fall 1987): 66.

59. Irigaray, *This Sex Which Is Not One*, 32.

60. Ibid.

61. Moi, *Sexual/Textual Politics*, 140 (Irigaray's emphasis).

62. In an interview, Irigaray stated that there is nothing other than masculine discourse. When the interviewer said, "I don't understand what 'masculine discourse' means," Irigaray retorted, "Of course not, since there is no other" (Irigaray, *This Sex Which Is Not One*, 140).

63. Ibid., 29.

64. Dorothy Leland, "Lacanian Psychoanalysis and French Feminism: Toward an Adequate Political Psychology," *Hypatia* 3, no. 3 (winter 1989): 90–99.

65. Kelly Oliver, "Julia Kristeva's Feminist Revolutions," *Hypatia* 8, no. 3 (summer 1993): 101.

66. Julia Kristeva, "The Novel as Polylogue," in *Desire in Language,* eds. Thomas Gora, Alice Jardine, and Leon S. Roudiez, trans. Leon S. Roudiez (New York: Columbia University Press, 1990), 159–209.

67. Oliver, "Julia Kristeva's Feminist Revolutions," 98.

68. Julia Kristeva, *Powers of Horror*, trans. Leon Roudiez (New York: Columbia University Press, 1982), 205–206.

69. Leland, "Lacanian Psychoanalysis and French Feminism," 93.

70. Ibid., 94.

71. Ibid.

72. Cited in ibid., 95.

73. Ibid.

74. Ibid.

75. Ibid.

76. Emily Zakin, "Psychoanalytic Feminism," in *Stanford Encyclopedia of Philosophy* (Stanford, CA: University of Stanford Press, 2011), 12–18, http://plato.stanford.edu/entries/feminism-psychoanalysis.

77. Ibid., 23–25.

78. Judith Butler, *Gender Trouble: Feminism and the Subversion of Identity* (New York: Routledge, 1990).

79. Zakin, "Psychoanalytic Feminism," 12–18.

80. Ibid.

81. Ibid.

82. Ibid.

Chapter 7: Care-Focused Feminism

1. Carol Gilligan, *In a Different Voice* (Cambridge, MA: Harvard University Press, 1982).

2. Gilligan, *In a Different Voice*, 22–23.

3. Lawrence Kohlberg, "From Is to Ought: How to Commit the Naturalistic Fallacy and Get Away with It in the Study of Moral Development," in *Cognitive Development and Epistemology*, ed. Theodore Mischel (New York: Academic Press, 1971), 164–165.

4. Gilligan, *In a Different Voice*, 151–174.

5. Carol Gilligan, "Adolescent Development Reconsidered," in *Mapping the Moral Domain*, eds. Carol Gilligan, Janie Victoria Ward, and Jill McLean Taylor, with Betty Bardige (Cambridge, MA: Harvard University Press, 1988), xxii.

6. Nel Noddings, *Caring: A Feminine Approach to Ethics and Moral Education* (Berkeley: University of California Press, 1984), 1.

7. Susan Sherwin made a similar point in "A Feminist Approach to Ethics," *Dalhousie Review* 64, no. 4 (winter 1984–1985).

8. Noddings, *Caring*, 1.

9. Ibid., 2.

10. Ibid., 3.

11. Ibid., 9.

12. Ibid., 47.

13. Ibid.

14. Ibid., 83.

15. Ibid., 5.

16. Immanuel Kant, *Groundwork of the Metaphysics of Morals*, trans. H. J. Paton (New York: Harper Torchbooks, 1958).

17. Noddings, *Caring*, 83.

18. Ibid.

19. Fiona Robinson, *Globalizing Care: Ethics, Feminist Theory, and International Relations* (Boulder, CO: Westview Press, 1999), 15–20.

20. Susan J. Hekman, *Moral Voices, Moral Selves: Carol Gilligan and Feminist Moral Theory* (Cambridge, UK: Polity Press, 1995), 1.

21. Sandra L. Bartky, *Femininity and Domination* (New York: Routledge, 1990), 105.

22. Ibid., 104.

23. Ibid., 109.

24. Ibid.

25. Quoted in Robinson, *Globalizing Care*, 19.

26. Brian Barry, *Justice as Impartiality* (Oxford: Oxford University Press, 1995), 252–256.

27. Marilyn Friedman, "Beyond Caring: The De-moralization of Gender," in *Science, Morality, and Feminist Theory*, eds. Marsha Hanen and Kai Nielsen (Calgary: University of Calgary Press, 1987), 100.

28. Friedman, "Beyond Caring," 101–102.

29. Gilligan, *In a Different Voice*, 174.

30. Carol Gilligan, "Moral Orientation and Moral Development," in *Women and Moral Theory*, eds. Eva Feder Kittay and Diana T. Meyers (Totowa, NJ: Rowman & Littlefield, 1987), 25–26.

31. Claudia Card, "Caring and Evil," *Hypatia* 5, no. 1 (spring 1990): 122.

32. Ibid., 105.

33. Ibid. (our emphasis).

34. Ibid.

35. Ibid.

36. Sarah Lucia Hoagland, "Some Thoughts About *Caring*," in *Feminist Ethics*, ed. Claudia Card (Lawrence: University Press of Kansas, 1991), 73.

37. Sara Ruddick, "Maternal Thinking," in *Mothering: Essays in Feminist Theory*, ed. Joyce Trebilcot (Totowa, NJ: Rowman & Allanheld, 1984), 214.

38. Ibid.

39. Ibid., 215.

40. Ibid., 19.

41. Ibid., 67.

42. Ibid., 71, 73, 74.

43. Ibid., 98.

44. Ibid., 118.

45. Ibid., 123.

46. Virginia Held, *The Ethics of Care: Personal, Political, and Global* (New York: Oxford University Press, 2006), 64.

47. Held, "Feminism and Moral Theory," in Kittay and Meyers, *Women and Moral Theory*, 112–113.

48. Held, *The Ethics of Care*, 113.

49. Held, "Feminism and Moral Theory," 116–117.

50. Held, *The Ethics of Care*, 134–135.

51. Virginia Held, "The Obligation of Mothers and Fathers," in Trebilcot, *Mothering*, 53–54.

52. Ibid.

53. Eva Feder Kittay, *Love's Labor: Essays on Women, Equality, and Dependency* (New York: Routledge, 1999), 19.

54. Ibid., 158.

55. Ibid., 51.

56. Quoted in Kittay, *Love's Labor*, 59. For more, see Robert Goodin, *Protecting the Vulnerable* (Chicago: University of Chicago Press, 1985).

57. Quoted in Kittay, *Love's Labor*, 59. For more, see Goodin, *Protecting the Vulnerable* (Goodin's emphasis).

58. Kittay, *Love's Labor*, 55.

59. Ibid.

60. Ibid., 59.

61. Sarah Lucia Hoagland, "Some Concerns About Nel Noddings' *Caring*," *Hypatia* 5, no. 1 (spring 1990), 110.

62. Ibid., 251.

63. Ibid.

64. Ibid., 252.

65. Ibid., 253.

66. Jean Grimshaw, *Philosophy and Feminist Thinking* (Minneapolis: University of Minnesota Press, 1986), 251.

67. Ibid.

68. Patricia Hill Collins, *Black Feminist Thought: Knowledge, Consciousness, and the Politics of Empowerment* (Boston: Unwin Hyman, 1990), 215.

69. Quoted in ibid.

70. Quoted in ibid.

71. Ibid., 216.

72. Quoted in ibid., 217.

73. Ibid., 217.

74. Quoted in ibid.

75. Elizabeth Cady Stanton, *The Woman's Bible*, 2 vols. (New York: Arno, 1972; originally published 1895 and 1899).

76. Barbara Houston, "Rescuing Womanly Virtues," in Hanen and Nielsen, *Science, Morality, and Feminist Theory*, 131.

77. Sheila Mullett, "Shifting Perspectives: A New Approach to Ethics," in *Feminist Perspectives*, eds. Lorraine Code, Sheila Mullett, and Christine Overall (Toronto: University of Toronto Press, 1989), 119.

78. Ibid.

79. Ibid.

Chapter 8: Ecofeminism

1. Karen J. Warren, "The Power and the Promise of Ecological Feminism," in *Ecological Feminist Philosophies*, ed. Karen J. Warren (Bloomington: Indiana University Press, 1996), 20 (Warren's emphasis).

2. Karen J. Warren, "Feminism and the Environment: An Overview of the Issues," *APA Newsletter on Feminism and Philosophy* 90, no. 3 (fall 1991): 110–111.

3. The terms "cultural ecofeminist" and "nature ecofeminist" are from Karen J. Warren, "Feminism and Ecology: Making Connections," in *Readings in Ecology and Feminist Theology*, eds. Mary Heather MacKinnon and Marie McIntyre (Kansas City, KS: Sheed and Ward, 1995), 114. The terms "psychobiologistic ecofeminist" and "social-constructionist ecofeminist" are from Janet Biehl, *Rethinking Ecofeminist Politics* (Boston: South End Press, 1991), 11, 17.

4. Rosemary Radford Ruether, *New Woman/New Earth: Sexist Ideologies and Human Liberation* (New York: Seabury Press, 1975), 204.

5. Rachel Carson, *Silent Spring* (Boston: Houghton Mifflin, 1962), 16–23.

6. Robert Alter, trans. and comm., *Genesis* (New York: W. W. Norton, 1996).

7. Aldo Leopold, "The Land Ethic," in *A Sand County Almanac: With Other Essays on Conservation from Round River* (New York: Oxford University Press, 1987).

8. See John Hospers, *Understanding the Arts* (Englewood Cliffs, NJ: Prentice Hall, 1982).

9. Arne Naess, "The Deep Ecological Movement: Some Philosophical Aspects," *Philosophical Inquiry* 8 (1986): 10–13.

10. Quoted in George Sessions, "The Deep Ecology Movement: A Review," *Environmental Review* 9 (1987): 115.

11. Karen J. Warren, "Feminism and Ecology," *Environmental Review* 9, no. 1 (spring 1987): 3–20.

12. Ibid.

13. Ariel Kay Salleh, "Deeper Than Deep Ecology: The Ecofeminist Connection," *Environmental Ethics* 6, no. 1 (1984): 339.

14. Ibid.

15. Luc Ferry, *The New Ecological Order*, trans. Carol Volk (Chicago: University of Chicago Press, 1992), 118.

16. Carol J. Adams, *The Sexual Politics of Meat: A Feminist-Vegetarian Critical Theory*, 3rd ed. (New York: Continuum International Publishing Group, 2010), 27.

17. Ibid., 27.

18. Ibid., 75.

19. Ibid.

20. Ynestra King, "The Ecology of Feminism and the Feminism of Ecology," in *Healing the Wounds: The Promise of Ecofeminism*, ed. Judith Plant (Philadelphia: New Society Publishers, 1989), 22–23.

21. Sherry B. Ortner, "Is Female to Male as Nature Is to Culture?," in MacKinnon and McIntyre, *Readings in Ecology and Feminist Theology*, 40–41, 51.

22. Ibid., 52–53.

23. Ibid., 54.

24. Ibid., 54–55.

25. Mary Daly, *Pure Lust: Elemental Feminist Philosophy* (Boston: Beacon Press, 1984), 25.

26. Mary Daly, *Gyn/Ecology: The Metaethics of Radical Feminism* (Boston: Beacon Press, 1978), 63–64.

27. Ibid., 10–11 (our emphasis).

28. Ibid.

29. Ibid., 12–13.

30. Ibid., 21.

31. See David Macauley, "On Women, Animals and Nature: An Interview with Eco-feminist Susan Griffin," *APA Newsletter on Feminism* 90, no. 3 (fall 1991): 118.

32. Susan Griffin, *Woman and Nature: The Roaring Inside Her* (New York: Harper & Row, 1978), 226.

33. Ibid., 83–90.

34. Ibid., 67.

35. Ibid.

36. Macauley, "On Women, Animals and Nature," 117.

37. Griffin, *Woman and Nature*, 228.

38. Susan Griffin, *Pornography and Silence: Culture's Revenge Against Nature* (New York: Harper & Row, 1981), 2.

39. Macauley, "On Women, Animals and Nature," 117.

40. Deena Metzger, Gloria Orenstein, Dale Colleen Hamilton, Paula Gunn Allen, Margot Adler, Dolores LaChapelle, A. K. Salleh, and Radha Bratt are also considered spiritual ecofeminists.

41. Riane Eisler, "The Gaia Tradition and the Partnership Future: An Ecofeminist Manifesto," in *Reweaving the World: The Emergence of Ecofeminism*, eds. Irene Diamond and Gloria Feman Orenstein (San Francisco: Sierra Club Books, 1990), 23.

42. Starhawk, "Power, Authority, and Mystery: Ecofeminism and Earth-Based Spirituality," in Eisler, *Reweaving the World*, 86.

43. Starhawk, "Feminist, Earth-Based Spirituality and Ecofeminism," in Plant, *Healing the Wounds*, 176.

44. Ibid., 177.

45. Ibid., 178.

46. Ibid.

47. Ibid.

48. Ibid., 179.

49. Ibid., 180.

50. Rosemary Radford Ruether, *Integrating Ecofeminism, Globalization, and World Religions* (Lanham, MD: Rowman & Littlefield, 2005), 8.

51. Starhawk, "A Story of Beginnings," in Plant, *Healing the Wounds*, 115.

52. Carol Christ, *She Who Changes: Re-imagining the Divine in the World* (New York: Palgrave Macmillan, 2003), 240.

53. Dorothy Dinnerstein, "Survival on Earth: The Meaning of Feminism," in Plant, *Healing the Wounds*, 193.

54. Ibid. (Dinnerstein's emphasis).

55. Ibid., 174.

56. Marge Piercy, *Woman on the Edge of Time* (New York: Fawcett Crest Books, 1976).

57. Ibid., 105.

58. Warren, "The Power and the Promise of Ecological Feminism," 178.

59. Karen J. Warren, *Ecofeminist Philosophy: A Western Perspective on What It Is and Why It Matters* (Lanham, MD: Rowman & Littlefield, 2000), 97.

60. Ibid., 99.

61. Ibid., 100.

62. Ibid.

63. Ibid., 101.

64. Ibid.

65. Maria Mies, "The Need for a New Vision: The Subsistence Perspective," in *Ecofeminism*, eds. Maria Mies and Vandana Shiva (London: Zed, 1993), 247.

66. Ibid.

67. Ibid.

68. Ibid.

69. Adams, *The Sexual Politics of Meat*, 94.

70. Peter Singer, *Animal Liberation*, 4th ed. (New York: HarperCollins Publishers, 2009).

71. Tom Regan, *The Case for Animal Rights* (Berkeley: University of California Press, 1983).

72. Greta Gaard, "Vegetarian Ecofeminism: A Review Essay," *Frontiers: A Journal of Women Studies* 23, no. 3 (2002): 122.

73. Ibid., 123.

74. Grace Kao, "Consistency in Ecofeminist Ethics," *International Journal of the Humanities* 3 (2005/2006): 15.

75. Adams, *The Sexual Politics of Meat*, 94.

76. Anne Primavesi, *Sacred Gaia: Holistic Theology and Earth System Science* (London: Taylor & Francis, 2000).

77. Ibid., 94.

78. Ibid., 86.

79. Ibid., 87.

80. Ibid.

81. Ibid.

82. Ibid.

83. Ibid.

84. Biehl, *Rethinking Ecofeminist Politics*, 14.

85. Ibid., 16 (quoting Simone de Beauvoir).

86. Ibid.

87. Mies and Shiva, *Ecofeminism*, 19.

88. Ynestra King, "Engendering a Peaceful Planet: Ecology, Economy, and Ecofeminism in Contemporary Context," *Women Studies Quarterly* 23 (fall/winter 1995): 19.

89. Biehl, *Rethinking Ecofeminist Politics*, 1–27.

90. Ibid.

91. Ibid.

92. Warren, *Ecofeminist Philosophy*, 127.

93. Ibid.

94. Ibid.

95. Ibid., 130.

96. Editors of the International Forum on Globalization, "From Bretton Woods to Alternatives," in *Alternatives to Economic Globalization*, ed. International Forum on Globalization (San Francisco: Berrett-Koehler, 2002), 228–238.

Chapter 9: Existentialist, Poststructural, and Postmodern Feminisms

1. Margaret A. Simons and Jessica Benjamin, "Simone de Beauvoir: An Interview," *Feminist Studies* 5, no. 2 (summer 1979): 336.

2. Terry Keefe, *Simone de Beauvoir* (Totowa, NJ: Barnes & Noble, 1983).

3. Jean-Paul Sartre, *Being and Nothingness*, trans. Hazel E. Barnes (New York: Philosophical Library, 1956).

4. Jean-Paul Sartre, *Existentialism*, trans. Bernard Frechtman (New York: Philosophical Library, 1947), 115.

5. Sartre, *Being and Nothingness*, 364.

6. Ibid.

7. Ibid., 378–379.

8. Ibid., 380.

9. Ibid., 381.

10. Ibid., 393.

11. Ibid., 412.

12. Dorothy Kaufmann McCall, "Simone de Beauvoir, *The Second Sex*, and Jean-Paul Sartre," *Signs: Journal of Women in Culture and Society* 5, no. 2 (1980): 210.

13. Simone de Beauvoir, *The Second Sex*, ed. and trans. H. M. Parshley (New York: Vintage Books, 1974), 24.

14. Ibid., 41.

15. Ibid., 55.

16. Ibid., 64.

17. Ibid., 72.

18. Ibid., 89–90.

19. Ibid., 500.

20. Ibid., 502–503.

21. It is no secret that de Beauvoir was not enamored of motherhood as we know it. The following quotation is representative of her view: "As motherhood is today, maternity-slavery, as some feminists call it, does indeed want to be free and independent, for those who want to earn their living, for those who want to think for themselves, and for those who want to have a life of their own" (Simons and Benjamin, "Simone de Beauvoir," 241.

22. De Beauvoir, *The Second Sex*, 571 (de Beauvoir's emphasis).

23. Ibid., 761–763.

24. Ibid., 630.

25. De Beauvoir's view of the prostitute as an exceptional woman who dares to challenge the sexual mores of her society was rooted in several studies, especially those of ancient Greece describing the *hetaerae*. These studies described Athens as a center for prostitution, where the prostitutes were divided into at least three classes. Lowest on the status ladder were the *pornai*, who were checked over before their services were bought. Of slightly higher status were the *ayletrides*, or players, who entertained guests with their music as well as their bodies. Occupying the highest position were the *hetaerae*. In some ways these intellectually gifted and physically endowed women were more privileged than were respectable Athenian wives and mothers. They could amass great wealth and exert considerable power in the public domain through the men they entertained—this at a time when these men's wives and mothers were without economic and political power. See Will Durant, *The Life of Greece* (New York: Simon & Schuster, 1939).

26. De Beauvoir, *The Second Sex*, 700.

27. Ibid., 710–711.

28. Ibid., 748.

29. Simone de Beauvoir, *The Prime of Life*, trans. Peter Green (Harmondsworth, UK: Penguin Books, 1965), 291–292.

30. De Beauvoir, *The Second Sex*, 791.

31. Sartre, *Being and Nothingness*, 412.

32. Josephine Donovan, *Feminist Theory: The Intellectual Traditions of American Feminism* (New York: Frederick Ungar, 1985), 136.

33. Ibid., 137.

34. Meredith Tax, "Woman and Her Mind: The Story of an Everyday Life," in *Notes from the Second Year: Women's Liberation—Major Writings of the Radical Feminists* (April 1970), 12.

35. Sandra Bartky, "Narcissism, Femininity and Alienation," *Social Theory and Practice* 8, no. 2 (summer 1982): 137.

36. De Beauvoir, *The Second Sex*, 147.

37. Jean Bethke Elshtain, *Public Man, Private Woman: Women in Social and Political Thought* (Princeton, NJ: Princeton University Press, 1981), 306.

38. Simone de Beauvoir, *Memoirs of a Dutiful Daughter*, trans. James Kirkup (Harmondsworth, UK: Penguin Books, 1963), 131.

39. De Beauvoir, *The Second Sex*, 553.

40. For an interesting analysis of de Beauvoir's "linguistic ambivalence" about the terms "brotherhood" and "sisterhood," see Eléanor Kuykendall, "Linguistic Ambivalence in Simone de Beauvoir's Feminist Theory," in *The Thinking Muse*, eds. Iris Young and Jeffner Allen (Bloomington: Indiana University Press, 1989).

41. Jim Powell, *Postmodernism for Beginners* (Danbury, CT: For Beginners, LLC, 1998), 43.

42. Lydia Alix Fillingham, *Foucault for Beginners* (Danbury, CT: For Beginners, LLC, 1993).

43. Ibid.

44. Ibid., 80.

45. Madan Sarup, *Post-structuralism and Postmodernism*, 2nd ed. (Athens: University of Georgia Press, 1993), 74.

46. Michel Foucault, *The History of Sexuality*, vol. 1: *An Introduction*, trans. Robert Hurley (London: Allen Lane, 1979), 93.

47. Philip Barker, *Michel Foucault: An Introduction* (Edinburgh: Edinburgh University Press, 1998), 27.

48. Chris Weedon, *Feminist Practice and Poststructuralist Theory* (New York: Basil Blackwell, 1987), 119.

49. Foucault, *The History of Sexuality*, 25.

50. Sarup, *Post-structuralism and Postmodernism*, 74.

51. Barker, *Michel Foucault*, 32.

52. Michel Foucault, "The Discourse on Power," in *Remarks on Marx: Conversations with Duccio Trombardori*, trans. R. James Goldstein and James Cascaito (New York: Semiotext[e], Columbia University, 1991), 174.

53. Kathryn Pauly Morgan, "Women and the Knife: Cosmetic Surgery and the Colonization of Women's Bodies," *Hypatia* 6, no. 3 (fall 1991): 40.

54. Ibid.

55. Naomi Wolf, *The Beauty Myth: How Images of Beauty Are Used Against Women* (New York: William Morrow, 1991), 13, 14, 233.

56. Ibid., 233.

57. Debra L. Gimlin, "Cosmetic Surgery: Paying for Your Beauty," in *Body Work: Beauty and Self-Image in American Culture*, ed. Debra L. Gimlin (Berkeley: University of California Press, 2002), 95.

58. Sandra Lee Bartky, "Foucault, Femininity, and the Modernization of Patriarchal Power," in *Femininity and Domination: Studies in the Phenomenology of Oppression* (New York: Routledge, 1990), 81.

59. Judith Butler, *Gender Trouble: Feminism and the Subversion of Identity* (New York: Routledge, 1990), 8.

60. De Beauvoir, *The Second Sex*.

61. Judith Butler, "Variations on Sex and Gender: Beauvoir, Wittig and Foucault," in *Feminism as Critique: Essays on the Politics of Gender in Late-Capitalist Societies*, ed. Seyla Benhabib and Drucilla Cornell (Cambridge, UK: Polity Press, 1987), 131.

62. Sara Salem, *Judith Butler* (New York: Routledge, 2002), 50.

63. J. L. Austin, *How to Do Things with Words* (Cambridge, MA: Harvard University Press, 1962), 6.

64. Salem, *Judith Butler*, 89.

65. Ibid.

66. Martha C. Nussbaum, "The Professor of Parody: The Hip Defeatism of Judith Butler," *New Republic*, February 22, 1999, 41.

67. Ibid., 41.

68. Judith Butler, *The Psychic Life of Power: Theories in Subjection* (Stanford, CA: Stanford University Press, 1997).

69. Nussbaum, "The Professor of Parody," 43.

70. Ibid., 44.

71. Judith Butler, *Undoing Gender* (New York: Routledge, 2004), 204.

72. Ibid., 204–205.

73. Jacques Derrida, *Writing and Difference*, trans. Alan Bass (Chicago: University of Chicago Press, 1978).

74. Toril Moi, *Sexual/Textual Politics: Feminist Literary Theory* (New York: Methuen, 1985), 106.

75. Ibid.

76. Ibid.

77. Ann Rosalind Jones, "Writing the Body: Toward an Understanding of *l'Écriture Féminine*," *Feminist Studies* 7, no. 1 (summer 1981): 248.

78. Hélène Cixous and Catherine Clement, "Sorties," in *The Newly Born Woman*, trans. Betsy Wing (Minneapolis: University of Minnesota Press, 1986), 63, 65.

79. Ibid., 65.

80. Hélène Cixous, "The Laugh of the Medusa," in *New French Feminisms*, ed. Elaine Marks and Isabelle de Courtviron (New York: Schocken Books, 1981), 249.

81. Ibid., 245.

82. Ibid., 262.

83. Elaine Marks and Isabelle de Courtviron, "Introduction III," in *New French Feminisms*, ed. Elaine Marks and Isabelle de Courtviron (New York: Schocken Books, 1981), 36.

84. Cixous, "The Laugh of the Medusa," 256.

85. Ibid., 251, 259–260.

86. Ibid., 256.

87. Ibid., 259–260.

88. Elizabeth Grosz, "Sexual Difference and the Problem of Essentialism," in *The Essential Difference*, ed. Naomi Schor and Elizabeth Weed (Bloomington: Indiana University Press, 1994), 88.

89. Ibid., 89.

90. Ibid.

91. Ibid., 91.

92. Ibid., 91–92.

93. Ibid., 91.

94. Naomi Schor, introduction to Schor and Weed, *The Essential Difference*, vii.

95. Margaret Whitford, "Luce Irigaray and the Female Imaginary: Speaking as a Woman," *Radical Philosophy* 43 (summer 1986): 7.

96. Teresa de Lauretis, "The Essence of the Triangle or, Taking the Risks of Essentialism Seriously," in Schor and Weed, *The Essential Difference*, 3.

97. Ibid., 4.

98. Ibid.

99. Ibid., 10.

100. Teresa de Lauretis, *Technologies of Gender* (Bloomington: Indiana University Press, 1987), x.

101. Ibid., 48.

102. Genesis 2:19.

103. Lao-tzu, "The Tao-te-Ching," in *The Texts of Taoism*, ed. James Legge (New York: Dover, 1962).

104. Christine Di Stefano, "Dilemmas of Difference," in *Feminism/Postmodernism*, ed. Linda J. Nicholson (New York: Routledge, 1990), 75.

105. Ibid., 78 (our emphasis).

Chapter 10: Third-Wave and Queer Feminisms

1. Rebecca Walker, ed., *To Be Real: Telling the Truth and Changing the Face of Feminism*, ed. Rebecca Walker. New York: Anchor Books, 1995.

2. R. Claire Snyder, "What Is Third-Wave Feminism? A New Directions Essay," *Signs: Journal of Women in Culture and Society* 34, no. 1 (autumn 2008): 175.

3. Ibid., 176.

4. Ibid.

5. Ibid.

6. Leslie Heywood and Jennifer Drake, "Introduction," in *Third Wave Agenda: Being Feminist, Doing Feminism*, ed. Leslie Heywood and Jennifer Drake (Minnesota: University of Minnesota Press, 1997), 3

7. Kathryn T. Gines, "Race Women, Race Men and Early Expressions of Proto-intersectionality, 1830s–1930s," in *Why Race and Gender Still Matter*, ed. N. Goswami, M. O'Donovan, and I. Young (London: Pickering & Chatto, 2014), 13–25.

8. Tina Fernandes Botts, "The Concept of Intersectionality: Genealogy, Controversies and Viability," in *The Routledge Companion to Feminist Philosophy*, ed. Ann Garry, Serene J. Khader, and Alison Stone (New York: Routledge, forthcoming).

9. Leslie McCall, "The Complexity of Intersectionality," *Signs: Journal of Women in Culture and Society* 30, no. 3 (spring 2005): 1771–1800.

10. Laurie Shrage, ed., *You've Changed: Sex Reassignment and Personal Identity* (New York: Oxford University Press, 2009); Cynthia Levine-Rasky, *Whiteness Fractured* (Surrey, UK: Ashgate Publishing, 2013); Tina Fernandes Botts, *Philosophy and the Mixed Race Experience* (Lanham, MD: Lexington Books, 2016); Ann Garry, "Intersectionality, Metaphors, and the Multiplicity of Gender," *Hypatia* 26, no. 4 (2011): 826–850.

11. Sirma Bilge, "Intersectionality Undone: Saving Intersectionality from Feminist Intersectionality Studies," *Du Bois Review: Social Science Research on Race* 10, no. 2 (2013): 405–424.

12. Gines, "Race Women, Race Men and Early Expressions of Proto-intersectionality," 13–25; Kristin Waters, "Past as Prologue: Intersectional Analysis from the Nineteenth Century to the Twenty-First," in Goswami, O'Donovan, and Young, *Why Race and Gender Still Matter*, 27–41.

13. Sumi Cho, Kimberlé W. Crenshaw, and Leslie McCall, "Toward a Field of Intersectionality Studies: Theory, Applications, and Praxis," *Signs: Journal of Women in Culture and Society* 38, no. 4 (2013): 785–810.

14. Kimberlé Crenshaw, "Mapping the Margins: Intersectionality, Identity Politics, and Violence Against Women of Color," *Stanford Law Review* 43, no. 6 (July 1991): 1241–1299; Kimberlé Crenshaw, "Demarginalizing the Intersection of Race and Sex: A Black Feminist Critique of Antidiscrimination Doctrine, Feminist Theory, and Antiracist Politics," *University of Chicago Legal Forum* 140 (1998): 139–167.

15. Daisy Hernández and Bushra Rehman, eds., *Colonize This! Young Women of Color on Today's Feminism* (Berkeley, CA: Seal Press, 2002).

16. Ibid., xxvii.

17. Mireya Navarro, "Going Beyond Black and White, Hispanics in Census Pick 'Other,'" *New York Times*, November 9, 2003, A1, A21.

18. Chilla Bulbeck, *Re-orienting Western Feminisms: Women's Diversity in a Postcolonial World* (Cambridge: Cambridge University Press, 1997), 350.

19. Heywood and Drake, "Introduction," 8.

20. Ibid.

21. Rebecca Walker, ed., "Being Real: An Introduction," in *To Be Real: Telling the Truth and Changing the Face of Feminism* (New York: Anchor Books, 1995), xxxiii–xxxiv.

22. Ibid.

23. Quoted in Cathryn Bailey, "Unpacking the Mother/Daughter Baggage: Reassessing Second- and Third-Wave Tensions," *Women's Studies Quarterly* 3–4, no. 30 (fall 2002): 144.

24. Ann Braithwaite, "The Personal, the Political, Third-Wave and Postfeminisms," *Feminist Theory* 3, no. 3 (December 2002): 340.

25. Bailey, "Unpacking the Mother/Daughter Baggage," 145.

26. Donna Haraway, "A Cyborg Manifesto: Science, Technologies and Socialist Feminism in the Late Twentieth Century," in *Simians, Cyborgs, and Women: The Reinvention of Nature* (New York: Routledge, 1991).

27. Jim Powell, *Postmodernism for Beginners* (Danbury, CT: For Beginners, LLC, 1998), 29.

28. Ibid., 130.

29. Ibid.

30. Ibid.

31. Ibid., 134–135.

32. Ibid., 180.

33. Jennifer Baumgardner and Amy Richards, *Manifesta: Young Women, Feminism, and the Future* (New York: Farrar, Straus and Giroux, 2000).

34. Sally J. Scholtz, *Feminism: A Beginner's Guide* (Oxford, UK: Oneworld Publications, 2010), 130.

35. Ibid., 130–131.

36. Powell, *Postmodernism for Beginners*, 29.

37. Elizabeth Wurtzel, *Bitch: In Praise of Difficult Women* (New York: Doubleday, 1998).

38. Available at https://www.cbc.ca/news/canada/toronto/toronto-slut-walk-takes.

39. Tamara Strauss, "A Manifesto for Third-Wave Feminism," *AlterNet*, October 23, 2000, http://www.alternet.org/story/9986/a_manifesto_for_third_wave_feminism.

40. Baumgardner and Richards, *Manifesta*, 20.

41. Martha Rampton, "The Three Waves of Feminism," *Magazine of Pacific University* 41, no. 2 (fall 2008): 3.

42. Available at "Third Wave Foundation," International Human Rights Funders Organization, ihrfg.org/funder-directory/third-wave-foundation.

43. Kira Cochrane, ""The Fourth Wave of Feminism: Meet the Rebel Women," *Guardian*, December 10, 2013, https://www.theguardian.com/world/2013/dec/10/fourth-wave-feminism-rebel-women.

44. Alison L. Howry and Julie T. Wood, "Something Old, Something New, Something Borrowed: Themes in the Voices of a New Generation of Feminists," *Southern Communication Journal* 4, no. 66 (summer 2001): 324.

45. Ann Ferguson, "Sex and Work: Woman as a New Revolutionary Class," in *An Anthology of Western Marxism: From Lukacs and Gramsci to Socialist Feminists*, ed. Robert J. Gottlie (Oxford: Oxford University Press, 1989), 352.

46. Katie Roiphe, *The Morning After: Sex, Fear, and Feminism on Campus* (New York: Little & Brown, 1993); Camille Paglia, *Sex, Art, and American Culture: Essays* (New York: Random House, 1992); Rene Denfeld, *The New Victorians: A Young Woman's Challenge to the Old Feminist Order* (New York: Routledge, 1995).

47. Annamarie Jagose, "Queer Theory," Encyclopedia.com, 2005, http://www.encyclopedia.com/history/dictionaries-thesauruses-pictures-and-press-releases/queer-theory

48. Ibid.

49. Scholtz, *Feminism*, 121.

50. Ralph R. Smith, "Queer Theory, Gay Movements, and Political Communication," *Journal of Homosexuality* 44, nos. 2–4 (2003): 345–348 (Smith's emphasis).

51. J. Jack Halberstam, *Gaga Feminism: Sex, Gender, and the End of Normal* (Boston: Beacon Press, 2005).

52. "Queer Theory Timeline," shmoop, http://www.shmoop.com/queer-theory/timeline.html, 1.

53. Ibid., 1.

54. Ibid., 1–2.

55. Ibid., 2.

56. Ibid., 2–3.

57. Ibid., 3.

58. Ibid.

59. Ibid., 3–4.

60. "Eve Sedgwick Quotes," shmoop, http://www.shmoop.com/queer-theory/eve-sedgwick-quotes.html, 2.

61. David Gauntlet, *Media, Gender, and Identity: An Introduction* (London: Psychology Press, 2002).

62. Ibid.

63. Eve Kosofsky Sedgwick, *Epistemology of the Closet* (Berkeley: University of California Press, 1990).

64. "Queer Theory Introduction," shmoop, http://www.shmoop.com/queer-theory, 4.

65. Ibid.

66. Suzanna Danuta Walters, "From Here to Queer: Radical Feminism, Postmodernism, and the Lesbian Menace (or, Why Can't a Woman Be More like a Fag?")," *Signs: Journal of Women in Culture and Society* 21, no. 4 (summer 1996): 866.

67. Ibid., 865.

Conclusion

1. *United States v. Morrison*, 529 US 598, 31 (2000).

2. Christine Di Stefano, "Dilemmas of Difference," in *Feminism/Postmodernism*, ed. Linda J. Nicholson (New York: Routledge, 1990), 63–82.

Bibliography

Chapter 1: Liberal Feminism

Conceptual Roots

Abbey, Ruth. "Back Toward a Comprehensive Liberalism? Justice as Fairness, Gender, and Families." *Political Theory* 35 (2007): 5–28.

Baehr, Amy R. "Liberal Feminism." In *Stanford Encyclopedia of Philosophy*. Substantial rev. Stanford, CA: Stanford Center for the Study of Language and Information, 2013. Available at http://www.cal.stanford.edu/groups/stanford.

———, ed. *Varieties of Feminist Liberalism*. Lanham, MD: Rowman & Littlefield, 2004.

Berlin, Isaiah. *Two Concepts of Liberty*. Oxford, UK: Clarendon Press, 1961.

Brennan, Teresa, and Carole Pateman. "'Mere Auxiliaries to the Commonwealth': Women and the Origins of Liberalism." *Political Studies* 27, no. 2 (June 1979): 183–200.

Brockett, L. P. *Woman: Her Rights, Wrongs, Privileges, and Responsibilities*. 1869. Freeport, NY: Books for Libraries Press, 1970.

Dicker, Rory C. *A History of U.S. Feminisms*. Berkeley, CA: Seal Press, 2008.

Donovan, Josephine. *Feminist Theory*. 4th ed. London: Continuum, 2012.

Dworkin, Ronald. "Liberalism." In *Public and Private Morality*, edited by Stuart Hampshire, 113–134. Cambridge: Cambridge University Press, 1978.

Freedman, Estelle. *The Essential Feminist Reader*. New York: Modern Library, 2007.

Gutmann, Amy. *Liberal Equality*. New York: Cambridge University Press, 1980.

Jaggar, Alison M. *Feminist Politics and Human Nature*. Totowa, NJ: Rowman & Allanheld, 1983.

Kensinger, Loretta. "(In) Quest of Liberal Feminism." *Hypatia* 12 (1997): 178–197.

Nussbaum, Martha. *Sex and Social Justice.* New York: Oxford University Press, 2000.

Rawls, John. *A Theory of Justice.* Cambridge, MA: Harvard University Press, 1971.

Sabrosky, Judith A. *From Rationality to Liberation.* Westport, CT: Greenwood Press, 1979.

Scott, Joan W. "Feminism's History." *Journal of Women's History* 16, no. 2 (2004): 10–28.

Strauss, Leo. *Liberalism: Ancient and Modern.* New York: Basic Books, 1968.

Before the "First Wave": Equal Education

Botting, Eileen Hunt. *Family Feuds: Wollstonecraft, Burke, and Rousseau on the Transformation of the Family.* Albany: State University of New York Press, 2006.

Butler, Melissa A. "Early Liberal Roots of Feminism: John Locke and the Attack on Patriarchy." *American Political Science Review* 72, no. 1 (1978): 135–150.

Clark, Lorenne M. G. "Women and Locke: Who Owns the Apples in the Garden of Eden?." In *The Sexism of Social and Political Theory,* edited by Lorenne M. B. Clark and Lydia Lange. Toronto: University of Toronto Press, 1979.

Engster, Daniel. "Mary Wollstonecraft's Nurturing Liberalism: Between an Ethics of Justice and Care." *American Political Science Review* 95 (1995): 577–585.

Gerson, Gal. "Liberal Feminism: Individuality and Oppositions in Wollstonecraft and Mill." *Political Studies* 50 (2002): 794–810.

Kant, Immanuel. *Groundwork of the Metaphysics of Morals.* Translated by H. J. Paton. New York: Harper Torchbooks, 1958.

Martin, Jane Roland. *Reclaiming a Conversation: The Ideal of the Educated Woman.* New Haven, CT: Yale University Press, 1985.

Rousseau, Jean-Jacques. *Emile.* Translated by Allan Bloom. New York: Basic Books, 1979.

Wollstonecraft, Mary. *Memoirs of Mary Wollstonecraft.* Edited by W. Clark Durant. New York: Gordon Press, 1972.

———. *A Vindication of the Rights of Woman.* Edited by Carol H. Poston. New York: W. W. Norton, 1975.

"First-Wave" Liberal Feminism: Equal Liberty and the Suffrage

Adams, Katherine H., and Michael L. Keene. *Alice Paul and the American Suffrage Campaign.* Chicago: University of Illinois Press, 2008.

Baker, Jean H. *Sisters: The Lives of America's Suffragists.* New York: Hill and Wang, 2006.

Donner, Wendy. "John Stuart Mill's Liberal Feminism." *Philosophical Studies* 69 (1993): 155–166.

DuBois, Ellen Carol, ed. *Elizabeth Cady Stanton, Susan B. Anthony: Correspondence, Writings, Speeches.* New York: Schocken Books, 1981.

Evans, Sara M. *Born for Liberty: A History of Women.* New York: Free Press Paperbacks, 2005.

Flexner, Eleanor. *Century of Struggle: The Woman's Rights Movement in the United States.* Cambridge, MA: Belknap Press of Harvard University Press, 1975.

Fuller, Margaret. *Woman in the Nineteenth Century.* New York: W. W. Norton, 1971.

Gordon, Ann D., and Bettye Collier-Thomas, eds. *African American Women and the Vote, 1837–1965.* Amherst: University of Massachusetts Press, 1997.

———, eds. *The Selected Papers of Elizabeth Cady Stanton and Susan B. Anthony.* New Brunswick, NJ: Rutgers University Press, 1997.

Grimké, Sarah. *Letters on "The Equality of the Sexes" and "The Condition of Woman."* New York: Burt Franklin, 1970.

Gurko, Miriam. *The Ladies of Seneca Falls: The Birth of the Woman's Rights Movement.* New York: Schocken Books, 1976.

Hannam, June. *International Encyclopedia of Women's Suffrage.* Santa Barbara, CA: ABC-CLIO, 2000.

Harper, Ida Husted, ed. *History of Woman Suffrage.* Vol. 5. New York: National American Woman Suffrage Association, 1922.

Hole, Judith, and Ellen Levine, *Rebirth of Feminism.* New York: Quadrangle Books, 1971.

Jacobs, Jo Ellen, ed. *The Complete Works of Harriet Taylor Mill.* Bloomington: Indiana University Press, 1998.

———. *The Voice of Harriet Taylor Mill.* Bloomington: Indiana University Press, 2002.

Krouse, Richard. "Mill and Marx on Marriage, Divorce, and the Family." *Social Concept* 1, no. 2 (September 1983): 36–75.

Mill, John Stewart. "The Subjection of Women." In *Essays on Sex Equality*, by John Stuart Mill and Harriet Taylor Mill. Edited by Alice S. Rossi. Chicago: University of Chicago Press, 1970.

Rossi, Alice S. "Sentiment and Intellect: The Story of John Stuart Mill and Harriet Taylor Mill." In *Essays on Sex Equality*, by John Stuart Mill and Harriet Taylor Mill. Edited by Alice S. Rossi. Chicago: University of Chicago Press, 1970.

"Seneca Falls Declaration of Sentiments and Resolutions (1848)." In *Feminism: The Essential Historical Writings*, edited by Miriam Schneir. New York: Random House, 1972.

Smith, G. W. "J. S. Mill on What We Don't Know About Women." *Utilitas: A Journal of Utilitarian Studies* 12 (2002): 41–61.

Stanton, Elizabeth Cady. "Address to the New York State Legislature." In *Feminism: The Essential Historical Writings*, edited by Miriam Schneir. New York: Vintage Books, 1994.

Stanton, Elizabeth Cady, Susan B. Anthony, and Matilda Joslyn Gage, eds. *History of Woman Suffrage.* Vol. 1: *1848–1861.* New York: Fowler and Wells, 1881. Reprinted by New York: Arno Press, 1969.

Ten, C. L. "Reviewed Work: The Liberal Self: John Stuart Mill's Moral and Political Philosophy by Wendy Donner." *Canadian Journal of Philosophy* 24, no. 2 (June 1994): 327–335.

Walton, Mary. *A Woman's Crusade: Alice Paul and the Battle for the Ballot.* New York: Palgrave Macmillan, 2010.

"Second-Wave" Liberal Feminism: Equal Rights

Ackerman, Bruce. "Political Liberalisms." *Journal of Philosophy* 91, no. 7 (1994): 364–386.

Carden, Maren Lockwood. *The New Feminist Movement.* New York: Russell Sage Foundation, 1974.

Collins, Gail. *When Everything Changed: The Amazing Journey of American Women from 1960 to the Present.* New York: Little, Brown and Company, 2009.

Dworkin, Ronald. *Taking Rights Seriously.* Cambridge, MA: Harvard University Press, 1977.

Evans, Judith. *Feminist Theory Today: An Introduction to Second-Wave Feminism.* London: Sage, 1995.

Friedan, Betty. *The Feminine Mystique.* New York: Dell, 1974.

Gheaus, Anca. "Gender Justice." *Journal of Ethics and Social Philosophy* 6 (2012): 1–24.

Ireland, Patricia. "The State of NOW." *Ms.* (July/August 1992): 24–27.

Kanowitz, Leo. *Women and the Law: The Unfinished Revolution.* Albuquerque: University of New Mexico Press, 1969.

Kirp, David L., Mark Gayudoff, and Marleen Strong Franks. *Gender Justice.* Chicago: University of Chicago Press, 1986.

MacLean, Nancy. *The American Women's Movement, 1945–2000: A Brief History with Documents.* Boston: Bedford/St. Martin's, 2008.

Mayeri, Serena. *Reasoning from Race: Feminism, Law, and the Civil Rights Revolution.* Cambridge, MA: Harvard University Press, 2011.

Mendes, Kaitlynn. *Feminism in the News: Representations of the Women's Movement Since the 1960s.* New York: Palgrave Macmillan, 2011.

"NOW Bill of Rights." In *Sisterhood Is Powerful,* edited by Robin Morgan. New York: Random House, 1970.

Nussbaum, Martha. *Sex and Social Justice.* New York: Oxford University Press, 2000.

Reich, Robert, and Debra Satz, eds. *Toward a Humanist Justice: The Political Philosophy of Susan Moller Okin.* Oxford: Oxford University Press, 2009.

Rossi, Alice. "Equality Between the Sexes: An Immodest Proposal." *Daedalus* 93, no. 2 (1964): 607–652.

Sterba, James. "Feminism Has Not Discriminated Against Men." In *Does Feminism Discriminate Against Men? A Debate,* edited by Warren Farrell and James Sterba. New York: Oxford University Press, 2007.

Strossen, Nadine. "The American Civil Liberties Union and Women's Rights." *New York University Law Review* 66 (1961): 1940–1961.

Thomas, Tracy A., and Tracey Jean Boisseau, eds. *Feminist Legal History: Essays on Women and the Law.* New York: New York University Press, 2011.

Toward "Third-Wave" Liberal Feminism: Sameness Versus Difference, Egalitarianism, and Intersectionality

Andrews, Elizabeth S. "What Is the Point of Equality?." *Ethics* 109 (January 1999): 287–337.

———. *Women in the Front Line.* New York: Amnesty International Publications, 1991.

August, Louise. "It Isn't Over: The Continuing Under-Representation of Female Faculty." Paper presented at the Association for Institutional Research, Chicago, Illinois, May 2006.

Baehr, Amy R. "Toward a New Feminist Liberalism: Okin, Rawls, and Habermas." *Hypatia* 11, no. 1 (winter 1996): 49–66.

Benatar, David. "The Second Sexism." *Social Theory and Practice* 29 (2003): 177–210.

Bryson, Valerie. *Feminist Debates: Issues of Theory and Political Practice.* New York: New York University Press, 1999.

Card, Robert F. "Gender, Justice Within the Family, and the Commitments of Rawlsian Liberalism." *Public Affairs Quarterly* 15 (1999): 155–171.

———, ed. *On Feminist Ethics and Politics.* Lawrence: University Press of Kansas, 1999.

Cudd, Ann. "The Paradox of Liberal Feminism: Preference, Rationality, and Oppression." In *Varieties of Feminist Liberalism*, edited by Amy R. Baehr, 37–62. Lanham, MD: Rowman & Littlefield, 2004.

Eisenstein, Zillah R. *The Radical Future of Liberal Feminism.* Boston: Northeastern University Press, 1986.

Feldman, Gayle. "Women Are Different." *Self* (July 1997): 105–108, 154.

Ford, Lynne E. *Women and Politics: The Pursuit of Equality.* 3rd ed. Boston: Wadsworth, 2011.

Friedan, Betty. *The Fountain of Age.* New York: Simon & Schuster, 1993.

———. *The Second Stage.* New York: Summit Books, 1981.

Jensen, Pamela Grande, ed. *Finding a New Feminism: Rethinking the Woman Question for Liberal Democracy.* Lanham, MD: Rowman & Littlefield, 1996.

Kornblut, Anne E. *Notes from the Cracked Ceiling: Hillary Clinton, Sarah Palin, and What It Will Take for a Woman to Win.* New York: Crown Publishers, 2009.

Krook, Mona Lena, and Sarah Childs, eds. *Women, Gender, and Politics: A Reader.* New York: Oxford University Press, 2010.

Lawless, Jennifer L., and Richard L. Fox. *It Still Takes a Candidate: Why Women Don't Run for Office.* 2nd ed. New York: Cambridge University Press, 2010.

Lemon, J. "Political Theory and Social Criticism." *Politica* 20, no. 2 (2001): 111–118.

MacLean, Douglas, and Claudia Mills. *Liberalism Reconsidered.* Totowa, NJ: Rowman & Allanheld, 1983.

Morgan, Robin. "Light Bulbs, Radishes and the Politics of the 21st Century." In *Radically Speaking: Feminism Reclaimed*, edited by Diane Bell and Renate Klein. North Melbourne, Australia: Spinifex, 1996.

Nash, Kate. "Feminism and Contemporary Liberal Citizenship: The Undecidability of 'Women.'" *Citizenship Studies* 5, no. 3 (2001): 255–268.

Nussbaum, Martha C. "The Future of Feminist Liberalism." In *Varieties of Feminist Liberalism*, edited by Amy R. Baehr. Lanham, MD: Rowman & Littlefield, 2004.

Nye, Andrea. *Feminist Theory and the Philosophies of Man.* New York: Routledge, 1989.

Okin, Susan Moller. "'Forty Acres and a Mule' for Women: Rawlism and Feminism." *Politics, Philosophy and Economics* 4 (1998): 223–248.

———. *Justice, Gender, and the Family.* New York: Basic Books, 1989.

Pearsall, Marilyn, ed. *Women and Values: Readings in Recent Feminist Philosophy.* Belmont, CA: Wadsworth, 1986.

Reich, Robert, and Debra Satz, eds. *Toward a Humanist Justice: The Political Philosophy of Susan Moller Okin.* Oxford: Oxford University Press, 2009.

Richards, Janet Radcliffe. *The Skeptical Feminist.* London: Routledge & Kegan Paul, 1980.

Schneider, Elizabeth M., and Stephanie M. Wildman. *Women and the Law: Stories.* New York: Thomson Reuters/Foundation Press, 2011.

Smith, Andrew F. "Closer but Still No Cigar: On the Inadequacy of Rawls's Reply to Okin's 'Political Liberalism, Justice and Gender.'" *Social Theory and Practice* 30, no. 1 (2004): 59–71.

Sterba, James. "Feminism Has Not Discriminated Against Men." In *Does Feminism Discriminate Against Men? A Debate*, edited by Warren Farrell and James P. Sterba. Oxford: Oxford University Press, 2007.

Stopler, Gila. "Gender Construction and the Limits of Liberal Equality." *Texas Journal of Women and the Law* 15 (2005): 44–78.

Strossen, Nadine. "Fighting Big Sister for Liberty and Equality." *New York Law School Law Review* 30 (1993): 7–8.

Critiques of Liberal Feminism

Abbey, Ruth. *The Return of Feminist Liberalism.* Montreal: McGill-Queens University Press, 2011.

Amos, Valerie, and Pratibha Parmar. "Challenging Liberal Feminism." *Feminist Review* 17 (1984): 3–19.

Arneil, Barbara. *Politics and Feminism.* Oxford, UK: Blackwell Press, 1999.

Butler, Judith, and Joan W. Scott. *Feminists Theorize the Political.* New York: Routledge, 1992.

Card, Claudia. "The L Word and the F Word." *Hypatia* 21, no. 2 (2006): 223–229.

Elshtain, Jean Bethke. "Feminism, Family and Community." *Dissent* 29 (fall 1982): 442–459.

———. *Public Man, Private Woman: Women in Social and Political Thought.* Princeton, NJ: Princeton University Press.

Epstein, Barbara. *The Successes and Failures of Feminism.* Indianapolis: Indiana University Press, 2002.

Fox-Genovese, Elizabeth. *Feminism Without Illusions: A Critique of Individualism.* Chapel Hill: University of North Carolina Press, 1991.

Frazer, Elizabeth, and Nicola Lacey. *The Politics of Community: A Feminist Critique of the Liberal Communitarian Debate.* Toronto: University of Toronto Press, 1993.

Friedan, Betty. "Betty Friedan Critiques Feminism and Calls for New Directions." *New York Times Magazine,* July 5, 1981.

Groenhout, Ruth E. "Essentialist Challenges to Liberal Feminism." *Social Theory and Practice* 28, no. 1 (January 2002): 51–95.

Higgins, Tracy E. "Gender Why Feminists Can't (or Shouldn't) Be Liberals." *Fordham Law Review* 72 (2004): 1629.

Jaggar, Alison M. *Feminist Politics and Human Nature.* Totowa, NJ: Rowman & Allanheld, 1983.

Jensen, Pamela Grande, ed. *Finding a New Feminism: Rethinking the Woman Question for Liberal Democracy.* Lanham, MD: Rowman & Littlefield, 1996.

Johnson, Pauline. *Feminism as Radical Humanism.* Boulder: CO, Westview, 1994.

Klausen, Jytte, and Charles S. Maier, eds. *Has Liberalism Failed Women? Assuring Equal Representation in Europe and the United States.* New York: Palgrave, 2001.

Lay, Kathy, and James G. Dalsey. "A Critique of Feminist Theory." *Advances in Social Work* 8, no. 1 (2007): 49–61.

Pateman, Carole. *The Problem of Political Obligation: A Critique of Liberal Theory.* Berkeley: University of California Press, 1979.

Phillips, Anne. "Feminism and Liberalism Revisited: Has Martha Nussbaum Got It Right?." *Constellations* 8, no. 2 (2001): 250.

Sandel, Michael J., ed. *Liberalism and Its Critics.* New York: New York University Press, 1984.

Saul, Jennifer Mather. *Feminism: Issues and Arguments.* Oxford: Oxford University Press, 2003.

Schaeffer, Denise. "Feminism and Liberalism Reconsidered: The Case of Catharine MacKinnon." *American Political Science Review* 95, no. 3 (September 2001): 699–708.

Schwartzman, Lisa H. *Challenging Liberalism: Feminism as Political Critique.* University Park: Pennsylvania State University Press, 2010.

Stacey, Judith. "The New Conservative Feminism." *Feminist Studies* 9, no. 3 (fall 1983): 559–583.

Stafford, William. "Is Mill's 'Liberal' Feminism 'Masculinist'?." *Journal of Political Ideologies* 9, no. 2 (June 2004): 159–179.

Tomasi, John. "Can Feminism Be Liberated from Governmentalism?." In *Toward a Humanist Justice: The Political Philosophy of Susan Moller Okin*, edited by Robert Reich and Debra Satz. Oxford: Oxford University Press, 2009.

Venker, Suzanne, and Phyllis Schlafly. *The Flipside of Feminism: What Conservative Women Know—and Men Can't Say*. Washington, DC: WND Books, 2011.

Wendell, Susan. "A (Qualified) Defense of Liberal Feminism." *Hypatia* 2, no. 2 (summer 1987): 66.

Wolf, Christopher. *Liberalism at the Crossroad: An Introduction to Contemporary Political Theory and Its Critics*. 2nd ed. Lanham, MD: Rowman & Littlefield, 2004.

Chapter 2: Radical Feminism

Radical-Libertarian and Radical-Cultural Feminism in General

Alcoff, Linda. "Cultural Feminism Versus Poststructuralism: The Identity Crisis in Feminist Theory." *Signs: Journal of Women in Culture and Society* 13, no. 3 (spring 1988): 405–436.

Bell, Diane, and Renate Klein. *Radically Speaking: Feminism Reclaimed*. North Melbourne, Australia: Spinifex, 1996.

Card, Claudia. "Radicalesbianfeminist Theory." *Hypatia* 13, no. 1 (1998): 206–213.

Crow, Barbara A. *Radical Feminism: A Documentary Reader*. New York: New York University Press, 2000.

Daly, Mary. *Beyond God the Father: Toward a Philosophy of Women's Liberation*. Boston: Beacon Press, 1973.

———. *Gyn/Ecology: The Metaethics of Radical Feminism*. Boston: Beacon Press, 1978.

———. *Pure Lust: Elemental Feminist Philosophy*. London: Women's Press Ltd. 2001.

Dubriwny, Tasha N. "Consciousness-Raising as Collective Rhetoric: The Articulation of Experience in the Redstockings' Abortion Speak-Out of 1969." *Quarterly Journal of Speech* 91, no. 4 (November 2005): 395–422.

Echols, Alice. *Daring to Be Bad: Radical Feminism in America, 1967–1975*. Minneapolis: University of Minnesota Press, 1987.

———. "The New Feminism of Yin and Yang." In *Powers of Desire: The Politics of Sexuality*, edited by Ann Snitow, Christine Stansell, and Sharon Thompson. New York: Monthly Review Press, 1983.

Eisenstein, Hester. *Contemporary Feminist Thought*. Boston: G. K. Hall, 1983.

Eliot, Lise. *Pink Brain, Blue Brain: How Small Differences Grow into Troublesome Gaps—and What We Can Do About It*. New York: Houghton Mifflin Harcourt, 2009.

Firestone, Shulamith. *The Dialectic of Sex.* New York: Bantam Books, 1970.

French, Marilyn. *Beyond Power: On Women, Men, and Morals.* New York: Summit Books, 1985.

Goldberg, Michelle. "What Is a Woman? The Dispute Between Radical Feminism and Transgenderism." *New Yorker*, August 4, 2014, 1–13.

Hirsch, Marianne, and Evelyn Fox Keller. *Conflicts in Feminism.* New York: Routledge, 1990.

Hole, Judith, and Ellen Levine. *Rebirth of Feminism.* New York: Quadrangle Books, 1971.

Jaggar, Alison M., and Paula S. Rothenberg, eds. *Feminist Frameworks.* New York: McGraw-Hill, 1984.

Klein, Renate, and Deborah Lynn Steinberg. *Radical Voices: A Decade of Feminist Resistance from Women's Studies International Forum.* New York: Pergamon Press, 1989.

Koedt, Anne, Ellen Levine, and Anita Rapone, eds. *Radical Feminism.* New York: Quadrangle, 1973.

Lindsay, Robert. "Define Gender Feminism and Radical Feminism." *Beyond Highbrow*, July 12, 2012, https://robertlindsay.wordpress.com/2012/07/21/define-gender-feminism-and-radical-feminism.

Mandell, Nancy. *Feminist Issues: Race, Class, and Sexuality.* Scarborough, Ontario: Prentice Hall, 1995.

Morey-Gaines, Ann-Janine. "Metaphor and Radical Feminism: Some Cautionary Comments on Mary Daly's *Gyn/Ecology.*" *Soundings* 65, no. 3 (fall 1982): 347–348.

Napikoski, Linda. "New York Radical Women." Women's History, http://womenshistory.about.com/od/feminism/a/new_york_radical_women.htm.

Rhodes, Jacqueline. *Radical Feminism, Writing, and Critical Agency.* New York: State University of New York Press, 2005.

Rubin, Gayle. "The Traffic in Women." In *Toward an Anthropology of Women*, edited by Rayna R. Reiter. New York: Monthly Review Press, 1975.

Thompson, Denise. *Radical Feminism Today.* London: Sage Publishing, 2001.

Whittier, Nancy. *Feminist Generations: The Persistence of the Radical Feminist Movement.* Philadelphia: Temple University Press, 1995.

Controversies Between Radical-Libertarian and Radical-Cultural Feminists

SEXUALITY

Bushnell, Dana E., ed. *"Nagging" Questions: Feminist Ethics in Everyday Life.* Lanham, MD: Rowman & Littlefield, 1995.

Coward, Rosalind. *Patriarchal Precedents: Sexuality and Social Relations.* London: Routledge & Kegan Paul, 1983.

Dworkin, Andrea. *Letters from a War Zone*. Brooklyn, NY: Lawrence Hill Books, 1993.

———. *Our Blood: Prophecies and Discourses on Sexual Politics*. New York: G. Putnam, 1981.

———. *Right-Wing Women*. New York: Coward-McCann, 1983.

———. *Woman Hating: A Radical Look at Sexuality*. New York: E. Dutton, 1974.

Echols, Alice. "The Taming of the Id." In *Pleasure and Danger: Exploring Female Sexuality*, edited by Carole S. Vance. Boston: Routledge & Kegan Paul, 1984.

Epstein, Cynthia Fuchs. *A Woman's Place*. Berkeley: University of California Press, 1971.

Frye, Marilyn. *The Politics of Reality: Essays in Feminist Theory*. Trumansburg, NY: Crossing Press, 1983.

Linden, Robin Ruth, Darlene R. Pagano, Diana E. H. Russell, and Susan Leigh Star, eds. *Against Sadomasochism: A Radical Feminist Analysis*. East Palo Alto, CA: Frog in the Well Press, 1982.

MacKinnon, Catharine A., ed. *Women's Lives, Men's Laws*. Cambridge, MA: Belknap Press of Harvard University Press, 2005.

Millett, Kate. *Sexual Politics*. Garden City, NY: Doubleday, 1970.

Redstockings, ed. *Feminist Revolution*. New York: Random House, 1975.

Rubin, Gayle. "Thinking Sex: Notes for a Radical Theory of the Politics of Sexuality." In *Pleasure and Danger: Exploring Female Sexuality*, edited by Carole S. Vance. Boston: Routledge & Kegan Paul, 1984.

Shafer, Carolyn M., and Marilyn Frye. "Rape and Respect." In *Women and Values: Readings in Recent Feminist Philosophy*, edited by Marilyn Pearsall. Belmont, CA: Wadsworth, 1986.

Shulman, Alix Kates. "Sex and Power: Sexual Bases of Radical Feminism." *Signs: Journal of Women in Culture and Society* 5, no. 4 (summer 1980): 590–604.

Smart, Carol, and Barry Smart, eds. *Women, Sexuality, and Social Control*. London: Routledge & Kegan Paul, 1978.

Stein, Arlene. *Shameless: Sexual Dissidence in American Culture*. New York: New York University Press, 2006.

Valenti, Jessica. *He's a Stud, She's a Slut, and 49 Other Double Standards Every Woman Should Know*. Berkeley, CA: Seal Press, 2008.

Vance, Carole S., ed. *Pleasure and Danger: Exploring Female Sexuality*. Boston: Routledge & Kegan Paul, 1984.

PORNOGRAPHY AND PROSTITUTION

Assiter, Alison. *Pornography, Feminism, and the Individual*. London: Pluto Press, 1991.

Attwood, Feona. "Pornography and Objectification." *Feminist Media Studies* 4, no. 1 (March 2004): 7–19.

Bazelon, Emily. "Should Prostitution Be a Crime?." *New York Times Magazine*, May 8, 2016, 34–43, 55–57.

Berger, Ronald J., Patricia Searles, and Charles E. Cottle. *Feminism and Pornography*. New York: Praeger Publishers, 1991.

Blakely, Mary Kay. "Is One Woman's Sexuality Another Woman's Pornography?." *Ms.* (April 1985): 37–47.

Brison, Susan J. "Contentious Freedom: Sex Work and Social Construction." *Hypatia* 21, no. 4 (fall 2006): 192–200.

Bronstein, Carolyn. *Battling Pornography: The American Feminist Anti-pornography Movement, 1976–1986*. New York: Cambridge University Press, 2011.

Chancer, Lynn S. *Reconcilable Differences: Confronting Beauty, Pornography, and the Future of Feminism*. Berkeley: University of California Press, 1998.

Ciclitira, Karen. "Pornography, Women and Feminism: Between Pleasure and Politics." *Sexualities* 7, no. 3 (August 2004): 281–301.

Cornell, Drucilla. *Feminism and Pornography*. Oxford: Oxford University Press, 2000.

Donnerstein, Edward. *The Question of Pornography: Research Findings and Policy Implications*. New York: Free Press, 1987.

Dworkin, Andrea. *Pornography: Men Possessing Women*. New York: Perigee Books, 1981.

———. "Pornography's 'Exquisite Volunteers.'" *Ms.* (March 1981).

English, Deirdre. *The Politics of Porn: Can Feminists Walk the Line?* San Francisco, CA: Henry Schipper, 1980.

Griffin, Susan. *Pornography and Silence: Culture's Revenge Against Nature*. New York: Harper & Row, 1981.

Itzin, Catherine, ed. *Pornography: Women, Violence, and Civil Liberties*. Oxford: Oxford University Press, 1993.

KaeLyn. "Feminist Porn: Sex, Consent, and Getting Off." *Feministe*, July 23, 2008, http://www.feministe.us/blog/archives/2008/07/23/feminist-porn-sex-consent-and-getting-off.

Klein, Dorrie. "Violence Against Women: Some Considerations Regarding Its Causes and Elimination." *Crime and Delinquency* 27 (January 1981): 64–80.

Lederer, Laura, ed. *Take Back the Night: Women on Pornography*. New York: William Morrow, 1980.

Long, Julia. *Anti-porn: The Resurgence of Anti-pornography Feminism*. London: Zed Books, 2012.

MacKinnon, Catharine A. "Feminism, Marxism, Method, and the State: Toward Feminist Jurisprudence." *Signs: Journal of Women in Culture and Society* 8, no. 4 (summer 1983): 635–658.

———. "Francis Biddle's Sister: Pornography, Civil Rights, and Speech." In *Feminism Unmodified: Disclosures on Life and Law*. Cambridge, MA: Harvard University Press, 1987.

Malamuth, Neil, and Edward Donnerstein. *Pornography and Sexual Aggression*. New York: Academic Press, 1984.

McCarthy, Sarah J. "Pornography, Rape, and the Cult of Macho." *Humanist* 40, no. 5 (September/October 1980): 11–20.

Newland, Laura. "Not for Sale: Feminists Resisting Prostitution and Pornography." *Off Our Backs* 35, no. 7 (August 2005): 30.

Richards, David A. J. "Commercial Sex and the Rights of the Person: A Moral Argument for the Decriminalization of Prostitution." *University of Pennsylvania Law Review* 127 (May 1979): 1233.

Rodgerson, Gillian, and Elizabeth Wilson, eds. *Pornography and Feminism: The Case Against Censorship.* London: Lawrence & Wishart, 1991.

Rosenbreet, Charles, and Barbara J. Puriente. "The Prostitution of the Criminal Law." *American Cultural Law Review* 11 (winter 1973): 373.

Sabo, Anne. *After Pornified: How Women Are Transforming Pornography and Why It Really Matters.* Alresford, UK: Zero Books, 2012.

Segal, Lynne. *Sex Exposed: Sexuality and the Pornography Debate.* Piscataway, NJ: Rutgers University Press, 1993.

Sharpe, Laurie. "Feminist Perspectives on Sex Markets: Pornography." In *Stanford Encyclopedia of Philosophy.* Stanford, CA: Stanford Center for the Study of Language and Information, 2013.

Soble, Alan. *Pornography: Marxism, Feminism, and the Future of Sexuality.* New Haven, CT: Yale University Press, 1986.

———. *Pornography, Sex, and Feminism.* Amherst, NY: Prometheus Books, 2002.

Strossen, Nadine. *Defending Pornography: Free Speech, Sex, and the Fight for Women's Rights.* New York: New York University Press, 2000.

Taylor, Stuart, Jr. "Pornography Foes Lose New Weapons in Supreme Court." *New York Times,* February 25, 1986, 1.

Tong, Rosemarie. *Women, Sex, and the Law.* Totowa, NJ: Rowman & Allanheld, 1984.

Tyler, Meagan. *Selling Sex Short: The Pornographic and Sexological Construction of Women's Sexuality in the West.* Newcastle upon Tyne, UK: Cambridge Scholars Publishing, 2011.

Walkowitz, Judith R. "The Politics of Prostitution." *Signs: Journal of Women in Culture and Society* 6, no. 1 (autumn 1980): 128.

ARTIFICIAL REPRODUCTION VERSUS NATURAL REPRODUCTION

"A Surrogate's Story of Loving and Losing." *U.S. News & World Report,* June 6, 1983, 12.

Adams, Alice. *Reproducing the Womb: Images of Childbirth in Science, Feminist Theory, and Literature.* Ithaca, NY: Cornell University Press, 1994.

Atwood, Margaret. *The Handmaid's Tale.* New York: Fawcett Crest Books, 1985.

Baruch, Elaine, Amadeo D'Adamo, and Joni Seager, eds. *Embryos, Ethics, and Women's Rights: Exploring the New Reproductive Technologies.* New York: Harrington Park Press, 1988.

Brakman, Sarah-Vaughan, and Sally J. Scholz. "Adoption, ART, and a Re-conception of the Maternal Body: Toward Embodied Maternity." *Hypatia* 21, no. 1 (winter 2006): 54–77.

Corea, Gena. "Egg Snatchers." In *Test-Tube Women: What Future for Motherhood?*, edited by Rita Arditti, Renate Duelli Klein, and Shelley Minden. London: Pandora Press, 1984.

———. *The Mother Machine: Reproduction Technologies from Artificial Insemination to Artificial Wombs.* New York: Harper & Row, 1985.

Crossley, Mary. "Dimensions of Equality in Regulating Assisted Reproductive Technologies." *Journal of Gender, Race, and Justice* 9, no. 2 (winter 2005): 273.

Dresser, Rebecca. "Regulating Assisted Reproduction." *Hastings Center Report* 30 (2000).

Dworkin, Andrea. *Right-Wing Women.* New York: Coward-McCann, 1983.

Firestone, Shulamith. *The Dialectic of Sex.* New York: Bantam Books, 1970.

Goldberg, Michelle. *The Means of Reproduction: Sex, Power, and the Future of the World.* New York: Penguin Press, 2009.

Goslinga-Roy, Gillian M. "Body Boundaries, Fiction of the Female Self: An Ethnographic Perspective on Power, Feminism, and the Reproductive Technologies." *Feminist Studies* 26, no. 1 (spring 2000): 113–141.

Makus, Ingrid. *Women, Politics, and Reproduction: The Liberal Legacy.* Toronto: University of Toronto Press, 1996.

Moore, Lisa Jean. *Sperm Counts: Overcome by Man's Most Precious Fluid.* New York: New York University Press, 2007.

Naff, Clay Farris, ed. *Reproductive Technology.* Farmington Hills, MI: Greenhaven Press, 2006.

O'Brien, Mary. *The Politics of Reproduction.* Boston: Routledge & Kegan Paul, 1981.

Overall, Christine. "Access to In Vitro Fertilization: Costs, Care and Consent." *Dialogue* 30 (1991): 383–398.

———. *Ethics and Human Reproduction: A Feminist Analysis.* Boston: Allen & Unwin, 1987.

———. *Human Reproduction: Principles, Practices, Policies.* New York: Oxford University Press, 1993.

Parks, Jennifer. "Rethinking Radical Politics in the Context of Assisted Reproductive Technology." *Bioethics* 23, no. 1 (2009): 20–27.

Purdy, Laura M. *Reproducing Persons: Issues in Feminist Bioethics.* Ithaca, NY: Cornell University Press, 1996.

Rowland, Robyn. "Reproductive Technologies: The Final Solution to the Woman Question." In *Test-Tube Women: What Future for Motherhood?*, edited by Rita Arditti, Renate Duelli Klein, and Shelley Minden. London: Pandora Press, 1984.

Sherwin, Susan. *No Longer Patient: Feminist Ethics and Health Care.* Philadelphia: Temple University Press, 1993.

Solinger, Rickie. *Pregnancy and Power: A Short History of Reproductive Politics in America.* New York: New York University Press, 2005.

Wolf, Susan, ed. *Feminism and Bioethics: Beyond Reproduction.* Oxford: Oxford University Press, 1996.

BIOLOGICAL MOTHERHOOD:
NEGATIVE VERSUS POSITIVE ASSESSMENTS

Allen, Jeffner. "Motherhood: The Annihilation of Women." In *Women and Values: Readings in Recent Feminist Philosophy*, edited by Marilyn Pearsall. Belmont, CA: Wadsworth, 1986.

Alpert, Jane. "Mother Right: A New Feminist Theory." Pittsburg, PA: Know Inc. 1974.

Badinter, Elisabeth. *The Conflict: How Modern Motherhood Undermines the Status of Women.* New York: Metropolitan Books, 2010.

Blades, Joan, and Kristin Rowe-Finkbeiner. *The Motherhood Manifesto: What American Moms Want—and What to Do About It.* New York: Nation Books, 2006.

Blank, Robert H. *Mother and Fetus: Changing Notions of Maternal Responsibility.* New York: Greenwood Press, 1992.

Brewer, Rose. "Black Women in Poverty: Some Comments on Female-Headed Families." *Signs: Journal of Women in Culture and Society* 13, no. 2 (winter 1988): 331–339.

Brown, Ivana. "Mommy Memoirs: Feminism, Gender and Motherhood in Popular Literature." *Journal of the Association for Research on Mothering* 8, nos. 1–2 (September 2006): 72–83.

Cahill, Susan, ed. *Motherhood.* New York: Avon Books, 1982.

Chodorow, Nancy. *The Reproduction of Mothering: Psychoanalysis and the Sociology of Gender.* Berkeley: University of California Press, 1978.

Crittenden, Anne. *The Price of Motherhood: Why the Most Important Job in the World Is the Least Valued.* London: Metropolitan Books, 2001.

DiQuinzio, Patrice. *The Impossibility of Motherhood: Feminism, Individualism, and the Problem of Mothering.* New York: Routledge, 1999.

———. "The Politics of the Mothers' Movement in the United States: Possibilities and Pitfalls." *Journal of the Association for Research on Mothering* 8, nos. 1 and 2 (September 2006).

———. "Reconceiving Pregnancy and Childcare: Ethics, Experience, and Reproductive Labor." *Hypatia* 22, no. 3 (summer 2007): 204.

Ehrenreich, Barbara, and Deirdre English. *For Her Own Good.* New York: Anchor/Doubleday, 1979.

Ferguson, Ann. *Blood at the Root: Motherhood, Sexuality, and Male Dominance.* London: Pandora Press, 1989.

———. "Motherhood and Sexuality: Some Feminist Questions." *Hypatia* 1, no. 2 (fall 1986): 3–22.

Folbre, Nancy. *The Invisible Heart: Economics and Family Values.* New York: New Press, 2001.

Green, Fiona Joy. "Developing a Feminist Motherline: Reflections on a Decade of Feminist Parenting." *Journal of the Association for Research on Mothering* 8, nos. 1 and 2 (September 2006): 7–21.

Hattery, Angela. *Women, Work and Family: Balancing and Weaving.* Thousand Oaks, CA: Sage Publications, 2001.

Kinser, Amber E. *Feminism and Mothering.* Berkeley, CA: Seal Press, 2010.

Lintott, Sheila, and Maureen Sander-Staudt, eds. *Philosophical Inquiries into Pregnancy, Childbirth, and Mothering: Maternal Subjects.* New York: Routledge, 2012.

Lorber, Judith. "On *The Reproduction of Mothering*: A Methodological Debate." *Signs: Journal of Women in Culture and Society* 6, no. 3 (spring 1981): 482–486.

Mahowald, Mary Briody. *Women and Children in Health Care: An Unequal Majority.* New York: Oxford University Press, 1993.

Mendell, Betty Reid. *Where Are the Children? A Close Analysis of Foster Care and Adoption.* Lexington, MA: Lexington Books, 1973.

Middleton, Amy. "Mothering Under Duress: Examining the Inclusiveness of Feminist Mothering Theory." *Journal of the Association for Research on Mothering* 8, nos. 1 and 2 (September 2006).

Oakley, Ann. *Sex, Gender, and Society.* London: Temple Smith, 1972.

Piercy, Marge. *Woman on the Edge of Time.* New York: Fawcett Crest Books, 1976.

Purdy, Laura. *In Their Best Interest? The Case Against Equal Rights for Children.* Ithaca, NY: Cornell University Press, 1992.

Rich, Adrienne. *Of Woman Born.* New York: W. W. Norton, 1979.

Trebilcot, Joyce, ed. *Mothering: Essays in Feminist Theory.* Totowa, NJ: Rowman & Allanheld, 1984.

GENETIC, GESTATIONAL, AND REARING CONNECTIONS TO CHILDREN

Chesler, Phyllis. *Sacred Bond: The Legacy of Baby M.* New York: Times Books, 1988.

Cohen, Cynthia B. "'Give Me Children or I Shall Die!' New Reproductive Technologies and Harm to Children." *Hastings Center Report* 26, no. 2 (March/April 1996): 19–27.

Colb, Sherry F. *When Sex Counts: Making Babies and Making Law.* Lanham, MD: Rowman & Littlefield, 2007.

Donchin, Anne. "The Future of Mothering: Reproductive Technology and Feminist Theory." *Hypatia* 1, no. 2 (fall 1986): 131.

Goodwin, Michele. "Assisted Reproductive Technology and the Double Bind: The Illusory Choice of Motherhood." *Journal of Gender, Race, and Justice* 9, no. 1 (fall 2005): 1–55.

Ketchum, Sara Ann. "Selling Babies and Selling Bodies." In *Feminist Perspectives in Medical Ethics,* edited by Helen Holmes and Laura M. Purdy. Bloomington: Indiana University Press, 1992.

Mellown, Mary Ruth. "An Incomplete Picture: The Debate About Surrogate Motherhood." *Harvard Women's Law Journal* 8 (spring 1985): 231–246.

Mundy, Liza. *Everything Conceivable: How Assisted Reproduction Is Changing Men, Women, and the World.* New York: Alfred Knopf, 2007.

Raymond, Janice. *Women as Wombs: Reproductive Technologies and the Battle over Women's Freedom.* San Francisco: Harper & Row, 1993.

Rodin, Judith, and Aila Collins, eds. *Women and New Reproductive Technologies: Medical, Psychosocial, Legal and Ethical Dilemmas.* Hillside, NJ: Lawrence Erlbaum Associates, 1991.

Tong, Rosemarie. *Feminist Approaches to Bioethics.* Boulder, CO: Westview Press, 1997.

LESBIAN SEPARATIST FEMINISM

Allen, Jeffner. *Lesbian Philosophy: Explorations.* Palo Alto, CA: Institute of Lesbian Studies, 1986.

Atkinson, Ti-Grace. *Amazon Odyssey.* New York: Links, 1974.

———. "Lesbianism and Feminism." In *Amazon Expedition: A Lesbian-Feminist Anthology*, edited by Phyllis Birkby et al. Washington, NJ: Times Change Press, 1973.

———. "Radical Feminism: A Declaration of War." In *Women and Values: Readings in Recent Feminist Philosophy*, edited by Marilyn Pearsall. Belmont, CA: Wadsworth, 1986.

Beck, Evelyn Torton, ed. *Nice Jewish Girls: A Lesbian Anthology.* Watertown, MA: Persephone Press, 1982.

Brandt, Eric, ed. *Dangerous Liaisons: Blacks, Gays, and the Struggle for Equality.* New York: New Press, 1999.

Bulkin, Elly, Minnie Bruce Pratt, and Barbara Smith. *Yours in Struggle: Three Feminist Perspectives on Anti-Semitism and Racism.* New York: Long Haul Press, 1984.

Califia, Pat. *Sapphistry: The Book of Lesbian Sexuality.* Tallahassee: Naiad Press, 1983.

Card, Claudia, ed. *Adventures in Lesbian Philosophy.* Bloomington: Indiana University Press, 1994.

———. "Radicalesbianfeminist Theory." *Hypatia* 13, no. 1 (1998): 206–213.

Ciasullo, Ann M. "Making Her (In)visible: Cultural Representations of Lesbianism and the Lesbian Body in the 1990s." *Feminist Studies* 27, no. 3 (fall 2001): 577.

Clarke, Cheryl. "Being Pro-Gay and Pro-Lesbian in Straight Institutions." *Journal of Gay and Lesbian Social Services* 3, no. 2. (1995): 95–100.

———. "Knowing the Danger and Going There Anyway." *Sojourner: The Women's Forum* 16, no. 1 (1990): 14–15.

Cole, Johnnetta Betsch, and Beverly Guy-Sheftall. "Black, Lesbian, and Gay: Speaking the Unspeakable." In *Gender Talk: The Struggle for Women's Equality in African American Communities.* New York: One World Ballantine Books, 2003.

Cuomo, Chris J. "Thoughts on Lesbian Differences." *Hypatia* 13, no. 1 (1998): 198–205.

Daly, Meg. *Surface Tension: Love, Sex, and Politics Between Lesbians and Straight Women*. New York: Simon & Schuster, 1996.

Ettorre, E. M. *Lesbians, Women, and Society*. London: Routledge & Kegan Paul, 1980.

Faderman, Lillian. *Odd Girls and Twilight Lovers: A History of Lesbian Life in Twentieth-Century America*. New York: Columbia University Press, 1991.

Frye, Marilyn. "Do You Have to Be a Lesbian to Be a Feminist?." *Off Our Backs* 20, no. 8 (September 30, 1990): 21.

Fuss, Diane, ed. *Inside/Out: Lesbian Theories, Gay Theories*. London: Routledge, 1991.

Goodman, Gerre, et al. *No Turning Back: Lesbian and Gay Liberation for the '80s*. Philadelphia: New Society Publishers, 1983.

Grier, Barbara, and Coletta Reid, eds. *The Lavender Herring: Lesbian Essays from "The Ladder."* Baltimore: Diana Press, 1976.

Harne, Lynne, and Elaine Miller, eds. *All the Rage: Reasserting Radical Lesbian Feminism*. London: Women's Press, 1996.

Harris, Laura, and Elizabeth Crocker, eds. *Femme: Feminists, Lesbians, and Bad Girls*. New York: Routledge, 1997.

Hawthorne, Susan. "The Depoliticising of Lesbian Culture." *Hecate* 29, no. 2 (2003): 235.

Heller, Dana, ed. *Cross-Purposes: Lesbians, Feminists, and the Limits of Alliance*. Bloomington: Indiana University Press, 1997.

Jeffreys, Sheila. *The Lesbian Heresy: A Feminist Perspective on the Lesbian Sexual Revolution*. North Melbourne, Australia: Spinifex, 1993.

Johnston, Jill. *Lesbian Nation: The Feminist Solution*. New York: Simon & Schuster, 1974.

Kleindienst, Kris, ed. *This Is What a Lesbian Looks Like*. Ithaca, NY: Firebrand Books, 1999.

Koedt, Anne. "The Myth of the Vaginal Orgasm." *Notes from the Second Year: Women's Liberation—Major Writings of the Radical Feminists*, University of Illinois, Chicago, April 1970, http://www.uic.edu/orgs/caluherstory/CWLUArchive/vaginalmyth.html.

Laner, Mary R., and Roy H. Laner. "Sexual Preference or Personal Style? Why Lesbians Are Disliked." *Journal of Homosexuality* 5, no. 4 (1980): 339–356.

Law, Sylvia. "Homosexuality and the Social Meaning of Gender." *Wisconsin Law Review* 2 (1988): 187–235.

Mohin, Lilian, ed. *An Intimacy of Equals: Lesbian Feminist Ethics*. New York: Harrington Park Press, 1996.

Myron, Nancy, and Charlotte Bunch, eds. *Lesbianism and the Women's Movement*. Baltimore: Diana, 1975.

Nestle, Joan. *Persistent Desire: A Butch-Femme Reader*. Boston: Alyson Publications, 1992.

"New York Covens' Leaflet." In *Sisterhood Is Powerful*, edited by Robin Morgan. New York: Random House, 1970.

Phelan, Shane. *Identity Politics: Lesbian Feminism and the Limits of Community*. Philadelphia: Temple University Press, 1989.

"Redstockings Manifesto." In *Sisterhood Is Powerful*, edited by Robin Morgan. New York: Random House, 1970.

Rich, Adrienne. "Compulsory Heterosexuality and Lesbian Existence." In *Living with Contradictions: Controversies in Feminist Social Ethics*, edited by Alison M. Jaggar. Boulder, CO: Westview Press, 1994.

Rule, Jane. *Lesbian Images*. Trumansburg, NY: Crossing Press, 1982.

SAMOIS. *Coming to Power: Writings and Graphics on Lesbian S/M*. Palo Alto, CA: Up Press, 1981.

Shugar, Dana R. *Separatism and Women's Community*. Lincoln: University of Nebraska Press, 1995.

Tanner, Donna K. *The Lesbian Couple*. Lexington, MA: Lexington Books, 1978.

Valk, Anne M. "Living a Feminist Lifestyle: The Intersection of Theory and Action in a Lesbian Feminist Collective." *Feminist Studies* 28, no. 2 (2002): 303.

Weise, Elizabeth Reba, ed. *Closer to Home: Bisexuality and Feminism*. Seattle, WA: Seal Press, 1992.

Critiques of Radical Feminism

Ashe, Fidelma. *The New Politics of Masculinity: Men, Power, and Resistance*. New York: Routledge, 2007.

Bar On, Bat-Ami. "The Feminist Sexuality Debates and the Transformation of the Political." *Hypatia* 7, no. 4 (fall 1992): 49.

Corcoran, Terence. "Radical Feminism's Absurd Legacy." *Globe and Mail*, July 31, 1998.

Ferguson, Ann. "The Sex Debate in the Women's Movement: A Socialist-Feminist View." *Against the Current* (September/October 1983): 12.

———. "Sex War: The Debate Between Radical and Liberal Feminists." *Signs: Journal of Women in Culture and Society* 10, no. 1 (autumn 1984): 106–112.

Frederick, Danny. "Radical Feminism: An Expose!." Libertarian Alliance pamphlet, November 18, 1992.

Goldberg, Michelle. "What Is a Woman? The Dispute Between Radical Feminism and Transgenderism." *New Yorker*, August 4, 2014, 1–13.

O'Beirne, Kate. *Women Who Make the World Worse: And How Their Radical Feminist Assault Is Ruining Our Families, Military, Schools, and Sports*. New York: Sentinel, 2006.

Willis, Ellen. "Radical Feminism and Feminist Radicalism." In *No More Nice Girls: Countercultural Essays*, 117–154. Middletown, CT: Wesleyan University Press, 1992.

Chapter 3: Marxist and Socialist Feminisms

Some Traditional Marxist Concepts and Theories

Acton, Henry Burrows. *What Marx Really Said.* London: MacDonald, 1967.

Anderson, Kevin. *Marx at the Margins: On Nationalism, Ethnicity, and Non-Western Societies.* Chicago: University of Chicago Press, 2010.

Engels, Friedrich. *The Origin of the Family, Private Property, and the State.* New York: International Publishers, 1972.

Fine, Ben, Alfredo Saad-Filho, and Marco Buffo, eds. *The Elgar Companion to Marxist Economics.* Elgar Original Reference. Cheltenham, UK: Edward Elgar Publishing Limited, 2012.

Harvey, David. *A Companion to Marx's* Capital. London: Verso, 2010.

Heilbroner, Robert L. *Marxism: For and Against.* New York: W. W. Norton, 1980.

Lane, Ann J. "Woman in Society: A Critique of Friedrich Engels." In *Liberating Women's History*, edited by Berenice A. Carroll. Champaign: University of Illinois Press, 1976.

Lenin, V. I. *The Emancipation of Women: From the Writings of V. I. Lenin.* New York: International Publishers, 1934.

Mandel, Ernest. *An Introduction to Marxist Economic Theory.* New York: Pathfinder Press, 1970.

Marx, Karl. *Capital.* Vol. 3. New York: International Publishers, 1967.

———. *A Contribution to the Critique of Political Economy.* New York: International Publishers, 1972.

———. "Economic and Philosophic Manuscripts." In *Early Writings*. Edited and translated by T. B. Bottomore. New York: McGraw-Hill, 1964.

———. *Grundrisse: Foundations of the Critique of Political Economy,* translated and edited by T. B. Bottomore. New York: Vintage Books, 1973.

Marx, Karl, and Friedrich Engels. *The German Ideology.* In *The Marx-Engels Reader.* Edited and translated by Robert C. Tucker. New York: W. W. Norton, 1978.

McLellan, David. *Karl Marx.* New York: Penguin Books, 1975.

Phelps, Linda. "Patriarchy and Capitalism." *Quest* 2, no. 2 (fall 1975): 35–48.

Quick, Paddy. "The Class Nature of Women's Oppression." *Review of Radical Political Economics* 9, no. 3 (winter 1977): 42–53.

Sacks, Karen. "Engels Revisited: Women, the Organization of Production and Private Property." In *Toward an Anthropology of Women*, edited by Rayna R. Reiter. New York: Monthly Review Press, 1975.

Sargent, Lydia, ed. *Women and Revolution: A Discussion of the Unhappy Marriage of Marxism and Feminism.* Boston: South End Press, 1981.

Schmitt, Richard. *Introduction to Marx and Engels.* Boulder, CO: Westview Press, 1987.

Slaughter, Cliff. *Marx and Marxism: An Introduction.* New York: Longman, 1985.

Suchting, Wallis Arthur. *Marx: An Introduction.* New York: New York University Press, 1983.

Tabak, Mehmet. *Dialectics of Human Nature in Marx's Philosophy*. New York: Palgrave Macmillan, 2012.

Wood, Allen W. *Karl Marx*. London: Routledge & Kegan Paul, 1981.

Wright, Erik Olin. *Classes*. London: Verso, 1985.

Classical Marxist Feminism: General Reflections

Bennett, Judith M. *History Matters: Patriarchy and the Challenge of Feminism*. Philadelphia: University of Pennsylvania Press, 2006.

Flax, Jane. "Do Feminists Need Marxism?." In *Building Feminist Theory: Essays from "Quest," a Feminist Quarterly*. New York: Longman, 1981.

Foreman, Ann. *Femininity as Alienation: Women and the Family in Marxism and Psychoanalysis*. London: Pluto Press, 1977.

Guettel, Charnie. *Marxism and Feminism*. Toronto: Women's Education Press, 1974.

Holmstrom, Nancy. "A Marxist Theory of Women's Nature." *Ethics* 94, no. 1 (April 1984): 456–473.

Jackson, Stevi. "Marxism and Feminism." In *Marxism and Social Science*, edited by Andrew Gamble, David Marsh, and Tony Tant, 17. Champaign: University of Illinois Press, 1999.

Levine, Rhonda, ed. *Social Class and Stratification: Classic Statements and Theoretical Debates*. Lanham, MD: Rowman & Littlefield, 2006.

MacKinnon, Catharine A. "Feminism, Marxism, Method, and the State: An Agenda for Theory." *Signs: Journal of Women in Culture and Society* 7, no. 3 (spring 1982): 515–545.

Reed, Evelyn. *Problems of Woman's Liberation*. New York: Pathfinder Press, 1970.

———. "Women: Caste, Class, or Oppressed Sex?." *International Socialist Review* 31, no. 3 (September 1970): 15–17, 40–41.

Saffiote, Heleieth I. B. *Women in Class Society*. Translated by Michael Vale. New York: Monthly Review Press, 1978.

Waters, Mary-Alice. *Feminism and the Marxist Movement*. New York: Pathfinder Press, 1994.

Wright, Erik Olin. "Explanation and Emancipation in Marxism and Feminism." *Sociological Theory* 11, no. 1 (March 1993): 39–54.

WAGES FOR HOUSEWORK

Barrett, Michèle, and Mary McIntosh. "The Family Wage: Some Problems for Socialists and Feminists." *Capital and Class* 2 (1980): 51–57.

Beechey, Veronica. "Some Notes on Female Wage Labour in Capitalist Production." *Capital and Class* 3 (autumn 1977): 45–66.

Benston, Margaret. "The Political Economy of Women's Liberation." *Monthly Review* 21, no. 4 (September 1969): 13–27.

Berch, Bettina. *The Endless Day: The Political Economy of Women and Work.* New York: Harcourt Brace Jovanovich, 1982.

Coulson, Margaret, Branka Magaš, and Hilary Wainwright. "'The Housewife and Her Labour Under Capitalism': A Critique." *New Left Review* 89 (January/February 1975): 59–71.

Cowan, Ruth Schwartz. "The 'Industrial Revolution' in the Home: Household Technology and Social Change in the Twentieth Century." *Technology and Culture* 17, no. 1 (1976): 1–23.

Dalla Costa, Mariarosa, and Selma James. "A General Strike." In *All Work and No Pay*, edited by Wendy Edmond and Suzie Fleming. London: Power of Women Collective and Falling Wall Press, 1975.

———. *The Power of Women and the Subversion of Community.* Bristol, UK: Falling Wall Press, 1972.

Edmond, Wendy, and Suzie Fleming. "If Women Were Paid for All They Do." In *All Work and No Pay*, edited by Wendy Edmond and Suzie Fleming. London: Power of Women Collective and Falling Wall Press, 1975.

Garson, Barbara. *All the Livelong Day: The Meaning and Demeaning of Routine Work.* New York: Penguin Books, 1975.

Gerstein, Ira. "Domestic Work and Capitalism." *Radical America* 7, nos. 4–5 (July/October 1973): 101–128.

Glazer-Malbin, Nona. "Housework." *Signs: Journal of Women in Culture and Society* 1, no. 4 (1976): 905–922.

Hartmann, Heidi I. "The Family as the Locus of Gender, Class, and Political Struggle: The Example of Housework." *Signs: Journal of Women in Culture and Society* 6, no. 3 (1981): 366–394.

———. "Towards a Historical Sociology of Housework." *Women's Studies International Forum* 15, no. 2 (1992): 153–172.

Kaluzynska, Eva. "Wiping the Floor with Theory: A Survey of Writings on Housework." *Feminist Review* 6 (1980): 27–54.

Malos, Ellen, ed. *The Politics of Housework.* London: Allison & Busby, 1980.

Molyneux, Maxine. "Beyond the Domestic Labour Debate." *New Left Review* 116 (July/August 1979): 3–27.

Oakley, Ann. *Woman's Work: The Housewife, Past and Present.* New York: Random/Vintage, 1974.

Scott, Ann Crittenden. "The Value of Housework for Love or Money?." *Ms.* (June 1972): 56–58.

Secombe, Wally. "The Housewife and Her Labour Under Capitalism." *New Left Review* 83 (January/February 1973): 3–24.

Contemporary Socialist Feminism: General Reflections

Alaimo, Stacy, and Susan Hekman, eds. *Material Feminisms.* Bloomington: Indiana University Press, 2008.

Barrett, Michéle. "Words and Things: Materialism and Method in Contemporary Feminist Analysis." In *Destabilizing Theory: Contemporary Feminist Debates*, edited by Michèle Barrett and Anne Phillips. Cambridge, UK: Polity Press, 1992.

Beneria, Lourdes. "Capitalism and Socialism: Some Feminist Questions." In *The Women, Gender, and Development Reader*, edited by Visanthan Nalini, Lynn Duggan, and Nan Wiegersma. Atlantic Highlands, NJ: Zed Books, 1997.

Calhoun, Cheshire. "Taking Seriously Dual Systems and Sex." *Hypatia* 13, no. 1 (1998): 224–231.

Delphy, Christine. *Close to Home: A Materialist Analysis of Women's Oppression*. Edited and translated by Diana Leonard. London: Hutchinson, 1984.

Eisenstein, Zillah R., ed. *Capitalist Patriarchy and the Case for Socialist Feminism*. New York: Monthly Review Press, 1979.

Ferguson, Ann. "The Che-Lumumba School: Creating a Revolutionary Family-Community." *Quest* 5, no. 3 (February/March 1980).

Friedman, Marilyn. "Nancy J. Hirschmann on the Social Construction of Women's Freedom." *Hypatia* 21, no. 4 (fall 2006): 182–191.

Funk, Nanette, and Magda Mueller, eds. *Gender Politics and Post Communism*. New York: Routledge, 1993.

Gal, Susan, and Gail Kligman. *The Politics of Gender After Socialism*. Princeton, NJ: Princeton University Press, 2000.

———, eds. *Reproducing Gender: Politics, Publics, and Everyday Life After Socialism*. Princeton, NJ: Princeton University Press, 2000.

Haraway, Donna. "A Manifesto for Cyborgs: Science, Technology and Socialist Feminism in the 1990s." *Socialist Review* 15, no. 2 (March/April 1985): 65–107.

Hartmann, Heidi I. "Capitalism, Patriarchy, and Job Segregation by Sex." In *Capitalist Patriarchy and the Case for Socialist Feminism*, edited by Zillah R. Eisenstein. New York: Monthly Review Press, 1979.

———. "The Unhappy Marriage of Marxism and Feminism: Towards a More Progressive Union." In *Women and Revolution: A Discussion of the Unhappy Marriage of Marxism and Feminism*, edited by Lydia Sargent. Boston: South End Press, 1981.

Hennessy, Rosemary. *Materialist Feminism and the Politics of Discourse*. New York: Routledge, 1993.

Holmstrom, Nancy, ed. *The Socialist Feminist Project: A Contemporary Reader in Theory and Politics*. New York: Monthly Review Press, 2002.

———. "The Socialist Feminist Project: A Contemporary Reader in Theory and Politics." *Monthly Review* 54, no. 10 (March 2003): 1.

Jaggar, Alison M. *Feminist Politics and Human Nature*. Totowa, NJ: Rowman & Allanheld, 1983.

Kuhn, Annette, and Ann Marie Wolpe, eds. *Feminism and Materialism: Women and Modes of Production*. New York: Routledge & Kegan Paul, 1978.

Landry, Donna, and Gerald Maclean. *Materialist Feminisms.* Cambridge, MA: Blackwell, 1993.

Martin, Gloria. *Socialist Feminism: The First Decade, 1966–1976.* Seattle, WA: Freedom Socialist Publications, 1978.

Mitchell, Juliet. *Woman's Estate.* New York: Pantheon Books, 1971.

———. "Women: The Longest Revolution." *New Left Review* 40 (November/December 1966): 11–37.

Page, Margaret. "Socialist Feminism: A Political Alternative." *m/f* 2 (1978).

Penny, Laurie. *Meat Market: Female Flesh Under Capitalism.* Alresford, UK: Zero Books, 2011.

Radical Women's 23rd Anniversary Conference General Membership. *The Radical Women Manifesto: Socialist Feminist Theory, Program and Organizational Structure.* Seattle, WA: Red Letter Press, 2001.

Rowbotham, Sheila. *Woman's Consciousness, Man's World.* Baltimore: Penguin Books, 1973.

Rowbotham, Sheila, Lynne Segal, and Hilary Wainwright. *Beyond the Fragments: Feminism and the Making of Socialism.* London: Merlin Press, 1979.

Russell, Kathryn. *The Socialist Feminist Project: A Contemporary Reader in Theory and Politics,* edited by Nancy Holstrom. New York: Monthly Review Press, 2002.

Smith, Sharon. *Women and Socialism: Essays on Women's Liberation.* Chicago: Haymarket Books, 2005.

Taylor, Barbara. "Lords of Creation: Marxism, Feminism and 'Utopian Socialism.'" In *Reader in Feminist Knowledge,* edited by Sneja Gunew, 360–365. New York: Routledge, 1991.

Vogel, Lise. *Marxism and the Oppression of Women: Towards a Unitary Theory.* New Brunswick, NJ: Rutgers University Press, 1983.

———. *Woman Questions. Essays for a Materialist Feminism.* New York: Routledge, 1995.

Walby, Sylvia. *Patriarchy at Work.* Cambridge, UK: Polity Press, 1986.

———. *Theorizing Patriarchy.* Oxford, UK: Basil Blackwell, Ltd., 1990.

Young, Iris Marion. "Beyond the Unhappy Marriage: A Critique of Dual Systems Theory." In *Women and Revolution: A Discussion of the Unhappy Marriage of Marxism and Feminism,* edited by Lydia Sargent, 43–79. Boston: South End Press, 1981.

———. "Five Faces of Oppression." *Philosophical Forum* 19, no. 4 (summer 1988).

———. "The Ideal of Community and the Politics of Difference." In *Feminism/Postmodernism,* edited by Linda J. Nicholson, 300–323. New York: Routledge, 1990.

Contemporary Women's Labor Issues

Alonso-Zaldivar, Ricardo. "Care Homes Hiring More Foreigners." *Los Angeles Times,* October 20, 2005, http://articles.latimes.com/2005/oct/20/nation/na-immig20.

Amott, Teresa, and Julie Matthaei. "Comparable Worth, Incomparable Pay." *Radical America* 18, no. 5 (September/October 1984): 25.

———. *Race, Gender, and Work: A Multicultural Economic History of Women in the United States.* Boston: South End Press, 1981.

Bar-Lev, Abby. "Equal Pay Still Unequal." *Minnesota Daily*, November 30, 2006, http://www.mndaily.com/2006/11/30/equal-pay-still-unqual.

Bergmann, Barbara. *The Economic Emergence of Women.* New York: Basic Books, 1986.

Bettio, Francesca, and Alina Verashchagina, eds. *Frontiers in the Economics of Gender.* New York: Routledge, 2008.

Boserup, Ester. *Women's Role in Economic Development.* London: George Allen and Unwin, 1970.

Bowers, Katherine. "Ruling OKs Class Action Suit Against Wal-Mart." *Women's Wear Daily* 193, no. 29 (February 7, 2007): 39.

Bureau of Labor Statistics, US Department of Labor. "Median Weekly Earnings of Full-Time Wage and Salary Workers by Detailed Occupation and Sex." ftp://ftp.bls.gov/pub/special.requests/lf/aat39.txt.

Caraway, Teri L. *Assembling Women: The Feminization of Global Manufacturing.* Ithaca, NY: Cornell University Press, 2007.

Collins, Jane L., and Victoria Mayer. *Both Hands Tied: Welfare Reform and the Race to the Bottom in the Low-Wage Labor Market.* Chicago: University of Chicago Press, 2012.

Eisenstein, Hester. *Feminism Seduced: How Global Elites Use Women's Labor and Ideas to Exploit the World.* Boulder, CO: Paradigm Publishers, 2010.

Equal Pay Act of 1963 (Pub. L. 88-93) (EPA), as amended, as it appears in volume 29 of the United States Code, at section 206(d).

Feldberg, Roslyn L. "Comparable Worth: Toward Theory and Practice in the United States." *Signs: Journal of Women in Culture and Society* 10, no. 2 (winter 1984): 311–313.

Goodman, Jacqueline. *Global Perspectives on Gender and Work: Readings and Interpretations.* Lanham, MD: Rowman & Littlefield, 2010.

Gordon, David M., Richard Edwards, and Michael Reich. *Segmented Work, Divided Workers.* New York: Cambridge University Press, 1982.

Harley, Sharon, ed. *Women's Labor in the Global Economy: Speaking in Multiple Voices.* Piscataway, NJ: Rutgers University Press, 2011.

Hennessy-Fiske, Molly. "Gender Pay Gap Narrows—for Unexpected Reasons." *Los Angeles Times*, December 3, 2006, A23.

Hochschild, Arlie. "Global Care Chains and Emotional Surplus Valve." *Global Capitalism*, edited by Will Hutton and Anthony Giddens, 130–146. New York: New Press, 2000.

———. *Second Shift.* New York: Penguin, 2003.

Howes, Ruth H. *Their Day in the Sun: Women of the Manhattan Project.* Philadelphia: Temple University Press, 1999.

Joyce, Amy. "Unusual Job Title: A Sign of the Times." *Merced (California) Sun-Star*, December 23, 2006, 1.

Lamar, Jake. "A Worthy but Knotty Question." *Time*, February 6, 1984, 30.

Laughlin, Kathleen A. *Women's Work and Public Policy: A History of the Women's Bureau, U.S. Department of Labor, 1945–1970*. Boston: Northeastern University Press, 2000.

Ledbetter, Lilly, and Lanier Scott Isom. *Grace and Grit: My Fight for Equal Pay and Fairness at Goodyear and Beyond*. New York: Crown Archetype, 2012.

Murphy, Evelyn. *Getting Even: Why Women Don't Get Paid like Men—and What to Do About It*. New York: Touchstone, 2005.

Nussbaum, Karen. "Women Clerical Workers." *Socialist Review* 10, no. 1 (January/February 1980): 151–159.

"Part-Time Programs Do Help Firms Hold On to Women Lawyers." *Law Office Management & Administration Report* 7, no. 5 (May 2007): 3.

"Paying Women What They're Worth." *QQ Report from the Center for Philosophy and Public Policy* 3, no. 2 (spring 1983).

Pfister, Bonnie. "It's National Equal Pay Day—and U.S. Women Earn 77 Cents to a Man's Dollar." *San Antonio Express-News*, April 20, 2004.

Pratt, Geraldine. *Working Feminism*. Philadelphia: Temple University Press, 2004.

Pyle, Jean, and Kathryn Ward. "Recasting Our Understanding of Gender and Work During Global Restructuring." *International Sociology* 18, no. 3 (2003): 461–489.

Remick, Helen. "Major Issues in A Priori Applications." In *Comparable Worth and Wage Discrimination: Technical Possibilities and Political Realities*, edited by Helen Remick. Philadelphia: Temple University Press, 1984.

Scott, Hilda. *Working Your Way to the Bottom*. London: Pandora Press, 1984.

Sixel, L. M. "EEOC Alleges Unequal Pay for Same Work." *Houston Chronicle*, August 23, 2005, 94.

Stone, Pamela. *Opting Out? Why Women Really Quit Careers and Head Home*. Berkeley: University of California Press, 2007.

Thomas, G. Scott. "Where the Men, and Women, Work." *American City Business Journals*, April 19, 2004, http://www.bizjournals.com/edit_special/12/html.

US Department of Labor. "Employment Standards Administration Wage and Hour Division," January 1, 2007, http://www.dol.gov/esa/minwage/america.htm #content.

Weeks, Kathi. *The Problem with Work: Feminism, Marxism, Antiwork Politics, and Postwork Imaginaries*. Durham, NC: Duke University Press, 2011.

World Bank Group. "Globalization." http://go.worldbank.org/V7BJE9FD30.

Critiques of Marxist and Socialist Feminisms

Anyon, Jean. "The Retreat of Marxism and Socialist Feminism: Postmodern and Poststructural Theories in Education." *Curriculum Inquiry* 24, no. 2 (summer 1994): 115–133.

Barrett, Michèle. *Women's Oppression Today: Problems in Marxist Feminist Analysis.* London: Verso, 1980.

Beasley, Chris. *What Is Feminism?* London: Sage Publications, 1999.

Bettie, Julie. "Women Without Class: Chicas, Cholas, Trash, and the Presence/Absence of Class Identity." *Signs: Journal of Women in Culture and Society* 26, no. 1 (2000): 1–35.

Boxer, Marilyn J. "Rethinking the Socialist Construction and International Career of the Concept 'Bourgeois Feminism.'" *American Historical Review* 112, no. 1 (February 2007): 131–158.

Bryson, Valerie. *Feminist Debates: Issues of Theory and Political Practice.* New York: New York University Press, 1999.

Frazer, Nancy. *Justice Interruptus: Critical Reflections on the "Post-socialist" Condition.* New York: Routledge, 1997.

Gimenez, Martha E. "What's Material About Materialist Feminism? A Marxist Feminist Critique." *Radical Philosophy* 11 (May/June 2000): 18–28.

Grosz, Elizabeth. *Volatile Bodies: Toward a Corporeal Feminism.* Bloomington: Indiana University Press, 1994.

Hartmann, Heidi, and Ann R. Markusen. "Contemporary Marxist Theory and Practice: A Feminist Critique." *Review of Radical Political Economics* 12, no. 2 (summer 1980): 87–93.

Voronina, Olga. "Soviet Patriarchy: Past and Present." *Hypatia* 8, no. 4 (fall 1993): 107.

Weinbaum, Batya. *The Curious Courtship of Women's Liberation and Socialism.* Boston: South End Press, 1978.

Chapter 4: Women-of-Color Feminism(s) in the United States

Women-of-Color Feminism(s) and the "First Wave"

Cooper, Anna Julia. *A Voice from the South: By a Woman from the South.* New York: Oxford University Press, 1988.

Davis, Angela Y. *Women, Race, and Class.* New York: Random House, 1981.

Joseph, Gloria I. "Sojourner Truth: Archetypal Feminist." In *Wild Women in the Whirlwind*, edited by Jeanne Braxton and Andreen Nicola McLaughlin. New Brunswick: Rutgers University Press, 1990.

Mabee, Carleton. *Sojourner Truth: Slave, Prophet, Legend.* New York: New York University Press, 1993.

Spillers, Hortense J. *Comparative American Identities: Race, Sex, and Nationality in Modern Text.* New York: Routledge, 1991.

Stanton, Elizabeth Cady, Susan B. Anthony, and Matilda Joslyn Gage, eds. *History of Woman Suffrage.* Vol. 1: *1848–1861.* New York: Fowler and Wells, 1881. Reprinted by New York: Arno Press, 1969.

Women-of-Color Feminism(s) and the "Second Wave"

Cannon, Katie G. 1988. *Black Womanist Ethics.* Atlanta: Scholars Press, 1989.

Collins, Patricia. "What's in a Name: Womanism, Black Feminism, and Beyond." *Black Scholar* 26, no. 1 (1996): 9–17.

Combahee River Collective. "A Black Feminist Statement." In *All the Women Are White, All the Blacks Are Men, but Some of Us Are Brave: Black Women's Studies,* edited by Gloria T. Hull, Patricia Bell Scott, and Barbara Smith. New York: Feminist Press, 1982.

Davis, Angela Y. *Angela Davis: An Autobiography.* New York: International Publishers, 1988.

Giddings, Paula. *When and Where I Enter: The Impact of Black Women and Race and Sex in America.* New York: Bantam Books, 1984.

hooks, bell. *Ain't I a Woman: Black Women and Feminism.* New York: Routledge, 1987.

Hull, Gloria T., Patricia Bell Scott, and Barbara Smith, eds. *All the Women Are White, All the Blacks Are Men, but Some of Us Are Brave: Black Women's Studies.* New York: Feminist Press, 1982.

King, Deborah. "Womanist, Womanism, Womanish." In *Women's Studies Encyclopedia,* edited by Helen Tierney. Rev. exp. ed. New York: Greenwood Press, 1999.

Lorde, Audre. *I Am Your Sister: Black Women Organizing Across Sexualities.* New York: Kitchen Table/Women of Color Press, 1985.

———. *Sister Outsider: Essays and Speeches.* Berkeley, CA: Crossing Press, 1984.

———. *Zami, a New Spelling of My Name: A Biomythography.* Freedom, CA: The Crossing Press, 1982.

Pinkney, Alphonso. *Black Nationalism in the United States.* London: Cambridge University Press, 1976.

Ramazanoglu, Caroline. *Feminism and the Contradictions of Oppression.* London: Routledge, 1989.

Van Deburg, William L. *New Day in Babylon: The Black Power Movement and American Culture, 1963–1975.* Chicago: University of Chicago Press, 1992.

Walker, Alice. *In Search of Our Mothers' Gardens: Womanist Prose.* New York: Harcourt Brace Jovanovich, 1983.

Women-of-Color Feminism(s) and the "Third Wave"

Albrecht, Lisa, and Rose M. Brewer, eds. *Bridges of Power: Women's Multicultural Alliances.* Philadelphia: New Society Publishers, 1990.

Alcoff, Linda Martín. *Visible Identities: Race, Gender, and the Self.* Oxford: Oxford University Press, 2006.

———. "What Should White People Do?." *Hypatia* 13, no. 3 (summer 1998): 6–26.

Bailey, Alison, and Jacquelyn Zita. "The Reproduction of Whiteness: Race and the Regulation of the Gendered Body." *Hypatia* 22, no. 2 (spring 2007): vii–xv.

Bulkin, Elly, Minnie Bruce Pratt, and Barbara Smith. *Yours in Struggle: Three Feminist Perspectives on Anti-Semitism and Racism.* Ithaca, NY: Firebrand Books, 1984.

Chock, Phyllis Pease. "Culturalism: Pluralism, Culture, and Race in the *Harvard Encyclopedia of American Ethnic Groups.*" In *(Multi)culturalism and the Baggage of "Race."* Special issue, *Identities: Global Studies in Culture and Power* 1, no. 4 (April 1985): 301–324.

Crenshaw, Kimberlé. "Mapping the Margins: Intersectionality, Identity, Politics, and Violence Against Women of Color." In *Critical Race Theory: The Key Writings That Formed the Movement*, edited by Kimberlé Crenshaw, Neil Gotanda, Gary Peller, and Kendall Thomas. New York: New Press, 1995.

Crenshaw, Kimberlé, Neil Gotanda, and Gary Peller, eds. *Critical Race Theory: The Key Writings That Formed the Movement.* New York: New Press, 1996.

Davis, Angela Y. "Gender, Class, and Multiculturalism: Rethinking 'Race' Politics." In *Mapping Multiculturalism*, edited by Avery R. Gordon and Christopher Newfield, 40–48. Minneapolis: University of Minnesota Press, 1996.

———. *Women, Race, and Class.* New York: Random House, 1981.

Dicker, Susan. *Languages in America: A Pluralist View.* Philadelphia: Multilingual Matters Limited, 1966.

DuBois, Ellen Carol, and Vicki L. Ruiz, eds. *Unequal Sisters: A Multicultural Reader in U.S. Women's History.* New York: Routledge, 1990.

Eisenstein, Zillah R. *Hatreds: Racialized and Sexualized Conflicts in the 21st Century.* New York: Routledge, 1996.

Essed, Philomena, and Rita Gircour. *Diversity: Gender, Color, and Culture.* Amherst: University of Massachusetts Press, 1996.

Ferguson, Russell, Martha Gever, Trinh T. Minh-ha, and Cornel West, eds. *Out There: Marginalization and Contemporary Cultures.* New York: New Museum of Contemporary Art, 1991.

Fernandes Botts, Tina. "Hermeneutics, Race, and Gender." In *The Routledge Companion to Philosophical Hermeneutics*, edited by Jeff Malpas and Hans-Helmuth Gander. New York: Routledge, 2013.

Fernandez, Carlos. "La Raza and the Melting Pot: A Comparative Look at Multiethnicity." In *Racially Mixed People in America*, edited by Maria P. Root. Newbury Park, CA: Sage, 1992.

Fowers, Blaine J., and Frank C. Richardson. "Why Is Multiculturalism Good?." *American Psychologist* 51, no. 6 (June 1996): 609.

Frankenberg, Ruth. *White Women, Race Matters.* Minneapolis: University of Minnesota Press, 1993.

Fraser, Nancy, and Axel Honneth. *Redistribution or Recognition? A Political-Philosophical Exchange.* Translated by Joel Golb, James Ingram, and Christiane Wilke. London: Verso, 2003.

Fusco, Coco. *English Is Broken Here: Notes on Cultural Fusion in the Americas.* New York: New Press, 1995.

Glazer, Nathan, and Daniel Patrick Moynihan. *Beyond the Melting Pot: The Negroes, Puerto Ricans, Jews, Italians, and Irish of New York City.* 2nd ed. Cambridge: Massachusetts Institute of Technology Press, 1970.

Haraway, Donna J. *Private Visions: Gender, Race, and Nature in the World of Modern Science.* New York: Routledge, 1989.

Harris, Cheryl I. "Whiteness as Property." In *Critical Race Theory: The Key Writings That Formed the Movement,* edited by Kimberlé Crenshaw, Neil Gotanda, Gary Peeler, and Kendall Thomas. New York: New Press, 1995.

Hochschild, Jennifer. *Facing Up to the American Dream: Race, Class, and the Soul of the Nation.* Princeton, NJ: Princeton University Press, 1995.

Hollinger, David A. *Post-ethnic America: Beyond Multiculturalism.* New York: Harper Collins, 1995.

Kirk, Gwyn. *Women's Lives: Multicultural Perspectives.* New York: McGraw Hill, 2009.

Lee, Jung Young. *Marginality: The Key to Multicultural Theology.* Minneapolis: Fortress Press, 1995.

Matisons, Michelle Renee. "Feminism and Multiculturalism: The Dialogue Continues." *Social Theory and Practice* 29, no. 4 (October 2003): 655–664.

McIntosh, Peggy. "White Privilege and Male Privilege: A Personal Account of Coming to See Correspondences Through Work in Women's Studies." In *Critical White Studies: Looking Behind the Mirror,* edited by Richard Delgado and Jean Stefanic. Philadelphia: Temple University Press, 1997.

Mookherjee, Monica. "Review Article: Feminism and Multiculturalism—Putting Okin and Shachar in Question." *Journal of Moral Philosophy* 2, no. 2 (2005): 237–241.

———. *Women's Rights as Multicultural Claims: Reconfiguring Gender and Diversity in Political Philosophy.* Edinburgh: Edinburgh University Press, 2009.

Moya, Paula M. L. *Learning from Experience: Minority Identities, Multicultural Struggles.* Berkeley: University of California Press, 2002.

Newman, Louise Michele. *White Women's Rights: The Racial Origins of Feminism in the United States.* New York: Oxford University Press, 1999.

Okin, Susan M. *Is Multiculturalism Bad for Women?* Princeton, NJ: Princeton University Press, 1999.

Pearson, Jonna Lian. "Multicultural Feminism and Sisterhood Among Women of Color in Social Change Dialogue." *Howard Journal of Communications* 18 (2007): 88.

Phillips, Anne. "Multiculturalism, Universalism, and the Claims of Democracy." In *Gender Justice, Development, and Rights,* edited by Maxine Molyneux and Shahra Razavi. Oxford: Oxford University Press, 2002.

Powell, Timothy B. "All Colors Flow into Rainbows and Nooses: The Struggle to Define Academic Multiculturalism." *Cultural Critique* 55 (fall 2003): 152–181.

Raz, Joseph. "Multiculturalism: A Liberal Perspective." *Dissent* (winter 1994): 74.

Scheman, Naomi. *Engendering: Construction of Knowledge, Authority, and Privilege.* New York: Routledge, 1993.

Schlesinger, Arthur M., Jr. *The Disuniting of America.* Knoxville, TN: Whittle Books, 1990.

Schueller, Malini Johar. "Analogy and (White) Feminist Theory: Thinking Race and the Color of the Cyborg Body." *Signs: Journal of Women in Culture and Society* 31, no. 1 (autumn 2005): 63–92.

Spelman, Elizabeth V. *Inessential Woman: Problems of Exclusion in Feminist Thought.* Boston: Beacon Press, 1998.

Spinner-Halev, Jeff. "Feminism, Multiculturalism, Oppression, and the State." *Ethics* 112 (October 2001): 84–113.

Takaki, Ronald. *A Different Mirror: A History of Multicultural America.* New York: Oxford University Press, 1993.

Ware, Vron. *Beyond the Pale: White Women, Racism, and History.* New York: Verso, 1992.

Wiegman, Robyn. *American Anatomies: Theorizing Race and Gender.* Durham, NC: Duke University Press, 1995.

Wing, Adrien Katherine, ed. *Critical Race Feminism: A Reader.* New York: New York University Press, 1997.

Zack, Naomi. *Women of Color and Philosophy: A Critical Reader.* Oxford, UK: Blackwell Publishers, 2000.

Zinn, Maxine Baca, and Bonnie Thornton Dill, eds. *Women of Color in U.S. Society.* Philadelphia: Temple University Press, 1994.

Distinct Women-of-Color Feminism(s)

BLACK FEMINISM

Berry, Mary Frances. *My Face Is Black Is True: Callie House and the Struggle for Ex-Slave Reparations.* New York: Alfred A. Knopf, 2005.

Bobo, Jacqueline. *Black Women as Cultural Readers.* New York: Columbia University Press, 1995.

Carby, Hazel. *Reconstructing Womanhood: The Emergence of the Afro-American Woman Novelist.* New York: Oxford University Press, 1987.

Collins, Patricia Hill. *Black Feminist Thought: Knowledge, Consciousness, and the Politics of Empowerment.* Boston: Unwin Hyman, 1990.

———. "Learning from the Outsider Within: The Sociological Significance of Black Feminist Thought." In *Feminist Approaches to Theory and Methodology: An Interdisciplinary Reader*, edited by Sharlene Hesse-Biber, Christina Gilmartin, and Robin Lydenberg. New York: Oxford, 1999.

Higashida, Cheryl. *Black Internationalist Feminism: Women Writers of the Black Left, 1945–1995.* Champaign: University of Illinois Press, 2011.

hooks, bell. *Feminist Theory: From Margin to Center*. Boston: South End Press, 1984.
———. *Talking Back: Thinking Feminist, Thinking Black*. Boston: South End Press, 1989.
———. *Yearning: Race, Gender and Cultural Politics*. Boston: South End Press, 1990.
James, Stanlie M., and Abena P. A. Busia, eds. *Theorizing Black Feminisms: The Visionary Pragmatism of Black Women*. New York: Routledge, 1993.
Kim, Elaine H. *Asian American Literature: An Introduction to the Writings and Their Social Context*. Philadelphia: Temple University Press, 1984.
King, Deborah. "Multiple Jeopardy: The Context of a Black Feminist Ideology." In *Feminist Frameworks*, edited by Alison M. Jaggar and Paula S. Rothenberg. 3rd ed. New York: McGraw-Hill, 1993.
Lorde, Audre. "Age, Race, Class, and Sex: Women Redefining Difference." In *Race, Class, and Gender*, edited by Margaret L. Andersen and Patricia Hill Collins. 2nd ed. Belmont, CA: Wadsworth, 1995.
McDuffie, Eric. *Sojourning for Freedom: Black Women, American Communism, and the Making of Black Left Feminism*. Durham, NC: Duke University Press, 2011.
Mosley, Albert G. "Negritude, Nationalism, and Nativism: Racists or Racialists?." In *Racism*, edited by Leonard Harris. Amherst, NY: Humanity Books, 1999.
Smith, Barbara, ed. *Home Girls: A Black Feminist Anthology*. Latham, NY: Kitchen Table/Women of Color Press, 1983.
White, Aaronette M. *African Americans Doing Feminism: Putting Theory into Everyday Practice*. Albany: State University of New York Press, 2010.
———. *Ain't I a Feminist? African American Men Speak Out on Fatherhood, Friendship, Forgiveness, and Freedom*. Albany: State University of New York Press, 2008.
Zackodnik, Teresa C. *"We Must Be Up and Doing": A Reader in Early African American Feminisms*. Peterborough, Ontario: Broadview Press, 2010.

LATIN AMERICAN/LATINA/CHICANA FEMINISM

Alcoff, Linda Martín. *Visible Identities: Race, Gender, and the Self*. Oxford: Oxford University Press, 2006.
Alvarez, Sonia. "Latin American Feminism 'Go Global': Trends of the 1990s and Challenges for the New Millennium." In *Cultures of Politics/Politics of Cultures: Revisioning Latin American Social Movements*, edited by S. Alvarez, E. Dagnin, and A. Escobar, 93–115. Boulder, CO: Westview Press, 1998.
Anzaldúa, Gloria. *Borderlands/La Frontera: The New Mestiza*. San Francisco: Aunt Lute Books, 1999.
———, ed. *Making Face, Making Soul/Haciendo Caras: Creative and Critical Perspectives by Women of Color*. San Francisco: Aunt Lute Books, 1990.
Anzaldúa, Gloria, and Cherríe Moraga, eds. *This Bridge Called My Back: Writings by Radical Women of Color*. San Francisco: Aunt Lute Books, 1999.

Arredondo, Gabriela F., Aída Hurtado, Norma Klahn, Olga Nájera-Ramírez, and Patricia Zavella, eds. *Chicana Feminisms: A Critical Reader.* Durham, NC: Duke University Press, 2003.

Asencio, Marysol, and Katie Acosta. "Macho Men and Passive Women: Debunking Myths About the Sexualities of Latinos." *Conscience: The News Journal of Catholic Opinion* 28, no. 2 (summer 2007): 11–14.

Blea, Irene I. *La Chicana and the Intersection of Race, Class, and Gender.* Westport, CT: Praeger, 1992.

Dávila, Arlene. *Latinos, Inc.: The Marketing and Making of a People.* Berkeley: University of California Press, 2001.

Flores, William V., and Rina Benmayor. *Latino Cultural Citizenship: Claiming Identity, Space, and Rights.* Boston: Beacon Press, 1997.

Haney López, Ian F. "Race and Erasure: The Salience of Race to Latinos/as." In *The Latino Condition*, edited by Richard Delgado and Jean Stefancic. New York: New York University Press, 1998.

Lugones, Maria, and Elisabeth Spelman. "Have We Got a Theory for You! Feminist Theory, Cultural Imperialism, and the Demand for the Woman's Voice." In *Feminist Philosophies*, edited by Janet A. Kourany, James Sterba, and Rosemarie Tong. Englewood Cliffs, NJ: Prentice Hall, 1992.

Moraga, Cherríe. *Loving in the War Years: Lo Que Nunca Pasó por Sus Labios.* Boston: South End Press, 1983.

Oboler, Suzanne. *Ethnic Labels, Latino Lives: Identity and the Politics of (Re)presentation in the United States.* Minneapolis: University of Minnesota Press, 1995.

Ramirez, Deborah A. "It's Not Just Black and White Anymore." In *The Latino Condition*, edited by Richard Delgado and Jean Stefancic. New York: New York University Press, 1998.

Ramos, Juanita, ed. *Compañeras: Latina Lesbians.* New York: Latina Lesbian History Project, 1987.

Rosaldo, Renato. "Identity Politics: An Ethnography by a Participant." In *Identity Politics Reconsidered*, edited by Linda Martín Alcoff, Michael Hames-García, Satya P. Mohanty, and Paula M. L. Moya. New York: Palgrave Macmillan, 2006.

Saldívar-Hull, Sonia. *Feminism on the Border: Chicana Gender Politics and Literature.* Berkeley: University of California Press, 2000.

Schutte, Ofelia. "Cultural Alterity: Cross-Cultural Communication and Feminist Theory in North-South Contexts." In *Decentering the Center: Philosophy for a Multicultural, Postcolonial, and Feminist World*, edited by Uma Narayan and Sandra Harding. Bloomington: Indiana University Press, 2000. First published in *Hypatia* 13, no. 2 (spring 1998): 53–72.

———. *Cultural Identity and Social Liberation in Latin American Thought.* Albany: State University of New York Press, 1993.

Trujillo, Carla, ed. *Chicana Lesbians: The Girls Our Mothers Warned Us About.* Berkeley: Third Woman Press, 1991.

Zea, Leopoldo. "Identity: A Latin American Philosophical Problem." *Philosophical Forum* 20 (fall/winter 1988–1989): 33–42.

ASIAN AMERICAN FEMINISM

Asian Women United of California, eds. *Making Waves: An Anthology of Writings by and About Asian American Women.* Boston: Beacon Press, 1989.

Cha, Theresa Hak Kyung. *Dictee.* New York: Tanam Press, 1982.

Chen, Ya-chen. *The Many Dimensions of Chinese Feminism.* New York: Palgrave Macmillan, 2011.

Hongo, Garrett, ed. *Under Western Eyes: Personal Essays from Asian-Americans.* New York: Anchor Books, 1995.

Katjasungkana, Nursyahbani, and Saskia E. Wieringa, eds. *The Future of Asian Feminisms: Confronting Fundamentalisms, Conflicts and Neo-liberalism.* Newcastle upon Tyne, UK: Cambridge Scholars Publishing, 2012.

Kim, Elaine H., and Lilia V. Villanueva, eds. *Making More Waves: New Asian American Writing by Asian Women.* Boston: Beacon Press, 1997.

Kim, Elaine H., and Eui-Young Yu. *East to America: Korean American Life Stories.* New York: New Press, 1995.

Klasen, Stephan, and Claudia Wink. "A Turning Point in Gender Bias in Mortality? An Update on the Number of Missing Women." *Population and Development Review* 28, no. 2 (January 2002): 285–312.

Loomba, Ania, and Ritty A. Lukose, eds. *South Asian Feminisms.* Durham, NC: Duke University Press, 2012.

Lowe, Lisa. "Heterogeneity, Hybridity, Multiplicity: Making Asian American Difference." *Diaspora* 1 (1991): 24–44.

Marchetti, Gina. *Romance and the "Yellow Peril": Race, Sex, and Discursive Strategies in Hollywood Fiction.* Berkeley: University of California Press, 1994.

Okihiro, Gary. *Margins to Mainstreams: Asians in American History and Culture.* Seattle: University of Washington Press, 1994.

Sen, Amartya. "More Than 100 Million Women Are Missing." *New York Review of Books,* December 20, 1990, http://www.nybooks.com/articles/1990/12/20/more-than-100-million-women-are-missing.

Takagi, Dana Y. *The Retreat from Race: Asian-American Admissions and Racial Politics.* New Brunswick, NJ: Rutgers University Press, 1992.

Wong, Diane Yen-Mei. *Dear Diane: Letters from Our Daughters.* San Francisco: San Francisco Study Center, 1983.

Wu, Frank. *Yellow: Race in America Beyond Black and White.* New York: Basic Books, 2002.

INDIGENOUS FEMINISM

Allen, Paula Gunn. "Kochinnenako in Academe: Three Approaches to Interpreting a Keres Indian Tale." In *Feminist Theory: A Reader,* edited by Wendy K. Kolmar and Frances Bartkowski. New York: McGraw-Hill, 2013.

————. *The Sacred Hoop: Recovering the Feminine in American Indian Traditions.* Boston: Beacon Press, 1986.

————, ed. *Spider Woman's Granddaughters: Traditional Tales and Contemporary Writing by Native American Women.* Boston: Beacon Press, 1986.

Bataille, Gretchen, and Kathleen Mullen Sands. *American Indian Women: Telling Their Lives.* Lincoln: University of Nebraska Press, 1984.

Dearborn, Mary V. *Pocahontas's Daughters: Gender and Ethnicity in American Culture.* New York: Oxford University Press, 1986.

Green, Rayna. *Indians of North America: Women in American Indian Society.* New York: Chelsea House Publishers, 1992.

————. *Native American Women: A Contextual Bibliography.* Bloomington: Indiana University Press, 1983.

Guerrero, M. A. Jaimes. "'Patriarchal Colonialism' and Indigenism: Implications for Native Feminist Spirituality and Native Womanism." *Hypatia* 18, no. 2 (spring 2003): 58–69.

James, M. Annette, ed. *The State of Native America: Genocide, Colonization, and Resistance.* Boston: South End Press, 1992.

Kailo, Kaarina. *Wo(men) and Bears: The Gifts of Nature, Culture and Gender Revisited.* Toronto: Inanna Publications, 2008.

Lawrence, Bonita. "Gender, Race, and the Regulation of Native Identity in Canada and the United States: An Overview." *Hypatia* 18, no. 2 (spring 2003): 3–31.

Mihesuah, Devon Abbott. *Indigenous American Women: Decolonization, Empowerment, Activism.* Lincoln: University of Nebraska Press, 2003.

Pillow, Wanda. "Searching for Sacajawea: Whitened Reproductions and Endarkened Representations." *Hypatia* 22, no. 2 (spring 2007): 1–19.

Poupart, Lisa. "The Familiar Face of Genocide: Internalized Oppression Among American Indians." *Hypatia* 18, no. 2 (spring 2003): 86–100.

Sarris, Greg. *Keeping Slug Women Alive: A Holistic Approach to American Indian Texts.* Berkeley: University of California Press, 1993.

Sellers, Stephanie A. *Native American Women's Studies: A Primer.* New York: Peter Lang Publishing, 2008.

Silko, Leslie Marmon. *Yellow Woman and a Beauty of Spirit: Essays on Native American Life Today.* New York: Touchstone/Simon & Schuster, 1997.

Smith, Andy. "Not an Indian Tradition: The Sexual Colonization of Native Peoples." *Hypatia* 18, no. 2 (spring 2003): 70–85.

Suzack, Cheryl, Shari M. Huhndorf, Jeanne Perreault, and Jean Barman, eds. *Indigenous Women and Feminism: Politics, Activism, Culture.* Vancouver: University of British Columbia Press, 2011.

Vest, Jennifer Lisa. "Names." *Canadian Journal of Native Studies* 30, no. 1 (spring 2010): 155–160.

Waters, Anne. "Introduction: Indigenous Women in the Americas." *Hypatia* 18, no. 2 (spring 2003): ix–xx.

Critiques of Women-of-Color Feminism(s) in the United States

Chang, Robert S., and Jerome McCristal Culp Jr. "After Intersectionality." *UMKC Law Review* 71, no. 2 (2002): 485–491.

Ehrenreich, Nancy. "Subordination and Symbiosis: Mechanisms of Mutual Support Between Subordinating Systems." *UMKC Law Review* 71, no. 2 (2002): 251.

Gubar, Susan. "What Ails Feminist Criticism?." *Critical Inquiry* 24 (summer 1988): 878–902.

Loo, Lindsey. "Feminism and Race: Just Who Counts as a Woman of Color?." *Code Switch*, September 12, 2013, http://www.npr.org/sections/codeswitch/2013/09/12/221469077/feminism-and-race-just-who-counts-as-a-woman-of-color.

Warnke, Georgia. "Race, Gender, and Antiessentialist Politics." *Signs: Journal of Women in Culture and Society* 31, no. 1 (autumn 2005): 93–116.

Chapter 5: Women-of-Color Feminism(s) on the World Stage: Global, Postcolonial, and Transnational Feminisms

Global Feminism in General

Amnesty International. *Human Rights Are Women's Right.* New York: Amnesty International Publications, 1995.

Barber, Benjamin. *Jihad vs. McWorld: How Globalism and Tribalism Are Reshaping the World.* New York: Ballantine, 1995.

Barry, Kathleen. *The Prostitution of Sexuality: The Global Exploitation of Women.* New York: New York University Press, 1995.

Benhabib, Seyla. *Claims of Culture: Equality and Diversity in the Global Era.* Princeton, NJ: Princeton University Press, 2002.

Bunch, Charlotte. "Women's Rights as Human Rights: Toward a Re-vision of Human Rights." *Human Rights Quarterly* 12, no. 4 (November 1990): 486–498.

Burn, Shawn Meghan. *Women Across Cultures: A Global Perspective.* Mountain View, CA: Mayfield Publishing, 2000.

Cohen, Colleen Ballerino, Richard Wilk, and Beverly Stoeltje. *Beauty Queens on the Global Stage: Gender, Contests, and Power.* New York: Routledge, 1996.

Crystal, David. *English as a Global Language.* Cambridge: Cambridge University Press, 1997.

Ehrenreich, Barbara, and Annette Fuentes. *Women in the Global Factory.* Boston: South End Press, 1983.

Eisenstein, Hester. *Feminism Seduced: How Global Elites Use Women's Labor and Ideas to Exploit the World.* Boulder, CO: Paradigm Publishers, 2010.

Eschle, Catherine, and Bice Maiguascha. *Making Feminist Sense of the Global Justice Movement.* Lanham, MD: Rowman & Littlefield Publishers, 2010.

Ferguson, Ann. "Resisting the Veil of Privilege: Building Bridge Identities as an Ethico-politics of Global Feminisms." *Hypatia* 13, no. 3 (summer 1998): 95–113.

Ferree, Myra Marx. *Varieties of Feminism: German Gender Politics in Global Perspective*. Stanford, CA: Stanford University Press, 2012.

Freeman, Carla. *High Tech and High Heels in the Global Economy: Women, Work, and Pink-Collar Identities in the Caribbean*. Durham, NC: Duke University Press, 1991.

Friedman, Jonathan. "Global System, Globalization and the Parameters of Modernity." In *Global Modernities*, edited by Mike Featherstone, Scott Lash, and Roland Robertson. London: Sage, 1995.

Friedman, Thomas. *The Lexus and the Olive Tree: Understanding Globalization*. New York: Picador, 2012.

Ginsburg, Faye, and Rayna Rapp, eds. *Conceiving the New World Order: The Global Politics of Reproduction*. Berkeley: University of California Press, 1995.

Hellsten, Sirrku Kristiina. "From Human Wrongs to Universal Rights: Communication and Feminist Challenges for the Promotion of Women's Health in the Third World." *Developing World Bioethics* 1, no. 2 (2001): 108–109.

Jabri, Vivienne. "Feminist Ethics and Hegemonic Global Politics." *Alternatives* 29 (2004): 275.

Jaggar, Alison. "Globalizing Feminist Ethics." *Hypatia* 13 (1998): 7–31.

———. "Vulnerable Women and Neo-liberal Globalization: Debt Burdens Undermine Women's Health in the Global South." *Theoretical Medicine and Bioethics* 23, no. 6 (2002): 425–440.

King, Anthony D., ed. *Culture, Globalization and the World-System: Contemporary Conditions for the Representation of Identity*. Minneapolis: University of Minnesota Press, 2000.

Koggel, C. "Global Feminism." In *Oxford Handbook of Philosophy*, edited by William Edelglass and Jay L. Garfield, 540–559. Oxford: Oxford University Press, 2011.

Miller, S. "A Feminist Account of Global Responsibility." *Social Theory and Practice* 37, no. 3 (2011): 391–412.

Molyneux, Maxine, and Shahra Razavi, eds. *Gender Justice, Development, and Rights*. Oxford: Oxford University Press, 2002.

Nussbaum, Martha. *Women and Human Development: The Capabilities Approach*. Cambridge: Cambridge University Press, 2001.

———. "Women's Capabilities and Social Justice." In *Gender Justice, Development, and Rights*, edited by Maxine Molyneux and Shahra Razavi. Oxford: Oxford University Press, 2002.

Okin, Susan Moller. "Feminism, Women's Human Rights, and Cultural Differences." *Hypatia* 13, no. 2 (1998): 42.

———. "Inequalities Between Sexes in Different Cultural Contexts." In *Women, Culture, and Development*, edited by Martha Nussbaum and Jonathan Glover. Oxford, UK: Clarendon Press, 1995.

———. "Recognizing Women's Rights as Human Rights." *APA Newsletters* 97, no. 2 (spring 1998).

Paxton, Pamela M., and Melanie M. Hughes. *Women, Politics, and Power: A Global Perspective.* Thousand Oaks, CA: Pine Forge Press, 2007.

Peters, Julia, and Andrea Wolper, eds. *Women's Rights, Human Rights: International Feminist Perspectives.* New York: Routledge, 1995.

Peterson, Spike V., and Laura Parisi. "Are Women Human? It's Not an Academic Question." In *Human Rights Fifty Years On: A Radical Reappraisal,* edited by Tony Evans. Manchester, UK: Manchester University Press, 1998.

Robertson, Roland. *Globalization.* London: Sage, 1992.

————. "Globalization: Time-Space and Homogeneity-Heterogeneity." In *Global Modernities,* edited by Mike Featherstone, Scott Lash, and Roland Robertson, 27. London: Sage, 1995.

Shaw, Martin. *Global Society and International Relations.* Cambridge, UK: Polity Press, 1994.

Tsutsui, Kiyoteru. "Redressing Past Human Rights Violations: Global Dimensions of Contemporary Social Movements." *Social Forces* 85, no. 1 (2006): 331–354.

Walby, Sylvia. "Feminism in a Global Era." *Economy and Society* 31, no. 4 (2002).

Waller, Marguerite, and Sylvia Marcos, eds. *Dialogue and Difference: Feminisms Challenge Globalization.* New York: Palgrave Macmillan, 2005.

Wilson, Shamillah, Anassaya Sengupta, and Kristy Evans, eds. *Defending Our Dreams: Global Feminist Voices for a New Generation.* London: Zed Books, 2005.

Postcolonial Feminism in General

Abdulhadi, Rabab, Evelyn Alsultany, and Nadine Naber, eds. *Arab and Arab American Feminisms: Gender, Violence, and Belonging (Gender, Culture, and Politics in the Middle East).* Syracuse, NY: Syracuse University Press, 2011.

Abu-Lughod, Lila. *Writing Women's Worlds: Bedouin Stories.* Berkeley: University of California Press, 1993.

Afkhami, Mahnaz. *Women in Exile.* Charlottesville: University Press of Virginia, 1994.

Agathangelou, Anna M., and Heather M. Turcotte. "Postcolonial Theories as Critique and Challenge to 'First Worldism.'" In *Gender Matters in Global Politics: A Feminist Introduction to International Relations,* edited by Laura J. Shepard, 44–58. New York: Routledge, 2009.

Ahmed, Leila. *Women and Gender in Islam: Historical Roots of a Modern Debate.* New Haven, CT: Yale University Press, 1992.

Alexander, M. Jacqui, and Chandra Talpade Mohanty, eds. *Feminist Genealogies, Colonial Legacies, Democratic Futures.* New York: Routledge, 1996.

Alexander, Meena. *The Shock of Arrival: Reflections on Postcolonial Experience.* Boston: South End Press, 1996.

Alloula, Malek. *The Colonial Harem.* Minneapolis: University of Minnesota Press, 1986.

Bahadur, Gaiutra. "Should My People Need Me." *Ms.* 22, no. 1 (winter 2012): 40–42.

Bulbeck, Chilla. *Re-orienting Western Feminisms: Women's Diversity in a Postcolonial World.* Cambridge: Cambridge University Press, 1998.

Chaudhuri, Nupur, and Margaret Strobel, eds. *Western Women and Imperialism: Complicity and Resistance.* Bloomington: Indiana University Press, 1992.

Donaldson, Laura E. *Decolonizing Feminisms: Race, Gender and Empire Building.* Chapel Hill: University of North Carolina Press, 1992.

Etienne, Mona, ed. *Women and Colonization: Anthropological Perspectives.* New York: Bergin & Garvey Publishers, 1980.

Green, Mary Jean, Karen Gould, Micheline Rice-Maximin, Keith Walker, and Jack Yeager eds. *Post-colonial Subjects: Francophone Women Writers.* Minneapolis: University of Minnesota Press, 1996.

Harding, Sandra. *Sciences from Below: Feminisms, Postcolonialities, and Modernities.* Durham, NC: Duke University Press, 2008.

Lewis, Reinra, and Sara Mills, eds. *Feminist Postcolonial Theory: A Reader.* New York: Routledge, 2003.

Loomba, Ania. *Colonialism/Postcolonialism.* London: Routledge, 1998.

McClintock, Anne. *Imperial Leather: Race, Gender and Sexuality in the Colonial Contest.* New York: Routledge, 1995.

McClintock, Anne, Aamir Mufti, and Ella Shohat, eds. *Dangerous Liaisons: Gender, Nation, and Post-colonial Perspectives.* Minneapolis: University of Minnesota Press, 1997.

Mohanty, Chandra Talpade, Ann Russo, and Lourdes Torres, eds. *Feminism Without Borders: Decolonizing Theory, Practicing Solidarity.* Durham, NC: Duke University Press, 2003.

———. *Third World Women and the Politics of Feminism.* Bloomington: Indiana University Press, 1991.

———. "Under Western Eyes Revisited: Feminist Solidarity Through Anticapitalist Struggles." *Signs: Journal of Women in Culture and Society* 28, no. 2 (2003): 499–535.

———. "Women Workers and Capitalist Scripts, Ideologies of Domination, Common Interests, and the Politics of Solidarity." In *Feminist Genealogies, Colonial Legacies, Democratic Futures*, edited by M. J. Alexander and Chandra Talpade Mohanty, 3–29. New York: Routledge, 1997.

Narayan, Uma. *Dislocating Cultures: Identities, Traditions, and Third-World Feminisms.* New York: Routledge, 1997.

Narayan, Uma, and Sandra Harding. "Introduction. Border Crossings: Multicultural and Postcolonial Feminist Challenges to Philosophy (Part I)." *Hypatia* 13, no. 2 (spring 1998): 86–106.

———. "Introduction. Border Crossings: Multicultural and Postcolonial Feminist Challenges to Philosophy (Part II)." *Hypatia* 13, no. 3 (summer 1998): 1–5.

Seshadri-Crooks, Kalpana. "At the Margins of Postcolonial Studies." In *The Preoccupation of Postcolonial Studies*, edited by Fawzia Azfal-Khan and Kalpana Seshadri-Crooks. Durham, NC: Duke University Press, 2000.

Sharpe, Jenny. *Allegories of Empire: The Figure of Woman in the Colonial Text.* Minneapolis: University of Minnesota Press, 1993.

Spivak, Gayatri Chakravorty. *A Critique of Postcolonial Reason: Toward a History of the Vanishing Present.* Cambridge, MA: Harvard University Press, 1999.

Suleri, Sara. "Women Skin Deep Feminism and the Postcolonial Condition." *Critical Inquiry* 18, no. 4 (1992): 756–769.

Weedon, Chris. "Key Issues in Postcolonial Feminism: A Western Perspective." *Gender Forum: An Internet Journal of Gender Studies* 1 (2002).

Transnational Feminism in General

Brenner, Johanna. "Transnational Feminism and the Struggle for Global Justice." *New Politics,* 9, no. 2 (2003).

Chowdhury, Elora Halim. "Local Global Feminisms Elsewhere: Braiding US Women of Color and Transnational Feminism." *Cultural Dynamics* 21, no. 1 (March 2009): 51–78.

Conway, J. "Transnational Feminisms Guilding Anti-globalization Solidarities." *Globalizations* 9, no. 3 (2012): 379–393.

Enloe, Cynthia. *Bananas, Beaches, and Bases: Making Feminist Sense of International Politics.* Berkeley: University of California Press, 1989.

Ferree, Myra Marx, and Aili Mari Tripp, eds. *Global Feminism: Transnational Women's Activism, Organizing, and Human Rights.* New York: New York University Press, 2006.

Fonow, Mary Margaret. "Human Rights, Feminism and Transnational Solidarity." In *Just Advocacy? Women's Human Rights, Transnational Feminisms, and the Politics of Representation,* edited by Wendy G. Hasford and Wendy Kozol, 221–243. New Brunswick, NJ: Rutgers University Press, 2005.

Grewal, Inderpal. "On the New Global Feminism and the Family of Nations: Dilemmas of Transnational Feminist Practice." In *Talking Visions: Multicultural Feminism in a Transnational Age,* edited by Ella Shohat, 501–530. Cambridge: Massachusetts Institute of Technology Press, 1998.

———. *Transnational America: Feminisms, Diasporas, Neoliberalisms.* Durham, NC: Duke University Press, 2005.

Jaggar, Alison. "Transnational Cycles of Gendered Vulnerability: A Prologue to a Theory of Global Gender Justice." *Philosophical Topics* 37, no. 2 (2009): 359–377.

Jayawardena, Kumari. *Feminism and Nationalism in the Third World.* London: Zed Books, 1986.

Kaplan, Karen, Norma Alarcon, and Minoo Moallem, eds. *Between Woman and Nation: Nationalisms, Transnational Feminisms, and the State.* Durham, NC: Duke University Press, 1999.

Marciniak, Katarzyna, Anikó Imre, and Áine O'Healy, eds. *Transnational Feminism in Film and Media.* New York: Palgrave Macmillan, 2007.

Mendez, Jennifer Bickham. "Greater Alternatives from a Gender Perspective: Transnational Organizing for Maquila Workers' Rights in Central America." In *Women's Activism in Globalization: Linking Local Struggles and Transnational Politics*, edited by Nancy A. Naples and Maneshi Desai, 121–141. New York: Routledge Press, 2002.

Moghadam, Valentine M. *Globalizing Women: Transnational Feminist Networks*. Baltimore: Johns Hopkins University Press, 2005.

Robinson, Fiona. "After Liberalism in World Politics: Towards an International Political Theory of Care." *Ethics and Social Welfare* 4, no. 2 (2010): 130–144.

Roces, Mina, and Louise Edwards. *Women's Movements in Asia: Feminisms and Transnational Activism*. New York: Routledge, 2010.

Rupp, Leila J., and Verta Taylor. "Forging Feminist Identity in an International Movement: A Collective Identity Approach to Twentieth-Century Feminism." *Signs: Journal of Women in Culture and Society* 24, no. 21 (1999): 363–386.

Rutherford, Alexandra, Rose Capdevila, Vindhya Undurti, and Ingrid Palmary, eds. *Handbook of International Feminism: Perspectives on Psychology, Women, Culture, and Rights*. International and Cultural Psychology. New York: Springer, 2011.

Scholtz, Sally J. *Feminism: A Beginner's Guide*. Oxford, UK: Oneworld Publications, 2010.

Shohat, Ella. "Area Studies, Transnationalism, and the Feminist Production of Knowledge." *Signs: Journal of Women in Culture and Society* 26, no. 4 (2001): 1269–1272.

Sylvester, C. *Feminist Theory and International Relations in a Postmodern Era*. New York: Cambridge University Press, 1994.

Swarr, Amanda Lock, and Richa Nagar. *Critical Transnational Feminist Praxis*. Albany: State University of New York Press, 2010.

Thayer, Millie. *Making Transnational Feminism: Rural Women, NGO Activists, and Northern Donors in Brazil*. New York: Routledge, 2010.

Towns, Ann E. *Women and States: Norms and Hierarchies in International Society*. New York: Cambridge University Press, 2010.

Wiesner-Hanks, M. E. "Crossing Borders in Transnational Gender History." *Journal of Global History* 6, no. 3 (2011): 357–379.

Critiques of Global, Postcolonial, and Transnational Feminisms

Mendosa, B. "Transnational Feminism in Question." *Feminist Theory* 3, no. 3 (2002): 295–314.

Lim, Shirley Geok-lin. "Where in the World Is Transnational Feminism?." *Tulsa Studies in Women's Literature* 23, no. 1 (spring 2004): 7–12.

Tickner, J. Ann, and Laura Sjoberg, eds. *Feminism and International Relations: Conversations About the Past, Present and Future*. New York: Routledge, 2011.

Chapter 6: Psychoanalytic Feminism

Classical Psychoanalytic Thought: Focus on Sigmund Freud

Adler, Alfred. *Understanding Human Nature.* New York: Greenberg, 1927.

Beardsworth, Sara. "Freud's Oedipus and Kristeva's Narcissus: Three Heterogeneities." *Hypatia* 20, no. 1 (winter 2005): 54–77.

Benjamin, Jessica. *The Bonds of Love.* New York: Pantheon Books, 1988.

Bernstein, Anne E., and Gloria Marmar Warner. *An Introduction to Contemporary Psychoanalysis.* New York: J. Aronson, 1981.

Brennan, Teresa. *The Interpretation of the Flesh: Freud and Femininity.* New York: Routledge, 1992.

Cohen, Ira H. *Ideology and Unconscious: Reich, Freud, and Marx.* New York: New York University Press, 1982.

Erdelyi, Matthew Hugh. *Psychoanalysis: Freud's Cognitive Psychology.* New York: W. H. Freeman, 1984.

Freud, Sigmund. *Civilization and Its Discontents.* Translated by James Strachey. New York: W. W. Norton, 1962.

———. *Dora: An Analysis of a Case of Hysteria.* Edited by Philip Rieff. New York: Collier Books, 1963.

———. *The Standard Edition of the Complete Psychological Works of Sigmund Freud.* Edited and translated by James Stachey. Vols. 1–12. London: Hogarth Press, 1968.

Gay, Peter. *Freud: A Life for Our Time.* New York: W. W. Norton, 1988.

Hall, Calvin Springer. *A Primer of Freudian Psychology.* New York: New American Library, 1954.

Jones, Ernest. *The Life and Work of Sigmund Freud.* New York: Basic Books, 1961.

Laplanche, Jean. *The Language of Psychoanalysis.* New York: W. W. Norton, 1973.

Roazen, Paul. *Freud: Political and Social Thought.* New York: Alfred A. Knopf, 1968.

Anglo-American Critiques and Appropriations of Sigmund Freud: Focus on Dorothy Dinnerstein, Nancy Chodorow, and Juliet Mitchell

Chodorow, Nancy. *The Reproduction of Mothering: Psychoanalysis and the Sociology of Gender.* Berkeley: University of California Press, 1978.

———. "Toward a Relational Individualism: The Mediation of Self Through Psychoanalysis." In *Reconstructing Individualism: Autonomy, Individuality, and the Self in Western Thought,* edited by Thomas C. Heller, Morton Sosna, and David E. Wellbury. Stanford, CA: Stanford University Press, 1986.

Dinnerstein, Dorothy. *The Mermaid and the Minotaur: Sexual Arrangements and Human Malaise.* New York: Harper Colophon Books, 1977.

Mitchell, Juliet. *Psychoanalysis and Feminism.* New York: Vintage Books, 1974.

Ortner, Sherry B. "Oedipal Father, Mother's Brother, and the Penis: A Review of Juliet Mitchell's *Psychoanalysis and Feminism.*" *Feminist Studies* 2, nos. 2–3 (1975): 179.

Raymond, Janice. "Female Friendship: Contra Chodorow and Dinnerstein." *Hypatia* 1, no. 2 (fall 1986): 44–45.

Contemporary Psychoanalytic Thought: Focus on Jacques Lacan

Clément, Catherine. *The Lives and Legends of Jacques Lacan.* New York: Columbia University Press, 1983.

Copjec, Joan. *Read My Desire: Lacan Against the Historicists.* Cambridge: Massachusetts Institute of Technology Press, 1994.

Duchen, Claire. *Feminism in France: From May '68 to Mitterrand.* London: Routledge & Kegan Paul, 1986.

Gallop, Jane. *Reading Lacan.* Ithaca, NY: Cornell University Press, 1985.

Grosz, Elizabeth. *Jacques Lacan: A Feminist Introduction.* New York: Routledge, 1990.

Lacan, Jacques. *Écrits: A Selection.* Translated by Alan Sheridan. New York: W. W. Norton, 1977.

———. *The Language of the Self.* Baltimore: Johns Hopkins University Press, 1968.

———. *The Seminar of Jacques Lacan, Book I: Freud's Papers on Technique.* Translated by John Forrester. New York: Norton, 1991.

———. *The Seminar of Jacques Lacan, Book II: The Ego of Freud's Theory and in the Technique of Psychoanalysis.* Translated by Sylvia Tomaselli. New York: Norton, 1991.

———. *The Seminar of Jacques Lacan, Book III: The Psychoses.* Translated by Russell Grigg. New York: Norton, 1993.

———. *The Seminar of Jacques Lacan, Book VII: The Ethics of Psychoanalysis.* Translated by Dennis Porter. New York: Norton, 1992.

———. *The Seminar of Jacques Lacan, Book XI: The Four Fundamental Concepts of Psychoanalysis.* Translated by Alan Sheridan. New York: Norton, 1977.

———. *The Seminar of Jacques Lacan Book XX: On Feminine Sexuality: The Limits of Love and Knowledge.* Translated by Bruce Fink. New York: Norton, 1998.

Leland, Dorothy. "Lacanian Psychoanalysis and French Feminism: Toward an Adequate Political Psychology." *Hypatia* 3, no. 3 (winter 1989): 90–99.

Mitchell, Juliet, and Jacqueline Rose, eds. *Feminine Sexuality: Jacques Lacan and the École Freudienne.* Translated by Jacqueline Rose. New York: W. W. Norton, 1982.

Ragland-Sullivan, Ellie. *Jacques Lacan and the Philosophy of Psychoanalysis.* Chicago: University of Illinois Press, 1986.

Ragland-Sullivan, Ellie, and Mark Bracher. *Lacan and the Subject of Language.* New York: Routledge, 1991.

Roudinesco, Elisabeth. *Jacques Lacan.* Translated by Barbara Bray. New York: Columbia University Press, 1999.

Critique of Jacques Lacan

Gallop, Jane. *Feminism and Psychoanalysis: The Daughter's Seduction.* London: Macmillan, 1983.

Irigaray, Luce. "Cosi Fan Tutti." In *The Continental Aesthetics Reader*, edited by Clive Cazeaux, 377–386. New York: Routledge, 2011.

Rose, Jacqueline. "Introduction—II." In *Feminine Sexuality*, edited by Juliet Mitchell and Jacqueline Rose. New York: W. W. Norton, 1982.

———. *On Not Being Able to Sleep: Psychoanalysis and the Modern World.* London: Vintage, 2003.

Roudinesco, Elisabeth. *Jacques Lacan.* Cambridge: Polity Press, 1997.

Roustang, François, *The Lacanian Delusion.* Translated by Greg Sims. Oxford: Oxford University Press, 1990.

Sokal, Alan D., and Jean Briemont. *Fashionable Nonsense: Postmodern Intellectuals' Abuse of Science.* London: Profile Books, 2011.

Webster, Richard. "The Cult of Lacan: Freud, Lacan and the Mirror Stage," 1994, Richardwebster.net, http://www.richardwebster.net/thecultoflacan.html (accessed October 7, 2014).

"French" Psychoanalytic Feminism: Focus on Luce Irigaray and Julia Kristeva

Beardsworth, Sara. *Julia Kristeva: Psychoanalysis and Modernity.* Albany: State University of New York Press, 2004.

Brennan, Teresa, ed. *Between Feminism and Psychoanalysis.* New York: Routledge, 1989.

———, ed. *History After Lacan.* London: Routledge, 1993.

Burke, Carolyn, Naomi Schor, and Margaret Whitford, eds. *Engaging with Irigaray: Feminist Philosophy and Modern European Thought.* New York: Columbia University Press, 1995.

Butler, Judith. "The Body Politics of Julia Kristeva." In *Revaluing French Feminism*, edited by Nancy Fraser and Sandra Lee Bartky. Bloomington: Indiana University Press, 1992.

Chanter, Tina. *Ethics of Eros: Irigaray's Re-writing of the Philosophers.* New York: Routledge, 1995.

Chanter, Tina, and Ewa Ziarek, eds. *Revolt, Affect, Collectivity: The Unstable Boundaries of Kristeva's Polis.* Albany: State University of New York Press, 2005.

Cimitile, Maria, and Elaine Miller, eds. *Returning to Irigaray: Feminist Philosophy, Politics, and the Question of Unity.* New York: Routledge, 2007.

Fuss, Diana J. "'Essentially Speaking': Luce Irigaray's Language of Essence." In *Re-valuing French Feminism*, edited by Nancy Fraser and Sandra Lee Bartky, 94–112. Bloomington: Indiana University Press, 1992.

Gallop, Jane. *The Daughter's Seduction: Feminism and Psychoanalysis*. Ithaca, NY: Cornell University Press, 1982.

———. *A Politics of Impossible Difference: The Later Work of Luce Irigaray*. Ithaca, NY: Cornell University Press, 2002.

Grosz, Elizabeth, with Pheng Cheah. *Irigaray and the Political Future of Sexual Difference*. Baltimore: Johns Hopkins University Press, 1998.

Huntington, Patricia. *Ecstatic Subjects, Utopia, and Recognition: Kristeva, Heidegger, Irigaray*. Albany: State University of New York Press, 1998.

Irigaray, Luce. *Democracy Begins Between Two*. 1994. Translated by Kirsteen Anderson. New York: Routledge, 2001.

———. *An Ethics of Sexual Difference*. Translated by Carolyn Burke and Gillian C. Gill. Ithaca, NY: Cornell University Press, 1993.

———. "Is the Subject of Science Sexed?." Translated by Carol Mastrangelo Bové. *Hypatia* 2, no. 3 (fall 1987): 66.

———. "'Je—Luce Irigaray': A Meeting with Luce Irigaray." *Hypatia* 10, no. 2 (1995).

———. *Sexes and Genealogies*. Translated by Gillian C. Gill. New York: Columbia University Press, 1993.

———. "Sorcerer Love: A Reading of Plato's Symposium, Diotima's Speech." In *Revaluing French Feminism*, edited by Nancy Fraser and Sandra Lee Bartky, 64–76. Bloomington: Indiana University Press, 1992.

———. *Speculum of the Other Woman*. Translated by Gillian C. Gill. Ithaca, NY: Cornell University Press, 1985.

———. *Thinking the Difference*. Translated by Karin Montin. New York: Routledge, 1994.

———. *This Sex Which Is Not One*. Translated by Catherine Porter. Ithaca, NY: Cornell University Press, 1985.

Kozel, Susan. "The Diabolical Strategy of Mimesis: Luce Irigaray's Reading of Maurice Merleau-Ponty." *Hypatia* 11, no. 3 (summer 1996): 114–129.

Kristeva, Julia. *About Chinese Women*. Translated by Anita Barrows. New York: Marion Boyars, 1977.

———. *Black Sun: Depression and Melancholia*. Translated by Leon S. Roudiez. New York: Columbia University Press, 1989.

———. *Desire in Language*. Translated by Leon Roudiez. New York: Columbia University Press, 1982.

———. *In the Beginning Was Love: Psychoanalysis and Faith*. New York: Columbia University Press, 1987.

———. *Intimate Revolt: The Powers and Limits of Psychoanalysis*. Translated by Jeanine Herman. New York: Columbia University Press, 2002.

————. "The Novel as Polylogue." In *Desire in Language.* Edited by Thomas Gora, Alice Jardine, and Leon S. Roudiez. Translated by Leon S. Roudiez. New York: Columbia University Press, 1990.

————. *Powers of Horror.* Translated by Leon Roudiez. New York: Columbia University Press, 1982.

————. *Revolution in Poetic Language.* Translated by Margaret Waller. New York: Columbia University Press, 1984.

————. *Strangers to Ourselves.* Translated by Leon S. Roudiez. New York: Columbia University Press, 1991.

————. "The Subject in Progress." In *The Tel Quel Reader,* edited by Patrick French and Roland-François Lack. New York: Routledge, 1998.

————. *Tales of Love.* Translated by Leon S. Roudiez. New York: Columbia University Press, 1987.

————. "Women's Time." *Signs: Journal of Women in Culture and Society* 7, no. 1 (summer 1981): 13–35.

Kuykendall, Eléanor H. "Introduction to *Sorcerer Love* by Luce Irigaray." In *Revaluing French Feminism,* edited by Nancy Fraser and Sandra Lee Bartky, 60–63. Bloomington: Indiana University Press, 1992.

Margaroni, Maria. "The Lost Foundation: Kristeva's Semiotic Chora and Its Ambiguous Legacy." *Hypatia* 20, no. 1 (winter 2005): 78–98.

Meyers, Diana T. "The Subversion of Women's Agency in Psychoanalytic Feminism: Chodorow, Flax, Kristeva." In *Revaluing French Feminism,* edited by Nancy Fraser and Sandra Lee Bartky, 136–161. Bloomington: Indiana University Press, 1992.

Moi, Toril, ed. *The Kristeva Reader.* New York: Columbia University Press, 1986.

Nye, Andrea. "The Hidden Host: Irigaray and Diotima at Plato's Symposium." In *Revaluing French Feminism,* edited by Nancy Fraser and Sandra Lee Bartky, 77–93. Bloomington: Indiana University Press, 1992.

Oliver, Kelly, ed. *Ethics, Politics, and Difference in Julia Kristeva's Writing.* New York: Routledge, 1993.

————. "Julia Kristeva's Feminist Revolutions." *Hypatia* 8, no. 3 (summer 1993): 94–114.

————. *Reading Kristeva: Unraveling the Double-Bind.* Bloomington: Indiana University Press, 1993.

Schmitz, Bettina. "Homelessness or Symbolic Castration? Subjectivity, Language Acquisition, and Sociality in Julia Kristeva and Jacques Lacan." Translated by Julia Jansen. *Hypatia* 20, no. 2 (spring 2005): 69–87.

Sjoholm, Cecilia. *Kristeva and the Political.* New York: Routledge, 2005.

Stone, Alison. *Luce Irigaray and the Philosophy of Sexual Difference.* Cambridge: Cambridge University Press, 2006.

Whitford, Margaret, ed. *The Irigaray Reader.* Cambridge, MA: Blackwell, 1991.

————. *Luce Irigaray: Philosophy in the Feminine.* New York: Routledge, 1991.

———. "Luce Irigaray and the Female Imaginary: Speaking as a Woman." *Radical Philosophy* 43 (summer 1986): 7.

Critiques of Freudian, Lacanian, and Psychoanalytic Feminist Thought

Beauvoir, Simone de. *The Second Sex.* Translated and edited by H. M. Parshley. New York: Vintage Books, 1952.

Butler, Judith. *Gender Trouble: Feminism and the Subversion of Identity.* New York: Routledge, 1990.

Chesler, Phyllis. *Women and Madness.* Garden City, NY: Doubleday, 1972.

Cott, Nancy. *The Grounding of Modern Feminism.* New Haven, CT: Yale University Press, 1987.

Deutsch, Helene. *The Psychology of Women: A Psychoanalytic Interpretation.* New York: Grune & Stratten, 1944.

Eisenstein, Hester. *Contemporary Feminist Thought.* Boston: G. K. Hall, 1983.

Elshtain, Jean Bethke. *Public Man, Private Woman: Women in Social and Political Thought.* Princeton, NJ: Princeton University Press, 1981.

Fiorini, Leticia Glocer, and Graciela Abelin-Sas Rose, eds. *On Freud's "Femininity."* London: Karnac Books, 2010.

Firestone, Shulamith. *The Dialectic of Sex.* New York: Bantam Books, 1970.

Gallop, Jane. *The Daughter's Seduction: Feminism and Psychoanalysis.* Ithaca, NY: Cornell University Press, 1982.

Garrison, Dee. "Karen Horney and Feminism." *Signs: Journal of Women in Culture and Society* 6, no. 4 (1981): 672–691.

Gilligan, Carol. *In a Different Voice.* Cambridge, MA: Harvard University Press, 1982.

Grimshaw, Jean. *Philosophy and Feminist Thinking.* Minneapolis: University of Minnesota Press, 1986.

Harding, Sandra. "Two Influential Theories of Ignorance and Philosophy's Interests in Ignoring Them." *Hypatia* 21, no. 3 (summer 2006): 20–36.

Horney, Karen. "The Flight from Womanhood." In *Feminine Psychology.* New York: W. W. Norton, 1973.

Izenberg, Gerald N. *The Existentialist Critique of Freud: The Crisis of Autonomy.* Princeton, NJ: Princeton University Press, 1976.

Klein, Viola. *The Feminine Character.* London: Routledge & Kegan Paul, 1971.

Kofman, Sarah. *The Enigma of Women: Woman in Freud's Writings.* Translated by Catherine Porter. Ithaca, NY: Cornell University Press, 1980.

Miller, Jean Baker, ed. *Psychoanalysis and Women.* New York: Penguin Books, 1974.

Millett, Kate. *Sexual Politics.* Garden City, NY: Doubleday, 1969.

Moi, Toril. *Sexual/Textual Politics: Feminist Literary Theory.* New York: Methuen, 1985.

Reppen, Joseph, ed. *Beyond Freud: A Study of Modern Psychoanalytic Theorists*. Hillsdale, NJ: Analytic Press, 1985.

Rose, Jacqueline. "Introduction—II." In *Feminine Sexuality: Jacques Lacan and the École Freudienne*, edited by Juliet Mitchell and Jacqueline Rose. New York: Norton, 1982.

Thompson, Clara. "Problems of Womanhood." In *Interpersonal Psychoanalysis: The Selected Papers of Clara Thompson*, edited by M. Green. New York: Basic Books, 1964.

Voloshinov, V. N. *Freudianism: A Marxist Critique*. New York: Academic Press, 1976.

Chapter 7: Care-Focused Feminism

The Roots of Care-Focused Feminism

Baier, Annette C. "Caring About Caring." In *Postures of the Mind: Essays on Mind and Morals*. Minneapolis: University of Minnesota Press, 1985.

Barry, Brian. *Justice as Impartiality*. Oxford: Oxford University Press, 1995.

Bartkey, Sandra Lee. *Femininity and Domination*. New York: Routledge, 1990.

Behuniak, Susan M. *A Caring Jurisprudence*. Lanham, MD: Rowman & Littlefield, 1999.

Belenky, Mary Field, Lynne A. Bond, and Jacqueline S. Weinstock. *The Tradition That Has No Name: Nurturing the Development of People, Families, and Communities*. New York: Basic Books, 1997.

Benhabib, Seyla. "The Generalized and Concrete Other: The Kohlberg-Gilligan Controversy and Moral Theory." In *Women and Moral Theory*, edited by Eva Feder Kittay and Diana T. Meyers. Totowa, NJ: Rowman & Littlefield, 1987.

Blustein, Jeffrey. *Care and Commitment*. Oxford: Oxford University Press, 1991.

Botes, Annatjie. "A Comparison Between the Ethics of Justice and the Ethics of Care." *Journal of Advanced Nursing* 32, no. 5 (2000): 1071–1075.

Bowden, Peta. *Caring: Gender-Sensitive Ethics*. London: Routledge, 1997.

Brender, Natalie. "Political Care and Humanitarian Response." In *Feminists Doing Ethics*, edited by Peggy DesAutels and Joanne Waugh. Lanham, MD: Rowman & Littlefield, 2001.

Bubeck, Diemut. *Care, Gender, and Justice*. Oxford, UK: Clarendon Press, 1995.

Card, Claudia. "Caring and Evil." *Hypatia* 5, no. 1 (spring 1990): 101–108.

Clement, Grace. *Care, Autonomy, and Justice: Feminism and the Ethic of Care*. Boulder, CO: Westview Press, 1996.

Collins, Patricia Hill. *Black Feminist Thought: Knowledge, Consciousness, and the Politics of Empowerment*. Boston: Unwin Hyman, 1990.

Davion, Victoria. "Pacifism and Care." *Hypatia* 5 (1990): 90–100.

Deveaux, Monique. "Shifting Paradigms: Theorizing Care and Justice in Political Theory." *Hypatia* 10, no. 2 (spring 1995): 115–119.

England, Paula, and Nancy Folbre. "The Cost of Caring." *Annals of the American Academy of Political and Social Science* 561 (January 1999): 39–51.

Engster, Daniel. "Care Ethics and Natural Law Theory: Toward an Institutional Political Theory of Caring." *Journal of Politics* 66, no. 1 (February 2004): 113–135.

———. "Rethinking Care Theory: The Practice of Caring and the Obligation to Care." *Hypatia* 20, no. 3 (summer 2005): 51–74.

Faludi, Susan. *Caregiving: Readings in Knowledge, Practice, Ethics, and Politics.* Philadelphia: University of Pennsylvania Press, 1996.

Fisher, Berenice, and Joan Tronto. "Toward a Feminist Theory of Caring." In *Circles of Care*, edited by Emily Abel and Margaret Nelson. Albany: State University of New York Press, 1990.

Gilligan, Carol. *In a Different Voice.* Cambridge, MA: Harvard University Press, 1982.

———. "Moral Orientation and Moral Development." In *Women and Moral Theory*, edited by Eva Feder Kittay and Diana T. Meyers, 25–26. Totowa, NJ: Rowman & Littlefield, 1987.

Gilligan, Carol, Jill McLean Taylor, Betty Bardige, and Janie Victoria, eds. *Mapping the Moral Domain: A Contribution of Women's Thinking to Psychological Theory and Education.* Cambridge, MA: Harvard University Press, 1988.

Gilligan, Carol, and Grant Wiggins. "The Origins of Morality in Early Childhood Relationships." In *The Emergence of Morality in Young Children*, edited by Jerome Kagan and Sharon Lamb, 279. Chicago: University of Chicago Press, 1987.

Gordon, Suzanne, Patricia Benner, and Nel Noddings, eds. *Caregiving: Readings in Knowledge, Practice, Ethics, and Politics.* Philadelphia: University of Pennsylvania Press, 1996.

Halfon, Mark S., and Joram G. Haber, eds. *Norms and Values: Essays on the Work of Virginia Held.* Lanham, MD: Rowman & Littlefield, 1998.

Halwani, Raja. "Care Ethics and Virtue Ethics." *Hypatia* 18, no. 3 (fall 2003): 161–192.

Hamington, Maurice, and Dorothy C. Miller, eds. *Socializing Care: Feminist Ethics and Public Issues.* Lanham, MD: Rowman & Littlefield, 2006.

Hankivsky, Olena. "Imagining Ethical Globalization: The Contributions of a Care Ethics." *Hypatia* 2, no. 1 (June 2006): 91–110.

Hekman, Susan J. *Moral Voices, Moral Selves: Carol Gilligan and Feminist Moral Theory.* Cambridge, UK: Polity Press, 1995.

Held, Virginia. "Care and the Extension of Markets." *Hypatia* 17, no. 2 (spring 2002): 19–33.

———. *The Ethics of Care: Personal, Political and Global.* New York: Oxford University Press, 2006.

———. "Feminism and Moral Theory." In *Women and Moral Theory*, edited by Eva Feder Kittay and Diana Meyers, 112. Totowa, NJ: Rowman & Littlefield, 1987.

———. *Feminist Morality: Transforming Culture, Society, and Politics.* Chicago: University of Chicago Press, 1993.

———. "The Meshing of Care and Justice." *Hypatia* 10, no. 2 (spring 1995): 128–132.

Held, Virginia, and Alison Jaggar, eds. *Justice and Care: Essential Readings in Feminist Ethics.* Boulder, CO: Westview, 1995.

Jaggar, Alison M. "Caring as a Feminist Practice of Moral Reason." In *Justice and Care: Essential Readings in Feminist Ethics*, edited by Virginia Held. Boulder, CO: Westview Press, 1995.

Koehn, Daryl. *Rethinking Feminist Ethics: Care, Trust, and Empathy.* London: Routledge, 1998.

Kohlberg, Lawrence. "From Is to Ought: How to Commit the Naturalistic Fallacy and Get Away with It in the Study of Moral Development." In *Cognitive Development and Epistemology*, edited by Theodore Mischel. New York: Academic Press, 1971.

Kramer, Betty J., and Edward H. Thompson Jr. *Men as Caregivers: Theory, Research, and Service Implications.* New York: Springer, 2002.

Kroeger-Mappes, Joy. "The Ethic of Care Vis-à-Vis the Ethic of Rights: A Problem for Contemporary Moral Theory." *Hypatia* 9, no. 3 (summer 1994): 108–131.

Kuhse, Helga. *Caring: Nurses, Women and Ethics.* Oxford, UK: Blackwell, 1997.

Larrabee, Mary Jeanne, ed. *An Ethic of Care: Feminist and Interdisciplinary Perspectives.* New York: Routledge, 1993.

Li, Chenyang. "The Confucian Concepts of *Jen* and the Feminist Ethics of Care: A Comparative Study." *Hypatia* 9, no. 1 (1994): 70–89.

———. "Revisiting Confucian *Jen* Ethics and Feminist Care Ethics: A Reply to Daniel Star and Lijun Yuan." *Hypatia* 17, no. 1 (2002): 130–140.

Little, Margaret. "Seeing and Caring: The Role of Affect in Feminist Moral Epistemology." *Hypatia* 10, no. 3 (1995): 117–137.

Manning, Rita C. *Speaking from the Heart: A Feminist Perspective on Ethics.* Lanham, MD: Rowman & Littlefield, 1992.

McLaren, Margaret A. "Feminist Ethics: Care as a Virtue." In *Feminists Doing Ethics*, edited by Peggy DesAutels and Joanne Waugh. Lanham, MD: Rowman & Littlefield, 2001.

Miller, Sarah Clark. *The Ethics of Need: Agency, Dignity, and Obligation.* New York: Routledge, 2012.

———. "A Kantian Ethic of Care?." In *Feminist Interventions in Ethics and Politics: Feminist Ethics and Social Theory*, edited by Barbara S. Andrew, 111–127. Lanham, MD: Rowman & Littlefield, 2005.

Moody-Adams, Michele M. "Gender and the Complexity of Moral Voices." In *Feminist Ethics*, edited by Claudia Card, 193–198. Lawrence: University Press of Kansas, 1991.

———. "The Social Construction and Reconstruction of Care." In *Sex, Preference, and Family: Essays on Law and Nature*, edited by David Estlund and Martha Nussbaum, 3–17. New York: Oxford University Press, 1997.

Morris, Jenny. "Impairment and Disability: Constructing an Ethics of Care That Promotes Human Rights." *Hypatia* 16, no. 4 (fall 2001): 1–16.

Noddings, Nel. *Caring: A Feminine Approach to Ethics and Moral Education.* Berkeley: University of California Press, 1984.

———, ed. *Educating Citizens for Global Awareness.* New York: Teachers College Press, 2005.

———. *Peace Education: How We Come to Love and Hate War.* New York: Cambridge University Press, 2012.

———. *Starting at Home: Caring and Social Policy.* Berkeley: University of California Press, 2002.

———. *Women and Evil.* Berkeley: University of California Press, 1989.

Robinson, Fiona. "Care, Gender and Global Social Justice: Rethinking 'Ethical Globalization.'" *Hypatia* 2, no. 1 (June 2006): 5–25.

———. *Globalizing Care: Ethics, Feminist Theory, and International Relations.* Boulder, CO: Westview Press, 1999.

———. "Stop Talking and Listen: Discourse Ethics and Feminist Care Ethics in International Political Theory." *Millennium: Journal of International Studies* 39, no. 3 (2011): 845–862.

Sander-Staudt, Maureen. "The Unhappy Marriage of Care Ethics and Virtue Ethics." *Hypatia* 21, no. 4 (fall 2006): 21–39.

Sevenhuijsen, Selma. *Citizenship and the Ethics of Care: Feminist Considerations on Justice, Morality and Politics.* London: Routledge, 1998.

Shanley, Mary Lyndon. "Public Policy and the Ethics of Care." *Hypatia* 16, no. 3 (summer 2001): 157–160.

Simson, Rosalind S. "Feminine Thinking." *Social Theory and Practice* 31, no. 1 (January 2005): 1–26.

Slicer, Deborah. "Teaching with a Different Ear: Teaching Ethics After Reading Carol Gilligan." *Journal of Value Inquiry* 24 (1990): 55–65.

Slote, Michael. "Caring in the Balance." In *Norms and Values,* edited by Joram G. Haber and Mark S. Hatfon. Lanham, MD: Rowman & Littlefield, 1998.

Star, Daniel. "Do Confucians Really Care? A Defense of the Distinctiveness of Care Ethics: A Reply to Chenyang Li." *Hypatia* 17, no. 1 (2002): 77–106.

Stone, Deborah. "Why We Need a Care Movement." *Nation,* March 12, 2000, 13–15.

Tessman, Lisa, ed. *Feminist Ethics and Social and Political Philosophy: Theorizing the Non-ideal.* New York: Springer, 2009.

Tong, Rosemarie. "The Ethics of Care: A Feminist Virtue of Care for Healthcare Practitioners." *Journal of Medicine and Philosophy* 23, no. 2 (1998): 131–152.

———. *Feminine and Feminist Ethics.* Belmont, CA: Wadsworth, 1993.

———. "Gender-Based Disparities East/West: Rethinking the Burden of Care in the United States and Taiwan." *Bioethics* 21, no. 9 (2007): 488–499.

———. "Global Perspectives on Health Care: Some Feminist Visions." In *Globalizing Feminist Bioethics: Crosscultural Perspectives,* edited by Rosemarie Tong, with Gwen Anderson and Aida Santos. Boulder, CO: Westview Press, 2001.

———. "Long-Term Care for the Elderly: Whose Responsibility Is It?." *International Journal of Feminist Approaches to Bioethics* 2, no. 2 (2009): 5–30.

———. "Love's Labor in the Health Care System: Working Toward Gender Equality." *Hypatia* 17, no. 3 (summer 2002): 200–213.

Tong, Rosemarie, and Nancy Williams. "Gender Justice in the Health Care System: Past Experiences, Present Realities, and Future Hopes." In *Medicine and Social Justice: Essays on the Distribution of Health Care*, edited by Rosamond Rhodes, Margaret P. Battin, and Anita Silvers. Oxford: Oxford University Press, 2012.

Tronto, Joan. "Care as a Political Concept." In *Revisioning the Political: Feminist Reconstructions of Traditional Concepts in Western Political Theory*, edited by Nancy J. Hirschmann and Christine Di Stefano. New York: Free Press, 1996.

———. *Moral Boundaries: A Political Argument for an Ethic of Care*. London: Routledge, 1993.

———. "Woman and Caring: What Can Feminists Learn About Morality from Caring?." In *Justice and Care: Essential Readings in Feminist Ethics*, edited by Virginia Held, 101–115. Boulder, CO: Westview Press, 1995.

Warren, Karen J. "Care-Sensitive Ethics and Situated Universalism." In *Global Environmental Ethics*, edited by Nicholas Low, 131–145. London: Routledge, 1999.

West, Robin. "The Right to Care." In *The Subject of Care: Feminist Perspectives on Dependency*, edited by Eva Feder Kittay and Ellen Feder. Lanham, MD: Rowman & Littlefield, 2002.

White, Julie Anne. *Democracy, Justice, and the Welfare State: Reconstructing Public Care*. University Park: Pennsylvania State Press, 2000.

Yuan, Lijun. "Ethics of Care and Concept of *Jen*: A Reply to Chenyang Li." *Hypatia* 17, no. 1 (2002): 107–129.

The Roots of Maternal Ethics

Aronow, Ina. "Doulas Step in When Mothers Need a Hand." *New York Times*, August 1, 1993, 1.

Badinter, Elisabeth. *Mother Love: Myth and Reality*. New York: Macmillan, 1980.

Baraitser, Lisa. *Maternal Encounters: The Ethics of Interruption*. New York: Routledge, 2009.

Chodorow, Nancy. *The Reproduction of Mothering: Psychoanalysis and the Sociology of Gender*. Berkeley: University of California Press, 1978.

Collins, Patricia Hill. "The Meaning of Motherhood in Black Culture and Black Mother/Daughter Relationships." Berkeley, CA: Sage, 1987.

———. "Shifting the Center: Race, Class, and Feminist Theorizing About Motherhood." In *Mothering: Ideology, Experience, and Agency*, edited by E. Glenn, G. Chang, and L. Furcey. New York: Routledge, 1994.

Engster, Daniel. *The Maternal Factor: Two Paths to Morality*. Berkeley: University of California Press, 2010.

Goodin, Robert. *Protecting the Vulnerable.* Chicago: University of Chicago Press, 1985.

Gottlieb, Roger S. "The Tasks of Embodied Love: Moral Problems in Caring for Children with Disabilities." *Hypatia* 17, no. 3 (summer 2002): 225–236.

Gould, Carol, ed. *Beyond Domination: New Perspectives on Women and Philosophy.* Totowa, NJ: Rowman & Allanheld, 1983.

Hanisberg, Julia, and Sara Ruddick, eds. *Mother Troubles: Rethinking Contemporary Maternal Dilemmas.* Boston: Beacon Press, 1999.

———, eds. *On Behalf of Mothers: Legal Theorists, Philosophers, and Theologians Reflect on Dilemmas of Parenting.* New York: Beacon Press, 1999.

Held, Virginia. "The Obligation of Mothers and Fathers." In *Mothering: Essays in Feminist Theory*, edited by Joyce Trebilcot, 1. Totowa, NJ: Rowman & Allanheld, 1984.

Hewett, Heather. "Talkin' 'Bout a Revolution: Building a Mothers' Movement in the Third World." *Journal of the Association for Research on Mothering* 8, nos. 1–2 (September 2006).

Kittay, Eva Feder. "A Feminist Public Ethic of Care Meets the New Communitarian Family Policy." *Ethics* 111 (April 2001): 523–547.

———. "At the Margins of Moral Personhood." *Ethics* 116 (October 2005): 100–131.

———. "Human Dependency and Rawlsian Equality." In *Feminists Rethink the Self*, edited by Diana T. Meyers. Boulder, CO: Westview Press, 1996.

———. *Love's Labor: Essays on Women, Equality, and Dependency.* New York: Routledge, 1999, 19.

———. "Taking Dependency Seriously." *Hypatia* 10 (winter 1995): 29.

Kittay, Eva Feder, and Diana T. Meyers, eds. *Women and Moral Theory.* Totowa, NJ: Rowman & Littlefield, 1987.

Lorber, Judith. "On *The Reproduction of Mothering*: A Methodological Debate." *Signs: Journal of Women in Culture and Society* 6, no. 3 (spring 1981): 482–486.

Purdy, Laura M. *Reproducing Persons: Issues in Feminist Bioethics.* Ithaca, NY: Cornell University Press, 1996.

Romero, Mary. "Who's Taking Care of the Maid's Children?." In *Feminism and Families*, edited by Hilde Lindemann Nelson and Jamie Nelson. New York: Routledge, 1997.

Rossi, Alice. "On *The Reproduction of Mothering*: A Methodological Debate." *Signs: Journal of Women in Culture and Society* 6, no. 3 (spring 1981): 497–500.

Ruddick, Sara. "Care as Labor and Relationship." In *Norms and Values: Essays on the Work of Virginia Held*, edited by Mark S. Halfon and Joram C. Haber. Lanham, MD: Rowman & Littlefield, 1998.

———. "Injustice in Families: Assault and Domination." In *Justice and Care: Essential Readings in Feminist Ethics*, edited by Virginia Held, 203–223. Boulder, CO: Westview Press, 1995.

————. "Maternal Thinking." In *Mothering: Essays in Feminist Theory*, edited by Joyce Trebilcot, 214. Totowa, NJ: Rowman & Allanheld, 1984.

Ruddick, William. "Parenthood: Three Concepts and a Principle." In *Family Values: Issues in Ethics, Society and the Family*, edited by Laurence D. Houlgate. Belmont, CA: Wadsworth, 1998.

Trebilcot, Joyce, ed. *Mothering: New Essays in Feminist Theory*. Totowa, NJ: Rowman & Littlefield, 1987.

Critiques of Care-Focused Feminism and Maternal Ethics

Allmark, Peter. "Is Caring a Virtue?." *Journal of Advanced Nursing* 28, no. 3 (1998): 466–472.

Bartky, Sandra Lee. "Feeding Egos and Tending Wounds: Deference and Disaffection in Women's Emotional Labor." In *Femininity and Domination*, edited by Sandra Lee Bartky, 99–119. New York: Routledge, 1990.

Davis, Angela Y. *Women, Race, and Class*. New York: Random House, 1981.

Davis, Kathy. "Toward a Feminist Rhetoric: The Gilligan Debate Revisited." *Women's Studies International Forum* 15, no. 2 (1992): 219–231.

Ferguson, Ann. "Motherhood and Sexuality: Some Feminist Questions." *Hypatia* 1, no. 2 (fall 1986): 3–22.

Friedman, Marilyn. *Autonomy, Gender, Politics*. New York: Oxford University Press, 2003.

Hoagland, Sarah Lucia. "Some Concerns About Nel Noddings' *Caring*." *Hypatia* 5, no. 1 (spring 1990): 114.

————. "Some Thoughts About *Caring*." In *Feminist Ethics*, edited by Claudia Card, 250. Lawrence: University Press of Kansas, 1991.

Houston, Barbara. "Rescuing Womanly Virtues." In *Science, Morality, and Feminist Theory*, edited by Marsha Hanen and Kai Nielsen. Calgary, Alberta: University of Calgary Press, 1987.

Mullett, Sheila. "Shifting Perspectives: A New Approach to Ethics." In *Feminist Perspectives*, edited by Lorraine Code, Sheila Mullett, and Christine Overall. Toronto: University of Toronto Press, 1989.

Porter, Elisabeth. "Can Politics Practice Compassion?." *Hypatia* 21, no. 4 (fall 2006): 97–123.

Puka, Bill. "The Liberation of Caring: A Different Voice for Gilligan's 'Different Voice.'" *Hypatia* 5, no. 1 (spring 1990): 59.

Reverby, Susan. *Ordered to Care*. Cambridge: Cambridge University Press, 1987.

Scher, George. "Other Voices, Other Rooms? Women's Psychology and Moral Theory." In *Women and Moral Theory*, edited by Eva Feder Kittay and Diana T. Meyers, 188. Totowa, NJ: Rowman & Littlefield, 1987.

Stephens, Julie. *Confronting Postmaternal Thinking: Feminism, Memory, and Care*. New York: Columbia University Press, 2011.

Willett, Cynthia. *Maternal Ethics and Other Slave Moralities.* New York: Routledge, 1995.

Wong, Sau-ling C. "Diverted Mothering: Representations of Caregivers of Color in the Age of Multiculturalism." In *Mothering: Ideology, Experience, and Agency*, edited by Evelyn Nakano Glenn, Grace Chang, and Linda Rennie Forcey. New York: Routledge, 1994.

Chapter 8: Ecofeminism

Some Roots of Ecofeminism

Abram, David. *Becoming Animal: An Earthly Cosmology.* New York: Vintage, 2011.

———. *The Spell of the Sensuous: Perception and Language in a More-Than-Human World.* New York: Vintage, 1996.

Adorno, Theodor W. *Minima Moralia: Reflections from Damaged Life.* Translated by E. F. N. Jephcott. London: New Left Books, 1974.

Aiken, William. "Non-anthropocentric Ethical Challenges." In *Earthbound: New Introductory Essays in Environmental Ethics*, edited by Tom Regan. New York: Random House, 1984.

Brown, Charles S., and Ted Toadvine, eds. *Eco-phenomenology: Back to the Earth Itself.* Albany: State University of New York Press, 2003.

Caldecott, Leonie, and Stephanie Leland, eds. *Reclaim the Earth.* London: Women's Press, 1983.

Callicott, J. Baird. "Do Deconstructive Ecology and Sociobiology Undermine Leopold's Land Ethic?." In *Environmental Philosophy from Animal Rights to Social Ecology*, edited by Michael Zimmerman, George Sessions, Karen Warren, and John Clark, 145–164. Upper Saddle River, NJ: Prentice Hall, 1998.

Carson, Rachel. *Silent Spring.* Boston: Houghton Mifflin, 1962.

Curry, Patrick. *Ecological Ethics: An Introduction.* Cambridge, UK: Polity Press, 2011.

Ferry, Luc. *The New Ecological Order.* Translated by Carol Volk. Chicago: University of Chicago Press, 1992.

Kohák, Erazim. *The Embers and the Stars: A Philosophical Inquiry into the Moral Sense of Nature.* Chicago: University of Chicago Press, 1984.

Leopold, Aldo. "The Land Ethic." In *A Sand County Almanac: With Other Essays on Conservation from Round River.* New York: Oxford University Press, 1987.

McDaniel, Jay B. *Earth, Sky, God, and Mortals: Developing an Ecological Spirituality.* Mystic, CT: Twenty-Third Publications, 1990.

Naess, Arne. "The Deep Ecological Movement: Some Philosophical Aspects." *Philosophical Inquiry* 8 (1986): 10–13.

Salleh, Ariel Kay. "Deeper Than Deep Ecology: The Ecofeminist Connection." *Environmental Ethics* 6, no. 1 (1984): 339.

———. *Ecofeminism as Politics: Nature, Marx and the Postmodern.* New York: Zed Books, 1997.

Sessions, George. "The Deep Ecology Movement: A Review." *Environmental Review* 9 (1987): 115.

Shiva, Vandana. "Taking Empirical Data Seriously: An Ecofeminist Philosophy Perspective." In *Living with Contradictions: Controversies in Feminist Social Ethics*, edited by Alison M. Jaggar, 642–643. Boulder, CO: Westview Press, 1994.

Early Conceptions of Ecofeminism

Crittenden, Chris. "Subordinate and Oppressive Conceptual Frameworks: A Defense of Ecofeminist Perspectives." *Environmental Ethics* 20, no. 3 (fall 1998): 247–263.

Cuomo, Christine. "Toward Thoughtful Ecofeminist Activism." In *Ecological Feminist Philosophies*, edited by Karen J. Warren, 42–51. Bloomington: Indiana University Press, 1996.

———. "Unravelling the Problems in Ecofeminism." *Environmental Ethics* 14, no. 4 (winter 1992): 351–363.

Diamond, Irene, and Gloria Feman Orenstein, eds. *Reweaving the World: The Emergence of Ecofeminism.* San Francisco: Sierra Club Books, 1990.

Gebara, Ivone. *Longing for Running Water: Ecofeminism and Liberation.* Minneapolis: Fortress Press, 1999.

King, Ynestra. "The Ecology of Feminism and the Feminism of Ecology." In *Healing the Wounds: The Promise of Ecofeminism*, edited by Judith Plant. Philadelphia: New Society Publishers, 1989.

LaChapelle, Dolores. *Earth Wisdom.* Silverton, CO: Way of the Mountain Learning Center and International College, 1978.

Mellor, Mary. *Feminism and Ecology.* New York: New York University Press, 1997.

Merchant, Carolyn. *The Death of Nature: Women, Ecology, and the Scientific Revolution.* San Francisco: Harper & Row, 1980.

———. *Radical Ecology: The Search for a Livable World.* New York: Routledge, 1992.

Mies, Maria, and Vandana Shiva. *Ecofeminism.* London: Zed Books, 1993.

Ruether, Rosemary Radford. *New Woman/New Earth: Sexist Ideologies and Human Liberation.* New York: Seabury Press, 1975.

Warren, Karen J. "Feminism and Ecology." *Environmental Review* 9, no. 1 (spring 1987): 3–20.

Women, Nature, and Culture: Some Tensions

Datar, Chhaya. *Ecofeminism Revisited: Introduction to the Discourse.* Jaipur, India: Rawat Publications, 2011.

Estés, Clarissa Pinkola. *Women Who Run with the Wolves.* New York: Random House Publishing Group, 1992.

Gaard, Greta. *The Nature of Home: Taking Root in a Place.* Tucson: University of Arizona Press, 2007.

Gray, Elizabeth Dodson. *Green Paradise Lost.* Wellesley, MA: Roundtable Press, 1981.

Gruen, Lori. "Toward an Ecofeminist Moral Epistemology." In *Ecological Feminism,* edited by Karen J. Warren, 120–138. New York: Routledge, 1994.

Hyner, Bernadette H., and Precious McKenzie Stearns. *Forces of Nature: Natural(-izing) Gender and Gender(-ing) Nature in the Discourses of Western Culture.* Newcastle upon Tyne, UK: Cambridge Scholars Publishing, 2009.

Kheel, Marti. "The Liberation of Nature: A Circular Affair." *Environmental Ethics* 7, no. 2 (1985): 135–149.

King, Ynestra. "The Ecology of Feminism and the Feminism of Ecology." In *Healing the Wounds: The Promise of Ecofeminism,* edited by Judith Plant. Philadelphia: New Society Publishers, 1989.

Piercy, Marge. *Woman on the Edge of Time.* New York: Fawcett Crest Books, 1976.

Plant, Judith, ed. *Healing the Wounds: The Promise of Ecofeminism.* Philadelphia: New Society Publishers, 1989.

Plumwood, Val. *Feminism and the Mastery of Nature.* Opening Out: Feminism for Today. London: Routledge, 1993.

Roach, Catherine. "Loving Your Mother: On the Woman-Nature Connection." In *Ecological Feminist Philosophies,* edited by Karen J. Warren, 52–65. Bloomington: Indiana University Press, 1996.

Salleh, Ariel Kay. "Deeper Than Deep Ecology: The Ecofeminist Connection." *Environmental Ethics* 6, no. 1 (1984): 339.

Nature Ecofeminism

Daly, Mary. *Gyn/Ecology: The Metaethics of Radical Feminism.* Boston: Beacon Press, 1978.

———. *Pure Lust: Elemental Feminist Philosophy.* Boston: Beacon Press, 2001.

Griffin, Susan. *Pornography and Silence: Culture's Revenge Against Nature.* New York: Harper & Row, 1981.

———. *Woman and Nature: The Roaring Inside Her.* New York: Harper & Row, 1978.

Kheel, Marti. *Nature Ethics: An Ecofeminist Perspective.* Lanham, MD: Rowman & Littlefield, 2008.

Merchant, Carolyn. *Reinventing Eden: The Fate of Nature in Western Culture.* New York: Routledge, 2003.

Ortner, Sherry B. "Is Female to Male as Nature Is to Culture?." In *Readings in Ecology and Feminist Theology,* edited by Mary Heather MacKinnon and Marie McIntyre. Kansas City, KS: Sheed and Ward, 1995.

Spiritual Ecofeminism

Adams, Carol J., ed. *Ecofeminism and the Sacred.* New York: Continuum, 1994.

Allen, Paula Gunn. "The Woman I Love Is a Planet; the Planet I Love Is a Tree." In *Reweaving the World: The Emergence of Ecofeminism*, edited by Irene Diamond and Gloria Feman Orenstein. San Francisco: Sierra Club Books, 1990.

Anderlini-D'Onofrio, Serena. *Gaia and the New Politics of Love: Notes for a Poly Planet.* Berkeley: North Atlantic Books, 2009.

Christ, Carol. *She Who Changes: Re-imagining the Divine in the World.* New York: Palgrave Macmillan, 2003.

Dalton, Anne Marie. *Ecotheology and the Practice of Hope.* Albany: State University of New York Press, 2010.

Eisler, Riane. "The Gaia Tradition and the Partnership Future: An Ecofeminist Manifesto." In *Reweaving the World: The Emergence of Ecofeminism*, edited by Irene Diamond and Gloria Feman Orenstein. San Francisco: Sierra Club Books, 1990.

Gray, Elizabeth Dodson. *Sacred Dimensions of Women's Experience.* Wellesley, MA: Roundtable Press, 1988.

Grey, Mary C. *Sacred Longings: The Ecological Spirit and Global Culture.* Minneapolis: Fortress Press, 2001.

McDaniel, Jay B. *Of God and Pelicans: A Theology of Reverence for Life.* Louisville, KY: Westminster/John Knox Press, 1989.

Neu, Diann L. *Return Blessings: Ecofeminist Liturgies Renewing the Earth.* Cleveland, OH: Pilgrim Press, 2002.

Ruether, Rosemary Radford. *Integrating Ecofeminism, Globalization, and World Religions.* Lanham, MD: Rowman & Littlefield, 2005.

———. *New Woman/New Earth: Sexist Ideologies and Human Liberation.* New York: Seabury Press, 1975.

———, ed. *Women Healing Earth: Third World Women on Ecology, Feminism, and Religion.* Maryknoll, NY: Orbis Books, 1996.

Spretnak, Charlene, ed. *The Politics of Women's Spirituality.* Garden City, NY: Anchor, 1982.

Starhawk. *Dreaming in the Dark: Magic, Sex, and Politics.* Boston: Beacon, 1982.

———. *Rebirth of the Goddess: Finding Meaning in Feminist Spirituality.* New York: Routledge, 1997.

———. *She Who Changes: Re-imagining the Divine in the World.* New York: Palgrave Macmillan, 2003.

———. *The Spiral Dance: A Rebirth of the Ancient Religion of the Great Goddess.* San Francisco: HarperSanFrancisco, 1979.

———. *Truth or Dare: Encounters with Power, Authority, and Mystery.* San Francisco: Harper and Row, 1987.

———. *Webs of Power: Notes from the Global Uprising.* Gabriola Island, BC: New Society Publishers, 2002.

Transformative Ecofeminism

Curtin, Deane. "Toward an Ecological Ethic of Care." In *Ecological Feminist Philosophies*, edited by Karen J. Warren, 129–143. Bloomington: Indiana University Press, 1996.

Dinnerstein, Dorothy. "Survival on Earth: The Meaning of Feminism." In *Healing the Wounds: The Promise of Ecofeminism*, edited by Judith Plant. Philadelphia: New Society Publishers, 1989.

Gebara, Ivone. *Longing for Running Water: Ecofeminism and Liberation.* Minneapolis: Fortress Press, 1999.

Nhanenge, Jytte. *Ecofeminism: Towards Integrating the Concerns of Women, Poor People, and Nature into Development.* Lanham, MD: University Press of America, 2011.

Spretnak, Charlene. "Feminism and Ecology: Making Connections." In *Readings in Ecology and Feminist Theology*, edited by Mary Heather MacKinnon and Moni McIntyre. Kansas City, KS: Sheed and Ward, 1995.

Warren, Karen J. "Deep Ecology and Ecofeminism." In *Philosophical Dialogues: Arne Naess and the Progress of Ecophilosophy*, edited by Nina Witoszek and Andrew Brennan, 255–269. Lanham, MD: Rowman & Littlefield, 1999.

———. *Ecofeminist Philosophy: A Western Perspective on What It Is and Why It Matters.* Lanham, MD: Rowman & Littlefield, 2000.

Zabinski, Catherine. "Scientific Ecology and Ecological Feminism: The Potential for Dialogue." In *Ecofeminism: Women, Culture, Nature*, edited by Karen J. Warren, 314–324. Bloomington: Indiana University Press, 1997.

Global Ecofeminism

Chua, Amy. *World on Fire: How Exploring Free Market Democracy Breeds Ethnic Hatred and Global Instability.* New York: Anchor, 2003.

Cibreiro, Estrella, and Francisca López, eds. *Global Issues in Contemporary Hispanic Women Writers: Shaping Gender, the Environment, and Politics.* Routledge Studies in Contemporary Literature. New York: Routledge, 2012.

Cuomo, Christine. "Ecofeminism, Deep Ecology, and Human Population." In *Ecological Feminism*, edited by Karen J. Warren, 88–105. New York: Routledge, 1994.

Eaton, Heather, and Lois Ann Lorentzen. *Ecofeminism and Globalization: Exploring Culture, Context, and Religion.* Lanham, MD: Rowman & Littlefield, 2003.

"From Bretton Woods to Alternatives." In *Alternatives to Economic Globalization*, edited by International Forum on Globalization, 228–238. San Francisco: Berrett-Koehler, 2002.

Merchant, Carolyn. *Radical Ecology: The Search for a Livable World.* New York: Routledge, 1992.

Mies, Maria. "White Man's Dilemma: His Search for What He Has Destroyed." In *Ecofeminism*, edited by Maria Shiva and Vandana Shiva. London: Zed, 1993.

Moe-Lobeda, Cynthia. *Globalization and God: Healing a Broken World.* Minneapolis: Fortress Press, 2002.

Rocheleau, Dianne, Barbara Thomas-Slayter, and Esther Wangari, eds. *Feminist Political Ecology: Global Issues and Local Experiences.* New York: Routledge, 1996.

Salleh, Ariel. *Eco-sufficiency and Global Justice: Women Write Political Ecology.* London: Pluto Press, 2009.

Seager, Joni. *Earth Follies: Coming to Feminist Terms with the Global Environmental Crisis.* New York: Routledge, 1993.

Shiva, Vandana. *Biopiracy: The Plunder of Nature and Knowledge.* Boston: South End Press, 1997.

———. *Earth Democracy: Justice, Sustainability, and Peace.* Brooklyn, NY: South End Press, 2005.

———. *Staying Alive: Women, Ecology, and Development.* 2nd ed. Brooklyn, NY: South End Press, 2010.

———. *Stolen Harvest: The Hijacking of the Global Food Supply.* Boston: South End Press, 2000.

Vegetarian Ecofeminism

Adams, Carol J. *The Sexual Politics of Meat: A Feminist Vegetarian Critical Theory.* 3rd ed. New York: Continuum International Publishing Group, 2010.

Adams, Carol J., and Josephine Donovan, eds. *The Feminist Care Tradition in Animal Ethics.* New York: Columbia University Press, 2007.

Armstrong, Susan. *The Animal Ethics Reader.* 2nd ed. New York: Routledge, 2008.

Beauchamp, Tom L., and R. G. Frey, eds. *The Oxford Handbook of Animal Ethics.* Oxford: Oxford University Press, 2011.

Bekoff, Marc, ed. *Encyclopedia of Animal Rights and Welfare.* 2nd ed. Santa Barbara, CA: Greenwood Press, 2010.

Collard, Andrée, with Joyce Contrucci. *Rape of the Wild: Man's Violence Against Animals and the Earth.* Bloomington: Indiana University Press, 1988.

Corrigan, Theresa, and Stephanie Hoppe. *With a Fly's Eye, Whale's Wit, and Woman's Heart: Animals and Women.* Pittsburgh, PA: Cleis Press, 1989.

DeMello, Margo. *Animals and Society: An Introduction to Human-Animal Studies.* New York: Columbia University Press, 2012.

Dunayer, Joan. *Animal Equality: Language and Liberation.* Derwood, MD: Ryce Publishing, 2001.

Francione, Gary L. *Animals as Persons: Essays on the Abolition of Animal Exploitation.* Chichester, UK: Columbia University Press, 2008.

Gaard, Greta. "Vegetarian Ecofeminism: A Review Essay." *Frontiers: A Journal of Women Studies* 23, no. 3 (2002): 117–146.

Gaarder, Emily. *Women and the Animal Rights Movement.* Piscataway, NJ: Rutgers University Press, 2011.

Gruen, Lori, and Kari Weil, eds. *Hypatia.* Special issue, *Animal Others* 27, no. 3 (summer 2012).

Imhoff, Daniel, ed. *The CAFO Reader: The Tragedy of Industrial Animal Factories.* Berkeley: University of California Press, 2010.

Joy, Melanie. *Why We Love Dogs, Eat Pigs, and Wear Cows: An Introduction to Carnism.* San Francisco: Conari Press, 2010.

Kemmerer, Lisa, ed. *Animals and World Religions.* New York: Oxford University Press, 2011.

Kemmerer, Lisa, and Anthony J. Nocella II, eds. *Call to Compassion: Religious Perspectives on Animal Advocacy.* Brooklyn, NY: Lantern Books, 2011.

———. *Sister Species: Women, Animals, and Social Justice.* Chicago: University of Illinois Press, 2011.

McElroy, Susan Chernak. *All My Relations: Living with Animals as Teachers and Healers.* Novato, CA: New World Library, 2004.

Nussbaum, Martha C. *Frontiers of Justice: Disability, Nationality, Species Membership.* Cambridge, MA: Harvard University Press, 2006.

Regan, Tom. *The Case for Animal Rights.* 2nd ed. Berkeley: University of California Press, 2004.

Sanbonmatsu, John, ed. *Critical Theory and Animal Liberation.* Lanham, MD: Rowman & Littlefield, 2011.

Scully, Matthew. *Dominion: The Power of Man, the Suffering of Animals, and the Call to Mercy.* New York: St. Martin's Press, 2002.

Shevelow, Kathryn. *For the Love of Animals: The Rise of the Animal Protection Movement.* New York: Holt Paperbacks, 2008.

Singer, Peter. *Animal Liberation.* 4th ed. New York: HarperCollins Publishers, 2009.

Singer, Peter, and Jim Mason, eds. *The Ethics of What We Eat.* Emmaus, PA: Rodale, 2006.

Socha, Kim. *Women, Destruction, and the Avant-Garde: A Paradigm for Animal Liberation.* New York: Rodopi, 2011.

Steeves, H. Peter, and Tom Regan, eds. *Animal Others: On Ethics, Ontology, and Animal Life.* Albany: State University of New York Press, 1999.

Stibbe, Arran. *Animals Erased: Discourse, Ecology, and Reconnection with the Natural World.* Middletown, CT: Wesleyan University Press, 2012.

Sunstein, Cass R., and Martha C. Nussbaum, eds. *Animal Rights: Current Debates and New Directions.* Oxford: Oxford University Press, 2004.

Tompkins, Ptolemy. *The Divine Life of Animals.* New York: Three Rivers Press, 2010.

Environmental Ecofeminism

Alaimo, Stacy. "Cyborg and Ecofeminist Interventions: Challenges for an Environmental Feminism." *Feminist Studies* 20, no. 1 (spring 1994): 133–152.

King, Ynestra. "Engendering a Peaceful Planet: Ecology, Economy, and Ecofeminism in Contemporary Context." *Women's Studies Quarterly* 23 (fall/winter 1995): 19.

Lahar, Stephanie. "Ecofeminist Theory and Grassroots Politics." In *Ecological Feminist Philosophies*, edited by Karen J. Warren, 1–18. Bloomington: Indiana University Press, 1996.

Munroe, Jennifer, and Rebecca Laroche, eds. *Ecofeminist Approaches to Early Modernity: Literatures, Cultures, and the Environment*. New York: Palgrave Macmillan, 2011.

Primavesi, Anne. *Scared Gaia: Holistic Theology and Earth System Science*. London: Taylor & Francis, 2000.

Rich, Bruce. *Mortgaging the Earth: The World Bank, Environmental Impoverishment, and the Crisis of Development*. Boston: Beacon, 1994, 49–106.

Sarkar, Sahotra. *Environmental Philosophy: From Theory to Practice*. West Sussex, UK: John Wiley & Sons, 2012.

———. *Environmentalism in Popular Culture: Gender, Race, Sexuality, and the Politics of the Natural*. Tucson: University of Arizona Press, 2008.

Taylor, Paul W. *Respect for Nature: A Theory of Environmental Ethics*. Princeton, NJ: Princeton University Press, 1986, 2011.

Critiques of Ecofeminism

Auerbach, Judith. "The Intersection of Feminism and the Environmental Movement, or What Is Feminist About the Feminist Perspective on the Environment?." *American Behavioral Scientist* 37, no. 8 (August 1994): 1095.

Biehl, Janet. *Rethinking Ecofeminist Politics*. Boston: South End Press, 1991.

Cook, Julie. "The Philosophical Colonization of Ecofeminism." *Environmental Ethics* 20, no. 3 (fall 1998): 227–246.

Plumwood, Val. "Ecofeminism: An Overview and Discussion of Positions and Arguments." *Australian Journal of Philosophy* 64 (June 1986): 135.

Sturgeon, Noël. *Ecofeminist Natures: Race, Gender, Feminist Theory, and Political Action*. New York: Routledge, 1997.

Chapter 9: Existentialist, Poststructural, and Postmodern Feminisms

Existentialism: Focus on Jean-Paul Sartre

Aron, Raymond. *Marxism and the Existentialists*. New York: Harper & Row, 1969.

Barrett, William. *Irrational Man: A Study in Existential Philosophy*. Garden City, NY: Doubleday, 1958.

Caws, Peter. *Sartre*. Boston: Routledge & Kegan Paul, 1979.

Chiodi, Pietro. *Sartre*. New York: New Viewpoints, 1973.

————. *Sartre and Marxism*. Atlantic Highlands, NJ: Humanities Press, 1976.

Kaufmann, Walter Arnold, ed. *Existentialism from Dostoevsky to Sartre*. New York: New American Library, 1975.

Marino, Gordon. *Basic Writings of Existentialism*. New York: Modern Library, 2004.

Murphy, Julien S., ed. *Feminist Interpretations of Jean-Paul Sartre*. University Park: Pennsylvania State University Press, 1999.

Oaklander, Nathan L. *Existentialist Philosophy: An Introduction*. 2nd ed. Saddle River, NJ: Prentice Hall, 1995.

Sartre, Jean-Paul. *Being and Nothingness*. Translated by Hazel E. Barnes. New York: Philosophical Library, 1956.

————. *The Emotions: Outline of a Theory*. New York: Philosophical Library, 1948.

————. *Existentialism*. Translated by Bernard Frechtman. New York: Philosophical Library, 1947.

————. *Existentialism Is a Humanism*. Translated by Carol Macomber. New Haven, CT: Yale University Press, 2007.

Solomon, Robert C., ed. *Existentialism*. 2nd ed. New York: Oxford University Press, 2004.

Existentialist Feminism: Focus on Simone de Beauvoir

Arp, Kristana. *The Bonds of Freedom: Simone de Beauvoir's Existentialist Ethics*. Peru, IL: Carus Publishing Company, 2001.

Ascher, Carol. *Simone de Beauvoir: A Life of Freedom*. Boston: Beacon Press, 1981.

Beauvoir, Simone de. *Adieux: A Farewell to Sartre*. New York: Pantheon Books, 1984.

————. *The Ethics of Ambiguity*. New York: Citadel Press, 1967.

————. *Letters to Sartre*. Translated and edited by Quinton Hoare. New York: Arcade Publishing, 1990.

————. *Memoirs of a Dutiful Daughter*. Translated by James Kirkup. Harmondsworth, UK: Penguin Books, 1963.

————. *The Prime of Life*. Translated by Peter Green. Harmondsworth, UK: Penguin Books, 1965.

————. *The Second Sex*. Translated and edited by H. M. Parshley. New York: Vintage Books, 1952.

Bergoffen, Debra B. "Simone de Beauvoir and Jean Paul Sartre: Woman, Man and the Desire to Be God." *Constellations* 9, no. 3 (2002): 406–418.

Card, Claudia. *The Cambridge Companion to Simone de Beauvoir*. Cambridge: Cambridge University Press, 2003.

Cohen Shabot, Sara. "On the Question of Woman: Illuminating de Beauvoir Through Kantian Epistemology." *Philosophy Today* 51, no. 4 (2007): 369–382.

Fullbrook, Kate, and Edward Fullbrook. *Simone de Beauvoir and Jean-Paul Sartre: The Remaking of a Twentieth-Century Legend*. New York: Basic Books, 1994.

Heinamaa, Sara. "What Is a Woman? Butler and Beauvoir on the Foundations of the Sexual Difference." *Hypatia* 12, no. 1 (1997): 20–39.

Jardine, Alice. "An Interview with Simone de Beauvoir." *Signs: Journal of Women in Culture and Society* 5, no. 2 (1979): 224–236.

Keefe, Terry. *Simone de Beauvoir*. Totowa, NJ: Barnes & Noble, 1983.

Kuykendall, Eléanor H. "Linguistic Ambivalence in Simone de Beauvoir's Feminist Theory." In *The Thinking Muse*, edited by Iris Young and Jeffner Allan, 1–30. Bloomington: Indiana University Press, 1989.

Mahon, Joseph. *Existentialism, Feminism and Simone de Beauvoir*. New York: Palgrave Macmillian, 1997.

McCall, Dorothy Kaufmann. "Simone de Beauvoir, *The Second Sex*, and Jean-Paul Sartre." *Signs: Journal of Women in Culture and Society* 5, no. 2 (1979–1980): 209–223.

Noudelmann, François. "What Do Jean-Paul Sartre and Simone de Beauvoir Have to Say to Us Today?." *Diogenes* 54, no. 216 (2007): 35–39.

O'Brien, Wendy, and Lester Embree, eds. *The Existential Phenomenology of Simone de Beauvoir*. Dordrecht, Netherlands: Kluwer Academic Publishers, 2001.

Rowley, Hazel. *Tête-à-Tête: Simone de Beauvoir and Jean-Paul Sartre*. New York: HarperCollins Publishers, 2005.

Simons, Margaret A., and Jessica Benjamin. *The Philosophy of Simone de Beauvoir*. Special issue, *Hypatia* 14, no. 4 (fall 1999).

———. "Sexism and the Philosophical Cannon: On Reading Beauvoir's *Second Sex*." *Journal of the History of Ideas* 51 (1990): 487–504.

———. "Simone de Beauvoir: An Interview." *Feminist Studies* 5, no. 2 (summer 1979): 336.

Warren, Karen J. *An Unconventional History of Western Philosophy: Conversations Between Men and Women Philosophers*. Lanham, MD: Rowman & Littlefield, 2009.

Whitmarsh, Anne. *Simone de Beauvoir and the Limits of Commitment*. Cambridge: Cambridge University Press, 1981.

Zerilli, Linda M. G. "A Process Without a Subject: Simone de Beauvoir and Julia Kristeva on Maternity." *Signs: Journal of Women in Culture and Society* 8, no. 1 (1982): 111–135.

Critiques of Existentialist Feminism

Bertozzi, Alberto. "A Critique of Simone de Beauvoir's Existential Ethics." *Philosophy Today* 51, no. 3 (2007): 303–311.

Dietz, Mary G. "Introduction: Debating Simone de Beauvoir." *Signs: Journal of Women in Culture and Society* 18, no. 1 (1983): 74–88.

Elshtain, Jean Bethke. *Public Man, Private Woman: Women in Social and Political Thought*. Princeton, NJ: Princeton University Press, 1981.

Grene, Marjorie. *Dreadful Freedom: A Critique of Existentialism*. Chicago: University of Chicago Press, 1948.

Kuykendall, Eléanor H. "Linguistic Ambivalence in Simone de Beauvoir's Feminist Theory." In *The Thinking Muse*, edited by Iris Young and Jeffner Allen, 1–30. Bloomington: Indiana University Press, 1989.

Lloyd, Genevieve. *The Man of Reason: "Male" and "Female" in Western Philosophy*. Minneapolis: University of Minnesota Press, 1984.

Schutte, Ofelia. "A Critique of Normative Heterosexuality: Identity, Embodiment, and Sexual Difference in Beauvoir and Irigaray." *Hypatia* 12, no. 1 (winter 1997): 40.

Whitmarsh, Anne. *Simone de Beauvoir and the Limits of Commitment*. Cambridge: Cambridge University Press, 1981.

Poststructuralism: Focus on Michel Foucault

Barrett, Michele. *The Politics of Truth: From Marx to Foucault*. Stanford, CA: Stanford University Press, 1991.

Bartky, S. "Foucault, Femininity, and the Modernization of Patriarchal Power." In *Feminism and Foucault: Reflections on Resistance*, edited by I. Diamond and L. Quinby. Boston: Northeastern University Press, 1988.

Bartky, Sandra. "Foucault, Femininity, and the Modernization of Patriarchal Power." In *Femininity and Domination*, edited by Sandra Bartky, 63–82. New York: Routledge, 1990.

Christmas, Simon. "Michel Foucault." In *An Introduction to Modern European Philosophy*, edited by Jenny Teichman and Graham White. New York: Palgrave MacMillan, 1995.

Connolly, William. "Taylor, Foucault, and Otherness." *Political Theory* 13, no. 3 (1985): 365–376.

Diamond, Irene, and Lee Quinby, eds. *Feminism and Foucault: Reflections on Resistance*. Boston: Northeastern University Press, 1988.

Dreyfus, H., and P. Rabinow. *Michel Foucault: Beyond Structuralism and Hermeneutics*. Sussex, UK: Harvester Press, 1982.

Dudrick, David. "Foucault, Butler, and the Body." *European Journal of Philosophy* 13, no. 2 (2005): 226–246.

Eribon, Didier. *Michel Foucault*. Translated by Betsy Wing. Cambridge, MA: Harvard University Press, 1991.

Fahs, Breanne. *Performing Sex: The Making and Unmaking of Women's Erotic Lives*. Albany: State University of New York Press, 2011.

Foucault, Michel. *Archeology of Knowledge*. Translated by A. Sheridan Smith. New York: Harper & Row, 1972.

———. *The Birth of the Clinic*. Translated by A. Sheridan Smith. New York: Pantheon, 1973.

————. *Discipline and Punish: The Birth of the Prison.* London: Allen Lane, 1977.

————. *The History of Sexuality.* Vols. 1–3: *Introduction, The Uses of Pleasure, and Care of the Self.* Translated by Robert Hurley. New York: Vintage, 1988–1990.

————. *Madness and Civilization.* Translated by Richard Howard. New York: Pantheon, 1965.

————. *The Order of Things.* New York: Vintage, 1973.

————. *Power/Knowledge.* Edited by Colin Gordon. New York: Random House, 1981.

Gutting, G. *The Cambridge Companion to Foucault.* Cambridge: Cambridge University Press, 1994.

Hekman, S., ed. *Feminist Interpretations of Michel Foucault.* University Park: Pennsylvania State University Press, 1996.

McHoul, Alec, and Wendy Grace. *A Foucault Primer: Discourse, Power and the Subject.* New York: New York University Press, 1993.

McNay, Lois. *Foucault: A Critical Introduction.* Cambridge, UK: Polity Press, 1994.

————. *Foucault and Feminism and the Self.* Boston: Northeastern University Press, 1993.

Newman, Saul. "Universalism/Particularism: Towards a Poststructuralist Politics of Universality." *New Formations* 41 (2000): 95–108.

Ramazanoglu, Caroline, ed. *Up Against Foucault: Exploration of Some Tensions Between Foucault and Feminism.* London: Routledge, 1993.

Sawicki, J. *Disciplining Foucault: Feminism, Power, and the Body.* New York: Routledge, 1991.

————. "Feminism and the Power of Discourse." In *After Foucault: Humanistic Knowledge, Postmodern Challenges,* edited by J. Arac, 161–178. New Brunswick, NJ: Rutgers University Press, 1988.

————. "Feminism, Foucault, and 'Subjects' of Power and Freedom." In *The Later Foucault: Politics and Philosophy.* Thousand Oaks, CA: Sage Publications, 1998.

————. "Foucault, Feminism, and Questions of Identity." In *The Cambridge Companion to Foucault,* edited by G. Gutting. Cambridge: Cambridge University Press, 1994.

Taylor, Dianna, and Karen Vintges, eds. *Feminism and the Final Foucault.* Urbana: University of Illinois Press, 2004.

Poststructural Feminism: Focus on Judith Butler

Allen, Amy. "Dependency, Subordination, and Recognition: On Judith Butler's Theory of Subjection." *Continental Philosophy Review* 38 (2006): 199–222.

Butler, Judith. *Bodies That Matter: On the Discursive Limits of "Sex."* New York: Routledge, 1993.

————. *Excitable Speech: A Politics of the Performative.* New York: Routledge, 1997.

————. *Gender Trouble: Feminism and the Subversion of Identity.* New York: Routledge, 1990.

————. *The Psychic Life of Power: Theories in Subjection.* Stanford, CA: Stanford University Press, 1997.

————. *Subjects of Desire: Hegelian Reflections in Twentieth Century France.* New York: Columbia University Press, 1987.

————. *Undoing Gender.* New York: Routledge, 2004.

Butler, Judith, Elisabeth Beck-Gernsheim, and Lidia Puigvert, eds., *Women and Social Transformation.* New York: Routledge, 2003.

Magnus, Kathy Dow. "The Unaccountable Subject: Judith Butler and the Social Conditions of Intersubjective Agency." *Hypatia* 21, no. 2 (spring 2006): 81–103.

McNay, Lois. "Subject, Psyche, and Agency: The Work of Judith Butler." *Theory, Culture & Society* 16, no. 2 (1999): 175–193.

Mills, Catherine. "Contesting the Political: Butler and Foucault on Power and Resistance." *Journal of Political Philosophy* 11, no. 3 (2003): 253–272.

————. "Efficacy and Vulnerability: Judith Butler on Reiteration and Resistance." *Australian Feminist Studies* 159, no. 32 (2000): 265–279.

Osborne, Peter, and Lynne Segal. "Extracts from *Gender as Performance: An Interview with Judith Butler.*" Theory.org.uk, 1993, http://www.theory.org.uk/butint1.htm (accessed December 3, 1999).

Salem, Sara. *Judith Butler.* New York: Routledge, 2002.

Critiques of Poststructural Feminism

Alcoff, Linda. "Cultural Feminism Versus Poststructuralism: The Identity Crisis in Feminist Theory." *Signs: Journal of Women in Culture and Society* 13, no. 3 (spring 1998): 405–436.

Hailey, Janet. *Split Decisions: How and Why to Take a Break from Feminism.* Princeton, NJ: Princeton University Press, 2008.

Lurie, Susan, Ann Cvetkovich, Jane Gallop, Tania Modleski, Hortense Spillers, and Carla Kaplan. "Roundtable: Restoring Feminist Politics to Poststructuralist Critique." *Feminist Studies* 27, no. 3 (autumn 2001): 679–707.

Nussbaum, Martha C. "The Professor of Parody: The Hip Defeatism of Judith Butler." *New Republic,* February 22, 1999, 37–45.

Sarup, Madan. *An Introductory Guide to Post-structuralism and Postmodernism.* Athens: University of Georgia Press, 1993.

Webster, Fiona. "The Politics of Sex and Gender: Benhabib and Butler Debate Subjectivity." *Hypatia* 15, no. 1 (winter 2000): 1–22.

Weeden, Chris. *Feminist Practice and Poststructuralist Theory.* 2nd ed. Oxford, UK: Wiley Blackwell, 2000.

Williams, Joan C. "Review: Feminism and Poststructuralism." *Michigan Law Review* 88, no. 6 (1990): 1776–1791.

Xu, Judith Chuan. "Poststructuralist Feminism and the Problem of 'Daodejing' [unreproducible symbol]." *Journal of Feminist Studies in Religion* 19, no. 1 (spring 2003): 47–64.

Postmodernism: Focus on Jacques Derrida

Derrida, Jacques. *Of Grammatology.* Translated by Gayatri Chakravorty Spivak. Baltimore: Johns Hopkins University Press, 1974.

———. *Margins of Philosophy.* Translated by Alan Bass. Chicago: University of Chicago Press, 1982.

———. *Positions.* Translated by Alan Bass. Chicago: University of Chicago Press, 1982.

———. *The Post Card: From Socrates to Freud and Beyond.* Translated by Alan Bass. Chicago: University of Chicago Press, 1987.

———. *Spurs: Nietzsche's Styles.* Translated by Barbara Harlow. Chicago: University of Chicago Press, 1978.

———. *Writing and Difference.* Translated by Alan Bass. Chicago: University of Chicago Press, 1978.

Feder, Ellen K., Mary C. Rawlinson, and Emily Zakin, eds. *Derrida and Feminism.* New York: Routledge, 1997.

Howells, Christina. *Derrida: Deconstruction from Phenomenology to Ethics.* Cambridge: Polity Press, 1998.

Jones, Irwin. *Derrida and the Writing of the Body.* Surrey, UK: Ashgate Publishing, 2010.

Smart, Barry. *Postmodernity: Key Ideas.* New York: Routledge, 1993.

Wolin, Richard. "Modernism vs. Postmodernism." *Telos* 62 (1984–1985): 9–29.

Postmodern Feminism: Focus on Hélène Cixous

Agger, Ben. *Gender, Culture, and Power: Toward a Feminist Postmodern Critical Theory.* New York: Praeger Publishers, 1993.

———. "Philosophy Matters: A Review of Recent Work in Feminist Philosophy." *Signs: Journal of Women in Culture and Society* 25 (2000): 841–882.

Benhabib, Seyla. *Situating the Self: Gender, Community, and Postmodernism in Contemporary Ethics.* London: Routledge, 1992.

Bree, Germaine. *Women Writers in France.* New Brunswick, NJ: Rutgers University Press, 1973.

Brown, Wendy. "Feminist Hesitations, Postmodern Exposures." *Differences* 3, no. 1 (1991): 63–84.

Cahill, Ann J., and Jennifer Hansen. *Continental Feminism Reader.* Lanham, MD: Rowman & Littlefield, 2003.

Cixous, Hélène. *The Book of Promethea.* Translated by Betsy Wing. Lincoln: University of Nebraska Press, 1991.

————. "Castration or Decapitation?." *Signs: Journal of Women in Culture and Society* 7, no. 1 (summer 1981): 41–55.

————. *"Coming to Writing" and Other Essays.* Translated by Sarah Cornell et al. Cambridge, MA: Harvard University Press, 1991.

————. "The Laugh of the Medusa." In *New French Feminisms*, edited by Elaine Marks and Isabelle de Courtivron. New York: Schocken Books, 1981.

Cixous, Hélène, with Mireille Calle-Gruber. *Hélène Cixous, Rootprints: Memory and Life Writings.* Translated by Eric Prenowitz. New York: Routledge, 1997.

Cixous, Hélène, and Catherine Clément. "Sorties." In *The Newly Born Woman.* Translated by Betsy Wing. Minneapolis: University of Minnesota Press, 1986.

Duchen, Claire. *Feminism in France: From May '68 to Mitterrand.* London: Routledge & Kegan Paul, 1986.

Fauré, Christine. "Absent from History." *Signs: Journal of Women in Culture and Society* 7, no. 1 (1981): 71–80.

Fraser, Nancy. *Unruly Practices: Power, Gender, and Discourse in Contemporary Critical Theory.* Minneapolis: University of Minnesota Press, 1989.

Grosz, Elizabeth. *Sexual Subversions: Three French Feminists.* Sydney, Australia: Allen & Unwin, 1989.

Hekman, Susan. *Gender and Knowledge: Elements of a Postmodern Feminism.* Cambridge, UK: Polity Press, 1990.

————. *The Material of Knowledge: Feminist Disclosures.* Bloomington: Indiana University Press, 2010.

Ives, Kelly. *Cixous, Irigaray, Kristeva: The Jouissance of French Feminism.* Kent, UK: Crescent Moon Publishing, 2010.

Jones, Ann Rosalind. "Writing the Body: Toward an Understanding of *l'Écriture Féminine.*" *Feminist Studies* 7, no. 1 (summer 1981): 248.

Mann, Susan. *Doing Feminist Theory: From Modernity to Postmodernity.* New York: Oxford University Press, 2012.

Marks, Elaine. "Review Essay: Women and Literature in France." *Signs: Journal of Women in Culture and Society* 3, no. 4 (summer 1978): 832–842.

Nicholson, Linda, ed. *Feminism/Postmodernism.* London: Routledge, 1989.

Oliver, Kelly. *French Feminism Reader.* Lanham, MD: Rowman & Littlefield, 2000.

————. *French Feminist Thought: A Reader.* New York: Blackwell, 1987.

————. *Witnessing: Beyond Recognition.* Minneapolis: University of Minnesota Press, 2001.

Oliver, Kelly, with Lisa Walsh, eds. *Contemporary French Feminism.* New York: Oxford University Press, 2005.

Sellers, Susan, ed. *The Hélène Cixous Reader.* New York: Routledge, 1994.

Soper, Kate. "Feminism, Humanism, and Postmodernism." *Radical Philosophy* 55 (summer 1990): 11–17.

————. *Feminist Practice and Poststructuralist Theory.* 2nd ed. Oxford, UK: Blackwell, 2000.

Critiques of Postmodern Feminism

Benhabib, Seyla. "Feminism and Postmodernism." In *Feminist Contentions: A Philosophical Exchange*, edited by Seyla Benhabib, with Nancy Fraser and Drucilla Cornell, 17–34. New York: Routledge, 1994.

Bordo, Susan. "Feminism, Postmodernism, and Gender-Scepticism." In *Feminism/Postmodernism*, edited by Linda J. Nicholson, 133–156. New York: Routledge, 1990.

Brown, W. "Postmodern Exposures, Feminist Hesitations." In *States of Injury: Power and Freedom in Late Modernity*, Princeton, NJ: Princeton University, 1995.

Code, Lorraine. "Feminist Epistemology." In *A Companion to Epistemology*, edited by Jonathan Dancy and Ernst Sosa, 138–142. Oxford, UK: Blackwell, 1992.

Di Stefano, Christine. "Dilemmas of Difference." In *Feminism/Postmodernism*, edited by Linda J. Nicholson, 63–82. New York: Routledge, 1990.

Fausto-Sterling, Anne. *Myths of Gender: Biological Theories About Women and Men*. New York: Basic Books, 1985.

Flax, Jane. "Postmodernism and Gender Relations in Feminist Theory." In *Feminism/Postmodernism*, edited by Linda J. Nicholson. New York: Routledge, 1990.

Fraser, Nancy, and Linda J. Nicholson. "Social Criticism Without Philosophy: An Encounter Between Feminism and Postmodernism." In *Feminism/Postmodernism*, edited by Linda J. Nicholson. New York: Routledge, 1990.

Jardine, Alice, and Hester Eisenstein, eds. *The Future of Difference*. New Brunswick, NJ: Rutgers University Press, 1985.

Marchand, Marianne H., and Jane Parpart, eds. *Feminism/Postmodernism/Development*. New York: Routledge, 1994.

Moi, Toril. *Sexual/Textual Politics: Feminist Literary Theory*. New York: Methuen, 1985.

Powell, Jim. *Postmodernism for Beginners*. Danbury, CT: For Beginners, LLC, 1998.

Shildrick, Margrit. *Leaky Bodies and Boundaries: Feminism, Postmodernism and (Bio)ethics*. New York: Routledge, 1997.

Chapter 10: Third-Wave and Queer Feminisms

Third-Wave Feminism

Alfonso, Rita, and Jo Trigilio. "Surfing the Third Wave: A Dialogue Between Two Third Wave Feminists." *Hypatia* 12, no. 3 (summer 1997): 8–16.

Austin, S. Bryn, and Pam Gregg. "A Freak Among Freaks: The 'Zine Scene." In *Sisters, Sexperts, Queers: Beyond the Lesbian Nation*, edited by Arlene Stein, 81–95. New York: Penguin Books, 1993.

Bailey, Cathryn. "Making Waves and Drawing Lines: The Politics of Defining the Vicissitudes of Feminism." *Hypatia*. Special issue, *Third Wave Feminisms* 12, no. 3 (summer 1997): 17–28.

Baumgardner, Jennifer, and Amy Richards. *Grassroots: A Field Guide for Feminist Activism.* New York: Farrar, Straus and Giroux. 2005.

——. *Manifesta: Young Women, Feminism, and the Future.* New York: Farrar, Straus and Giroux, 2001.

Bayerl, Katherine: "Mags, Zines, and gURLs: The Exploding World of Girls' Publications." *Women's Studies Quarterly* 29, no. 3–4 (fall/winter 2000): 287–292.

Carlip, Hillary. *Girl Power: Young Women Speak Out!* New York: Warner Books, 1995.

Cashen, Jeanne. "The Revolution Is Mine: Grrrl Resistance in a Commodity Culture." Unpublished manuscript, University of New Orleans, 2002.

Cornstock, Michelle. "Grrrl Zine Networks: Re-composing Spaces of Authority, Gender, and Culture." *JAC* 21, no. 2 (2001): 383–409.

Denfeld, Rene. *The New Victorians: A Young Woman's Challenge to the Old Feminist Order.* New York: Routledge, 1995.

Dicker, Rory, and Alison Piepmeier, eds. *Catching a Wave: Reclaiming Feminism for the 21st Century.* Boston: Northeastern University Press, 2003.

Doncombe, S. "Let's All Be Alienated Together: Zines and the Marketing of Underground Community." In *Generations of Youth: Youth Cultures and History in the Twentieth-Century,* edited by Joe Austin and Nevin Michael Willard, 427–251. New York: New York University Press, 1998.

Edut, Ophira, ed. *Adios Barbie: Young Women Write About Body Image and Identity.* Seattle, WA: Seal Press, 1998.

Ensler, Eve. *The Vagina Monologues.* London: Virago Press, 2001.

Findlen, Barbara, ed. *Listen Up: Voices from the Next Generation.* Seattle, WA: Seal Press, 1995.

Fixmer, Natalie, and Julia T. Wood. "The Personal Is Still Political: Embodied Politics in Third Wave Feminism." *Women's Studies in Communication* 28, no. 2 (fall 2005).

Fraser, M. L. "Zines and Heard: Fringe Feminism and the Zines of the Third Wave." *Feminist Collections* 23, no. 4 (summer 2002): 6–10.

Garrison, Ednie Keah. "U.S. Feminism—Grrl Style! Youth (Sub)cultures and the Technologies of the Third Wave." *Feminist Studies* 26, no. 1 (spring 2000): 141–170.

Gillis, Stacy, Gillian Howie, and Rebecca Munford, eds. *Third Wave Feminism: A Critical Exploration.* Basingstoke, UK: Palgrave Macmillan, 2007.

Gilmore, Stephanie. "Looking Back, Thinking Ahead: Third Wave Feminism in the United States." *Journal of Women's History* 12, no. 4 (winter 2001): 215–221.

Goode, Jennie. "Adios, Assumptions–'Young' Feminists Publish." *Alternative Library Literature, 1998/1999: A Biennial Anthology,* edited by Sanford Berman and James P. Danky. Jefferson, NC: McFarland, 2000.

Green, Eileen, and Alison Adam. *Virtual Gender: Technology, Consumption and Identity.* London: Routledge, 2001.

Halstead, Ted. "A Politics for Generation X." *Atlantic Monthly* 284, no. 2 (August 1999): 33–42.

Hernández, Daisy, and Bushra Rehman, eds. *Colonize This! Young Women of Color and Today's Feminism.* Berkeley, CA: Seal Press, 2002.

Heywood, Leslie. *The Women's Movement Today: An Encyclopedia of Third-Wave Feminism.* Westport, CT: Greenwood Press, 2006.

Heywood, Leslie, and Jennifer Drake, eds. *Third Wave Agenda: Being Feminist, Doing Feminism.* Minneapolis: University of Minnesota Press, 1997.

Hollows, Joanne. *Feminism, Femininity and Popular Culture.* Manchester, UK: Manchester University Press, 2000.

hooks, bell. *Feminism Is for Everybody: Passionate Politics.* Boston: South End Press, 2000.

Howry, Allison L., and Julia T. Wood. "Something Old, Something New, Something Borrowed: Themes in the Voices of a New Generation of Feminists." *Southern Communication Journal* 4, no. 66 (summer 2001): 324.

Inness, S. A., ed. *Running for Their Lives: Girls, Cultural Identity, and Stories of Survival.* Lanham, MD: Rowman & Littlefield Publishers, 2000.

Jervis, Lisa, and Andi Zeisler, eds. *BITCHfest: 10 Years of Cultural Criticism from the Pages of Bitch Magazine.* New York: Farrar, Straus and Giroux, 2006.

Johnson, Merri Lisa. *Third Wave Feminism and Television: Jane Puts It in a Box.* London: I. B. Tauris & Co. Ltd., 2007.

Kaplan, E. Ann. "Madonna Politics: Perversion, Repression, or Subversion? Or Masks and/as Master-y." In *The Madonna Connection: Representational Politics, Subcultural Identities, and Cultural Theory,* edited by Cathy Schwichtenberg. Boulder, CO: Westview Press, 1993.

Karp, Marcelle, and Debbie Stoller, eds. *The BUST Guide to the New Girl Order.* New York: Penguin Books, 1999.

Kenny, Lorraine Delia. *Daughters of Suburbia: Growing Up White, Middle Class, and Female.* New Brunswick, NJ: Rutgers University Press, 2000.

Kinser, Amber. "Negotiating Space For/Through Third-Wave Feminism." *NWSA Journal* 16, no. 3 (2005): 124–153.

Koyama, Emi. "The Transfeminist Manifesto." In *Catching a Wave: Reclaiming Feminism for the 21st Century,* edited by Rory Dicker and Alison Piepmeier, 244–259. Boston: Northeastern University Press, 2003.

Kunin, Madeleine M. *The New Feminist Agenda: Defining the Next Revolution for Women, Work, and Family.* White River Junction, VT: Chelsea Green Publishing, 2012.

Labaton, Vivien, and Dawn Lundy Martin, eds. *The Fire This Time: Young Activists and the New Feminism.* New York: Anchor Books, 2004.

Leonard, Marion. "'Rebel Girl, You Are the Queen of My World': Feminism, 'Subculture' and Grrl Power.'" In *Sexing the Groove: Popular Music and Gender,* edited by Sheila Whiteley, 230–255. London: Routledge, 1997.

Meyers, Marian, ed. *Mediated Women: Representations in Popular Culture.* Cresskill, NJ: Hampton Press, 1999.

Miya-Jarvis, Lisa, and Andi Zeisler, eds. *BITCHfest: 10 Years of Cultural Criticism from the Pages of Bitch Magazine.* New York: Farrar, Straus and Giroux, 2006.

Navarro, Mireya. "Going Beyond Black and White, Hispanics in Census Pick 'Other.'" *New York Times*, November 9, 2003, A1, A21.

Rosenberg, Jessica, and Gitana Garofalo. "Riot Grrrl: Revolutions from Within." *Signs: Journal of Women in Culture and Society* 23, no. 3 (1998): 809–841.

Rowe-Finkbeiner, Kristin. *The F-Word.* New York: Avalon Publishing Group, 2004.

Shehyn, Audrey. *Picture the Girl: Young Women Speak Their Minds.* New York: Hyperion, 2000.

Shugart, Helene A. "Isn't It Ironic? The Intersection of Third-Wave Feminism and Generation X." *Women's Studies in Communication* 24, no. 2 (fall 2001).

Siegel, Deborah, and L. Siegel. "The Legacy of the Personal: Generating Theory in Feminism's Third Wave." *Hypatia* 12, no. 3 (1997): 46–75.

———. *Sisterhood, Interrupted: From Radical Women to Grrls Gone Wild.* New York: Palgrave Macmillan, 2007.

"SlutWalk Toronto: What?." Available at http://slutwalktoronto.com/about/what (accessed July 2016).

Snyder, R. Claire. "What Is Third-Wave Feminism? A New Direction Essay." *Signs: Journal of Women in Culture and Society* 34, no. 1 (September 2008): 175–196.

Springer, Kimberly. "Third Wave Black Feminism?." *Signs: Journal of Women in Culture and Society* 27, no. 4 (summer 2002): 1059–1082.

Wald, Gayle. "Just a Girl? Rock Music, Feminism, and the Cultural Construction of Female Youth." *Signs: Journal of Women in Culture and Society* 23, no. 3 (1998): 576–609.

Walker, Rebecca. "Becoming the Third Wave." *Ms.* (January 1992): 39–41.

———, ed. *To Be Real: Telling the Truth and Changing the Face of Feminism.* New York: Anchor Books, 1995.

Williams, Greg. "And Still I Rise—a Meeting with Madonna: The Last Pop Giant on Earth." *Arena* (January/February 1999): 38–46.

Wurtzel, Elizabeth. *Bitch: In Praise of Difficult Women.* New York: Doubleday, 1998.

Zaslow, Emilie. *Feminism, Inc.: Coming of Age in Girl Power Media Culture.* New York: Palgrave Macmillan, 2009.

Zeilinger, Julie. *A Little F'd Up: Why Feminism Is Not a Dirty Word.* Berkeley, CA: Seal Press, 2012.

Zita, Jacquelin N. "Introduction." *Third Wave Feminisms.* Special issue, *Hypatia* 12, no. 3 (summer 1997): 1–6.

Critiques of Third-Wave Feminism

Bailey, Cathryn. "Unpacking the Mother/Daughter Baggage: Reassessing Second- and Third-Wave Tensions." *Women's Studies Quarterly* 3–4, no. 30 (fall 2002): 144.

Berger, Melody. *We Don't Need Another Wave: Dispatches from the Next Generation of Feminists.* Berkeley, CA: Seal Press, 2006.

Cockrane, Kria. "The Fourth Wave of Feminism: Meet the Rebel Women." *Guardian*, December 10, 2013, https://www.theguardian.com/world/2013/dec/10/fourth-wave-feminism-rebel-women.

Denfeld, Rene. *The New Victorians: A Young Woman's Challenge to the Old Feminist Order.* New York: Routledge, 1995.

Gillis, Stacy, Gillian Howie, and Rebecca Munford, eds. *Third Wave Feminism: A Critical Exploration.* Basingstoke, UK: Palgrave Macmillan, 2007.

Henry, Astrid. "Feminism's Family Problem: Feminist Generations and the Mother-Daughter Trope." In *Catching a Wave: Reclaiming Feminism for the 21st Century*, edited by Rory Dicker and Alison Piepmeier, 209–231. Boston: Northeastern University Press, 2003.

———. *Not My Mother's Sister: Generational Conflict and Third-Wave Feminism.* Bloomington: Indiana University Press, 2004.

Mantilla, Karla. "Backlash and a *Feminism* That Is Contrary to *Feminism*." *Off Our Backs* 37, no. 1 (2007): 58–61.

McRobbie, Angela. *The Aftermath of Feminism: Gender, Culture and Social Change.* London: Sage Publications, 2009.

Paglia, Camille. *Sex, Art, and American Culture: Essays.* New York: Random House, 1992.

Quinn, Rebecca. "An Open Letter to Institutional Mothers." In *Generations: Academic Feminists in Dialogue*, edited by Devoney Looser and Ann Kaplan. Minneapolis: University of Minnesota Press, 1997.

Roiphe, Katie. *The Morning After: Sex, Fear, and Feminism on Campus.* New York: Little & Brown, 1993.

Wlodarczyk, Justyna. *Ungrateful Daughters: Third Wave Feminist Writings.* Newcastle upon Tyne, UK: Cambridge Scholars Publishing, 2010.

Feminist Queer Theory

Berlant, Lauren, and Michael Warner. "What Does Queer Theory Teach Us About X?." *PMLA: Publications of the Modern Language Association of America* 110, no. 3 (May 1995): 343–349.

Butler, Judith. *Bodies That Matter: On the Discursive Limits of "Sex."* New York: Routledge, 1993.

———. "Critically Queer." *GLQ: A Journal of Lesbian and Gay Studies* 1, no. 1 (1993): 17–32.

———. *Gender Trouble: Feminism and the Subversion of Identity.* New York: Routledge, 1990.

———. "Imitation and Gender Insubordination." In *Inside/Out: Lesbian Theories, Gay Theories*, edited by Diane Fuss, 13–31. London: Routledge, 1991.

De Lauretis, Teresa. "Queer Theory: Lesbian and Gay Sexualities." *Differences: A Journal of Feminist Cultural Studies 3*, no. 3 (1991): iii–xviii.

Diamond, Morty, ed. *Trans/love: Radical Sex, Love, and Relationships Beyond the Gender Binary*. San Francisco: Manic D Press, 2011.

Edelman, Lee. *Homographesis: Essays in Gay Literary and Cultural Theory*. New York: Routledge, 1994.

Grosz, Elizabeth. *Volatile Bodies: Toward a Corporeal Feminism*. Bloomington: Indiana University Press, 1994.

Halberstam, J. Jack. *Gaga Feminism: Sex, Gender, and the End of Normal*. Boston: Beacon Press, 2012.

Halperin, David M. *Saint Foucault: Towards a Gay Hagiography*. New York: Oxford University Press, 1995.

Harper, Phillip Brian. "Gay Male Identities, Personal Privacy, and Relations of Public Exchange: Notes on Directions for Queer Culture." *Social Text* 52–53 (fall/winter 1997): 5–29.

Jagose, Annamarie. *Queer Theory: An Introduction*. New York: New York University Press, 1996.

Marinucci, Mimi. *Feminism Is Queer: The Intimate Connection Between Queer and Feminist Theory*. London: Zed Books, 2010.

Morland, Iain, and Annabelle Willox, eds. *Queer Theory*. New York: Palgrave Macmillan, 2005.

Robertson, Pamela. *Guilty Pleasures—Feminist Camp from Mae West to Madonna*. London: I. B. Tauris, 1996.

Weed, Elizabeth, and Naomi Schor, eds. *Feminism Meets Queer Theory*. Bloomington: Indiana University Press, 1997.

Critiques of Feminist Queer Theory

Bergman, David. "Something About Eve: Eve Kosofsky Sedgwick's Closet Drama." Review of *Epistemology of the Closet* by Eve Sedgwick. *Raritan* 11, no. 1 (1991): 115–131.

Biddy, Martin. "Lesbian Identity and Autobiographical Differences." In *The Lesbian and Gay Studies Reader*, edited by Henry Abelove, Michele Aina Barale, and David M. Halpern, 274–293. New York: Routledge, 1993.

Daumer, Elisabeth D. "Queer Ethics: Or, the Challenge of Bisexuality to Lesbian Ethics." *Hypatia* 7, no. 4 (1992): 91–105.

Goldberg, Michelle. "What Is a Woman? The Dispute Between Radical Feminism and Transgenderism." *New Yorker*, August 4, 2014, 1–13.

Hale, Jacob. "Are Lesbians Women?." *Hypatia* 11, no. 2 (spring 1996): 94–121.

Harper, Phillip Biran, E. Francis White, and Margaret Cerullo. "Multi/queer/culture." *Radical America* 24, no. 4 (1993): 27–37.

Morgan, Tracy. "Butch-Femme and the Politics of Identity." In *Sisters, Sexperts, Queers: Beyond the Lesbian Nation*, edited by Arlene Stein, 35–46. New York: Routledge, 1993.

Nunokawa, Jeff. "Identity Crisis: Queer Politics in the Age of Possibilities." Interview by Alisa Solomon. *Village Voice*, June 30, 1992.

Roy, Camille. "Speaking in Tongues." In *Sisters, Sexperts, Queers: Beyond the Lesbian Nation*, edited by Arlene Stein, 6–12. New York: Plume/Penguin, 1993.

Sedgwick, Eve Kosofsky. "Across Gender, Across Sexuality: Willa Cather and Others." *South Atlantic Quarterly* 88, no. 1 (1989): 53–72.

———. *Epistemology of the Closet*. Berkeley: University of California Press, 1990.

———. "How to Bring Your Kids Up Gay." *Social Text* 29 (1991): 80–27.

———. *Tendencies*. Durham, NC: Duke University Press, 1993.

Walters, Suzanna Danuta. "From Here to Queer: Radical Feminism, Postmodernism, and the Lesbian Menace (or, Why Can't a Woman Be More like a Fag?)." *Signs: Journal of Women in Culture and Society* 21, no. 4 (summer 1996): 830–868.

Whisman, Vera. "Identity Crises: Who Is a Lesbian Anyway?." In *Sisters, Sexperts, Queers: Beyond the Lesbian Nation*, edited by Arlene Stein, 47–60. New York: Plume/Penguin, 1993.

Zita, Jacquelyn N. "Gay and Lesbian Studies: Yet Another Unhappy Marriage?." In *Tilting the Tower: Lesbians Teaching Queer Subjects*, edited by Linda Garber, 258–276. New York: Routledge, 1994.

———. "The Male Lesbian and the Postmodernist Body." *Hypatia* 7, no. 4 (1992): 106–127.

Index